Is It Really Just
A Small World?

Also by Sandra Ghost

The Mustard Seed
(Co-authored with Chuck Mottley,
Dr. Charles M.. Mottley)

Why 2K?
When the Chips Are Down, Is It a Hoax?

The Turnaround—From 0-10 To 10-0
(Co-authored with Chuck Mottley)

Wings Of Terror—The Bird Flu Pandemic
(Co-authored with Chuck Mottley)

Is It Really Just A Small World?

THERE ARE NO COINCIDENCES!

Sandra Boyce Ghost

WestBow
PRESS
A DIVISION OF THOMAS NELSON

WestBow Press books may be ordered through booksellers or by contacting:

WestBow Press
A Division of Thomas Nelson
1663 Liberty Drive
Bloomington, IN 47403
www.westbowpress.com
1-(866) 928-1240

Because of the dynamic nature of the Internet, any web addresses or links contained in this book may have changed since publication and may no longer be valid. The views expressed in this work are solely those of the author and do not necessarily reflect the views of the publisher, and the publisher hereby disclaims any responsibility for them.

Any people depicted in stock imagery provided by Thinkstock are models, and such images are being used for illustrative purposes only.

Certain stock imagery © Thinkstock.

Scripture taken from the New King James Version. Copyright 1979, 1980, 1982 by Thomas Nelson, inc. Used by permission. All rights reserved.

ISBN: 978-1-4497-2220-3 (e)
ISBN: 978-1-4497-1659-2 (sc)
ISBN: 978-1-4497-2221-0 (hc)

Library of Congress Control Number: 2011927541

Printed in the United States of America

WestBow Press rev. date: 9/22/2011

Preface

hough I've had a track record of four other books, and many ghostwriting
endeavors, I found I suffered industrial strength writer's block in trying to
write about myself as the glitzy, glamorous, self-centered singer and recording
artist of the past. I just couldn't seem to portray the reality of that part of my
life in the first person. I could only begin to rerun the subconscious tape of my
memories by writing in the third person—at arm's length from the person I used
to be. Please keep this in mind as Part One unfolds.

There is no way that this book would have ever made it into print without
the brilliant assistance of Esther Stevenson and her daughter, Ashlee. The story
was originally done on a typewriter. Years ago, I had purchased a bright orange
Adler typewriter, once owned by Rod Serling, who had pounded out many of
the Twilight Zone television episodes on it. I had written two other books on
the Adler and Part One of this book that then lay in a drawer for many years.
Esther and Ashlee undertook to be anointed scribes in lovingly transferring
all the typewritten pages into a computer program so that I could continue.
There are no words of gratitude equal to expressing my appreciation to them
and to my own daughter, Lisa, for her masterful excellence in editing.

Is It Really Just A Small World? is lovingly dedicated to son, Kent, as it is
more *his* story than mine!

SANDY GHOST

Chapter One

⟳

*I*t was the final performance on the Jazz Concert printed program. Technicians abruptly killed the auditorium house and stage lights. In total darkness, Sandy slipped out of the wings to the microphone at center stage. Red, glowing exit lights were the only illumination -- the concert audience responded with a surprised hush.

On cue, at the sound of the first note, a small, pin spotlight centered on just her face alone. The face floated in the velvet of darkness, as she sang the verse a cappella and one chorus of Peggy Lee's hit, "Fever". The mic magnified the sound of her fingers snapping crisply in time to the music. A soft murmur of approval sifted toward her from the crowd.

At the top of the second verse, her voice was bolstered by a deep resonant acoustic bass that now joined in. They modulated up a half step to a new key that added bright, fresh interest. The pin spot broadened to frame head and shoulders.

"Fever started long ago"...

Another verse--up another half step--drums now punctuated the sensuous rhythm, and the spotlight grew larger, glinting off the gold sequins on her dress, causing tiny pinwheels of flashing light to wink at the audience.

"Captain Smith and Pocahontas, had a very mad affair
When her Daddy tried to kill him
She said, Daddy-o don't you dare
He gives me fever...

Keyboards now lent a solid foundation line; they modulated up another half-step. The spotlight expanded again as the snapping fingers of the audience resounded like thousands of crickets in the darkness, clicking in cadence.

"Fever! In the morning...fever all through the night"...

Up another half step, Sandy had counted on staging and modulation to build excitement in what could have been a monotonous song. She always leaned on staging to cover up what she considered to be her mediocre voice; however, the reaction of the crowd now seemed to build to a fever of its own. Approval rolled across the footlights, that now blazed into glaring multi-colored light. Five, gutsy saxophones began a swaggering, sexy riff in support of the melody.

"Fever yeah I burn forsooth"

And still up another half--the trombone section stood, slides gleaming as

1

they added a full, rich bass line on the next chorus. The audience was standing too, clapping in time to the music.

On the final chorus, five trumpets began a wailing, brassy riff. Sandy wriggled sexily across the stage, mic in hand, wishing the moment would never end. The excitement was contagious; some stood on their seats.

"Chicks were born to give you fever
Be it Fahrenheit or Centigrade, they give you fever"...

She had planned a dramatic finish. On the last note, the stagehands again killed all the lights. The contrast of darkness and silence stunned the crowd--she exited stage right, tripping over an instrument wire, and grabbed the green velvet stage curtains to keep from falling.

Simultaneously, a mental picture presented itself. She could vividly see herself in a sprawl of sequins and spraddled legs on the floor, when the technicians would hit the lighting switch again. *I'm such a klutz,* she told herself. *My big moment, and I almost have a prat fall--typical of me!*

There seemed to be no way she could reconcile that a fluke of fate had turned her from a frumpy housewife into a glamorous singer as though with a wave of a fairy godmother's wand. Wiping beads of perspiration off her upper lip, she steadied herself with several deep breaths in anticipation of the curtain call.

As the house, stage and footlights blazed back on, the crowd began to whistle, applaud and cheer. The emcee walked to the microphone and announced, "You voted her Cleveland's Jazz Vocalist of 1960...Sandy Ghost. Sandy, come out and take a bow. You've worked us to a fevered pitch--we love you!"

The tight gold dress dictated tiny steps, much like those of a geisha whose feet had been bound in childhood. It hindered a full bow, but Sandy threw kisses with both hands to the crowd, "I love you, too!" she breathed into the microphone.

She noticed even the recording technicians in the orchestra pit were applauding. There was to be a record of the live performance, which would later be produced for public sale. How could all this be happening to her, she wondered?

Now that she could see the audience, her eyes automatically swept the crowd for her husband, Bill. He hadn't come tonight. She still couldn't seem to perform well under his sarcastic scrutiny. There seemed to be an inner button she could press in the wings and become "Sandy Ghost, entertainer", but when Bill was in the audience, or the children, that button was almost unreachable. She felt like "Sandy Ghost, housewife" just up there making a complete fool of herself. The warmth from the crowd felt almost tangible as she wrapped herself in the glow of their response and tiptoed off stage.

Chalky white paint peeled off the walls of the chilly backstage dressing room. Although a huge, rusty radiator snored loudly, the room was frigid and she hastily changed into a heavy, blue wool sweater and slacks. There was a shelf, covered with flowered oilcloth, that served as a dressing table, and she quickly creamed off the theatrical makeup, then reapplied a tamer shade of lipstick. False eyelashes lay on top of a plastic container looking like two ugly centipedes mating. The surroundings were sordid, but as Sandy looked in the mirror, they were transformed into grandeur by the excitement that still lingered in the air, much like ozone after a thunderstorm.

She smiled at this new "Alice In The Looking Glass" and the image even looked different--confident and beautiful. Her long brown hair had been pulled to one side and draped over one shoulder so that it cascaded down, almost covering one breast. The vivid blue eyes were her best feature, she decided, but the nose was too large. "Roman" some called it, but she sensed that was only in kindness. Sandy determined then and there to have cosmetic surgery at the first opportunity. She turned to look at her profile just as there was a knock on the dressing-room door.

"Ya' decent, Ghost?" Chuck Hitmar eased into the room smiling self-consciously. He pushed thick glasses back up onto his nose with the hand that wasn't holding a tenor saxophone. "You're the guest of honor at the Jazz Society banquet...can't be late. You'll have to follow us to the club. By the way, it's Black and Tan." He bent to look in the mirror and ran a hand over his blond burr haircut. "That bother you?"

She raised an eyebrow, "'Black and Tan'? You mean the building?"

"A racially mixed crowd, Ghost, wise up."

"I don't care if everybody's purple with pink polka dots." Shrugging into a short, fake fur jacket she declared, "I've never felt such love...such appreciation. But, Chuck, it was your arrangement that made it a good performance--not my singing. Your arrangements are always sensational." She picked up a yellow wardrobe bag and turned out the light.

Chuck Hitmar, in spite of all his musical strength and talent, wore a cloud of shyness and naivete like most people wore sunglasses. She could see his flush of embarrassment in the light of the hall.

"Come on, we'll be late. Follow the guys in the band," he said gruffly and then added, "Why can't you ever seem to take any credit when you deserve it, Sandy? Stop putting yourself down. You've got a great career ahead of you."

Do I really? She hugged the thought to herself as they stepped out into the snow covered parking lot. The exquisite triumph of this night transformed the icicles on the light poles into tiny cornucopias of diamonds.

The two hour drive alone from Cleveland, Ohio to Greenville, Pennsylvania seemed endless as she reminded herself that on four hours sleep she'd have to get

Eric and Lisa up and dressed. *I promise not to be "Monster Mom"*, she resolved. *A glass of orange juice and Cocoa Puffs in a bowl, how bad can it be?*

Maybe "Ding Dong School" and Miss Frances on TV would keep them entertained enough to catch a quick nap on the couch. The only trouble was that prissy old Miss Frances always told them to, "Go get your Mommy" when the commercial came on. *If I keep singing*, she thought, *next year will be harder as Eric will be in school--hot breakfasts and packing lunches will be the order of the day. We'll see...*

A heavy crisp snow began to fall. It slanted obliquely in front of the headlights and she fought the hypnotic effect with the remembrance of how a tiny coincidence in time had changed everything. Switching on the defrosters, her mind swirled back to another snowy night, just five years earlier, when the portrait of her life had been painted with black strokes of loneliness and despair.

***

An icy wind had howled mournfully that night in 1955. It had angrily rattled the windows of the tiny, one bedroom house in the country with the incessant fury of an angry prowler demanding entry. As the snowstorm mounted in intensity, the wind angrily pushed drifts to the south, then moments later bulldozed them to a new position, much as a discontented housewife rearranges furniture. It had seemed to Sandy, alone with a newborn baby, as if the wind were writing threatening messages on the windows with a frosty finger which probed to gain entrance.

Where *was* Bill? He had called from work and said he'd be a "little late", but it was now 10:00 o'clock at night. She scratched enough frost from the kitchen window to peer out at the highway. A car laboriously churned through the snow. The icy lane of tracks was quickly obliterated by the swift hand of the wind that seemed to jealously resent the intrusion in its nervous decorating scheme.

While the highway had not been plowed, it was obviously still open to traffic. The house was only two miles outside of Greenville, but could there have been an accident? Sandy shivered and glanced at the clock again just as the telephone rang.

"Well, I won't be home for dinner," Bill chuckled and added, "just thought I'd call and let you know." His voice was faltering--the words thick-tongued.

She could hear a woman's laughter in the background, people talking; music blared from a jukebox. A rush of hot anger boiled upward dissolving her former fear. "You call me at 10:00 o'clock at night to tell me you're not coming home to dinner? I already *know* you're not coming home to dinner!"

There was silence on the other end. She could almost see his silly grin. The jukebox switched songs. Jo Stafford smoothly sang, "You Belong to Me." *Pretty lousy timing for that song*, she thought. *He doesn't belong to me.*

"Bill, are you there? You left me alone through the whole pregnancy. Now we've got a son who is a month old. When will you grow up?"

"Making a big dramatic production out of this, Sandy?" The words were slurred and he chuckled again.

"I'm terrified being alone in this snowstorm with the baby," she implored. "What if something happens...I have no car...what if...", and at that moment Eric began to cry for his 10:00 o'clock feeding.

"You just take your little index finger," the knifing sarcasm in Bill's voice cut slashes in her self-esteem, "and you put it in those little holes in the 'phone and dial for help."

"But, where are you, Bill?" The line went dead.

Blindly blinking back tears, she put a bottle on to heat and went to the bedroom. Suddenly, she couldn't help laughing; Eric lay in the bassinet, smacking his lips as though he were eating already.

"Well, little man, I think a diaper change might be in order here." She reached for a fresh one and the can of talcum powder. Task performed, she hugged the baby to her and went to the kitchen.

A sudden burst of wind violently shook the house and she tucked the receiving blanket around Eric's head to protect him from drafts while he ate. The pewter gray kitchen walls seemed to close in on them as the storm raged outside. The only sounds were the second hand of the round kitchen clock tapping a metronome to the concert the wind performed.

As little Eric took his bottle, a kaleidoscope of past events insinuated themselves into the quicksand of self-pity that now mired Sandy's mind:

She saw herself as a teenager in a home that floated on the swirling currents of a river of alcohol. It was like living on the edge of being swept over rapids which ran smooth at times, then suddenly, with no provocation, could erupt into threatening, churning waters.

And then, Chelie came along when Sandy was sixteen--a tiny, blonde sister to play with like a doll baby. But the hysterectomy that their mother had to have immediately following giving birth at forty-three, plunged Gaye into further emotional imbalance. Both children lived on top of a powder keg that threatened to explode at any minute.

In the passing collage of events, now swirling by Sandy's mind in the kitchen that night, she saw herself trying to make it up to Chelie, as her high school schedule and homework permitted. She was so involved with the baby the other kids teased, suggesting Chelie was really Sandy's baby, born out of wedlock. This tore large holes in the fabric of her already tattered self-esteem.

And then a sly escape presented itself. At one of the rare parties she was allowed to attend, Sandy met Brad. He was not particularly handsome, in fact, bald, portly and thirty-five years old. Because of his age, he was the only one driving. Brad told her two weeks later that when she walked in front of his Chevrolet's headlights that night, he determined, "That's the girl I'm going to marry."

For some unknown reason, Gaye promoted the relationship of her daughter, who was then just a junior in high school, and a thirty-five year old man who had recently been discharged from the Navy. Sandy and Brad were served cocktails as Gaye bragged that, "We would rather have Sandy drinking at home, or smoking at home, than have her do it behind our back. In fact, we bought her the first pack of cigarettes."

Brad nodded approval at such a modern approach to parenting; however, Sandy had begun to run with a fast crowd, when she was allowed out of the house at all. She laughed inwardly at the rationale of her mother's statement, and took a canapé from the silver tray. She eyed Brad closely, trying to assess why he had paid her so much attention in past weeks. It was "neat-o" to ride around in his car; he had really "been around", and she was now the envy of all her girl friends, who suspected they were "doing it".

They were wrong. While smoking and drinking were permissible, sex was expressly forbidden. Gaye's admonishments on the subject were better than any chastity belt. In one of her better moments, perhaps precipitated by the fact that her daughter was dating an older man, she turned a "girl-talk chat" into a hell fire and brimstone sermon which would have made a Baptist minister envious.

In conclusion she added, "Never, never give away your 'virtue'." Sandy winced. She inwardly felt her grandmother had a better handle on it. Grammy had told her, "A man never continues to run after a bus if he's already caught it." That made more sense than what her mother said.

Gaye had continued, "I cannot watch everything you do when you leave this house, Sandra, but God sees everything!"

She wasn't even sure there *was* a God. *If so, He certainly is too busy holding up the stars to waste His time spying on me,* she told herself. *But what if there is a God?* Apparently, He was someone to be feared even more than she feared her mother...and she was terrified of her mother.

Perhaps because Brad couldn't "catch the bus", or perhaps because Sandy saw his proposal of marriage as an escape from her stringent home life, marriage plans began to unfold. She would quit school at the end of her junior year.

As the second hand of the kitchen clock noisily brought her back to the present, Sandy burped the baby and continued to give him the rest of the bottle.

The thread of memory continued to weave its spell of despair. She realized that marrying Brad had only traded a river of alcohol for a sea of jealous physical abuse. She shook her head sadly at the thought, and wiped a dribble of milk from little Eric's mouth. Brad, insecure at having married someone much younger, not only dominated, but wanted to jealously possess her.

"I don't ever want children," he said. "They might come between us." She was not allowed to have friends either, or go to the grocery store alone. Brad was to be the sole focus of her attention, so she modeled herself after the housewives she saw on television, and tried to tie a crisp white apron around her mind.

The marital charade culminated one day in a furious explosion of Brad's temper. It had all begun so innocently. Kitty Ryan, wife of their landlord, was from Florida. The Ryans lived in a studio apartment over the carriage house of the large Victorian home that had been divided into apartments. Kitty came by to pick up the rent check. The girls talked for a few minutes and she confessed how homesick she was for Florida. Sandy invited her in for coffee.

Later, when Brad came home from work, the first thing he spotted was the two china cups and saucers on the coffee table by the fireplace. He lit a cigarette and walked into the small kitchen. "So, who was here?"

Sandy was stirring spaghetti sauce, "Just Mrs. Ryan. She seemed so lonely, I asked her in for coffee". She reached for some oregano seasoning.

At that moment, Brad put the cigarette between his thumb and index finger and shot it into her face. It burned her and fell into the sauce. He grabbed her by the arm, dragging her to the living room where he threw her on the couch. "You little brat! Don't you *ever* have anyone in here without asking me, you understand?" He spat out a string of expletives.

"But it was just a cup of coffee, only another woman, Brad. I didn't do anything wrong." she implored.

At that, Brad walked toward the coffee cups and smashed them against the marble of the fireplace. He picked up the mahogany coffee table, which had been a wedding present, smashing it too against the wall.

As she watched in horror, he advanced toward her, and she ran screaming from the apartment.

"Come and get me, Daddy," she begged from the telephone booth on the corner. Her father made it from Greenville to Meadville in record time.

They found Brad had left, as she and her father stepped over a pile of splintered pieces of furniture to get to the bedroom and pack. "Good grief, what would he have done to you, honey, if you hadn't run?" Her father was obviously shaken by the devastation of the apartment.

"He looked like he was going to murder me. All I did was have coffee with a girl friend...not even a friend at that, just the landlord's wife." She snapped a suitcase closed.

"Is he *that* eaten up with jealousy?"

She scooped a jewelry box into a paper bag, "Daddy, you have no idea. He's consumed by it." She was surprised to find herself talking intimately with her father, but she had always been closer to him. He was funny, and loving, and sensitive--when he wasn't drinking.

He carried the suitcases to the front door and turned to view the living room again, "I'd like to wring his neck! This is really sick," he pronounced, forgetting how many door jambs he had splintered himself. "Let's take you home, sweetheart."

She hugged him tightly. He was her rescuer, though in her heart she knew he needed rescuing too.

***

Out of the river, into the sea and back into the river. And now I'm drowning again, Sandy thought as she rocked little Eric back and forth. The kitchen clock now said "11:10" and still no abatement in the snowstorm. And still no husband, Bill...

Her mind couldn't seem to stop the litany of self-pity it had begun. She saw herself going back to Meadville after Brad begged forgiveness that first time. Her mother insisted she was obliged to try to make it work; however, continued incidents of violence finally escalated into physical abuse. After two years of marriage, a kindly, old Episcopalian priest encouraged her to get a divorce.

She moved back home at Christmas time and filed for divorce. In her mind's eye, she remembered the fragrance of evergreen boughs behind pictures and on the mantel. Red candles in brass holders flickered in competition with a crackling log in the fireplace. Sitting next to her mother at the piano, she turned the pages of the music as Gaye played a few carols and then started to sing, "I'll be home for Christmas."

Choking back sobs, Sandy felt a bittersweet thankfulness to be home. A heavy weight of failure on her nineteen-year-old shoulders further constricted her self-esteem. The only one overjoyed was tiny Chelie, who snuggled in her lap.

Her little sister made more sense than most adults. Sandy, having moved again into the role of surrogate mother, found that Chelie had developed her own vocabulary. A butterfly was a "flutter-by"--much more reasonable than the word itself; a nightgown was a "night down"--you put it on when you went "down" for the night, so that made much better sense. And a "lollypop" was christened a "candy pop"-- who had ever eaten a "lolly"?

The two sisters, so far apart in age, clung steadfastly together against the torrent of emotional outbursts and stony silences in their home. When Gaye threatened suicide, swallowing a handful of pills while Bill watched, Sandy took Chelie to her room and read, "Winnie-the-Pooh", with varying voices for Pooh, Piglet and all the characters getting increasingly louder as diversion in an attempt to cover the noises of the rescue squad.

Sandy went back to finish high school and was considered a freak by her classmates. She had been married, was two years older, and it was a demeaning experience to have boys stop her in the hall and taunt, "I'm available, darling. And don't you forget it." She wanted to vomit.

At this point in time, Chelie developed two imaginary friends to fill the daytime void while her big sister was in school. Gaye had been doing their chemical company's accounting at home, and Chelie christened her new imaginary friends, "Debit" and "Credit".

After their daughter's graduation, Gaye and Bill took lengthy sales trips together. Sandy was a built-in babysitter. "Someday I'll pay you back when you have children of your own. But for now, you owe us...we paid for your divorce, took you back in, you know." And off they would go for weeks at a time.

The peacefulness in the house was a blessed relief, but with Sandy in full charge, it further fueled the gossip in Greenville that Chelie was really *her* child. "Sometimes I just feel like a punching bag," she confessed to her best friend, Patty.

And then Bill Ghost rode into her life, not on a white horse, but in a white Buick with four holes on either side of the hood that pronounced it was a 1952 status symbol. He was a total opposite of Brad, slender, handsome, with curly brown hair and hazel eyes that danced with fun. A strange coincidence surrounded their meeting. Bill's father was an osteopath: Sandy's grandmother's doctor.

Doctor Ghost was adored by his patients--not only for his medical expertise--but because he cared deeply about his patients. He had delivered a majority of the babies in Greenville, and his kind heart would dismiss a bill when low income patients left a bushel of potatoes, jams, jellies, apples or other produce on his back porch. During a house call to Sandy's grandmother, he mentioned his son had graduated from Penn State and was now back in Greenville looking for a job. Grammy, sensing a "bus chase" might be in the offing for her granddaughter, jumped on the opportunity and suggested Bill Ghost meet Sandy.

It could have been an awkward meeting, but Bill's dry sense of humor and relaxed manner put her at ease. They began dating and Gaye, impressed that he was a doctor's son, allowed her oldest daughter more free time.

Bill seemed infatuated. Sandy declared to all that would listen that she finally knew what real love was. He wasn't possessive, even seemed to be totally indifferent about what she did, or where she went. Sparks flew when they were together.

At the conclusion of a date, as he kissed her "goodnight" in the white Buick, Gaye would flash the front porch light to signal disapproval. *If she's afraid I'll lose my "virtue", guess what? I've already lost it, I've been married for Pete's sake,* Sandy wryly thought, but obediently she'd push Bill away and go in the house. She still feared her mother.

Bill began work in Elyria, Ohio with a large auto manufacturer as a Time and Motion Specialist, but came back to Greenville every weekend. Sandy seemed to live in a parenthesis during the week. As Halloween approached, she got a card in the mail with Bill Ghost's Ohio address in the upper left-hand corner of the envelope.

It was a card displaying a ghost on the cover, wearing an impish grin. Inside it read:

"If a ghost drops by on Halloween
Don't be a fuddy duddy
Just pucker up to get a kiss
For in your hands he's putty".

At the bottom, he wrote, "Dinner Saturday night at Shusters?" Sandy slept with the card under her pillow. Almost all of their dates had taken place at the different bars and roadhouses near Greenville, or at the drive-in theater. The drinking age in Pennsylvania was twenty-one; therefore, Sandy had cokes. Bill always put away several beers. This bothered her, but she kept silent about it because he was so affable, cute and funny. It was not at all like the personality change she had observed in her parents when they were drinking.

Shusters Restaurant was famous for their steaks—definitely not their atmosphere. Tables with white linen cloths were placed in double rows of precise, rigidly straight lines on each side of the huge dining room. The rows of tables, sitting on flooring of large black and white squares of linoleum, gave a stark appearance of two armies of chess pieces that faced each other. Patrons had to speak in whispers or their conversations would ricochet like bowling balls across a room that was devoid of even a drapery to dampen the acoustics.

Shusters, however, was *the* place to go and Sandy anticipated something special. She wore a black, slightly off the shoulder dress with a full skirt. After dinner, a band played for dancing. Bill held her very close on the dance floor, his fingers sensually played games with her spine.

"Having fun?" he whispered in her ear as he seated her back at the table.

"Oh, yes. The band's great." She smiled across the table, hoping to look provocative.

"The place is a barn," Bill waved a hand expansively. "The music's great if you don't mind it sounding like it's being played through a police bullhorn." He signaled to the waitress for another beer.

Sandy laughed and shook her head, "You are so funny, Bill." The waitress served his beer without bothering to pick up the other bottles. She willed herself not to count them, but there were now five on the table arranged in a neat, brown line like a fortress between them.

"How would you like to be a Ghost?" Bill lit a cigarette. The lid of the Zippo lighter snapped shut with a reverberating ring that echoed across the room.

Remembering the card, she asked, "You mean for Halloween?"

"Nope, I mean for life." He reached into his suit coat pocket, removing a small blue velvet box. Flipping open the lid, he extended the box across the table.

There, nestled in white satin, was a diamond engagement ring. Two smaller diamonds flanked the large solitaire on each side.

"Oh, yes, Bill, yes!" she looked into his eyes and saw a future brimming with romance, laughter, children, and beautiful homes, as he put the ring on the finger of her left hand. The young lovers had no idea at that time what the significance of the four small diamonds in the ring would mean, and the message they would send at a later date.

Bill ordered a bottle of champagne and she sneaked sips from his glass. She felt as effervescent as the bubbles that shimmered in the light.

Later that night, Gaye waited by her sentry post beside the front porch light switch. When she saw the Buick pull up by the house, she counted to one hundred, "Enough time for a *proper* goodnight," she muttered and began flicking the switch like a lighthouse keeper preventing boats from crashing on the rocks.

Bill had spent two years in the Navy. "Jeez, your mother missed her calling. She should have been on a destroyer, signaling Morse code." He walked her to the door and they risked one more kiss, knowing full well that Gaye was on the other side breathing sighs of disapproval.

Once inside, Sandy proudly showed her mother the ring. Gaye walked toward the kitchen trailing words, "Well, December would be a nice month...a Christmas wedding. You could wear ice blue, can't be white, you know."

Virtue loss again rears its ugly head, Sandy thought.

"Let's see, it will have to be a small wedding. Can't flaunt the fact you've been married before--the reception here." Gaye poured herself a drink. "I'll have Lil do the cooking and Jimmy will serve."

Sandy wistfully remembered the lavish reception her grandparents had given her before at the posh Iroquois Club in Conneaut Lake.

Her mother prattled on barely pausing for a breath, "I'll call Father Paul in the morning and see if he can perform the ceremony," she consulted a calendar on the kitchen wall. "December 4th, that's a good date," she circled the "4th" and began waving the pencil like a baton as she continued orchestrating details.

Sandy sank into a kitchen chair. She resisted a sudden urge to cover her ears. "Don't you think we ought to consult Bill and his family first before we set a date?" she asked wearily.

An obstinate look entered Gaye's blue eyes, turning them to steel gray. Her daughter had seen that look many times before. "You just listen here, young lady, your father and I are the ones paying for this. And don't you forget we have already paid for one wedding--and a divorce too. If we say it's the fourth of December, it's the fourth of December." She punctuated her statement with a flourish of the yellow pencil.

Later, as she climbed into bed, Sandy realized her mother had managed to puncture the ballooning thrill of this night with the point of her waving yellow pencil. *I can't even plan my own wedding,* she brooded. She lay on her back, staring toward the dark ceiling. The street light outside illuminated only her desk and the flowered chintz skirt of the dressing table. Shadows of tree branches dipped and glided silently across the wall, as the warm night wind gently coached their dance.

The tips of her fingers sought the card under her pillow for reassurance. "How would you like to be a Ghost?" he had said. The feeling of love and excitement returned momentarily, but was quickly replaced by a twinge of fear. Could it be a warning? She saw Bill clearly in her mind's eye behind the stockade of brown beer bottles. *He just had to bolster his courage a bit to ask me to marry him* she reasoned, dismissing the image and the eerie feeling it had somehow held portentous meaning. She closed her eyes and willed sleep to come.

The warning signal came again, however, just a month later, with all the shrill clarity of a civil defense siren.

The beginning of November, they went to State College, Pennsylvania for Penn State's homecoming game. Bill's frat house served as the center for all the festive activities; the rathskeller bar in the basement was jammed with "brothers" pounding each other on the back in greeting, toasting each other with beer steins.

Not having gone to college, Sandy felt intimidated by the surroundings. She hoped she wouldn't embarrass Bill in any way and had dressed carefully in a brown wool tweed suit, which had a matching reversible coat with huge pockets as part of the sporty design. The social hour at the rathskeller preceded the game. Bill was well on the way to becoming drunk before the game and after the game as he continued to drink, Sandy resolved to break off the engagement. She gave him back his ring the following day.

Her mother accepted the news of the broken engagement with the grace of a small volcanic eruption. Instead of feeling sorry for her daughter's demeaning experience, and reinforcing her decision, Gaye shook her by the shoulders, "The engraved wedding invitations have already been paid for and sent out. The flowers are ordered, Father Paul's reserved the church and we've paid for the reception food. You cannot back out now, Sandra!"

"I'll get a job and pay you back." She had been babysitting Chelie to pay back the first marriage and divorce.

"You'd better wake up and take hold of your life. He's a great catch--handsome, good sense of humor, so what if he drinks too much. What makes you think *you're* so perfect?" Gaye walked out of the room.

She knew she wasn't perfect--in fact, she felt pretty worthless, wondered what Bill had seen in her to begin with. But she couldn't make many more mistakes with one marriage shot down before the age of nineteen. *I am trying to take hold of my life,* Sandy reasoned. Did her confessed fear of Bill's drinking hit a personal raw nerve with her mother? Or was she frivolously ungrateful for all her parents had done for her? Maybe she should reconsider. She knew she deeply loved Bill, maybe marriage would change him and he'd settle down.

They were married on December 4, 1954. Dainty, blonde Chelie was a bridesmaid and stole the show by furiously chewing gum through the entire ceremony. Sandy felt she was abandoning her sister a second time to the volatile environment at home, but as Bill had taken a job in Greenville, she'd be able to still try to be a positive influence in her life.

They rented a one bedroom house in the country across from Greenville's only Country Club. Bill joked about living across from "the Club", but he spent all his free hours on the links, hunting with "the guys", or getting "bombed with the boys" at Cianci's bar. Eric was born on their first anniversary, proudly delivered by his grandfather, Dr. Ghost, while another doctor stood in attendance as that was protocol when it was a family member.

Gaye was furious. Sandy had promised to take her parents to the airport in Pittsburgh and then unexpectedly, her water broke and labor began. Their chemical company had taken bankruptcy; they were moving to Florida where Sandy's dad had taken a job as Vice President of Tatum Chemical in Miami. Gaye insinuated she had purposely started labor to avoid driving them to Pittsburgh.

The hospital in Grove City was on the way to Pittsburgh. She begged them to at least stop on the way to see their new grandson. A cab waited outside as they viewed baby Eric through the glass of the nursery and kissed Sandy on the cheek. Wryly she remembered her mother's words, "When you have children of your own I'll pay you back for all the babysitting", and on the very same day, they were now moving to Florida. *What an ironic coincidence,* Sandy thought.

Chelie tried to crawl into the hospital bed with her. "I don't want to go," she cried. "I wanna stay with Sandy."

Sandy thought her heart would break. She stroked Chelie's hair, what would become of her so far away?

***

With a start, Sandy was pulled back from remembrance by the ticking of the second hand on the kitchen clock. The wind still howled outside and the kitchen had become very cold. She realized hot tears were spilling down onto Eric's little owl-like face. His large eyes regarded her quizzically.

"Oh, sweetheart, I'm so sorry," she wiped away her tears from his face with a corner of the receiving blanket. She hugged the baby tightly. What would become of them? Her father was in Florida, he couldn't be her rescuer again. Was there no one to help her? At that moment in time, Sandy could not have even imagined the events that were lining up to create a new life.

Chapter Two

———————— ◌ᵥ◌ ————————

As Sandy continued to travel back to Greenville from the Jazz Concert in Cleveland, memories were suppressed into quietly treading water as the heavily falling snow required her driving attention, but then they would suddenly bob to the surface serving up a fresh picture from the past with new intensity. So much had happened since that night when Eric was just a month old...

Spring had brought promise to the Pennsylvania countryside by painting wildflowers from a pastel palette, and caressing fields of hay with the same gentle hand that tickled the clouds. Now, summer flamed onto the scene, scorching the hay, wilting the flowers and torching tempers with unbearable heat and humidity.

"I can't stand it anymore! I'm sick to death of living in the country!" Sandy muttered to herself, slamming the ant covered cherry pie into the garbage can. She stomped on the trail of ants that marched across the kitchen floor, and then worried about the noise wakening Eric as he napped. *I'm planted here in the country with the baby and the crops.* Her mind cooked up a hash of bitterness. *If we could just move to town...I could at least take Eric for a walk on a sidewalk.*

She took her glass of iced tea to the living room, and opening the front door for a cross draft, wilted onto the couch. The Chinese red accents and heavy, black lacquered furniture of the room seemed to magnify the smothering heat. The only fan was in the bedroom where the baby was sleeping.

It was too hot and oppressive to even think. Her feet and fingers were swollen. She removed her blouse, fanning herself with a magazine. *Well, why not? The front door is on the opposite side of the house from the driveway. Nobody ever comes out here anyway,* she thought. Taking off her slacks too, she began to walk across the living room, in bra and pants, to turn on the television. Suddenly, without the whisper of a sound, there was a man standing at the front door.

They both gasped at the same time. His eyes grew huge and his mouth made soundless guppy-like motions. *A rapist...*was the first thing to come to mind as she lunged behind the front door, attempting to close it.

Just then he found his voice, "I...I'm selling Bibles," he stammered.

She peered around the door. He still looked like he might swallow his Adam's apple. "Not interested." She slammed the door and locked it.

The episode worked in her favor, however. Using her vulnerability in the country as a platform of appeal, Sandy related the incident at dinner. She passed Bill the bowl of mashed potatoes. "I could have been raped or murdered," she lifted Eric into his highchair and tied a terrycloth bib under his chin.

"By a Bible salesman?" Bill laughed so hard he choked on a piece of meat.

"That's not the point. I'm here alone most of the time. Anything could happen."

"You make such a big stinkin' deal out of everything, Sandy. Relax!" He really liked being so close to the golf course, even though it was just nine holes.

She interrupted his thoughts, "Couldn't we move to town? Frankly, I hate it here...I've got claustrophobia being cooped up like this."

"Now that makes a whale of a lot of sense," he waved an arm expansively. "You've got claustrophobia in the country. I was a psychology major. Believe me you don't even know what the word means."

"It's just that I feel planted here," she fed Eric a spoonful of mashed potatoes, that he promptly took out of his mouth and wiped across the highchair tray. He continued to finger paint potatoes across his arms and into his hair, but Sandy was staring at the pewter gray kitchen walls as though she could see through them.

"If we could just find a little house in town to rent, I could walk Eric on sidewalks, walk to the store, or to a friend's house in the daytime." It was as though she had painted a blissfully happy scene on the kitchen wall. She smiled...until she looked at the baby.

"Oh, good grief... Mr. Potato Head in person." She grabbed a washcloth.

"I wondered when you'd wake up and see the devastation. Remember when Reb came home from Korea?"

She nodded. Her brother-in-law had been wounded there; shipped back home with a Purple Heart.

Bill chuckled. "He said he'd been able to stomach bloated dead bodies in ditches, but he couldn't stand to watch his kid eat. He was right." Bill pushed back from the table. "Gotta go hit a few balls before it gets dark."

"But would you just think about moving? We can't stay in this tiny house much longer with Eric's crib in our bedroom."

He smiled--it was his signature one-two punch--not that it was contrived, but people always seemed to come around to his way of thinking when he smiled at them. "If you're that unhappy here, I'll think about it," he promised.

After Eric's first birthday, after Christmas, and after the Country Club had closed for the season, they moved to town the following April. It was a comfortable, old two-story home with white clapboard siding. The front porch wore a green striped awning like an awkwardly frivolous hat, but it had a broad porch swing to rock babies. An arbor was laden with morning glory flowers in the spring. They unfolded their pale blue delicacy, lifting faces to greet each day, and then shyly folded like a southern belle's coquettish fan in the heat of the afternoon.

The freedom Sandy had been denied by her mother, then Brad, and the confinement of country living, was now excitingly available. They just had one car; therefore, she could be seen walking with Eric's little hand in hers, or pushing him in the stroller if the trip to the store was too far for chubby little legs. *I can walk to Patty's house, or even to Bill's Mom and Dad's house,* she told herself happily. It was like being let out of a cage.

Mom Ghost had now become the understanding, loving mother Sandy had reached out for all her life. There was a certain wisdom, strength and stability in Isabel Ghost which was surprising, perhaps because she was so tiny. A halo of tight brown curly ringlets framed a high forehead and sensitive face. Her rippling laughter was contagious.

"Today we're going to can tomatoes," Isabel tied a red checked apron around her waist, and reached in the drawer for a flowered one for Sandy. Eric had been put down for his nap in a playpen in the senior Ghost's dining room.

"I really appreciate this. I never learned these things at home, Mom. If there was anything canned, it was my father getting fired from his job."

Isabel giggled like a teenager. She put a boiling pan of water on the kitchen counter and dipped the plump red tomatoes in the scalding water. The silver paring knife flashed in the sunlight from the window as the tomatoes were scalped with ease.

"I got it. Here let me do that." Sandy took the knife and promptly sliced a gash in her finger. "Oh, I'm such a klutz, can't seem to do anything right." She blinked back tears, not that the gash hurt, but the cutting words she had just uttered did.

"You're a wonderful mother--a lovely wife, dear." Isabel's fingertips wiped away the tears on Sandy's cheeks that couldn't seem to be held back. Something was definitely bothering her daughter-in-law.

"I know I'm a good mother, but I'm not sure about the wife part." She grabbed a paper towel and dabbed at her eyes. "Mom, I'm trying to be. If I show affection, I get fluffed off. Bill just can't seem to show his feelings." She couldn't believe she was telling his mother these things, but the torrent of words seemed to spill like a waterfall. "He hardly pays any attention to me or the baby. You know I told you, Brad was smothering...but this is worse. I feel like I'm just there to fix meals, clean the house and be there when he wants me physically." She wished she could put a piece of duct tape over her mouth. Why was she telling his mother these things?

17

Isabel shook her head. Tears of empathy could be detected behind her glasses. "He leaves you alone too much. I'll see if I can talk to him." Her arms folded lovingly around Sandy. "Have you prayed about this?" Her voice was almost a whisper.

Sandy pushed back from her mother-in-law. "Prayed about it? Mom, I hate to tell you, but I'm not even sure there is a God, and if there is, He's surely too busy throwing fireballs around the firmament to be bothered with our marriage."

"Let's put the tomatoes on hold...there's a story I want to tell you." The cooking lesson was forgotten as Isabel turned off the stove. She poured two glasses of iced tea, and returned the pitcher to the refrigerator.

They sat at the red formica and chrome kitchen table like two best friends. Isabel circled the cold glass with tiny hands, knuckles gnarled from arthritis. "Okay, now you said you weren't even sure you believed in God. But I know personally that He's real because of an experience I had." A new depth seemed to come into her deep brown eyes. She hugged some memory to herself that she was about to share. "I haven't told many people about this, or they'd think I was peculiar... ditzy." She smiled.

Sandy wondered what could have happened. She knew she would believe anything Mom told her.

"You remember that Reb was in Korea?"

She nodded. "Bill just mentioned it the other day."

"Well, I was playing golf the day Reb was shot. Suddenly, I was overcome by an overwhelming fear for Reb. It was as though an audible voice were telling me to pray for him. I dropped to my knees right there on the golf course and pleaded with God to spare him. When we found out later the exact time when he was wounded; it was at that precise moment, halfway around the world, that I was prompted to pray for him."

"But, Mom, that could have just been a coincidence. It was...it was just a coincidence."

"No one will ever convince me of that. I know full well that I was 'told' to pray for him at that moment. I really feel if there hadn't been intercession, he would have died. But I understand," she patted Sandy's hand. "I guess you have to have you own experience to know for sure."

Not me, she thought later as she pushed Eric toward home in the stroller. *Maybe somebody as good as Mom could be called upon...if there's a God up there to do the calling.* Obviously, her mother-in-law had confused a total coincidence with some mystical, religious experience. She promptly relegated the strange story to happenstance and hung it in the closet of her subconscious.

Over the weeks her depression deepened. One minute she would be laughing over Eric stuffing spinach up his nose, and the next minute she found herself crying if she broke a handle on a cup.

Bill had now been elected President of the local chapter of the Jaycees. This further compounded his absence from home at night. She watched television in the evenings, and began reading books on hypnosis, thinking perhaps self-hypnosis would cure this strange emotional pain she was experiencing--or at least tell her what was the cause. Her best friend, Patty, offered a suggestion.

They were drinking cokes, watching Eric ride the small, red tractor he had gotten for his second Christmas. The large living room with hardwood floors was perfect for speeding between couches, chairs and tables. "Slow down, Farmer Brown, you'll have a wreck," Sandy admonished. She turned to Patty, who was sitting on a loveseat in the path of Eric's demolition derby, "How good is your insurance? Bill can sell you some." He had just been hired as the local agent for a large, national insurance company.

Patty giggled and wrinkled her nose. "I think I've got enough coverage if I'm hit by a miniature tractor." She looked around the room. "You've rearranged the furniture again."

"Yep, the desk was over there," she gestured toward the wall by the stairs. "And I moved the conversational grouping over here. But would you believe it, even with a major change like this, Bill never said a word? I waited two weeks and then asked him if he noticed anything different. He said, 'You're wearing a new dress?'"

"Well, what do you expect? He's never here long enough to see anything but the shower and the bed." Patty took a long drink of coke and rearranged the ice cubes with one finger.

"You haven't heard the half of it, yet. When I told him, he looked around and had the audacity to say he didn't like it...after two weeks!"

"I see you haven't changed it back," Patty observed dryly.

"Well, no. Apparently I'm the only one who has to live with it." She shrugged her shoulders, wondering if she should tell Patty just how emotional she had become lately.

"You're going to explode if you don't get some help soon, Sandy. It's written all over your face. Can't you go to Dr. Ghost? Just tell him you're depressed if you don't feel free to talk about your marriage."

"Maybe I should," she realized her hands were shredding the paper napkin into small pieces, "this is not fair to little Eric, bursting into tears at the drop of a hat."

"And what about not fair to yourself? You don't have much of a marriage, and you don't really have much of a life from my viewpoint. So what if he looks like James Garner?"

"He really does, especially when he smiles. You know, I can sit here all evening seething over being left alone, and if I'm still up when he gets home, all he has to do is smile and my anger melts. Unless he's had too much to drink." She stubbed out her cigarette in the ashtray. "He's like Dr. Jekyll and Mr. Hyde, Patty, just a different person when he's drinking."

"Well, if you want to continue living this way, you're gonna' have to take Valium, or something. Go make an appointment with your father-in-law, hon," she retrieved her purse from the coffee table and stood up to leave.

She took Patty's advice two weeks later. It's been said that most women fall slightly in love with their doctor. In Sandy's case, it was not the typical crush felt by some women patients, but a deep well of respect due to Doctor Ghost's personal reservoir of kindness and caring.

Allen Ghost's medical knowledge, first-hand experience of treating ranges of ages, and seeing all manner of diseases over the years, made him an excellent diagnostician. While Osteopathy is a branch of the medical profession that believes the body has the ability to heal itself through external manipulation, there is also the belief that in the proper situation, prescription medicine is appropriate.

He was over six feet tall, with a lean masculine build that wears clothing well. He could be in hunting clothes and still look like he had just walked out of a haberdashery. His glasses helped to disguise the fact that one eye was slightly crossed. It was the only thing that made Sandy uncomfortable. When talking to him, she found herself not knowing which eye to look into. She proudly bragged to all her friends that he had delivered his own grandson by natural childbirth. Sandy felt secure in Dr. Ghost's compassionate care. What she didn't feel secure about was telling him what she felt was the *cause* of her nervousness--his son.

She sat on the treatment table in his office and looked at the now familiar pastel green walls and stainless steel tables holding various instruments. Three rooms, with separate entrance, housed his office in the tall, stately brick home across from the downtown park in Greenville.

Dr. Ghost wore a white coat over his daily clothes. He patted her on the arm, "I've drawn blood to be sent out for tests, and we should have results back in a few days. Don't worry, now." He patted her arm again. "I promise we'll find out if something is medically wrong. In the meantime, I'm going to administer a Vitamin B-12 shot for a pick-me-up. An MD, whom I sometimes work with, recommends a new tranquilizer that's just come out."

He squinted as he held a syringe upward toward the overhead light, filling it with Vitamin B-12. "He'll telephone the prescription to the drug store." At that time, Osteopathic Physicians were not permitted to prescribe drugs.

Bill picked up the prescription and brought it home at dinnertime. She was about to take the first two pills when the telephone rang.

"Sandy, don't take that prescription!" her father-in-law's voice warned sternly.

"What? Dad, what's wrong? I was just about to take the first dose."

"I'm not really sure," Allen sounded strangely troubled. "I just feel somehow it's wrong. Don't take them," he said mysteriously and hung up.

She put the bottle of pills on the top shelf of the medicine cabinet so that Eric couldn't reach them. A week later, her father-in-law called her into his office. She again sat on the treatment table waiting her turn; he was finishing up with another patient.

He walked into the room and washed his hands with antiseptic at the small sink. Drying them on a paper towel, he folded his arms against his chest and smiled knowingly. "I know what's wrong with you. I got the tests back. You're pregnant, Sandy."

"Pregnant? No, that can't be right. I haven't missed..."

"Well, you're going to make me a grandfather again." He was filling another syringe with B-12. "Pregnancy makes pretty radical hormonal changes in the system. I suspect the rush of hormones is what's causing the nervousness and the nervousness is what's bringing on continued periods."

"The joke's on us. We thought it was rabies, and here it was babies!"

They both laughed as she hugged the idea to herself. She would love another baby. But would Bill?

"Now that we know you're pregnant, I definitely do not want you taking those tranquilizers, understand?"

She nodded affirmatively.

"In fact, I want you to throw them out."

But Sandy, not convinced that pregnancy alone was causing her nervousness, did not throw them out. She resolved, however, not to take the pills as long as she carried another life inside her.

She had planned to tell Bill the news that night, but he didn't come home until after she was asleep. The following morning the smell of coffee percing and bacon cooking filled the small kitchen. "Only got time for coffee," Bill announced as he came to the table wrestling with a tie.

"I fixed biscuits with your mother's elderberry jam...your favorite." She tried to buy more time as she poured his coffee.

"I've got an 8:30 appointment for a life policy," he reached for the cream, "gotta go." She sat down at the table and looked at him. How would he take this? After phrasing and re-phrasing the words, rehearsing them in romantic terms, now the words just seemed to take on a life of their own, bulldozing their way into the room. She blurted out, "I'm pregnant."

21

Bill's coffee cup clattered down onto the saucer as he stared at her. "That's wonderful!" He grinned broadly, and then a small frown began to cloud the handsome smile. "We're scarcely making it now financially. Another baby's going to wipe us out."

She sat on his lap. A baby would put him under a lot more pressure she realized. Maybe she needed to be more sensitive to what he was feeling. "We'll make it, honey, don't worry," she stroked his cheek and kissed him gently.

"Up, up, up," Bill pushed back his chair. "Way to go kid! But you're probably going to have to get a job."

"At least, there won't be a doctor bill." But the words were said to his retreating back and she didn't know if he had even heard them.

Two months later Sandy brought the newspaper in from the front porch, checked on a pie in the oven and spread the pages out on the kitchen table. Her eyes rested on an article on the front page, "Thalidomide Suspected to Cause Deformity in Babies". As she read on, she winced at statistics of children born with deformed arms and legs. The FDA proclaimed it was studying results in pregnant mothers. Something insistently pulled at her mind. Somehow the word "thalidomide" sounded familiar--but it couldn't be.

She slowly climbed the stairs and retrieved the forgotten bottle of tranquilizers from the medicine cabinet. She held the small print of the label to the light. "Take two as needed", it instructed. "Thalidomide." The word seemed to jump off the label. She dropped the pill bottle as the impact presented itself with startling clarity. The bottle clattered around in the sink.

"I just feel somehow it's wrong. Don't take them," Dad had said. *At that time he didn't even know I was pregnant,* Sandy remembered. She went to the telephone and dialed.

"Dad, have you seen tonight's paper?" She could tell from the preoccupied way in which he answered the phone that he had.

"I've seen it. Thank God you never took that prescription." There was a slight tremor in his voice.

"But did you *know* something, is that why you warned me?"

"No, not really." There was a pause. "I just had a strong inner feeling that it would be terribly wrong for you to take the prescription." His words came slowly. "Didn't even know you were pregnant when I had the feeling." He seemed to be talking more to himself than to Sandy, hesitantly sifting through the whole experience.

"Oh Dad, thank you. What a lucky coincidence, I just can't imagine..." Her words trailed off into thoughtfulness as she pictured their baby with no arms or deformed legs.

"Coincidence? Yes, well...if you want to call it that." It was as though he was still having trouble focusing on her end of the conversation.

22

"I love you, Dad."

"I love you too," he said and the line went dead.

She couldn't wait to tell Bill about it--show him the newspaper article. He'd agree it was probably the luckiest coincidence they could possibly ever have in their lives.

Little did she know that it was the beginning of a pattern that would slowly begin to unfold.

Chapter Three

⌒◇⌒

Whispers of soft spring rain coaxed the morning glories to bloom again as whispers of the life within Sandy caused her to have what she referred to as "bloomin' morning sickness". She popped the huge pink and blue natal capsules in her mouth, washing them down with a large glass of milk. It had become an evening ritual she hated.

Taking the large basket of clean clothes into the living room, she snapped on the small, black and white television set. A sexy-looking dark haired guy was singing and playing guitar. Obviously, he was gyrating wildly from the waist down; however, the camera only showed a close up. "Why can't they show the bottom part?" Sandy wondered aloud, and found herself dancing around the living room with a clean bath towel as a partner. Women in the audience screamed loudly as the song ended, chanting, "Elvis! Elvis!"

"Wow", she said aloud, as she collapsed onto the couch. The music and excitement of the rhythm had made a startling mood transformation for her. Moments earlier she had faced the doldrums of another evening alone. Somehow the music had ignited some strange spark of promise as though beckoning to her.

She folded another towel as a woman singer was announced on the musical program. The first notes of the song "Summertime" drifted toward her and the pile of laundry. Almost as if in a daze, Sandy picked up a ruler off the desk nearby, and holding it like a microphone, sang with the television. There was an antique Bulls Eye mirror hanging over the fireplace that reflected the entire room into a convex distorted image. As she viewed herself in the mirror, envisioning herself on stage, the lyrics of the song seemed to dictate the moves to make with her hands and body. At the end, she pretended the applause was for her and bowed to the image in the mirror.

"Good Lord, I'm losing my mind!" she exclaimed. She scrambled back to the couch. "Talking to myself out loud, singing to a pretend audience in the mirror--if Bill had come in while that idiocy was going on, he'd have me committed." She quickly returned to the laundry, as if to hastily fold the embarrassment of her impetuous actions into the reality of clean towels.

He might have considered having her committed had he seen her make believe performance; however, ultimately, he was used as the initial catalyst to cause it to materialize.

"The Jaycees are hosting a three night home talent show at the high school

24

in two months," he announced as he buttered a roll at dinner several nights later. "We need help producing it, Sandy." He took a bite.

She nodded in affirmation as she'd seen the posters in stores.

"You did a few stints with the Theater Guild in high school, didn't you?" He cut into a slice of roast beef.

"Yes. I did some production--also had a few roles."

"Casting and rehearsals start next week. Mom says she'll babysit Eric on rehearsal nights. Okay?"

Immediately she wanted to jump at the chance; however, a rush of belittling scenes at home presented themselves. Past experience checked her answer. "Well, I don't know."

"What do you mean, 'I don't know'?" The words were steeped in sarcasm. "You have a chance to get out and a built in babysitter."

"I want to, I really do. It's just that... you put me down here at home all the time...about my cooking, the way I iron your shirts. I'll die of embarrassment if you put me down in front of the cast." Conflicting emotions played tug of war with her mind. It could be so much fun, but not worth public embarrassment.

"Are you going to start a fight over *this*? I just thought you need to get out of the house more, but just forget it." Bill tossed his napkin onto the table.

Now that the door of opportunity threatened to slam shut, she realized how badly she wanted to do it. "I'm sorry. I really would love it." She began to clear the table. Maybe if she did well, Bill would be proud of her. It never seemed to occur to her that she had transferred to her husband the pattern of striving to win her mother's approval.

He seemed bewildered by her sudden shift in gears and lashed out, "You're a total enigma--impossible to understand! Suit yourself, but I need help."

"I'll do it. I said I'd love to." She kissed his cheek.

Eric, who had brought a small, stuffed toy to the table held it up to her. "Kiss doggie," he instructed. She leaned over and complied. He patted her stomach. "Baby in there." She wasn't in maternity clothes yet, but they had told Eric he would have a brother or sister.

Bill laughed, "Time to tell him the facts of life soon."

As if to reinforce his father's statement, Eric now patted his own stomach and proclaimed, "Baby in here."

"No, just squash and roast beef in there, sweetheart." She picked him up, setting him on her lap. "It's a little early. He's only two. We can't overwhelm him with sex facts he's not ready to understand yet. Haven't you ever heard the story about the five year old who came to his parents and asked where he came from?"

"I'm not sure." Bill impatiently looked at the clock.

She shifted Eric's weight on her lap. "Well, the parents went to the library and took out every book they could on explaining sex to a young child. They spent every evening reading the books to him, showing him fairly explicit pictures and at the end of the sessions finally asked, 'Tommy, now do you know where you come from?' The kid just looked at them and said, 'Jimmy comes from Pittsburgh, I just wanted to know where I come from.'"

Eric slid down off her lap, picking up a small red ball from the kitchen floor. "Play ball, Daddy."

"Not now, son. Daddy's got to go to work." Bill looked again at the clock over the kitchen sink.

She wondered how many nighttime insurance appointments he would schedule once rehearsals started. It was pretty hard to swallow that evening appointments could last until midnight. She suspected he usually met friends at a bar afterwards; but she kept silent, not wanting to precipitate another quarrel.

The following Monday night, the high school auditorium was a seething mass of pandemonium. Most of the Jaycees had brought their wives. Non-members, responding to an ad in the paper, showed up to be in the production and nobody seemed to be in charge. Bill stepped up on stage and yelled, "Settle down, people. Settle down." When there was reasonable quiet he continued, "This is to be an old time minstrel. We have scripts here to pass out." He handed Sandy a stack of mimeographed scripts and waved her in the direction of the crowded auditorium seating.

"There is an 'Oleo' portion which precedes the actual minstrel itself. We'll be auditioning for the talent for that tonight. So if you juggle, jiggle, sing, dance or whatever you can do, you'll be considered for the first portion of the show." There was a scattering of sporadic self-conscious laughter.

"The show will run for three nights; rehearsals will be Monday through Thursday every week for two months, so if you can't commit for that length of time, please don't waste our time auditioning." Several people filtered out through the exits.

"We need six 'End Men'...they're the ones who keep the comedy rolling in the minstrel portion. And we need eight big, heavy guys for a 'Beef Trust'. That's a chorus of guys dressed up like the Radio City Rockettes who'll prance around a bit." More giggles from those who were looking over the scripts.

What in the world have I gotten myself into? Sandy wondered as she took a seat at the long oak library table which had been placed on stage. Bill hadn't said this was a minstrel show. Inwardly, Sandy cringed at the idea of "blackface" as being racially demeaning. It was not a concept she had been taught at home. In fact, her thoughts wandered back to a time when she was a little girl and they had moved to Virginia. She remembered her father saying that now they lived in the south they could "kick the Negroes off the sidewalks". From some well of understanding deeper than experience, the words had stabbed her, even though he'd said it in a kidding manner. She had run from the room sobbing. Hopefully, the minstrel would be done tastefully, she reasoned, after all it was an art form in itself.

A beautiful brunette in a black sweater and slacks sat at the end of the table. A long fuchsia scarf was draped dramatically over one shoulder. Huge silver hoop earrings constantly fought entanglement in her long hair as her head bobbed from side-to-side while she sized up the candidates for audition. She flashed a dazzling smile in Sandy's direction. "I'm Joyce Redding with Home Talent Productions," she said. There was a trace of a New York accent. "I understand you'll be my assistant."

"I'll try...just let me know what you want done." Sandy liked her instantly.

"We'll try to whip this thing together," she stuck a pencil over one ear and Sandy watched in fascination as the bobbing pencil now vied with the animated hoop earrings. "We bring all the costumes with us, do the production and keep the `gate`, the Jaycees make their money on the program advertising. Let's get the auditions going." She shoved a yellow legal pad in Sandy's direction. "Get them to sign up. You know most of these people?"

"Some of them."

"Get them to put their name and type of act. We'll take 'em in sequence." Joyce smiled and whispered behind her hand, "Frankly, I think this is going to be a cattle call."

Sandy laughed and hurried off with the sign-in pad. This was going to be fun, after all, even if she would just be a "go-fer"; however, as the auditions progressed, Joyce conferred with her about each act, asking her opinion. They watched two brothers who juggled; a girl who sang badly off-key; a lady who tap danced very well; a prominent doctor with a sensational tenor voice; and a teenage boy who did an outstanding magic act.

"If he could just make his acne disappear like that rabbit, I'd take him on the road," Joyce made a notation on her script.

The next candidate for audition was an extremely voluptuous girl. Her large endowment strained at the fabric of a tight red sweater. "I wonder what *she* does?" Joyce looked amused.

"Maybe she just crawls out on stage and tries to stand up," Sandy whispered.

Joyce put her head down on her arms on the table and tried to fight laughing aloud. "Sorry, I'm just very tired," she shouted across the stage at the girl. "You can begin now." Miss Voluptuous handed the accompanist her music and surprised them both with how well she sang. "That's a keeper!" Joyce made another notation on the script.

"She's really good," Sandy agreed. "But her material's rather bland for the way she looks. She'd bring down the house with something like 'My heart belongs to Daddy' or maybe 'Whatever Lola Wants, Lola Gets'."

Joyce raised one eyebrow and looked at Sandy as though seeing her with new eyes. "You're absolutely right. See if we can get that sheet music, or see if Lynn, the accompanist, knows it. You seem to know music, do you sing?"

"No, heavens no, I've just loved music ever since I was little. Lyrics are easy for me to remember, that's all. I'll talk to Lynn about Barb Franklin's music."

As they wrapped up the auditions, Joyce added a new assignment. "I have a piece of music I want you to consider finding a very pretty girl to sing. I haven't seen just the right person here tonight. Have you ever heard Pearl Bailey's song, 'That's Good Enough For Me'?"

"I love it."

"Find me someone to sing it, okay? Put your thinking cap on and come up with someone by tomorrow night."

After rehearsal, flashes of heat lightening illuminated boxy brick ranch houses, squatting side-by-side with tall, proud Victorian homes wearing lacey gingerbread trim like fussy old maids. Thunder rumbled faintly in the distance speaking muffled dark secrets of discontent to the night. As Bill drove home, Sandy looked unseeingly out the car window. Eric slept on her lap. She felt a strange, unnamed excitement brewing within her. Could she possibly ask to audition for the Pearl Bailey number herself? Thoughts of actually singing on that stage, where she had sat at the library table with Joyce, confronted her with a harsh mental slap. Excitement dissolved immediately into stark inhibition. Her thoughts swirled back to rumors that her sister was really her baby--her divorce--the embarrassment of returning to high school. *I don't need to set myself up for further ridicule in this small town,* she thought, and swept the short-lived, hazy cobwebs of her dream into a dustpan of rejection.

"Do you remember Julie Burt who was in the Miss Pennsylvania contest?" She broke the silence in the car.

Bill chuckled. "There's probably not a man in Greenville who doesn't remember Julie as the prettiest girl in town. That's like saying, 'Is the Pope Catholic'?" In his mind's eye he pictured her smile first--beguiling dimples, full sexy lips. The picture widened to include a figure like a goddess--long, brown hair which begged to be touched.

"Joyce Redding is looking for a pretty girl to sing a Pearl Bailey song for the show. What would you think about Julie?"

"It would sure be a home run for the show to have her in the cast. Good idea, but can she sing?"

"I don't know, but I'll find out. Julie borrowed my prom gown for the Miss

28

Pennsylvania contest when she was runner-up for the title. I'll call her tomorrow and see. Maybe I can talk her into it." She laughed, "She owes me for the use of the dress. I'll twist her arm if I have to."

A telephone call the following afternoon produced success on the assignment Joyce had given her. Julie had sung with the chorus in high school and agreed to be at rehearsal that night.

"Ya' done good, kid!" Joyce flashed a smile in Sandy's direction as Julie walked on stage, her spike heels clicking crisply across the bare wood of the stage floor. Shiny brown hair was pulled back sleekly, before it cascaded gracefully down her back into a frothy pony-tail. The affect accentuated the high cheekbones and picture-perfect features of her face.

Sandy leaned over to Joyce and whispered, "If I dared to wear my hair like that I'd look just like George Washington."

Joyce collapsed on her arms as she had the night before, trying to quell her laughter before the girl approached the table. She handed Julie the sheet music and asked, "Do you read..." And after a slight pause, "music, that is?"

Julie's dimples appeared fetchingly as she smiled, "Yes, sure do."

"Great! Take all the time you want to go over it. We'll go on with other auditions until you're ready. Come on back up here when you think you want to try it."

"Julie, we really appreciate this, thanks so much for coming." Sandy briefly patted her arm. "You'll do great!"

A pair of young male tap dancers auditioned in silver sequin costumes, with top hats and canes. Their music was Ravel's "Bolero". The rapid paced music resulted in twin blurs of flashing out-of-step silver. They resembled two rapidly whirling silver balls on a dance hall ceiling, throwing out rays of revolving light.

Joyce started to scratch them off her list until Sandy suggested, "Maybe the music's wrong. Why don't we see if they can do the same routine to say...'I'm a Yankee Doodle Dandy'? They've got the top hats and the canes for it."

Joyce set her soda bottle down and cocked her head, staring at Sandy strangely as she had the night before. "Great idea!" She called the performers back on stage. "Lynn, do you know 'Yankee Doodle Dandy'?

In answer, Lynn began to play it. Joyce motioned to the tap dancers. "Try it at this tempo," she told them.

After a few hesitant false starts, they got in step and the result was astonishing. Canes tapped in unison with their clicking toes and heels, top hats were doffed as though in mirrored image. Those already selected as cast began to applaud and cheer. They finished with broad smiles, obviously proud of their own performance.

Joyce stood and applauded also. "You're in, guys," she said and then turned to Sandy. "You're holding out on me!" she accused. "You've either danced or sung before, haven't you?"

"Nope, I haven't...honest. I've just always liked music." Sandy wondered herself about the source of these ideas. It was almost as if they were being dropped into her consciousness from an unknown source.

The tap dancers were followed by a painfully thin, adolescent girl whose mother shoved her out on stage. Long, spindly legs seemed to grow out of a short pink tulle ballet skirt. She stood timidly on stage, looking not unlike a baby flamingo about to take flight. Her mother lighted a gasoline soaked baton in the wings and handed it to her. For a moment, the girl looked at the baton in shock as though she'd never seen it before. Slowly she began to twirl as the fire whizzed around in large circles, just missing wisps of her drab blonde hair.

Joyce's eyes widened in horror as the circles of fire came nearer to the stage curtains. "Oh, no!" she said under her breath. And then shouted, "That's enough! That's enough! Thank you very much, dear, but it's not an appropriate act for this type of show."

The child looked immensely relieved. She stood immobile, holding the fiery baton aloft like the Statue of Liberty's torch until her mother snuffed it out with a large, black cap. A cloud of smoke lingered on stage as the mother angrily shepherded her daughter into the wings. Sandy smiled wondering if it lingered from the extinguished fire, or had it come from the mother's almost tangible seething huff?

Joyce consulted her audition sheet. "Stage mothers," she muttered, "I could have spared that little one some embarrassment if I'd known what kind of act that was. Good grief! Under type of act it says 'Blaze of Glory'. I didn't catch that. It could have been a four alarm blaze of glory if those curtains had caught fire." She shook her head and the silver hoop earrings flashed from the depths of her dark hair.

Julie approached the table and indicated she was ready to try the Pearl Bailey number. She took the sheet music to Lynn and posed by the piano.

"Wait until I move the mic," Sandy brought it over to her. "It lifts out of the stand if you want to use it as a hand mic," she told her. "Go get 'em, gal," she whispered.

The introduction was a "vamp", the same chords continuously played in succession, until the song began. Julie seemed to be waiting for something more. "Just jump in anywhere," Lynn instructed from the piano.

"I don't want a genius for a husband
Or a guy who's big financially
I want a simple little fellow
Like, Joe Lewis, that's good enough for me."

Julie's voice was high and rather thin, warbling with vibrato. While it was not the low, sexy rendition Pearl Bailey gave it, her appearance made up for the voice. Males in the cast began to whistle enthusiastically. She rewarded them with a dimpled smile across the footlights, took a deep breath, and started the second chorus.

Joyce whispered behind one hand, "I want you to work with her, Sandy. Coach her on hand movements. Don't let her sing the whole thing. Talk some of it like Pearl Bailey does."

"*Me?* You've got to be kidding, I can't coach her...I don't know what to do."

"Your instincts are right. Go on, girl, just do it!" Her smile belied the harsh words.

"Well, I'll try, but just being around her makes me feel like my grandmother's cleaning lady."

As the weeks progressed, Joyce always seemed to confer with her on production decisions; trying most of her suggestions they found them workable, much to Sandy's surprise. As Joyce worked to smooth out the timing on the comedy end of the program between the End Men, the direction of most of the single musical acts were entrusted to Sandy. If she couldn't sing herself, then this new role was extremely fulfilling, plus there could be no chance for conflict between her and Bill as he was an End Man, under Joyce's direction. Some nights he dropped her off at home after rehearsal and went out again, but there seemed to be a new comradeship between them.

Julie took direction well, pliably mimicking the moves Sandy made with her hands and body. "Let the lyrics tell you what to do." They found a full-length mirror in the girls' locker room and in tandem they practiced the song. "Sexier, slower...slightly sarcastic now," Sandy encouraged, "hand on your hip. Great!"

There is an old backstage adage that says: "Good dress rehearsal--bad performance." Dress rehearsal went as smoothly as a professional production; therefore, opening night was doomed before the curtain even went up.

"Come on, lighten up people!" Joyce had never seen such a case of communal jitters. The problem was they kept taking turns peeking out at the audience through the curtain. As the auditorium was now almost filled to capacity, nerves on the backstage side began to tremble like the ground before an earthquake. "People, you've been rehearsing for two months now.

If I were asking you to go out there on stage, in front of your friends buck-naked, I could understand you might be nervous." This was received with a few restrained giggles. "But you're in costume--you're not yourself anymore. You're a performer, now go get 'em--break a leg!"

Sandy heard just snatches of her pep talk as she was sewing up the seat of the doctor's tux pants--with the tenor in them. Dr. Hill weighed almost three hundred pounds and when his cummerbund fell off, he had bent down to pick it up. "Hold still, George," she admonished. "At least you don't have to perform surgery from the underside of your patients." He continued to wipe his sweating hands down the satin stripe of the pants. The orchestra was now playing the overture for the Oleo. "Okay, doc, the surgery was a success." She tied off the thread and snipped it with a pair of scissors.

The doctor jumped, "Careful with those scissors! I don't need my number transposed to a soprano key." He was joking, but she sensed how nervous he was. He had performed in churches and concerts all over the state; therefore, his obvious stage fright surprised her. He was the first performer to go on.

His act was flawless. The applause echoed backstage as he took three curtain calls. *Don't bow, George! Whatever you do, don't bow*, Sandy thought as she adjusted the silver sequined vests and handed canes to the two tap dancers. "Break a leg, guys!" she whispered, keeping tradition with the notion that it was taboo to wish "good luck" for a performance. As the orchestra began "Yankee Doodle Dandy", they tapped out to center stage. And then the taller boy slipped and promptly fell. "Jeez, I didn't mean for them to really break a leg," she covered her mouth and looked toward Joyce, who was biting her lip.

The boy's recovery was phenomenal. He jumped up and fell right into step. There was thunderous applause. "Go get Julie prepped," Joyce said, looking back toward the lighting board. "Where in the world is she?"

Sandy made a dash for the girls' locker room. Julie Burt stood before the mirror. She looked stunning in a long black strapless dress, tight to the knees, which accentuated her figure. The dress then flared into a flounce that made her look like a slightly modern mermaid. The affect was breathtaking...until Sandy looked closely at her face. Smudged mascara ran in two black trails from her eyes. "Julie, what's wrong, hon?" Sandy began to panic. Did she have the jitters? Was she in pain?

"I can't do it...I just can't do it," she sobbed.

"Of course you can," Sandy began hastily wiping away the mascara tracks, applying more makeup and powder.

"It was different when just the cast was here. But all those people out there...I just can't." She began to cry again. Sandy could hear the final chorus being played in stop time for the tap dancers. She had to do something fast. Grabbing Julie's arm, she yanked her out the door of the locker room toward the wings.

"The footlights are very bright, hon, you won't be able to see the people." She tried to reason with her, but Julie froze into a rigid pillar. "Now just stop this," she shook her by the shoulders with no response. The tap dancers were taking their bows. There was no time now as the dancers had come off stage into the wings, and were being congratulated by the rest of the cast.

The orchestra began Julie's vamp introduction. Hopefully the familiar sound would motivate her. Sandy continued to shake her and plead, but she was almost in a catatonic state.

The vamp introduction continued on and on, waiting for someone to come in--there was a small, restless murmur from the audience. They realized something was wrong. Sandy knew she had to go on in Julie's place to keep the show from bogging down. She was the only one who knew the song.

A surprised audience now saw Sandy, in blue jeans, tee shirt and tennis shoes, swagger sexily toward the mike as she had coached Julie to do. She had to sing it a full octave lower, but the throaty sound of her own voice, when miked, resonated through the auditorium and didn't sound too bad.

There was no time for nerves. The memory from coaching rang in her head, "Let the lyrics tell you what to do....sexier...slower. Hand on hip now."

She was aware people were consulting their programs. This was supposed to be Julie Burt. She found it helped to pretend she actually *was* Julie...She must look ridiculous strutting around, making those moves in blue jeans...No time to think of that...remember the lyrics.

It was over. She bowed as she had taught Julie to do. To her astonishment they were giving her a standing ovation! She looked upward toward the balcony. They were standing and applauding also. The orchestra in the pit stood and applauded. She exited stage left and was met by a large segment of the cast who pounded her shouting congratulations.

"You saved us. And you sounded so professional." Joyce embraced her in a bear hug. "Get out there and take another bow, the crowd's still applauding." She shoved her toward the stage.

Now that it was over, a massive case of nerves set in. As Sandy walked toward center stage her mouth seemed full of cotton. Could she keep her knees from knocking as she took another bow? She couldn't wait to get off stage.

Were they applauding because her singing was good, or because she was brave enough to step in and abort an emergency? She was to have a solid answer to that question in one more day; however, accolades from the cast now flowed over her like soothing balm to her suddenly frayed nerves.

Julie, who had rallied, hugged her impromptu substitute. "You were absolutely fabulous! I'm so sorry I let you down. Sorry for that, but not sorry you went on, Sandy. You were perfect--I bequeath my dress to you. You're doing the act for the next two nights."

Sandy motioned for the magician to go on. "No way! I'm not going out there again." She remembered the feeling of cotton in her mouth. What if that happened when she tried to sing? She shivered at the thought.

Joyce had been listening to the exchange. "Julie's right." Her dark eyes flashed as though defying a challenge to her statement. "You're doing the number--no excuses."

Bill, in red coat and blackface makeup, held a tambourine. Waiting to go on with the other End Men, he put one arm around his wife. "Didn't know you had it in you. You were great." He squeezed her shoulders. Bill never showed affection in public. For the first time, she actually experienced a measure of pride in what she had done. If her singing had Bill's approval, perhaps it hadn't been too bad. Maybe she should consider doing the act the next two nights. It would certainly be easier in the slinky black dress than it had been in blue jeans and tennis shoes.

The audience seemed to love the minstrel portion of the show, laughing whole heartedly in all the proper places, and a few improper places when "Mr. Bones" forgot his lines. There were accidentally broken banjo strings, and purposefully broken "G"-strings in the Beef Trust, as eight burly, hairy men did high kicks in a chorus line, threatening to destroy the flooring of the stage with their weight. The bright, happy music and snappy jokes overshadowed a slightly ragged performance of ill-timed entrances and forgotten lines.

At the curtain call, the Interlocutor silenced the audience and made announcement: "Our assistant producer, Sandy Ghost, filled in spontaneously for Julie Burt tonight. Let's bring her out here!"

Joyce gave her a shove toward the stage. As she came out to take a place with the cast, the audience again rose and applauded. She mimicked a curtsey, holding out the sides of her jeans, which brought a laugh.

She could not stop talking on the way home. "I really wanted to do that number when Joyce first mentioned it, but I was scared to volunteer for it...I never told you that... so I got Julie instead. I still can't believe this happened...I'm pinching myself, Bill."

He nodded. "You sure thought on your feet to step in like that. It took guts."

"Not really. If I'd stopped to think, I probably wouldn't have gone out there. It was just kind of an automatic reflex or something. I feel bad Julie didn't get to perform, but what a fluke the way it worked out." She gazed thoughtfully out the window, remembering the pretense of singing before an audience in the Bulls Eye mirror. It had almost been prophetic.

She turned and made certain the garment bag was still hanging correctly. But tomorrow night she wouldn't be a hero, filling in to save the performance. Even with the help of the slinky black dress, could she pull it off on her own?

Chapter Four

⟨⟩

he following morning, the alarm clock shrilly insisted it was just another
day. Sun bathed the living room in its pronouncement of just another day,
sending fingers of twirling sunbeams to point in fussy disapproval at formerly
unrevealed patches of undusted furniture. It was not just another day, however,
it was a day of foreboding misgivings for Sandy. She knew somehow she had to
back out of performing that night. Could she use her pregnancy as an excuse?
As if in answer, it came as a surprise that there had been no morning sickness
this day. Actually, she felt in excellent health.

Mental pictures of embarrassment in letting Joyce and the cast down,
compared themselves to the scenario of exposing herself to public ridicule
on stage. As a consequence, there were household casualties in this war of
emotions: two broken cup handles and an accidental drowning of the U. S.
mail, which happened to be in the target zone of a gallon bottle of milk that
slipped out of her hands.

Perhaps her decision was centered in branching roots of subconscious
desire to win the approval of her mother, now transferred to Bill, or in a solid
sense of commitment to the show's production and cast. Ultimately, she realized
to "chicken out" would leave her in a hen house of scarred self-esteem and
unfulfilled dreams. Therefore, after lunch she put Eric down for a nap, dusted
the living room, plumped the pillows on the couch, and her resolve.

She would rehearse until the song no longer threatened her. Stage fright
couldn't overtake a body so schooled by repetition that it moved by rote, she
reasoned. The convex image in the mirror over the fireplace distorted her
practice session with a surrealistic quality that actually helped. "I'd better run
through it wearing the dress," she told the singer in the mirror. Taking the
garment bag from the hall closet, she slipped into the gown, zipping it up the
back.

There was a surprising mental surge from viewing this new image. The
black dress clung to her thighs like a second skin, curving sensuously from
her small waist. Her pregnancy didn't show at all. She moved back and forth
in front of the mirror, assuming poses the lyrics dictated. "The shoes...I've got
to have the shoes," she said aloud and stepped into the black high-heels. This
time, as she rehearsed the song, the image seemed to take on an astonishing life
of its own. She listened and viewed it apart from reality, as though watching
an intangible personality on television. She added long, rhinestone earrings
and even that small enhancement seemed to improve the performance. Had

she found a secret key to unlock a closet of resources she hadn't been aware of? If she could manage to assume the identity of the singer in the mirror, firmly implant the image in her mind, she might be able to pull it off after all. "What colossal bull!" she said aloud.

Shaking her head, she hastily unzipped the dress. But how could a simple housewife be expected to know she had inadvertently stumbled upon a device used by many professionals?

If nervousness could be measured in kilowatts, the entire cast was on overload before curtain-time. One of the Beef Trust chorus had popped the hooks on his lacy, red bra. A quick repair was imperative. Miss Voluptuous, Barbara Franklin, had lost the long, feathered boa for her number, "My Heart Belongs to Daddy".

"If I had a figure like yours, I wouldn't cover it up with a boa," Sandy told her. "You're better off without it."

"I don't know what to do with my hands if I can't clutch the boa," she wailed.

"Take this fan as a prop. Practice flirting a bit with the audience, snap it open and closed to punctuate your lines. Barb, you project sex like Marilyn Monroe. By comparison, I look like I need a training bra. And you're worried about your *hands*!"

Barb's smile was winsome. She headed for the dressing room, the fan in her left hand fluttering limply like a dying moth on a leash.

Sandy dashed around in jeans, trying to put out last minute fires with an extinguisher of encouragement. She passed Bill and fluffed out his floppy bow tie. "In three years of marriage, I've never seen you do as much sewing as I have this week," he observed. "Remember my asking if we had to throw my dress shirts out when the buttons came off?"

"Could we talk about this later?" He had been great about not putting her down in front of the cast as she'd originally feared, she thought. His timing was lousy to start now when her nerves were already standing on tiptoe. "Break a leg," she whispered and throwing him a kiss, headed off to the next crisis.

The overture began. Joyce grabbed her by the shoulders. "You'd better get changed, girl. We've got standing room only out there. Hot doggies!" She rubbed her hands together and Sandy remembered Home Talent Productions' proceeds came from the "gate".

"Why you greedy, money hungry wench!" Sandy teased. It was surprising how rapidly a bond had developed between them. She would never have thought, when they first met, that such familiarity was possible. In fact, the shared experience of the production had seemed to fuse the entire cast together with a weld rod of exceptional closeness. At the time, it was like receiving the gift of an entirely new family she thought while dashing toward the dressing room.

Would the microphone pick up the pounding of her heart? She could actually hear it in her ears as she rapidly dressed, applied stage makeup, and clipped on the large, glittering earrings. There was no time to dwell on stage fright. She was needed backstage to deal with production problems. She could hear the doctor's beautiful tenor voice which filtered past the closed door.

Hurrying toward the lighting board, she was stopped by Joyce. "I can't believe it! Turn around," she commanded. "Sandy, you'll dazzle them if you don't even open your mouth!"

"Get outta' here, you silver-tongued devil. You'd try to charm the socks off anybody for a good performance...I'm on to you now, lady."

Joyce suddenly grew serious. "I'm going to say something from a professional standpoint, Sandy, and also from a viewpoint of the friendship I feel between us. With your voice, appearance and instinctive production talent, you should consider making singing a career."

The tap dancers were on the final stop time chorus. Warm applause encouraged their finale. There wasn't much time left before she went on. "You're so sweet," she told Joyce, "but that's impossible. Besides I think I stink on ice." She dismissed the complimentary words as nothing more than encouragement to build her up before she had to face an audience. She honestly did feel she wasn't very good--but she knew the alter ego of her image in the mirror *was* good. If she could just become that other person before she stepped on stage.

The vamp introduction began and she started into the sultry walk to the microphone. The blinding, hot footlights camouflaged the presence of the audience, allowing her to visualize only the image in the mirror.

"Now, I don't want a genius for a husband,
"Or a guy who's big financially,
"I want a simple little fellow like...

(The line was "Joe Lewis", who at the time was one of the most famous boxers in the world; however, she substituted the name of the local mayor. And as she did so, she wondered where that had come from so spontaneously.) There was a roar of laughter from the audience.

"That's good enough for me," she sang, marveling at how relaxed she felt.
"And when it comes to things,
Like, well...charge accounts"
*(Remember to talk this...hand on hip now...*she coached herself mentally.)
"To me...to me that's utterly rash, honey. 'Cause I don't want to bother my escorts with no signatures on the check, money orders endorsements, that kind of thing...(an exaggerated wave of the hand now as she leaned closer to the

microphone as if confiding in the audience). In a sassier voice she said, "Just let him buy his merchandise in cash...cash...that'll be good enough for me!"

Another burst of laughter rewarded her.

Two more choruses and it was over. Now, she allowed the mirror image to dissolve between her and the audience. To her surprise, they were giving her another standing ovation. They continued to applaud until she came out of the wings for additional bows.

Joyce pounded her on the back, "What a show stopper that was!"

Bill beamed proudly, his teeth dazzlingly bright in contrast to the blackface makeup, "Way to go! Where did you get that mayor thing? That was great!"

As before, the nerves caught up with her afterward. She realized her hands were trembling as she shook hands with the doctor who told her, "That was a great piece of business naming the mayor. You sounded terrific...what a sexy voice."

Her mind whirled with the compliments as she changed back into blue jeans; however, Bill's words were the ones she hugged to her remembrance. He had thought she was "great".

It was sweltering backstage. Most of the cast crowded into the wings, not just waiting to go on, but trying to see what was happening on stage.

"Sorry guys," Sandy motioned with one hand held aloft, "got to herd you into the locker rooms until your curtain time. I'll need a railroad car of powder to keep all your makeup from running if you don't move out of here fast!" She dusted a fresh coat on Barb and handed her a mirror, "More lipstick, hon," she said giving her a tube to apply. "You look sensational. Let me see how you use the fan."

She opened it with a crisp snap and lifted it coquettishly to her face, then let it fall to her side.

"Try the same move, but instead of holding it to your face, hold it over your bust line, then give the audience a peek."

Barb giggled and tried it.

"Terrific!" Joyce pronounced as she joined them. "Keep that move in, you'll wow them."

The orchestra began the intro to "My Heart Belongs to Daddy". Sandy squeezed her hand. "You'll kill 'em, break a leg."

Of course, the first glimpse of Barb the audience had was her well endowed bust line, which proceeded from behind the curtain at least a full second before the rest of her body. She sauntered sexily toward the microphone in the tight red strapless dress. There were whistles and cheers before she ever began the song, and the bust-covering move with the coquettish fan teased the audience into more wolf whistles.

"That girl exudes sex from every pore," Joyce observed, "too bad she can't sing very well."

"Who needs to sing if you look like *that!*" There was no doubt Barb's act was a crowd pleaser.

"Wrong! You may think this is just a 'Mickey Mouse' production with hometown talent exploited, but I belonged to Actors' Equity for years and was professional. Take it from me, Sandy, you have the looks and voice to make it as a professional. You need to go for it!"

For the first time, she realized Joyce wasn't just trying to bolster her performance. "I can't possibly. I've got a two year old at home and I'm pregnant," she confided.

"Pregnant? You sure don't show it. No matter! You can be married with kids and still be a singer."

"But, I'm just a housewife," she stammered. "I've had no training...I'm just kind of fakin' it, you know."

"You've got superb instincts, and talent whether you realize it or not. Get that through your jug head!"

Barb was taking bows now. The wolf whistles followed her off stage. "Fantastic job!" Sandy told her.

"You bet...great...just great," Joyce chimed in as the orchestra began to play "Alexander's Ragtime Band". The minstrel chorus in brilliant blue robes filed onstage singing. That was her cue to go on to conduct the chorus. Just before stepping out from the wings, Joyce looked toward Sandy, and putting one hand over her heart, crossed her eyes. Barb and Sandy struggled to muffle their laughter.

"When all this nonsense is over, maybe we could get together sometime for coffee. I don't live far from you," Barb offered.

"I'd love it," she replied as she helped Eddie Filer into his End Man suit coat.

Eddie, who was a car dealer, weighed in at about three hundred pounds. He was an unassuming, loveable teddy bear of a man, always jovial, and a perfect candidate for both the Beef Trust and as an End Man. The dual role posed a problem--getting Eddie out of the chorus girl costume and into blackface in time to make the transition from the Oleo to the Minstrel portion of the show. The teamwork resembled a pit crew changing a tire in a car race. He flashed a shy smile, "All of you want to come out to the farm and help me get dressed to go to work in the morning? I'd appreciate it a heap."

Sandy struggled to apply the blackface makeup from the tube. "Hold still," she admonished, trying to apply the heavy dark makeup, as others worked on adjusting his wide, yellow suspenders. "You know you couldn't have done both parts if the End Man role had come first. We'd have never gotten this makeup washed off in time to go from End Man to chorus girl." She handed him a tambourine. "We made it!"

They had modified the script for Eddie to come on last, with the other End Men yelling he was late. He shuffled lazily onstage, taking his place in one of the chairs in the first row, in front of the chorus, "Ah's comin'. Jack Benny asked me to park his Studebaker." The line always brought a laugh. Eddie Filer was the local Studebaker dealer.

With the minstrel portion well underway, Sandy went back to the dressing room to change back into her costume for the curtain call. Joyce's words sifted slowly back through her consciousness, "You have the looks and talent to make it as a professional," she had said.

She couldn't possibly entertain such thoughts, she had a husband, a son, a house and another baby on the way to care for.

"No matter! You can be married with kids and still be a singer." The words rang in her head as though Joyce were standing there in person arguing with her. She thought about all her lonely nights at home. Combing her hair slowly, she applied more lipstick. "It's too late in life to embark on a career now," she whispered softly, "even though I would have loved it." She again clipped on the dangling earrings and viewed her image wistfully. "Don't expect any standing ovations at the curtain call tonight, old girl," she told herself. "They loved you because you stepped in and took Julie's place, not because you performed so well. It was 'mercy applause', that's what it was." She turned out the dressing room light and made her way to the wings.

Banjos and mandolins came in on the last chorus of "Alabama Jubilee". The bright, happy tempo spilled across the footlights infecting the crowd, who now clapped in time to the music as though they were part of the show. Tambourines flashed as spotlights swept the stage, enveloping the cast in small fireworks of amber light. It was the finale.

The Oleo cast began lining up in the wings for their curtain call. The Interlocutor now began announcing each act in the Oleo in sequence of performance. "And now, Sandy Ghost, leaving production duties long enough to sing, "That's Good Enough for Me". She took her place in the line of acts, joining hands with the tap dancers. As she watched, clusters of people began to rise in different sections of the theater as they applauded. And then, to her amazement, the entire audience was again on their feet.

Later that evening, after Eric was tucked in for the night and Bill was out with the cast for drinks, she sat on the side of her bed sifting through each treasured incident of the evening: her confidence on stage; the standing ovation; the compliments and Joyce's words. Fondling each memory like a precious rosary bead, she became too elated to sleep, but turned out the light. Could she do it again tomorrow night? She knew she couldn't, but she had discovered a secret--the mirror image could.

The final night of the show was a better performance than the former had been, and again, Sandy received two standing ovations. "Too bad it's over," she told Joyce, "just when we got the whole thing fine-tuned."

"Story of my life, that's always the case when I do these shows." She slung an arm around Sandy's shoulders. "If you'll let me, I'd like to help you get a start on a career, gal."

"I just can't. Even though it's tempting...I just can't. I've got to settle down now and focus on having a baby. You've been wonderful Joyce, just knowing you...sharing this with you. I can't express what all this has meant to me." They probably wouldn't see each other again, and it was painful to break the close-knit bond that had been so solidly formed between them. She was going back to New York and wouldn't attend the cast party.

"Write to me," she handed her a card. "Something will happen to change your mind. I just don't want to lose touch. When you become rich and famous, I want to be able to say Home Talent Productions gave you your start. Got that?"

Sandy laughed, "Don't hold your breath." She hugged her tightly and whispered, "I'll really miss you."

At the time, she never would have dreamed that the "something" to change her mind would softly creep into her life that very evening, because it tiptoed in with such veiled subtlety that she failed to recognize what was happening.

She and Bill always left by the backstage outside exit door, but this night, by some coincidence, the door was locked and they had to go out through the auditorium. Small remnants of the audience remained in clusters chatting.

The band busily packed up their instruments in the orchestra pit. Holding the garment bag over one arm, Sandy descended the stairs and called to the band, "You were wonderful--all of you! Thanks so much for your help."

"Wait a minute!" Norman Mossman called out, as he zipped up the cover over his acoustic bass. Norman walked toward them, after disentangling his lanky frame from bchind the drummer's trap cases. His wife Lynn, the piano player, followed behind. She carried a thick, unruly stack of sheet music, and began tamping the edges back into order with the heel of one hand as she walked.

"Hey, Mose--good job, man," Bill said as they shook hands.

"Your wife's the one who should get the praise," Norman smiled broadly and turned toward Sandy. "You need to know, Lynn and I've been talking behind your back. We want to know if you've sung professionally before?"

41

"Good grief, no! I don't even sing lullabies to our son...never sang in a choir...don't even sing in the bathtub."

Norman's small, intense brown eyes pierced through her small talk. He was known as an excellent musician, who made his living playing professionally in a small group with his wife, and with a popular big band--Johnny Martin's Orchestra. He waved a hand in the air as though erasing her words, "Well, Lynn and I think we'd like to work with you. Our group plays at the VFW on Saturday nights, why don't you come on out and sit in sometime?"

"'Sit in'?" Sandy's eyebrows lifted. "You mean sit with you?"

When Lynn laughed, two deep dimples appeared. She spoke with a slight lisp, which becomingly gave her a little-girl quality. "Don't mind Mose. He thinks everyone understands musician lingo. That means to sing or play with a band on an impromptu basis."

Norman wiped his high forehead with a handkerchief and shrugged out of his suit jacket. "I'm wasted with this heat," he explained. "Look here," his voice took on a cut-to-the-chase, no nonsense tone, "there are no good vocalists in this area...only one and she works with our big band. We decided we want to work with you, Sandy."

It was a tremendous compliment, she knew, because of their reputation, but the offer was still unthinkable. She looked from one to the other. "I just couldn't. I don't know anything but that one song." As the words came out of her mouth, she was checked that it was a small misrepresentation of truth. Lyrics had just seemed to stick in her head from the time she was little. "And besides, I'm expecting," she added.

"What's that got to do with your vocal chords," Norm said in his typically terse manner, "*they're* not pregnant, are they?" They all laughed.

"I'll work with you," Lynn offered. "We'll establish good keys for you on some of the standards. We could do that out at our house so you'd feel comfortable before you sit in with the band."

Sandy looked at Bill to see how he was taking the idea. He shrugged, "Why not?"

"I have to tell you, I'm overwhelmed at the compliment. Can I think about it? I'd hate to have you waste your time with me, Lynn, and then not be able to follow through...you know, chicken out on you."

Norm slung his suit jacket over one shoulder, "With 'pipes' like you've got, lady, it'll be a waste if you don't try."

She took Lynn's hand, "May I call you? Thanks so much for your vote of confidence."

The deep dimples showed again as she smiled, "You bet, we're in the 'phone book."

"Are you going to the cast party?" Bill asked.

"No way," Norm told them. "I just want to get out of these wet clothes and into a dry martini."

"Come on, Mose, don't give me that bull. I know you don't drink." Bill playfully punched his shoulder.

Later, at the cast party Sandy sat by herself at one of the long tables. Bill had gone to the bar to get another beer. Mimi had gone to the ladies room, and Barb was dancing with her husband, Winston, or "Win" as everyone called him.

Large parties had always made her feel uncomfortable. She loved being with all these people--they had become like family, but now in this setting it was different somehow. She wondered if she was becoming a prude, and then decided it was just that she disliked not being able to really talk to people. Snatches of sentences, shouted over top of loud music and boisterous laughter, were not her idea of a conversation. She could never seem to truly enter in, didn't know what to say in that type of atmosphere. Suddenly she saw the irony of her discomfort. *Here I am squirming inside, and not an hour ago, I was considering singing with a band. What craziness! I'd subject myself to feeling awkward constantly if I did that...it's one thing to sing on stage...quite another to perform in a club.* She hadn't even thought about that facet of Norman and Lynn's suggestion before. That could be a monumental stumbling block.

Several months had passed since the show, when one morning Sandy received a telephone call from Lynn Mossman.

"Norm told me to call you." She giggled like a little girl. "In his typical fashion he said, 'She's had enough time to think about it. Give her a call.' So, are you going to come out to work on some keys for standards?"

"Oh, Lynn, I'm sorry I've left you two hanging. I should have called you before this." She hadn't really thought much more about it, except sometimes during long evenings when she was at home alone. At those times, she secretly relived the three nights of being on stage. "What would be a good time for you?"

"I give piano lessons in the afternoon. How about some morning?"

"Maybe Bill's Mom could babysit Eric for me. Let me see if I can work it out for Monday morning, okay?"

Isabel, as usual, was very supportive of her daughter-in-law. She felt it would be good if there were some outside interests and even offered her car as the Mossmans lived in the country.

Their new, modern house had spacious cathedral ceilings and vast expanses of glass. Musical instruments of many varieties blended with comfortable, contemporary furnishings. Lynn, sensing her guest was nervous, made coffee and they sat at the kitchen table talking for awhile.

"Norm's really impatient to get you started," she stirred two cubes of sugar into her cup.

43

"But look at me, I'm big as a house. The other day, I was wearing a yellow dress, walked past a school bus stop and twelve kids tried to board me!"

Lynn's laughter produced the two deep dimples.

"I can't go on a bandstand in maternity clothes."

"Don't worry about it," she told her, "we'll just go about this at your own pace."

They scheduled weekly sessions which Sandy began to look forward to, counting the days off impatiently in between. Not only was it fun, but occasionally Norman came home to lend a special magic with suggestions on breathing and phrasing. She knew her voice was growing stronger, technique improving, and her facility to remember lyrics always seemed to surprise her.

When Norman pressed for her to actually work with them in a club, her negative response now stemmed more from her unwieldy appearance in pregnancy than from a total lack of confidence. Just prior to Christmas, he began urging her to work a company Christmas party with them and New Years Eve.

"Norm, get serious. That's impossible. I'm due to have this baby next month. What do I wear, a gown by Omar-the-Tentmaker?"

Turning a dining room chair around, he straddled it backwards, John Wayne fashion. "You're just another instrument up there on the stand, Sandy. People are going to listen to you--not look."

She hadn't really considered that aspect, but realized suddenly it was truth. Lynn patted her hand. "There's no rush, he's just impatient about everything. Have the baby, get back on your feet, and when you're ready the timing will be just right."

Lisa was born on January 27, 1958, a perfectly formed, dainty baby girl with wisps of curly blonde hair. Dr. Ghost stood by Sandy's hospital bed sporting a wide, proud smile as she counted fingers and toes, examining the baby's perfect limbs. "When I think about what could have happened...that we could have had a deformed child, if you hadn't had a funny feeling about those pills..." Her eyes brimmed with grateful tears.

"Hush, don't think about that now. Get some rest, your labor was harder and longer this time." He took the baby, handing the small bundle to a nurse. But she did think about it now--it was *all* she could think of as sleep wouldn't come. What if their daughter had been born with no arms to hold her own baby when the time came? No legs to run and play like other children? Arms so short she could never be able to do her own hair, or apply makeup when she grew to be a teenager? Sharing those thoughts with Bill after he had seen the baby in the hospital nursery, he agreed they had been very lucky. But was it really luck, or had there been some intervening force, she wondered?

44

Chapter Five

*O*nce they were home from the hospital, Eric appropriated the new baby as though she belonged solely to him. He proudly brought safety pins for diapering and talcum powder. When not being asked to provide assistance, he promptly invented his own guidelines of service by covering Lisa with a sacrifice of stuffed animals.

"And we were worried he might be jealous of the new baby. Boy, were we wrong! He thinks we went off to a toy store and bought the baby for him." Sandy rinsed a glass, putting it in the dish drainer.

"I told you we should have told him the facts of life," Bill said as he put an oxblood shade of shoe polish on one of his loafers and attacked it with a brush.

"That's hardly the point I was trying to make. I just meant he adores his new little sister." She wished Bill would take more interest in the baby. Somehow she had envisioned the typical storybook masculine melting once there was a little girl in the house. She had thought fathers re-evaluated their lives when they had a daughter--made new vows, became filled with a misty-eyed sense of protectiveness. *Not Bill,* she thought. *He doesn't pay any more attention to Lisa than he did to Eric when he was a baby.*

He smeared more shoe polish on the right shoe and brushed it vigorously. As if perceiving her thoughts, he muttered, "Shall I get a soapbox for you to stand on? I feel a speech coming on."

"It's just that...I wish you'd hold her once in awhile. Give her a bottle. She's so adorable."

He finished with the brush and viewed each shoe from all angles to survey his work.

"Elizabeth Taylor could put her makeup on looking into the finish on those shoes, Bill. Are you listening to me at all?"

"I hear you." He slipped his feet into the loafers. "I'm just not very good with babies. Wait until she grows up a bit and has a personality."

"By then she won't know *you*! She's got a personality *now*, if you'd just take time to discover it."

"Can we put the soapbox away now? I've got an appointment at 7:30 tonight."

"Do you have appointments Friday night?"

He looked at her as though expecting a trap, "Why?"

She took a deep breath and wiped a fork with the dish towel. "Because I'm going to work with Norm and Lynn's band on Saturday night. You could go too. It'll be fun." The words were said in a rush.

"Okay...so what's with Friday night?" His tone was laced with suspicion.

"I thought maybe you could babysit Friday night. We're going to rehearse. I'll have the babies in bed before I have to leave. You might have to give Lisa her 11:00 o'clock bottle, but that's all."

"So that's the underlying reason for all the preaching on not paying attention to the baby!"

"That's not true at all...and it's not fair. I really am concerned about your disregard of both children. You can claim you just aren't good with babies, but you don't even take your son into the backyard to play ball."

"I'm busy." His remark snapped like a rubber band.

"You're never here." Her eyes flashed. "I'm here night after night. All I'm doing is asking you to babysit one night."

"Not me, Love!" The last word dripped with sarcasm. "Get Mom, or pay a sitter--I'm busy." He grabbed his suit jacket from the back of a kitchen chair, and left.

The local VFW had been transformed into a higher measure of class for Saturday night with white table cloths and candles on each table.. Barb and Win had been invited to keep Bill company. They appropriated a table in front of the bandstand, and promptly ordered drinks as Sandy joined the band, who were busy setting up. Norm placed a chair by the piano; Sandy would sit on the stand through each set as her vocals were interspersed between the instrumentals.

Lynn arranged pages of sheet music in proper order, and set her 'bible' on the floor beside the piano stool. "You look lovely," she said.

The gold satin dress shimmered in the light of the one spot that was center focused, lined up with the microphone stand. "Bill's Mom made the dress, thank you." And then, "I'm so nervous," she whispered. "I'll bet you're sick of hearing it."

Lynn's smile was warm. "You don't have a thing to worry about. I see you brought your own cheering section." She gestured toward the table just off to the left.

"That's half the problem," she confessed. "I think I'd be better off if they weren't here."

"Well, why did you ask them if you felt they'd make you feel self-conscious?" Norm asked, as he adjusted the reed on his alto saxophone. The logic of his question compelled her to sort out her feelings. "I more-or-less had to ask Bill. It wouldn't have been right to leave him sitting at home."

Norm smirked, "And what about the Sex Pot?"

"She's my best friend," she said defensively, "of course, I had to ask her." Actually, she would have been more comfortable without any of them there.

"Look, this is a job. You're being paid, kid. If you had a secretarial job, would you lug Miss Blessed-With-Bountiful-Bosoms to work with you to watch you type?" He laughed. It was not said in the form of a rebuke, but as a supportive suggestion in an attempt to help her.

"Point well taken," Sandy laughed so hard her mascara ran. She took a small, silver compact from her evening bag to use the mirror for cosmetic repairs. Her mother had given the compact to her as a birthday present years before. Would her mother approve of what she was doing, she wondered? Probably not. But the month before they had moved even farther away than Florida. Topps Chemical had transferred her father to Los Angeles. She experienced a sudden heart wrench, as she realized it could be years before she might see Chelie again. *Don't think about this now,* she told herself as the band began to play the first selection in the set. Several couples got up to dance.

She jiggled one foot in time to the music, snapped her fingers, smiled, looked enthusiastic, wondered if the crowd could see up her dress from that height, crossed her legs, rearranged her skirt, wondered if her perspiration was staining the satin dress, applauded at choruses taken in solo by each member of the band...and then, began the sequence all over again.

She felt like a piece of furniture sitting up there. She smiled at Bill, he smiled back. They seemed to be having a good time.

The next song up was "Lady Is a Tramp". Norm approached the microphone, "You may have noticed we've dressed the band up a bit by the addition of a vocalist. Let's all welcome Sandy Ghost to the mic. 'The Lady Is a Tramp'," he'd meant to introduce the song, but it didn't come off that way. He stepped back to the mic, "Ah...that's the name of the song, you guys...not a disparaging remark!"

There was applause as Sandy approached the microphone, Norm's timing, whether contrived or accidental, had broken the ice. Rather than embarrassing her, the humorous introduction massaged her nerves. Conversations stopped, drinks were set aside as the people politely listened, then rendered a favorable verdict by enthusiastic applause at the end. She went back to her chair. "Great!" Lynn whispered. "Just terrific."

From her vantage point, candles flickered in the dark like large fireflies on a summer night. She watched as couples danced to a slow ballad, remembering that when she had been a little girl that building had been Shuster's first restaurant. She and her father had danced the "Beer Barrel Polka" on that same dance floor. When she couldn't keep up, he had told her to place her small feet on top of his. They had whirled around that very room until she was dizzy and giddy with delight. She missed him very much, she realized, wondering

47

why all this was putting her in such a reflective mood. Perhaps because there wasn't anything to do except jiggle your foot, rearrange your skirt, cross your legs, uncross your legs...

There was no announcement of her second number. Norm just signaled it was coming up next. It surprised her that this time, people paid little attention. Glasses clinked, people talked and laughed, waitresses cleared tables, and couples danced. There was a scattering of applause at the end. As she returned to her chair this time, she wondered what had gone wrong. At intermission, she asked Norm and Lynn.

"They don't applaud each number the band does. You're just another instrument up there, remember?" He drained a glass of ginger ale.

"It was terrific," Lynn added. "When they're out there having fun, we're just kinda' background for that fun to take place."

"Sure is different from doing a show, isn't it?"

"Totally," Lynn agreed as she headed for the ladies room.

Sandy sat down beside Bill at the table. "You know, you sounded really good with the group," he told her. He patted her hand.

"I'm not really comfortable up there. I feel like a fixture or a piece of furniture on a set."

"Nonsense!" Win ate the olive in his martini, then licked his fingers. "You look good, you sound good--you didn't look nervous."

"You could move around a little more," Barb suggested.

"You know, you're right." In concentrating on phrasing and tone, she had forgotten about movement. She hadn't thought to apply the principles she'd coached the singers on in the show--the principles she'd practiced in the mirror. She hugged Barb, "Leave it to you to keep me straight!" She sipped at a coke as they talked.

The band had come back from break, and it was time to return to the stand. For the balance of the evening, Sandy tried to remember to move and gesture. People seemed to pay a little more attention when she did, but it wasn't easy to try to sell a song when you were just background for drinking, talking and dancing. In some respects, it was disappointing; however, the pay was excellent. She had pleased Bill, and particularly when he saw how much she was paid--that had seemed to impress him. And the experience of being able to work with such excellent musicians was a privilege. She hoped the time would never come, however, when she had to admit--she couldn't even read one single note of music. Perhaps as time passed, she could devise some method to wake up an audience--make them want to pay attention. She was soon to discover the answer, as fragments of that formula presented themselves to her like secrets whispered in her ear.

Chapter Six

Sandy had been singing with Norm and Lynn's group on a regular basis for almost six months when Norm called and said the vocalist for the big band, Johnny Martin's orchestra, was quitting as she was pregnant. He suggested she audition for the job. Johnny Martin's orchestra was well-known as one of the most popular bands in a tri-state area. Bill said that he didn't mind her singing with them. "As long as you don't ever have to drive," he added, "I need the car for appointments."

"This whole conversation is probably academic." She had told him while pouring orange juice into three, small glasses. "I'm sure I won't get it anyway if I have to audition."

"Well, we can use the extra money. It's about time we start looking for a house to buy instead of rent. We need another bedroom. If we'd had another boy, they could have bunked in together."

Sandy threw a hot pad into the air. "Yes! A house of our very own!" The hot pad landed on the kitchen table in front of Eric, who stared wide-eyed at his mother and then at the flying object, which had narrowly missed attacking his oatmeal. "When can we start looking?" She threw her arms around Bill.

"Probably Saturday. I made an appointment to look at a few possibilities." He wiped one corner of his mouth with a napkin. "Better get a sitter. Don't get too enthused. We can't afford anything expensive."

"But a house of our very own!" Sandy repeated. "I had no idea you were even thinking about it. I can't wait." Why hadn't he mentioned it before now, she wondered? Apparently he'd discussed it with a real estate agent, before he even thought to suggest it to her. No matter, they were going together to pick out their new home.

As her hands washed the breakfast dishes, her mind painted delicious pictures of their beautiful new home. It would be a cozy, Cape Cod with a quaint picture window. A picket fence--no, wrought iron, would surround it with loving arms, so the children could play safely in the yard. The gray house, with white shutters would be on one floor so that she wouldn't have to run up and downstairs so much. The kitchen would sparkle with long rows of gleaming white cabinets. She envisioned thick, pale green wall-to-wall carpeting spanning the floors and a glistening, colonial chandelier in the dining room. She stared out the kitchen window as she dried the dishes, and rashly added random width pegged floors in the living room, and a colonial fireplace. "A double Dutch door might be nice," she said aloud.

The gods of real estate must have been listening--and taking notes. They must have rubbed their hands together, laughed heartily and produced a house with all the lines and architectural grace of an empty refrigerator box. It was a tall, narrow white house with tall, narrow windows and tall, narrow stairs to the second floor, which would have given a mountain goat a heart attack. Thin, tan indoor-outdoor carpeting spanned sagging floors, caused by bowed basement supports, crippled by the arthritis of age. But there were three bedrooms, a big backyard, a large dining room and Sandy had already transformed it with her eyes. They signed the contract and applied for a loan with the bank.

The following Monday night, she auditioned for the job as big band vocalist. All the way to the rehearsal hall, Norman fired off suggestions and crisp advice with the rapidity of a Gattling gun. She sensed he was nervous for her and this acted to set off a daisy chain reaction of internal misgivings. She missed the sensitivity of Lynn's support in tandem with Norm's. Lynn did not play with Johnny Martin's orchestra as there was a male, who played keyboards. With a start, she realized the vocalist was the only female with the band. She laced her fingers tightly together to disguise her trembling hands.

The rehearsal hall echoed cavernously in a cacophony of instruments being tuned. "Sounds like the background for a spooky, psychological film," she commented as they walked across the long hardwood floor. Norman managed a nod in affirmation as he carried the large acoustical bass toward the end of the room, where some musicians were set up. Others struggled to erect metal music stands, or tuned up. Sandy counted eighteen pieces in all: five saxophones, who doubled on clarinet; five trombones; five trumpets; electronic piano, bass and drums. She wished she could just snap her fingers and disappear.

Norman introduced her to the leader, who suggested she sit with the other candidates--there were two other girls sitting on folding chairs. It was explained that they would all audition to the same arrangement of "Sentimental Journey". There would be three choruses: the vocalist would take the first; second would be instrumental; and then, the vocalist would take it out on the third chorus. The band would rehearse for awhile before the auditions began. With those instructions, Johnny turned and abruptly left. "Do you have the feeling you'd rather be someplace else?" Sandy asked the other girls.

Both giggled. Further conversation was impossible as the band began to play "In the Mood". The full rich sound held an uncanny resemblance to all the big band era music Sandy had always adored--Glenn Miller arrangements, Tommy Dorsey, Harry James. She realized tiny goose pimples had erupted on her arms. She was mesmerized by the beautiful, mellow sound as they segued into "String of Pearls". Her nervousness faded into the excitement of the music...until they began to call for the auditions.

The candidates were to begin in turn, and as she was last to arrive she found herself with the advantage of watching the other two go first. The petite blonde sounded very good, but appeared to be extremely uncomfortable; she stood ramrod straight with no gestures or movement. *Remember that when you're up there*, Sandy told herself.

The second candidate may have had an excellent voice, but the key was wrong for her. That was one piece of advice Norman had stressed. With eighteen instruments and written arrangements, music couldn't be transposed like he and Lynn had so often done for her. "Like it or lump it, you'll do it in the key as written," he had said. They both worried that with her low range, some material might be unsuitable.

Thank God they picked "Sentimental Journey" for the audition song, she thought. Fortuitously, it was arranged in a lower key than most. And now it was her turn...

The rich tones of the introduction seemed to envelop her in a vibrant cloud. It was as though the voice she heard now was one from her childhood, when she had played the record so many times the grooves had become worn. As she sang, she remembered World War II, when her father was in the army--the loneliness, the fear of war, the spirit of patriotism that swept the country even affecting her as a small child.

"Gonna take a sentimental journey
To renew old memories..."

The song itself lifted her onto a magic carpet of remembrance and she was surprised when it was over so quickly. The band broke into applause and as she smiled at Norman, Johnny said, "Lady, you sure sold that song! You're in."

During the drive home, she shared with Norman exactly what had happened to her while she sang. "I got so carried away by the music; it was almost as if I wasn't really there. What if they had picked another song for the audition? What if it had been something else in a bad key? Wasn't it luck, it was 'Sentimental Journey'?"

Norman raised one eyebrow, "Do you believe in luck?" he asked.

She bit her lip and stared into the darkness beyond the windshield. Street lamps cast eerie misshapen images beyond the headlights.

"I'm not sure what I believe," she responded.

There had to be several rehearsals prior to Sandy's first big band job, and this was to be the night they worked at the posh Franklin Club. Cocktail length formals were the new style, worn with a bouffant half slip, which made the skirt stand out. Her dress was black--off the shoulder. The only adornment was a nosegay of flowers, just above the hem, where the skirt had been lifted to reveal an inset froth of ruffled lace.

As the band's caravan of cars and station wagons entered Franklin, Pennsylvania, Sandy remembered that the town had gotten its start because of oil drilling, similar to the first discovery of oil at the Drake Well in Titusville. The opulence the ensuing wealth had engendered was evident in the mansions and beautiful homes they passed. Slender, two-story Georgian colonial columns proudly guarded the entrance to the Franklin Club like rigid sentries. Two stories of colonnaded porches enfolded the front and sides of the building. Inside, richly polished parquet floors were interrupted by thick oriental carpets and burnished cherry Queen Anne tables.

"Wow!" Sandy said, borrowing Eric's word.

"You betcha'," Norm agreed. He carried the bass, while Sandy carried the music. They entered the large banquet room with dance floor, which had been set up to accommodate approximately two hundred at round tables. There were flowers everywhere: azure cornflowers interspersed with vivid red hibiscus in cut crystal vases decorated the individual tables; bronze chrysanthemums and yellow dahlias tumbled from cornucopias on the banquet tables; silver urns, positioned around the room, held stately salmon colored gladioli.

"It's gorgeous," Sandy clapped her hands together.

"Smells like a stinkin' funeral in here," Norman observed dourly, as he began to set up his music stand.

Sandy learned that the flimsy metal music stands used for rehearsal were not the ones actually used for a job. These large cream colored stands were solid to the floor. Brass music lights fastened to the top and each bore a burgundy monogram, "J/M". Even the band members looked different from rehearsal, as each wore a black tux with burgundy cummerbund.

She choked back the urge to say, "Wow!" again, but wanted to pinch herself to be sure she really was a part of such a prestigious, professional musical group.

Members began to file into the room from the dining room. It was like a fashion show of elegant formal clothes. Long pearls appeared to be the accessory statement. Sandy wished she had worn hers, and then remembered they were pop beads.

She stifled a laugh as her mind wove a picture of what could have happened had she worn them. In her mind's eye, dancers whirled around the floor as she sang. As she gestured with one hand, it became caught in the imitation pearls that immediately popped--sending tiny ball bearings of chaos onto the dance floor. She pictured blue haired matrons slipping and falling, bringing their escorts crashing down on top of them. Waiters with glass laden trays skated across the beads trying to maintain their balance, until tall men in tuxes rolled into them like bowling balls making a strike.

She thanked her lucky stars she had left them at home. But the mental picture had acted as a leveler of sorts to make her feel much more comfortable in such posh surroundings. The lighting of the crystal chandeliers dimmed, and Johnny Martin's Orchestra began their first set.

The music was received enthusiastically by the guests. They applauded at the end of each number, jitterbugged to "Chattanooga Choo Choo". These were the songs of their era--the music which brought back memories, whether you lived in a mansion and had teethed on old oil money, or in a bungalow paid for by the sweat of a job in a steel mill. It was a common denominator between classes.

Johnny introduced her first number, "Route 66" that was basically blues arranged for big band. People stopped dancing, gathered around the bandstand and listened. They applauded vigorously and to her surprise, some gentlemen broke with the decorum of the room and whistled while clapping.

Her next vocal was "Embraceable You", which was in the middle of a medley of ballads. She moved toward the microphone as the intro began and sang her heart out. There was no applause other than scattered polite appreciation, as people returned to their tables.

What was the difference? she wondered, as she returned to her seat. It had to be the introduction. It was almost as if you had to coach an audience in how to respond. As "Pennsylvania 6-5000" livened up the room, she remembered to shout with the rest of the band in the proper places, but her mind swirled, searching in corners for an answer she just couldn't seem to pin down.

It was the same with Norman and Lynn's band. When she was introduced, the crowd paid attention--they ignored her when her vocals came as part of the set or medley. That might be a part of the answer. She made mental note to keep score on that point for awhile, examine different crowd reactions. While nothing could be done to change the big band's approach as it was all so heavily scripted, maybe Norman and Lynn would try the experiment with her. She remembered their answer when she asked what she had done wrong that first night, when there was no applause, "You're just another instrument up there, remember?" It would almost seem that an introduction somehow separated her from being "just another instrument". She would make it a point to find out.

She picked up the claves, two hollow mahogany sticks that clicked in a precise tempo. The Latin, "Cherry Pink and Apple Blossom White" was next. Norman had taught her how to play the claves, but warned her she must join the musician's union. That week she had applied to the American Federation of Musicians as a "Latin Percussionist". Was that a hoot--she couldn't even read music!

Later as she paid the sitter, checked on the children and put her gown on a hanger, she felt like Cinderella who had been to the ball. Bill wasn't home yet and she was bursting to share the evening with him--the elegance of the Franklin Club, the gleaming silver, abundance of flowers, crisp white linen, sparkling chandeliers and polished parquet floors. She was awed by the moneyed families who had struck it rich years ago in oil.

At that moment, as she drifted off to sleep, had she been able to see into the future, she would have seen herself singing at the Petroleum Club in Tulsa, Oklahoma--where only those who owned oil stock could belong. The top two floors of the Petroleum Building were connected by a massive, curved stairway the width of a small highway. On the top floor, fountains of champagne and sparkling burgundy were surrounded by fine crystal glasses. The extravagant decor would look like the lavish set of a Cecil B. DeMille movie.

But, of course, she couldn't see into the future. There is the kindness of a velvet veil between the present and what is to come. Had it been a gossamer veil, she would also have been able to see the devastating heartbreak in store...

Chapter Seven

*O*ne evening a year later, a full, harvest moon danced in the dark sky and lovingly laid a golden blanket of muted light over the silhouetted Pennsylvania countryside. Gently rolling hills were transformed into splendid majesty, as they wore this golden gift from the moon like a regal mantle. Small puffs of fog, touched by moonbeam madness, sensuously swirled and bowed to the moon. The caravan of cars and station-wagons traveled silently together after a job at a private club in Erie. Sandy's conversation with Norm, who was driving, seemed to resurrect the continuing enigma of applause. While a piece of the puzzle seemed to decidedly be the dynamics of an introduction versus just coming in on a chorus like another instrument, it was not the entire answer. There seemed to be other pieces to the puzzle which continued to elude her. Norman and Lynn had cooperated with the experiment. It was predictable that when Norman introduced her, people paid attention--always applauded. It was equally predictable that not introducing her brought lukewarm applause, or no reaction at all. There had been no opportunity to make that same analogy with Johnny Martin's orchestra.

She leaned her head back against the passenger seat. "You know, I really do feel like just another instrument with the big band, Norm. It's exciting to be a part of such a great sound, but we don't get anything *back* from the people. I find myself wanting to interact with them more...I don't just mean applause, I mean..." She searched for just the right words, "I feel like I'm reaching out to them and I want them to reach back to me."

Norman squinted at approaching headlights distorted by the fog. "I think you're growing bored, Sandy. Frankly, I think you won't be happy until you find the key to the crowd psychology you keep searching for."

"I'm deeply grateful for what I'm doing. It's just that..." Her voice trailed into thoughts. Just what was she searching for? Something within kept nudging that there was more to be discovered. "Do you think I'm silly?" she asked.

He scowled into the rear view mirror as a car approached from behind. Its bright lights blazed. The car sped past, its tail lights fading into two red pinpoints in the night. "I'm not putting you down for what you're feeling, Sandy. I think maybe you're ready to grow a bit more."

She giggled. "Is it growing pains I'm experiencing?"

"Just so it's not labor pains--don't get pregnant. You've got a great career going for you."

"We don't plan on it. Bill and I have our boy and our little girl."

He grew thoughtful. "You know, Gary Sweigart's been bugging me to work out with a jazz group that's just starting. He'd like you to work with them too, but mentioned it to me instead of you, as he didn't want there to be a conflict of interest."

"Jazz group? Anybody I know?"

"Just Gary on drums. Really brilliant tenor, alto, baritone sax--Chuck Hitmar, guy by the name of Joe Straka on piano, and the leader is a musician who calls himself Frankie Mann, but his real name is Frank Mango. He plays accordion."

"Accordion?" Sandy raised her eyebrows and began to laugh. She pictured a polka band, or Lawrence Welk. "Ah-one, and ah-two, and ah..."

He smiled and raised one hand, "Hold it, Champagne Lady! You've never heard an amplified jazz accordion--sounds like an organ. Mango plays like Ray Charles."

"So are you going to go sit in with them?"

"Next Sunday afternoon in Masury, Ohio. Want to come?"

"I thought you'd never ask! Let me see if I can get a sitter."

"How many insurance appointments can Bill have on a Sunday afternoon? Let's get real here!"

It was one thing to confide in Barb, but she didn't want to let Norm know there were problems at home. "We have a deal. He doesn't baby sit."

"They're his kids too, but suit yourself." He shrugged his shoulders. "This jazz group might be just the change you're looking for. Certainly would give you a chance to grow musically."

It was just an innocent remark, but prophetic. Neither of them realized that this group, the Frankie Mann Quartet, would be the stepping stone onto a pathway of dazzling glamour far beyond the horizon of any of her dreams... but she was to find that stepping stones can be slippery--sometimes leading to a serious fall.

The rehearsal at Melody Lane was an eye-opener. Frank Mango and the other musicians offered them both a place with the band and she knew she was really going to enjoy working with this group. *Working a "gig"*, she told herself and rolled the word around in her mind. While she had been exposed to the word for the last two years, she had never used it herself. What was different now? Perhaps she had begun to accept herself as really being a singer, instead of just play-acting at a part-time job. She realized she could never have come this far if it hadn't been for Norman and Lynn, but she felt like a second-grader thrust into a high school class with this band. Could she possibly live up to their standard of musicianship? She was bursting to tell Barb and Bill about the Frankie Mann Quartet.

She got back home in time to pay the sitter, get a roasting chicken in the oven, make a salad and set the table for Sunday dinner. "Mommy will set the kitchen table, don't worry, sweetheart." The dining room table was covered with Lincoln Logs.

Lisa was sitting up in bed, playing with a green, rubber Gumby doll. Her blonde hair, still damp from sleep, wound itself into tight curly ringlets They walked down the steep stairs hand-in-hand just as Bill came in the front door.

"I can't wait to tell you about rehearsal today." She watched Lisa run toward Eric and the Lincoln Log project in the dining room. She cringed, waiting for Eric's protests that Lisa was bulldozing his village.

"Was it a good one?" Bill snapped on the television and switched channels to find a football game.

"Terrific! We're going to start working with the Frankie Mann Quartet at Melody Lane in Masury--Friday and Saturday nights."

"What about the big band?"

"They'll get substitutes for Norm and me on nights we have to work with the big band. Bill, this group is so talented. And it's going to give me a chance to grow...to develop more musically."

"Yes!" he yelled, but not in response to her words. There had been a fumble.

"You can go with me on these jobs--after all, it will be both nights of every weekend."

He punched the palm of one hand. "Gettem! Get him!" he yelled.

"We could get Barb and Win to go one night...and maybe Mimi and Ed could go another night. This will be fun, you'll see."

"Make it!" he yelled. "Make that lousy first down!" He lit a cigarette.

Realizing he was not listening to one word she continued, "And the President of the United States is going to be there," she said in the same tone of voice. "And there will be strippers at intermission time to entertain the audience," she paused to catch his reaction.

He watched the pass and held his breath.

"I'll be singing a duet with Elvis Presley."

He nodded his head.

"In the nude."

"That's great." He took off his shoes and massaged one foot. "Now run it this time!" he yelled.

"It's an audition for Ed Sullivan, isn't that neat?"

He frowned and looked slightly perplexed. "What did you say?"

"I said it's time to eat!" She shrugged and left the room.

At dinner, he agreed to go Saturday night. That would work out well as

Lynn was going Saturday night too. They'd be company for each other while Norm and Sandy were on the bandstand.

Melody Lane was a large, frame "L"-shaped building--the huge bar, that had its own entrance, formed the foot of the "L". The dining room, with large dance floor and raised bandstand was plain, but clean and well maintained. Unless it was packed with people, the acoustics were terrible. However, their first night had been advertised extensively in all the newspapers and there was a good response.

For the first time, Sandy saw her name advertised in print, "The Frankie Mann Quartet with Sandy Ghost, Vocalist, appearing Friday and Saturday." She cut the ad out to send to her mother in California, who, to this point in time, had not been impressed that she was singing. She looked around the room as the band set up and realized if her mother could have actually seen Melody Lane, she would have been appalled. She could hear her voice, "A roadhouse--nothing but a gin mill! To think a daughter of mine..." The thought trailed off as Frankie approached her.

"Norm's going to introduce your numbers," he said. "We have you up for three per set."

What a sweetheart, she thought, *he must have asked to have introductions for me.* It just was not customary with most bands. "That's great," she said aloud.

She left the bandstand to visit with Lynn and Bill. "I've missed you so much." She hugged Lynn. "I hate it that you're not playing with us."

"I miss you too," she pushed Sandy back from the hug and took a long look at her, "but look at you, girl, you're fulfilling all the dreams Norman and I knew you could."

"This isn't exactly Blues Alley or Carnegie Hall," Sandy laughed and gestured around the room.

"No, but you'll get there. You're moving up. Isn't she, Bill?"

Bill lifted his glass in a mock toast to his wife.

"Lynn, I want some honest critiques tonight. Tell me anything I'm doing wrong. I'm so glad you're here." She hugged her again. This was her mentor, along with Norman, and while it made her nervous to be performing under Lynn's scrutiny, she knew any criticism would come from a caring sensitivity.

"You know I'll help in any way I possibly can."

Pink spotlights now illuminated the stage. Sandy excused herself and climbed the steps to the bandstand. They had agreed the opener would be "Primrose Lane", which they would all sing in parody:

"Melody Lane
Life's a holiday at Melody Lane...

Just a holiday at Melody Lane
With you..."
Frankie stepped to the microphone. "The Frankie Mann Quartet with vocalist Sandy Ghost, playing for your dancing enjoyment."

There was polite applause as people acknowledged the somewhat corny announcement. The long tables were filling up. Waitresses took drink and dinner orders. Some carried huge trays, held aloft, over the heads of those standing. The first couple got up to dance to "Blue Velvet", a Bobby Vinton song that was popular.

They were off and running...

Midway through the set, Norman approached the microphone, "Ladies and Gentlemen, we have a special treat for you this evening...Sandy Ghost, here to haunt you, (there was scattered laughter) to put a bewitching spell on you with the familiar ballad, 'Bewitched, Bothered and Bewildered.'" He handed her the mic--the intro had already begun behind him.

The omni-directional Astatic microphone lent a wonderful fullness to her voice. People came out of the bar, carrying drinks, to listen. The pink spotlights shimmered across the black velvet gown, turning the silver sequins to tiny amethysts. She moved across the stage and leaned toward the people crowding in from the bar. The crowd whistled and cheered in the middle of the song, spurred by the innuendo of the lyrics. She caught a glimpse of Lynn and Bill, both grinning broadly. Lynn nodded her head "yes".

Chuck Hitmar took a chorus on the alto saxophone. She swayed, watched him, still holding the microphone in one hand, as though he played for her alone. Normally she hated an instrumental chorus in the middle of a vocal. It left her standing awkwardly, waiting to come back in, while she tried to figure out what to do with herself in the interim. But with this band, it was different--she could easily lose herself in a solo by any of them.

No one danced, yet they had gathered around the bandstand to watch and listen as she sang the last chorus. And then an amazing thing happened. At the end of "Bewitched", the applause lasted so long that the band had to scramble their numbers for the set. Frankie, normally so at ease, suave and in control, flipped hastily through his music, "Satin Doll. Get 'Satin Doll' up!" he yelled. That was another one of her numbers, to come later in the set, but he was calling it now.

Norman moved toward the mike again, "By popular demand...", he smiled broadly. There was a ripple of laughter again, as the crowd could easily see what was happening. "We'll bring Sandy back. Our own satin doll...Sandy Ghost, but she's wearing velvet tonight," he added, and handed her the microphone. They began to play the intro in a sexy, backbeat temp.

"Cigarette holder which wigs me

Over his shoulder he digs me
Out cattin'...
My satin doll..."

She moved across the stage in much the same manner as she had done in the Pearl Bailey number back in the minstrel show. The crowd loved it---but she loved it more! She wasn't just an instrument. She was reaching out to them, and they were reaching back. They were interacting. She saw Lynn and Bill had moved closer and were standing with the crowd in order to be able to see. She mustn't look at Bill--she knew she'd lose it if she did. *Pretend he's not here,* she told herself.

And it happened again. They wouldn't let her sit down. Again, Frankie scrambled sheet music. "Lady Is a Tramp"! he yelled, wondering if they were ever going to get a chance to play "Green Dolphin Street", which should have been the number up after "Bewitched".

As she sang, out of the corner of one eye, she saw a lady, dressed in the bonnet and uniform of the Salvation Army. She silently passed a tambourine among the remaining few, who still sat on stools in the bar. Gruff-looking, bearded men and preppie college seniors alike contributed coins or bills. Was it dictated by a sense of guilt that they had money to be out drinking, while others had no food? As she finished the final chorus, the uniformed lady departed.

In an attempt to get the set back in order, Sandy left the stage while the audience was still applauding. She made her way through the crowd, accepting compliments as she went, and headed for the table where Lynn and Bill had been sitting. The empty chair on the bandstand, where she should have been, spoke of desertion, but she knew her instincts were right to leave the stand.

"Good grief--that was sensational." Lynn shook her head. "You ended up doing a show up there. You realize that, don't you?"

"I hope Frankie isn't mad," she said apologetically.

"Mad? He won't be mad. He called up the numbers himself in response to the crowd's reaction."

"Well, I'm supposed to be sitting on the stand. I left the stage to get things back on track."

"And your instincts were right on target, as usual," she took a sip of her coke. "During intermission we need to talk to Mose. Maybe they should let you do your own set--a show. Then the rest of the time play for dancing." She wiped a ring of moisture from the table with a paper napkin.

Bill returned to the table, carrying a fresh beer. "You turned 'em upside down, kid," he told her. "Aren't you supposed to be sitting up there?" He jerked a thumb in the direction of the stage.

"Well, yes, but I thought it best to leave the stage, after so many numbers in a row."

"And you always know best, don't you?" The tone was caustic.

Lynn shuffled her feet. "Excuse me, I'm going to find the ladies' room before the rush at intermission."

"Wait for me," Sandy took the opportunity to escape with her.

As they stood at the mirror repairing makeup, Lynn remarked, "It's none of my business, but does Bill resent your singing?"

"He doesn't seem to care one way or the other, but he does like the extra income." She combed her hair and tightened one, long earring.

"Any time I've ever been around him, he puts you down terribly. How do you take it?"

"It doesn't have a thing to do with the singing, Lynn. He was doing that long before I started singing. If anything, I've gained a bit of his respect, I think."

Lynn snapped her compact shut. "It's hard for me to keep my mouth shut when he starts in on you. I've seen him do it before when he came along on our band's jobs."

When they returned to the table, the band had ordered drinks and was on a twenty-minute break.

"I hope you guys aren't mad at me. I left the stand to try to get us back on track. I'll go back the next set and sit up there."

"You were fantastic--you did exactly the right thing," Frankie told her.

Bill raised his eyebrows like Groucho Marx.

"I don't mean to interfere," Lynn began, "but can I make a suggestion here?" They all knew she was a polished musician in her own right. "Maybe you need to feature Sandy. Lump all her numbers together--let her do a show. Play her on...play her off."

"Right on!" Gary Sweigart agreed.

Chuck Hitmar cleaned his glasses with a paper napkin. "I think you're absolutely right," he nodded his head and replaced the glasses. As the room came back into focus, he smiled a shy, engaging smile. "Play her off and on to Satin Doll".

"It works for me," Frankie said.

Norman smiled, "Do you realize this is what you've been searching for, Sandy? You've said all along you wanted more crowd reaction, more inter-play with them. You got it tonight!"

"I got it--but can I keep it?" She laughed. "Really, it all kind of evolved like a coincidence--the crowd inspired it."

It was decided from that point forward she would not sit on the stage again. Her material would be arranged into four separate shows. They would announce her, play her on just before each of the four intermissions.

The Frankie Mann Quartet played Melody Lane to packed crowds for six months. During that time, more staging secrets were whispered in Sandy's ear; they just seemed to drop in her lap from some unknown source. She discovered her actions broadcast to an audience how to react: if she raised an arm at the end of a song, it signaled applause; if she moved around the stage, they clapped in time to the music. She learned to telegraph the response she wanted from a crowd. Some of these staging ploys even worked with the big band, but now working with them was so bland by comparison, that she gave her notice to Johnny Martin's Orchestra, staying until they could audition a vocalist to replace her.

She bought a long, eighty-foot microphone cord to use at Melody Lane. If the room was not crowded, she came to them, working from the dance floor-- singing table-to-table.

She learned pacing. Start with an upbeat, excitement generating piece of music, then a ballad, then moderate tempo, and always go out with something upbeat again.

Experimenting with patter between songs, she improvised her own introductions to songs, telling in what Broadway shows songs had been featured, and put together a medley of music on girl's names, which turned out to be a crowd-pleaser. She kibitzed with the crowd, laughed with them--became a part of them while performing.

But the one frivolous, silly, little thing that helped the most was a pair of long, white opera gloves. The first time she wore them they made her feel different--professional, somehow. It was as though they reminded her she was an entertainer, and she actually sang better when she wore them. The long rhinestone earrings had performed the same kind of mental magic during the minstrel show. They were minor crutches, but major perception image builders.

There was one curious thread in the six months of entertaining. Every time Sandy sang, "Lady Is a Tramp", the Salvation Army lady, in her black uniform, opened the door to the bar and passed the tambourine. Sandy had mentioned it to the band after the first few times, and they began to watch for her too. Without fail, it happened every time. Was it coincidence, or did she wait in the parking lot for her cue, tighten the strings on her bonnet and polish her tambourine until they played "her song"? They joked about it until the entire band had to struggle to keep from cracking up when they saw her. It happened so often, however, that Sandy wondered if it held any particular significance. There had been so many strange things happening in the last two years.

Winter released its snowy grip on western Pennsylvania and one rainy spring Friday night, Frankie rushed into the club with the force of a small tornado. He took the stage steps two-at-a-time. Water scattered everywhere from his rain soaked, yellow mackintosh as he threw it backstage.

"Hey, man. You're hosing down the instruments," Norm chided him.

Frankie took out a handkerchief and wiped his face. "Have I got news for you!" His handsome face radiated excitement. "An agent caught us the other night. He's coming again tonight to talk with us about a record! This may be a big break for the band, and you too, Sandy. He really liked you."

"You're kidding!" She'd never expected exposure like that.

"Are you connin' us, man?" Joe Straka was always the last to accept anything new. He reminded Sandy of Eeore in the Winnie-the-Pooh stories she read to Lisa and Eric. Eeore was the donkey, who always looked at the dark side of situations, never quite believing he deserved anything good that might happen to him.

Frankie flashed his perfect smile. "I'm telling you, Straka, this guy thinks we're fantastic. His name is Jimmy Williams. He's an independent agent and record producer from Cleveland."

Chuck and Gary both tried to talk at once. They stopped and then started in again on top of each other. Gary won out with a drum roll. They all laughed. "What time is he coming?"

"He didn't say, but just be on your toes and give the best performance possible."

"What's he look like?" Chuck finally got to say, apparently hoping to spot the agent in the audience.

"Now, how am I supposed to know, dummy? I talked to him on the telephone. He called me." Frankie said good-naturedly.

Sandy was thankful she had brought a form-fitting gold lame gown. Actually, her mother-in-law had taken a gold lame bathing suit and sewn a lame flounce around the bottom, turning it into a flashy theatrical dress. While she and Dr. Ghost seldom saw Sandy perform because clubs were not a part of their life-style, Isabel had continued to make wardrobe for her and babysit when she could. During fittings, she bounced staging suggestions off her mother-in-law, who seemed to have the ability to assess ideas clearly, helping her avoid what ultimately could have come across as slapstick pitfalls. "Let's just do our best, and let the chips fall where they may," she told the band.

"Buffalo chips," Straka muttered as he began playing arpeggios.

"Chocolate chips," Chuck giggled and began to tune up his baritone sax.

As the evening progressed, the band scrutinized every lone man who came in and sat down by himself. At the second intermission, Straka declared, "Not gonna show, man. He's not gonna show."

Frankie took a long drink of his Tom Collins. "He's coming. Just not here yet."

They were all nervous, including Sandy. "He's coming in the disguise of a Salvation Army lady," she joked.

They had just started their third set when a short, balding man in a tan trench-coat appeared in the archway between the bar and dining room. He leaned against the wall, holding a highball glass in one hand, a clipboard in the other. Between songs, he ambled toward an empty table and sat down, placing the raincoat over the back of one of the empty chairs. An unspoken signal passed between the members of the band, which was missed by Sandy who was changing in the ladies' room. She had instituted a new practice of changing wardrobe before each of her four shows. Luckily, the gold lame was next on the agenda.

She put finishing touches on her makeup just as the beginning few bars of "Satin Doll" were being played. She climbed the steps to the stage as Norman announced her. Perhaps it was fortuitous that there was no chance for anyone to tell her the agent was in the audience.

They kicked off her show with "Yes, Indeed" a rollicking Ray Charles song, where the band vocally sang a riff of "Yes, indeed" behind her. Chuck Hitmar had cleverly written an arrangement similar to the Charles record, which made the four pieces sound like a big band. The next up was the ballad, "Willow Weep for Me", another Hitmar arrangement, then the standard, "Makin' Whoopee".

She did the first chorus on stage and then, taking the mike out of the stand, came down off the stage, working table-to-table. She was working in front of the agent's table, when it suddenly dawned on her who he was. She almost forgot the lyrics. "Are you Jimmy Williams," she whispered between phrasing. He nodded "yes" and smiled. She returned the smile and moved on to the next table, but her heart was beating faster.

At intermission, Jimmy came up to the bandstand and introduced himself. They all went back to his table. "You've got a unique sound," he told them. "I'm willing to finance a recording session. We'll press a master and distribute to a local market. If it gets some good air play, we'll talk about a contract." The words were all wreathed in haloes of smoke from the cigar that perched in the corner of his mouth. He turned to Sandy, "You're a class act, lady. You've got real crowd appeal. I wish I could bottle it--I'd make a fortune."

She couldn't believe her ears and stammered, "Thank you very much, Mr. Williams."

"Jimmy," he corrected her. The cigar bobbed twice--once for each syllable.

Three days later, Norman telephoned. The recording session had been set up for 8:00 AM the following Thursday at Embassy studios in Cleveland.

In rapid succession, she dialed Bill at work, Mom, and then Barb. "Put on the coffee, I'm on my way over," Barb told her. "I've got to hear all the details."

Later, after Sandy had described what happened, including almost losing it in the middle of a song, when she realized who he was, Barb asked, "And there will be a contract if the record does well?"

"That's what he promised. He also paid me a great compliment, said I was a 'class act' and that I had 'real crowd appeal', if he could bottle it he'd 'make a fortune'. Imagine!"

Barb raised one eyebrow, "Better be careful. Sounds like he might try to get you on an auditioning couch!"

"Oh, come on! The guy's short, fat and bald… with dandruff," she added. "How will I ever cut a record at eight o'clock in the morning? You know I'm a night person. Norm suggested I stay up all night."

"That's a thought."

But she was terribly worried about trying to sing so early in the morning. In fact, she was positive she couldn't do it.

Chapter Eight

———————— ⌀⅂⅂⅁ ————————

*T*he reception room of the recording studio reeked with pungent cigar smoke, announcing that Jimmy Williams was already there, before they had a chance to see him. The walls were papered in heavy, tan grass cloth. Thick, chocolate broadloom carpeting was interrupted by glass tables and groupings of butternut leather chairs. Jimmy waved the cigar in the air like a drum major's baton, "Right this way," he said, marching off down a dark hall toward a brightly lit room in the back. The cigar tip glowed fiercely like a beacon in front of them, as Sandy and the band followed, struggling to keep instrument cases from banging against the walls of the narrow hallway.

They emerged into a room that resembled a tiered high school band rehearsal hall; however, upon closer observation, they were actually in a large booth with acoustical walls and ceiling tiles. Engineers sat at a large control board on the other side of a glass wall. There were no windows. Jimmy closed the vault-like door to the hallway and automatically a red light illuminated above it.

"Oh, Norm...help...I've got claustrophobia. I feel like I can't breathe," Sandy whispered to Norman. He continued to unpack his instruments. "How can I sing if I can't breathe?" She wiped perspiration from the palms of her hands down the sides of her red slacks.

Before he could answer, Jimmy led her away. "Now, we'll do the vocal first." He took her to a separate corner of the room that had been boxed in with acoustical material. At that moment, it resembled an upright coffin to Sandy. A microphone was suspended from the ceiling--under it, a high stool with tall chrome legs suggested this could be a long, tiresome procedure. He handed her a set of earphones. "Put these on," the cigar bobbed up and down in his mouth. "So, it'll mess your hair a little, so what." He smiled, waving a pudgy hand.

"But...but, you mean I'll be singing back here in this box? I can't even *see* the band from here." Smothering doubts became overwhelming, threatening suffocation. She had always received her energy from the band. How could she perform with just the impersonal sound of them coming through the headset?

"That's the way it's done, honey. Don't worry, you'll be fine." He was gone like a bald genie, disappearing in a cloud of smoke

But she wasn't fine. She sat on the stool, looking at a wall that resembled white pegboard. She nervously picked at threads on her slacks.

She was suddenly jarred by an unfamiliar voice in the headset that asked, "Ready, Sandy?" She pushed the stool back and stood up, remembering

66

Norman and Lynn's advice to never sit while singing--the position depressed the diaphragm--or was it a reflex action to get away from the stool? She could hear the familiar intro in the headset. They had chosen "Gone With The Wind", a soft ballad done in a Latin tempo. Her voice sounded abstract, lifeless, in the headset. She attempted to conjure up some device to rescue the situation, pump some animation into the impersonal voice, but it just seemed to drone blandly on. The ending was a tag, mechanically faded.

When they listened to the play back, everyone, including Jimmy, seemed pleased--except Sandy. "It has all the personality of a limp dishrag," she complained. "I sound like I'm sitting in a coffin with a toe tag on!"

"You wanna' do another take?" Jimmy made a circle in the air toward the control booth.

"Let's try something. I just can't seem to work to a blank wall. I know I'm new at this, and the engineers will probably think I'm a real hick, but could you stand in front of me in the booth, Jimmy? If I can sing *to* somebody maybe it will come off better."

He grinned and bit the tip off another cigar. "Let's try it." They readied for another take.

It was just the deceptive device needed. The playback came to life this time. "Leave it alone guys, we're not going to lay down additional tracks," Jimmy told the control room engineers. "Just press the Master with that take!"

"Tracks? What are 'tracks'?" Sandy questioned.

"Additional recordings, like if we wanted to flesh out the instrumental portion, we'd have the band record harmony to themselves, or even have you sing harmony to your first track. The audio engineers would then mix those tracks with what we've got now."

"And what's a 'Master'?"

"The finished product becomes a Master and that's actually pressed, then the records are duplicated off that Master. If I wanted to, I could make you sound like the Mormon Tabernacle Choir, singing with a big band as backup." He laughed and flicked a huge cigar ash into a wastebasket. "But I like the quality just like it is. Your sexy voice comes through better that way--it's more intimate."

"Thanks, but I was afraid I just couldn't pull it off until you agreed to let me sing directly to you." She smiled and shook her head.

"Yah' got good instincts, kid! Yah' knew how to work it out," Jimmy pounded her on the back, gagging her with a mushroom cloud of cigar smoke. "We gotta' talk sometime soon. Gimme me your 'phone number."

As she scribbled the number, Barb's warning about the "auditioning couch" surfaced in a red flag of caution. *Could he want her telephone number for some dark purpose of his own?* He wore a gold wedding band, but she had never heard him speak of his wife. She handed him the piece of paper and said rather haughtily, "I would think anything you had to say to me, Jimmy, could be said in front of the band."

"Not really," the cigar bobbed twice. "I may have some work for you without them," he told her.

Oh boy...here it comes, she thought and struggled to keep a lewd picture from her mind of a pudgy, Jimmy Williams dribbling cigar ashes all over a woman he was kissing.

"Kid, the money's not in just being another instrument up there with the band. The money is in doing a nightclub act--that's where the real bucks are. Now, I think you've got what it takes to put an act together. You've got sparkle, and with a little bit of coaching, some professional pictures...the right promotion," he took a handkerchief out of his pocket, and wiped his sweaty forehead, "I think you've got the potential to be a first class act."

"Really?" she said, but with a measure of reserve. "I appreciate the compliment."

"I wouldn't kid you, Sandy. I'm perfectly serious," he smiled and re-lit his cigar with a lighter the size of a flame thrower. "First of all, I want you to meet my wife Patty. She used to be an entertainer. She can give you a few pointers. Then, we'll take you up to Buffalo, New York to have promo pictures taken-- best doggone theatrical photographic studio in the country--Gene LaVerne. He could make Minnie Pearl look like a glamour queen!"

Her laughter made the band look toward their direction. "And your wife would go with us to Buffalo?"

"Yeah, sure." He took out a pen knife and cleaned under his thumbnail.

She felt small enough to crawl under the stool in the sound booth. Weighing his words, she felt she had seriously misjudged the agent, when all he really had in mind was her career...and, of course, ultimately a piece of the "real money."

The engineers were beginning to cue up for the instrumental side of the recording now, which prohibited further conversation. Frankie adjusted the straps on his accordion, but kept nervously wiping the palms of his hands on his slacks. Straka stubbed out a cigarette and hunched over the keyboard, poised for the countdown, while Norman and Chuck Hitmar seemed riveted to watching the engineers in the control room. Gary seemed to be the only one unaffected by jitters. He lazily cleaned an ear with the tip of one drumstick.

The dark and swarthy audio engineer, behind the glass window, pointed at Frankie, who mouthed the words, "One...two...one, two, three, four." The full, distinctive sound of the Frankie Mann Quartet filled the studio.

Now that her own personal pressure was off, Sandy began to feel like Snow

White, wakened from a long sleep by the kiss of a prince. She looked around the studio with new eyes as the words, *We're really, truly cutting a record* made circles in her mind like the chant of some mantra. She heard the band with the discernment of new ears, as though the record were already getting air play on a radio station. Her broad smile seemed to encourage the band as this wave of newly found excitement swirled past her toward the small group of musicians.

As they reached the top of the last chorus, Frankie smiled back and nodded "yes"; Chuck Hitmar looked out over top of his thick glasses, and smiled with his eyes; Norman, eyes closed, swayed to the music as his strong fingers flashed across the strings of the bass.

When they were finished, even the engineers in the sound booth applauded. Jimmy breathed a sigh of relief when it was decided to go with the first take--he was the one paying for studio time. As they listened to both playbacks one last time, the excitement was infectious. Even Norman, the perfectionist, admitted it was good--had potential to gain them professional attention. But would the public render the same verdict?

Three weeks later, she was making peanut butter and jelly sandwiches for Eric and Lisa when the telephone rang, "They just announced 'Greenville's own Sandy Ghost' on the Greenville radio station!" Lynn yelled the words into the telephone excitedly and clicked off the line. Sandy slammed down the receiver and told the kids, "Listen, guys! It's Mommy on the radio!" She wildly spun the dial to Greenville just as the introduction was playing.

Eric's eyes grew wide as he listened to the music. He looked from her to the radio and back again, smiling broadly. Lisa giggled, clapping her hands, "Mommy's in the radio box," she proclaimed.

At the end of the cut, the announcer said, "I think we've got another Julie London, right here in little 'ole Greenville. That was 'Gone With The Wind' by vocalist, Sandy Ghost."

"Who's Julie London?" Eric asked.

"She's a beautiful lady who is a very popular singer, honey. That was a nice compliment." But why hadn't the announcer said it was good? She just wanted someone to say it was "good". "I wish Daddy had been here too, but surely they'll play it again."

"Daddy in the box too?" Lisa took a bite of her sandwich.

"No, just Mommy, sweetheart," she laughed and poured two glasses of milk as the telephone rang.

"Can I have your autograph?" It was Barb. "Your record's on the Youngstown, Ohio station. Right now! Call you back."

Sandy searched for the Youngstown station just as it was ending. "That was 'Gone With The Wind' by vocalist Sandy Ghost with the Frankie Mann

Quartet, and now the news." The announcer immediately launched into a local newscast, as the telephone rang again.

"Sensational, hon... just great." This was the first time Barb had heard the record.

"You'd say that whether it was or not," Sandy told her, "You're obliged to say that because you're my best friend. Your opinion doesn't count!"

"Best friends tell the truth. I'd tell you if it stunk," she laughed. "This should kick off a national career. Are you going to Buffalo for professional pictures?"

Sandy stretched the telephone cord to its limit and washed dishes as they talked, "I guess so. I haven't told the band anything about it yet. I want their opinion first--especially Norman and Lynn."

"Why? Seems to me you're a big girl now. Spread your wings and fly. Take advantage of the agent's offer."

"You don't understand, Barb," she rinsed a glass. "I owe them, especially Norm and Lynn. None of this would be happening if they hadn't groomed me for it, worked hard to teach me... and I would be running off and leaving them."

"Come on! This is what they wanted for you."

"Part of me wants to do it, but the other half is scared to death. I'll talk to the band Friday night during intermission."

"You're crazy. You don't need their permission. What about Bill? What does he think?"

"Oh, you know," she waved a wet hand and soap bubbles floated down onto the counter, capturing tiny rainbows of color from the sunny kitchen window. "He seems impressed about the record... maybe will be even more so when he actually hears it playing on the radio."

"But what does he think about you traveling--doing a night club act?"

"It's okay, I guess. I assured him I wouldn't even think of it if I couldn't remain in control of the time I spent with him and the kids."

There was a long pause, then, "I don't care what the band says. If you don't at least try this, you'll wonder the rest of your life if it was a missed opportunity."

"I know you're right," she sighed, "but I'm still scared to death. I almost hope the band's indignant--mad at me, so I can call Jimmy and tell him, 'thanks, but no thanks'."

But the band was not indignant, nor angry with her. They encouraged Sandy to explore the opportunity. Lynn had come to listen that Friday night. Seeing a hint of tears in Sandy's eyes she reached across the table, covering her hand with her own, "Don't you realize, you silly goose, this is just another stepping stone to the potential we all saw in you?"

"You're not abandoning us," Frankie chimed in. "If you make it big, it's good for us too because we recorded with you."

That following night, Sandy arranged her middle show to finish with "Lady Is a Tramp" as the last song, hoping to close off the show quickly and catch up with the Salvation Army lady. It had become an obsession to talk with her and as their time at Melody Lane was coming to a close, it was imperative to find out the woman's motivation for always coming in when that song was played. Was it coincidence, or did she do it to make a point?

Out of the corner of her eye, on the opening bars of the song, she spotted the lady. It was hard to concentrate on the lyrics as she watched the bonneted woman as she passed the tambourine from person-to-person around the bar. Her long black dress swished gracefully as she approached clusters of people standing in groups watching the show. They appeared to treat her with deference, responding by reaching in pockets for bills and change. She never smiled, but seemed to thank them with a slight nod of the head causing the bow of the bonnet, tied under her chin, to bob up and down. Did the bonnet smell like french fries, smoke and beer when she hung it up at home, Sandy wondered?

The show was over. She took abbreviated bows and sprinted through the crowd to the parking lot. The Salvation Army lady had disappeared out the door on the last note. She saw her at the end of the parking lot, the long black dress mingling with the shadows.

"Wait! Please wait..." she shouted. Her gold high heels clicked crisply across the asphalt.

The woman hesitated, then waited.

Sandy ran toward her wondering what she would say when she finally had a chance to talk to her. "I'm sorry..." she was out of breath, "but I have a question to ask you."

"Yes?" The woman's voice was soft, melodious.

"It's just that... well," she stammered, "it seems like every time I sing 'Lady Is a Tramp' you appear. Is it a coincidence?"

The woman smiled, but didn't reply.

She was beginning to feel like a fool, but continued to press the point. "Do you do it on purpose? I'm not mad, or anything... I just want to know."

As she tilted her head slightly, the parking lot lights illuminated her face that had been hidden by the shadow of her bonnet. She was smiling broadly, "I have something for you, Sandy." She reached into a deep pocket in her long skirt and pulled out a piece of paper folded into a small square. "Read it when you're alone," she said mysteriously, handing it to Sandy. "God bless you," she said softly as she got into the passenger side of the waiting car.

In the garish florescent light of the Ladies' Room, Sandy unfolded the lined piece of paper. The words, "Do you know Jesus?" were written in a childish penciled scrawl on the blue lines of the notebook paper. "He loves you very much," was the rest of the message.

The small, creased piece of paper seemed to burn a hole in her hand. She looked at her image in the mirror. Bright red sequins winked off her reflection. *Me? God loves me? Surely not!* Thoughts pressed themselves into her mind. Was the woman really giving her a message from God, or did she carry that piece of paper around to give to anyone, much like a tract handed out by religious people on the street? But what if God had really lead this sweet woman to write the note just for her?

Intermission was over. The band was playing again. She caught sight of her show biz image in the mirror again. "Oh, come on, Ghost! You're reading more into this than it deserves. She probably carries that around in her pocket every night, hoping to give it to anybody she thinks needs '*saving*'," she flung the words aloud toward her image in the mirror.

She remembered that night, now four years in the past, when with a harsh stomp of the gold high heel, she had stepped on the lever that opened the waste can and dropped the note onto a bed of crumpled, wet paper towels. In her mind's eye, she could still see the lid of the waste can snap shut. Why after all these years and experiences did this seem so important tonight?

***

Her mind abruptly spun back to the present. The headlights of an approaching snow plow stopped her from tracing all the events which had lead up to her triumph of being named Jazz Singer of the year at the concert that night. The snow that slanted obliquely in the headlights had now stopped. Sandy shut off the windshield wipers that had been beating a cadence for the last eighty miles. She had almost reached Greenville and the crisp snowfall frosted the fields with a smooth marshmallow icing. She hadn't thought about the Salvation Army lady for months, but something inside her seemed to be warning she shouldn't have thrown the note away.

Chapter Nine

*T*he incident was soon forgotten again in a swirl of promotion pictures taken, rehearsing different acts and getting together "charts"--the arrangements done by Chuck Hitmar. Her first booking was a posh club in Pittsburgh. She developed a "patter" to introduce her own songs, sprinkled with occasional jokes, and leaned heavily on "kibitzing" with the crowd in an exchange between her listeners. Agents in most cities, whom Jimmy split commission with, began to tout her to supper clubs as "someone who can take a room full of people and make them have a good time."

These were still just weekend jobs in Cleveland, Erie, Pittsburgh or surrounding towns and suburbs, but she was always well-received and booked back for a return engagement. According to Jimmy and Patty, his wife, she was earning her "dues". Under their instructions, she joined AGVA, the Actors' Guild of Variety Artists union.

Occasionally, there was an afternoon appearance on a television program to promote the club in the city where she might be appearing. Mike Douglas had an afternoon talk and music show in the afternoons on KYW TV in Cleveland and she appeared on that program. The name "Ghost" always seemed to be something the producers wanted to work around and use. The set on *The Mike Douglas Show* was similar to that of the *Tonight Show* and many others, with the host sitting at a desk. Lounge chairs for guests were to the left; the studio band was situated to the right. The director had a unique idea: to have Sandy singing her first song, "Mack the Knife" as the show title and credits ran at the inception of the program. She would actually be on a separate camera from the cover shot, positioned at a standup microphone to the side, but superimposed over top of an empty standup microphone in the shot showing the band and host. The studio announcer was scripted to say, "...featuring our guest vocalist, Sandy Ghost!" just as the song ended. With those words, the director would kill the camera she was on...and poof...she would disappear.

This particular show was videotaped for replay, and she was actually back home in Greenville on the afternoon it aired. Before the days of cable, Cleveland reception was spotty in Greenville, but the neighbors across the street could receive it as they had a motor to direction their antenna.

"Hurry up, kids." Sandy had them by the hand as they crossed the street. "We're going to see Mommy on TV."

Lisa's chubby little legs churned to keep up. "Just like Miss Frances," she lisped.

"Miss Frances doesn't sing," Eric said in his usual tone of superiority he reserved for his little sister.

Sandy wished Bill could be with them. He'd never seen her on television either, but he had to work. His appointments were mostly scheduled outside the office. She wondered why he couldn't have taken fifteen minutes to run by when it meant so much to her.

She set those thoughts aside as the program began. They sat on the floor as close to the set as possible. The video reception was poor, but the audio was good. Her neighbor, Janie, seemed to be excited too. The disappearing act worked great, but it looked like she was evaporating from view in a heavy snow storm. Lisa and Eric clapped their hands. Lisa's large hazel eyes widened, "Where did you go, Mommy, up to heaven?"

She sang "I Enjoy Being a Girl" later in the program. It was done up-tempo, and seemed to come off well, although it had been a matter of concern to Mike Douglas, who actually had been an accomplished singer himself. He didn't like her "jazzy" version, wanted it "more feminine--like Julie Andrews would do it". It taped in the first take, however. Now, Sandy wondered if he hadn't been right, but her neighbor and the kids loved it.

As her career took wing, bookings for a week at a time in posh hotels and clubs across the country began to be presented to her by some of the top agencies. At first, she refused, not wanting to be away from her husband and the children for any length of time; however, the money was so tempting. It was hard to turn down several thousand dollars for one weekly appearance. "Once in awhile wouldn't hurt. We sure could use the extra money," Bill told her. They decided to put an ad in the newspaper for a part-time nanny.

From a profile view, Grace Brakeman had the thin face, sharp pointed chin, and long, pointed nose of the woman who stole Dorothy's dog, Toto, and later rode her bicycle to Oz in the vortex of the cyclone. When she laughed there was the hint of a cackle, but there the similarity between her and the wicked witch abruptly ended. She had the pronounced hump on her shoulders that was the signature of many women who experienced a lack of calcium. Gray hair was pulled back stiffly into a bun with wisps that constantly escaped, forming the suggestion of a salt and pepper halo. Her vivid blue eyes twinkled mischievously behind thick glasses. "Brakie" had had nine children of her own, and was a registered nurse who adored children. Her no-nonsense attitude, laced with love and high-spirited fun were a perfect blend.

Satisfied the children would be well cared for, Sandy began to free-lance. One of the first bookings was at the Clifton Hotel in Niagara Falls, Ontario,

Canada. For the following several years, she was booked into Niagara Falls for the entire month of June to open their honeymoon season.

The Marty Conn Agency booked her in the mid-west, Sid Friedman in Pittsburgh took care of weekend club dates in the Erie, Pittsburgh, Cleveland area when she was in off the road. Alert Theatrical in Buffalo booked her into Canada, and the William Morrison Agency handled bookings out west.

She always sent newspaper clippings, or reviews to her mother in California, still hoping for a word of encouragement. The only response, or even acknowledgment to her singing career came in the form of a rather terse letter advising Sandy that Lawrence Welk was looking for a new "Champagne Lady". Taking this as a slender sign of approval, she shot back a letter explaining that her voice and style of material wouldn't fit their criteria, but that she appreciated the lead. Gaye's answer to her daughter was one heavy with reproof, suggesting that perhaps she should change her style to measure up to higher standards.

She shared the letter with her friend Barb, lamenting, "Can't I ever win her approval in anything?"

"No, you're looking at it wrong," Barb told her. "Can't she ever stop trying to manipulate you into what *she* wants?"

"I guess you're right. The way I'm working using different agencies is perfect. If I want to go for a week, I can. And then if I want to stay home with Bill and the kids for three weeks straight I just tell any agencies that call that 'I'm booked', even though I may just be playing with the kids for three weeks. Lately though I've been feeling so very tired—nauseous."

The tiredness and nausea continued for two weeks. All she wanted to do was sleep. Brakie talked her into a professional appointment with Dr. Ghost, who put her through a battery of tests. Allen Ghost called her two days later. "Well, Sandy, guess what?" and before she had a chance to answer he resumed, "You're pregnant."

There was a long silence as Sandy tried to deal with the news. "That's terrific! Unexpected... unplanned, but terrific!"

"Now look, you know I'm trying to retire. Frankly, I'd appreciate it if you found yourself a good OBGYN man. I've enjoyed delivering grandbabies, but you're on your own this time. Okay?" He chuckled.

"Okay," she agreed, wondering how to break the news to Bill, wondering if now she would have to retire from singing. It was a relief when he actually seemed elated with the idea, and thought it humorous when Sandy found out her female gynecologist was also pregnant on the foam birth control product she had recommended to all her patients.

Her career continued until it was time to wear maternity clothes, and in the last three months of pregnancy she lamented to Barb, "I'm as big as a rhinoceroses. People watch me lumber across the room at a party and heave a corporate sigh of relief when I sit down!" It was about that time that Sid Friedman called, asking Sandy to sing in a concert in Pittsburgh.

"You know I've taken maternity leave, and I'm the size of the William Penn Hotel."

"Doesn't matter, sweetheart. It's a concert."

"But Sid, I'm a mess and I can't even breathe right."

"Hey, do it for old Sid, okay? Do it as a favor for me. We've got to have you sing this number to fill out the production."

"Fill it out is right! What song is it that's so important?"

"You Made Me Love You."

A ludicrous picture took shape in her mind. "Get real! Can't you just see me up there singing, 'You made me love you, I didn't want to do it' and I'm eight months *pregnant*?"

There was dead silence on the other end of the line...then snickers that turned into snorts of laughter. "I...ah...uh..(another fit of snorts) never thought of it like that. Guess you're right. It wouldn't be in (snort, snort) good taste."

Two weeks before her due date, Sandy's doctor decided an X-ray might be in order, but didn't tell her why. She had weighed 95 pounds before pregnancy and now weighed in at 140. Rolling around the X-ray table like a beached whale, she accepted help from the technicians in order to change positions.

The doctor bustled into the room after the films were developed. "Well, look here," he told her, holding the plate to the light overhead. "Here's the head and the backbone...and here's the *other* head and the *other* backbone." He beamed at her proudly.

"What?" The meaning of the cryptic message on the doctor's order she had handed to the X-ray technician slowly began to dawn on her. "Number of passengers" it had said.

"Get outta' here, Ted," she told her doctor. "That's somebody else's X-ray!"

"Not a chance. You're going to have twins. You're carrying them one in front of the other. That's why I've only been hearing one heart beat."

The room swirled around her. *Two weeks to get ready for two babies not one!* How would they be able to cope? And then the warmth of the realization struck--it was like a miracle. "Two peas in a pod," she murmured while caressing her stomach..."two beautiful babies." Would they be boys or girls, or one of each? In 1963, Ultrasound had not yet been developed, or was not being used yet to determine sex of a fetus.

And while she pondered the miracle of two babies at the time, she had no way of knowing that one of them would be used as a messenger from God.

Chapter Ten

*B*ill appeared to be button-popping proud at the idea of fathering twins; however, he still maintained a cool distance from his wife, and balked at having any part in the preparation for the babies' arrival. Dr. Ghost informed them both that "twins ran in the family" to which Sandy laughingly replied, "Nobody ever told me that when I married Bill. Gee, thanks a bunch for the warning, Dad!"

Brakie's daughter loaned them another bassinet. They loaded up on more baby clothes and diapers. Sandy finally gave up on trying to get Bill involved in the excitement of getting things ready; however, Eric and Lisa more than made up for his lack of interest. They couldn't wait for the babies to get there and Lisa put in an order for one boy and one girl so that she could "have" the girl and her brother could "have" the boy.

One morning at breakfast Sandy tried to pin Bill down on his favorite names. He was spending more time away in the evenings and breakfast seemed to be the only time to talk with him. "Well, let's see, we could call them Benedict and Arnold," he smiled around a coffee cup, "or Cain and Abel."

"Get serious, I'm overdue already," she sank into a kitchen chair and supported her stomach with both hands. "We had decided 'Kurt' if it's a boy. What about 'Kent' if it's two boys, they kinda go together?"

"Sounds good to me." He scooted the kitchen chair back and got ready to leave.

"Couldn't you please just take a little more interest, Bill?"

"Don't start!" He held up one hand as if to ward off any more statements. "I'm outta' here. Late now."

"But what if it's two girls, or a boy and a girl?"

"We'll cross that bridge when we come to it." He waved goodbye to Eric and Lisa.

"You mean wait until they're *born*?" But he was out the side door and into the driveway.

A wave of sadness washed over her. It seemed that her pregnancy had only amplified their problems. At least when she had been singing, they had gotten along better. Would she ever be able to go back to her career now?

She could scarcely walk and the doctor ordered her to go to bed for the rest of the term. "And if you don't deliver by Easter, I'm going to induce them. Don't like to do it with twins... but we don't have a choice here."

Sandy struggled to her feet in preparation to leave his office. "They do seem to want to stay where they are until they come out with college degrees in their hands."

"We'll induce them the 15th--the day after Easter--three days from today. Don't eat anything from midnight on."

Because even maternity clothes wouldn't fit, on Easter Sunday she put on a huge man's shirt and pants. She had Eric find her Easter hat from the year before, crunched it onto her head and asked Bill to take a cheesecake pose of her sitting on a garbage can in that get up. While it was a joke, sadly it was a statement of how she felt about her appearance.

The following morning, after she was settled in the hospital bed with the IV drips running, contractions began. The room was near a stairway to the cafeteria and the aroma of bacon and coffee beckoned. She didn't know which was worse--the hunger pains or the contractions.

"Can't I just have one tiny cup of coffee?" she begged the doctor when he came in to check the IV.

"Absolutely not." Turning to Bill who was sitting in a chair beside the bed reading a *MAD MAGAZINE*, "I want you to time her contractions. Write them down so you don't lose track, and when they get to two minutes--which should be fairly soon--ring for the nurse. Okay?" He handed Bill a pen. The doctor had turned up the rapidity of the drips, and the pains were getting harder--closer together.

After about thirty minutes, Bill tossed the pen, watch and magazine onto the bed. "Here! Keep your own score. I'm going downstairs to get some breakfast," he said.

Her eyes plaintively followed him out of the room. She picked up the pen as a crushing pain hit. They had wheeled her to delivery by the time he returned.

She had insisted on natural childbirth as Eric and Lisa had both been delivered that way. "Baby A" was born at 1:10 PM--a big boy at 7 pounds 4 ounces. And everything stopped--no pains, no contractions...nothing. She watched the second hand going around on the large black and white clock on the wall...nothing. Ten minutes passed.

"The second one's breach," the doctor said. "We'll have to turn this baby."

She could hear her first twin squalling in the background. Suddenly a black mask came down over her mouth and nose. She had taken one breath before she ripped it off and the room seemed to slip away. When she came to, her doctor announced proudly, "You have two big fraternal twin boys, Sandy. Seven pounds, four ounces and six pounds four and one-half ounces. I think that's a record so far for Greenville Hospital as the largest twins." Both babies

78

were crying as they laid them on her stomach. Later, after Bill had viewed them he slipped back into her room.

"Good job, kid!" he told her. They decided Baby A (as the hospital had penned on the card above his bassinet) would be named "Kurt"; Baby B's name would be "Kent".

The following day, her doctor's wife brought in a double orchid that had bloomed in her greenhouse. "This seldom happens, Sandy, just a coincidence, I guess," she told her. "I thought it appropriate to bring it to you in celebration of the twins."

The first nurse to attend her after the delivery pulled the sheet back and gasped, "Are you the mother of those great big twins?"

Amazingly, she was back to ninety-five pounds. "It was all water and babies, Barb!" she told her best friend that evening during visiting hours.

Once home it was a scramble to take care of the babies. Kurt was on a four hour schedule for feeding; Kent's schedule was every three hours. Bill insisted that the bassinets be placed in the dining room instead of in their bedroom upstairs so that his sleep wouldn't be disturbed. Sandy would have to sleep on the couch in the living room in order to get up with them. Tired from the delivery itself, many nights she found herself changing and feeding the same baby twice.

"Could you please just take them for one night so I could get just one whole night's rest?" she asked.

"I have to get up for work... can't do it." The reply was terse, closing the door to any further discussion.

"But, could I get Brakie to help then? Bill, I've got to get one full night's sleep."

"Brakie is paid by you, when you're working." The words were weighted with sarcasm. "And *are* you working, Sandy?"

She slowly shook her head 'no'. She had received a congratulatory card from her first agent, Jimmy Williams and his wife, Patty, in that morning's mail. Tucked in with the card was an embossed bookmarker with a poem called, "Don't Quit". Was it a sign of some kind? Or was it just their way of urging her to go back to work? It was certainly out of the question now. She couldn't leave the babies.

As the twins grew, they began to develop different personalities: Kent was the more passive of the two, quietly staring wide-eyed at the new world around him; Kurt made his needs known quickly and was the first to smile in recognition of his mother. After the first two months, Sandy was besieged by agents with bookings, and took limited engagements. Brakie was in seventh

79

heaven acting as nursemaid. She adored the twins and Eric and Lisa were excited to have her back in the "family".

Sandy's parents and Chelie made a trip back east from California. The novelty of twin grandsons propelled Gaye into a visit. It had been eight years since they had seen each other. Chelie had grown into a beautiful and vivacious, blonde teenager. She and Sandy had seen pictures of each other, talked on the telephone, but the strong, clinging bond of love between the two sisters had naturally tarnished with time and distance.

"I have a huge hole in my heart feeling cheated for all the time we missed together. I didn't get to watch you grow up," Sandy said as she hugged her sister. "You've become so beautiful...and I missed watching it happen."

Chelie wanted to see all her sister's reviews and promo pictures, pumped her on the different kinds of shows she'd done. Gaye, pragmatic as usual, told them, "Put away all that stuff and let's get dinner on the table. Your father's starved."

But having the twins had affected the shattering of a huge barrier between mother and daughter. Sandy had finally done something right in her mother's eyes.

When they left to return to California, tears basted Sandy's "goodbyes" particularly with her sister.

Shortly after they left, Sandy's Cleveland, Ohio agent booked her into Annarino's Supper Club in Dayton. She opened her act on New Year's Eve, worked that week's contract and then was held over for another week. It seemed to be important to her not to be away from her family for more than two weeks. The balance of January was spent at home and then she took another booking in Akron, Ohio at a posh supper club the second week of February. But it was different now that she had babies at home. She couldn't wait to get back to Greenville, however, that night snowy roads dictated cautious driving.

The full-bodied strains of Aker Bilk's deep clarinet filtered into the car from the radio. "Stranger on the Shore" seemed to resonate like some inner tuning fork with Sandy, wrapping her in a strange cloak of melancholy. She began to sense she had become a stranger to herself--three people wrapped into one. There was the entertainer whose career was racing at full throttle; there was the mother, who never seemed to be able to schedule enough time with her children; and then there was the wife. Something was definitely wrong with this role. No matter how hard she tried she couldn't please Bill. And as she pondered these things she realized that they had indeed become strangers standing far apart on a shore of indifference.

The car radio kept her awake on the snowy nighttime journey from Akron,

Ohio. Three shows a night for a week at the chic Lemon Tree nightclub had been so successful that the club owner had tried to hold her over for another week. "I'm booked solid for the next month", she had told him while thinking, *booked solid to play with my babies.* She couldn't wait to get home, cuddle Lisa, help Eric with homework and admire the twins' newest tricks.

Kent seemed to love music and would sit in his playpen snapping his fingers in perfect time to a jazz tune. Kurt tried to do everything first including talk; however, Kent reserved his first word for an unusual speech preference—not "Mama" but the word "tickle" just seemed to explode from him one day. He loved to be tickled at bath time. Just remembering this helped to dispel the waves of unhappiness that had overtaken her as she took her suitcase out of the car and greeted Brakie.

"Eric fixed the radio," Grace Brakeman's eyes flashed as she made this announcement. "They're all sound asleep, but Eric worked all day at getting the radio working."

"You've got to be kidding...the thing hasn't worked for months and it's almost as old as I am." Sandy walked over to the large black console and turned the knob. Music immediately began to play. She collapsed into a chair. "Brakie, my parents had that old radio and recording unit when I was a kid. They recorded Roosevelt's declaration of war on steel records on that! And Eric fixed it?"

"He's a determined nine year old." She smiled proudly.

"I've missed the kids terribly, Brakie. I never worry about them when you're caring for them. Can't tell you how deeply I appreciate you." She hugged her.

The divide between Bill and Sandy had seemed to deepen into a chasm. There was no affection, little communication and Sandy didn't know how to fix it. However, it was still a shock when one crisp March day, Bill announced he had taken a job in Louisville, Kentucky. The news was stunning—it was alarming.

"You can't just leave your family, Bill. You can't just walk off and leave us."

"You'll be fine. You have your singing jobs." He continued to weed out ties he wasn't going to take. "If it works out the family can come down later. Don't worry." He examined a tweed jacket with leather patch elbows and folded it neatly.

"How will you get down there?"

"Well, how do you think? I'm going to drive." Sarcasm seasoned the words.

"You're taking the car?"

"Yep."

"But, my grandmother made the down payment on that car for us. How will I get groceries.... milk? How will I work?"

He threw a green plaid tie into the box of clothes to go to the Salvation Army. "I've made all the payments on the car and I'm taking it. Guess you'll have to rent one when you work, kiddo."

"But the twins first birthday will be next month and you won't even be here," She tried to think of any anchor to hold him, but he had already accepted the job as traffic manager with a large manufacturing firm and she was powerless to dissuade him from going.

"I'll come back some weekends," he told Eric and Lisa. But he never did and the next time she saw him was when she went through Louisville on a Greyhound bus to Birmingham, Alabama.

Lack of a car was a cumbersome hindrance in taking care of four children. Dr. Ghost and a neighbor took turns making treks to the local dairy for milk. Jackson's Grocery still delivered daily if Sandy telephoned them with a list by 11:00 AM; however, doctor's appointments, PTA meetings or school events were always an imposition on someone else. Club dates in Erie, Pittsburgh or Cleveland required a car rental and that, plus Brakie's pay, cut into what Sandy brought home. She found herself making all the mortgage payments and household expenses. Bill didn't seem to feel any of this was his responsibility and therefore sent no money back to Pennsylvania for the family. Feeling like a bit of a traitor, Sandy showed Bill's father how this had put them in a financial dilemma. Several times his loans pulled them out of a problem. And while he and Mom Ghost tried to help and were aware of what had happened to the marriage, Sandy felt that for the most part they were in denial.

As months dragged by Sandy's attitude toward the marriage became even more brittle. Now, more than ever, she didn't want to spend prolonged periods of time away from home; however, finances were pressing her to take more jobs. She signed a contract with the Morrison Agency to do a tour of six weeks with the Starlight Revue. The show was to be put together in Birmingham, Alabama, then perform at Army and Air Force bases out West, with pickup dates in between. There was a dancer, Ginny Loring, booked out of Boston, and the comic was booked out of Chicago. They would be accompanied by a four piece band and travel in a rental nine passenger station wagon pulling a trailer with the instruments, luggage and costumes. After rehearsals in Birmingham, the show would open in Tulsa, Oklahoma at The Petroleum Club.

Sandy had never ridden a Greyhound bus before, but now took one from Youngstown, Ohio to Birmingham. She arranged to have two days with Bill in Louisville en route. One hundred proof Kentucky bourbon did little to help stave off the awkwardness of this meeting and nothing was settled between them. Later, looking out the window of the bus as it raced toward

Alabama, Sandy's thoughts scrolled back over the last two days. It seemed all she could remember in the miasma of the bourbon was Bill's dreary one bedroom apartment on the second floor of an old Louisville red brick row house. The dingy furnished rooms smelled of a slight gas leak in the fireplace and musty overstuffed furniture. How could he possibly be happier here than with his family, she wondered? The miles whizzed past as her mind poked into old corners of remembrances, trying to figure out where their marriage had turned the corner that pitted them for disaster. She knew that alcohol had played a major role in Bill's attitude ever since they had become engaged. Perhaps they never should have gotten married... but then, what about Eric, Lisa and the twins? She couldn't imagine living without ever having been mother to them.

As they finally entered the outskirts of Birmingham, she realized she couldn't wait to check into the hotel, take a shower, and wash off the days on the crowded bus and heavy sadness of her two days with Bill in Louisville.

While the other performers and musicians were extremely professional, the tour was grueling. They worked Officer's and NCO clubs with pickup dates in between such as the prestigious Petroleum Club in Tulsa. Crossing into New Mexico, they stopped and walked over a black lava field and she picked up pieces of obsidian to send home to Lisa and Eric. She purchased a cowboy suit for Eric, and Indian dress for Lisa in Texas. Though she talked with Brakie and the children almost every day, she found herself missing them terribly and couldn't wait for the tour to end. The itinerary of the tour took them through Arizona, Nevada, Utah, Wyoming and then up into Rapid City, South Dakota. She had given her notice to the agency that she planned on fulfilling her six week contract in Rapid City and wanted to go home from there. The agency offered to fly her home for Easter and then fly her back to rejoin the tour and do North Dakota, Washington, Oregon and California.

"I'm bleeding inside because I need my children", she told them. "There's not enough gold in Fort Knox to lure me back, but thanks for the compliment."

While she couldn't wait to get home, little did she know the frightening situation that awaited her back in Greenville.

Chapter Eleven

*I*t was late the following night when she arrived home. The children were sleeping. After peeking in at them, planting kisses on pudgy cheeks, she and Brakie settled in the living room with cups of coffee.

"I took it upon myself to protect you from something, Sandy". Brakie frowned slightly and tucked up a whisp of gray hair.

"Protect me? From what?"

"Well, it just happened two days ago...and I knew you were on your way back so it didn't make any sense to alarm you, dear."

"Brakie, you're scaring me to death! What is it? "

"It's just that... well, the sheriff was here and tacked a sheriff's sale sign on the front porch."

"What? That can't possibly be. Brakie, I've paid all the mortgage payments to the bank. Paid them on time. Always! I was in such a hurry to get in the house I didn't even see it." She got up, opened the front door and turned on the porch light. The sign was tacked to the left of the front window. A sudden dark fear rose up constricting her breath.

"I've got to call the bank first thing in the morning. Can you stay one more night, Brakie? I may have to go down to the bank in the morning. How can this be happening?"

"You know I'm here for you, dear. You sure don't need this on top of everything else."

It was almost impossible to sleep that night, even though Sandy was in her own bed for the first time in six weeks. The twins' cribs were in the same room and their soft breathing finally lulled her to sleep. She couldn't wait to hold them in the morning.

She was awakened by Eric and Lisa pouncing on the bed, which, of course, wakened the twins. Soon all five of them wrestled on the double bed, hugging each other as Sandy produced the gifts from out west. Eric beat on the Indian Tom Tom until Sandy begged him to stop, realizing she needed at least one cup of coffee to cope with the noise.

After breakfast she called Nelson Morten (name changed), the President of the bank where their mortgage was held. Nelson was her father-in-law's best friend and therefore she felt she was on a first name basis with him.

"Nelson, I've just come back from a six week tour out west and there's a sheriff's sale sign on my house. I've made all my mortgage payments on time... what's with this action?" She was indignant but tried to suppress her anger.

"Now... now... don't get upset, Sandy. You may not know this, but your mortgage is not a regular mortgage note. It's a Demand Note and the bank has made the decision to call the note."

"But why, Nelson? I've never missed a payment. They've always been made on time."

"Yes, but we've decided that you're not really a good financial risk."

"What in the world do you mean? I'm gainfully employed. I'm making all the payments on time. What do you mean I'm not a 'good financial risk'?"

"Well, dear..." , Nelson's tone became rather conspiratorial like he was taking her into his confidence, "why don't you just be a good little girl, pack up your children and go down to Kentucky to join your husband?"

"Join my husband? Join my husband? What if he doesn't *want* us down there? Is the small town gossip fomenting this, Nelson? Is my father-in-law instigating this with you?"

"No... no... now don't get upset. Maybe we can work out something," he told her.

"I'm getting an attorney!" she told him and hung up. She called Michael Armstrong, a local attorney, and explained the circumstances. He said he'd contact the bank as they had not properly "called" the note and therefore the sheriff sale was improper. He explained they had the right to call the loan, make demand, but had to notice her first and give her proper allowance time by law to pay the note in full. They had totally bypassed that legal stipulation. This last piece of information seemed to confirm that it wasn't a Board decision, but a personal ploy to push her out of town to squelch any small town gossip. But, he explained that by putting them on notice, it would only accomplish buying her more time. If they continued with the action she would still have to come up with the money or lose the house.

"Pay the note in full", Sandy echoed the words later to Brakie. "How in heaven's name can I possibly pay off the whole house all by myself? Brakie, I'm being forced out of town because of gossip. If I take the children and move to Louisville it will look like we've reconciled and the wagging tongues will stop."

"What can you do?" Brakie picked up Kent and put him in his playpen. He giggled and immediately began snapping his fingers in perfect time to music that was playing on the radio.

"Gonna' be a musician, for sure, aren't you?" Sandy ruffled his blond hair. "He absolutely loves music, doesn't he?"

Brakie nodded and placed Kurt in his own playpen. Occasionally the twins needed to be fenced into a corral.

"There is no way I can raise thousands of dollars." Hot tears burned her eyes. "I'm going to lose my home, aren't I?"

Brakie reached out motherly arms and enfolded her.

Four days later, in a scheduled meeting with Nelson Morten, he granted an extension in taking possession of the house. If Sandy would agree to putting the house up for sale, she and the children could continue to live in it until it sold; however, she would need to continue making the payments. Once the house sold, this would satisfy the Demand Note and remove the lien. Nelson lowered his voice as he stipulated the last condition, "You understand that we are extending this generous offer to you with the proviso that you will not just rent another home in Greenville. You will take your children and move to Louisville."

It was outright blackmail, but what could she do? She agreed to the terms so they wouldn't put her and the children out on the street. The bank carried a big stick and there was no fight left in her after a telephone conversation with Bill. He had denied having anything to do with the pressure the bank was putting on her. She believed him because he really didn't sound like he particularly wanted them in Louisville.

The Morrison Agency who had booked her on the six week tour called and wanted her to do a six week USO show in Europe the following month and while that would help financially with paying off the demand note, it wouldn't be enough. When she broached the subject with Bill his reaction was, "Just try to do it and I'll slap you with a custody suit for the children!"

"If that's the way you feel, that's an unthinkable solution then," she told him. "I won't go, but what's your answer to this?"

"I can't pay it. Don't look to me to buy you a house!" The sarcastic tone infused every word.

"Don't you understand your parents are pushing for us to be a family again, Bill? That's what's really going on here."

Silence on the other end of the line.

"Bill, what do you want? What do you want me to do?"

More silence.

He sounded weary...downtrodden himself, like Sandy felt. "I guess I could find a house to rent down here," he finally said. "There's time yet. Are you going to contact a realtor and list the house?"

"I have to or get thrown out on the street by Nelson Morten's so-called 'generous offer'."

"Well, I guess we'll cross this bridge when we come to it," Bill told her. The following day, the sheriff's sale sign came down and a realtor's for sale sign replaced it.

Sandy accepted weekend club dates in Pittsburgh, Erie and Cleveland. She took agency calls, but told them she was booked on any dates they wanted at a distance. Realtors were now bringing strangers through the house and she wanted to be there herself. There were several house offers over the months, but none that matched the asking price so she felt validated in turning them down. And then, in the month of July, an offer was presented for the full price. There was no way to avoid it; she had to accept. There was a closing scheduled for forty-five days. She tried to buy a little more time, but the bank seemed to hover over her shoulder through the process with the realtor and said she'd just have to "get on with it".

Bill received this news by telephone with the warmth of a large polar iceberg. "So now what? You want me to find a house down here, is that the game plan?"

"I feel like we're pawns on the bank's chessboard, Bill. Nobody here seems to care what we want. Do you want us down there? Be truthful."

A long silence and then, "Well... what will happen if you don't come down here?"

"The bank's made it clear that I have to go to Louisville, Bill. I can't stay in Greenville... go rent another house here. I gave my word when they allowed us to remain in the house until it sold. I can't go back on my word."

More silence.

"Hello! Say something, Bill."

"I'm thinking. I guess I'll try to find a house for rent," his tone was that of a man resigned to being told he had a terminal disease.

"You'll have to fly up here and help me with the twins on the plane, Bill."

"Whatever."

The realtor expressed the contract for you to sign tomorrow. You'll have to over night it back to her."

"Whatever," he repeated, didn't say goodbye and hung up the telephone.

Sandy felt sorry for him in a way. He was being pushed into a corner, but so was she.

Brakie helped her pack up everything and contact movers and after two weeks Bill called to say he had rented a house on Cornell Place in St. Matthews, a suburb of Louisville. He said it was an older home with four bedrooms and two baths. That sounded positive and Sandy was encouraged, but leaving Brakie was the hardest part of all for Sandy and the children. She had been substitute mother to all of them. She was best friend, advisor, mother image—Sandy's sounding board and defender. How could she leave her behind? They would pack for awhile and then one or the other would start to tear up and soon find themselves weeping in each others' arms.

Moving day finally came and last goodbyes were said. As Sandy watched

Brakie's car drive away, her loss plunged to a new depth. Losing her best friend Barb too would create a deep scar. The loss of Brakie's support and love cut an additional heart laceration. She had never felt so alone. It seemed as though everyone she loved was always being ripped away from her. Her deep sadness at that juncture reflected more than just dark fleeting thoughts--they were actually a portentous warning of events to come.

Chapter Twelve

*E*ric and Lisa had never flown before and excitement bounced back and forth between them like arcing electricity. Eric sat at a window seat with Bill who held Kent on his lap. Lisa had the window seat on the other side of the aisle with Sandy holding Kurt.

Lisa kept leaning forward looking under her seat. Finally Sandy asked, "Sweetheart, what are you doing?"

"Lookin' for my parachute," her lisp was pronounced. "Where is it, Mommy?"

"You don't have a parachute on a commercial plane, honey."

The hazel eyes squinted slightly, "But... but... what if something happens? I want my parachute!" she wailed.

Kurt, sensing something was wrong with his sister, started to cry in a wailing duet.

"Lisa, it's okay, honey. Nothing's going to happen." But the more Lisa insisted, the more Sandy began to feel that maybe her seven year old daughter was absolutely right. They *all* needed parachutes. Bill laughed and shook his head. Once they were airborne the twins went to sleep and Eric and Lisa were fascinated watching the fleecy clouds.

Sandy grew reflective as the rays of the sun blazed through the window. Hopefully this was a sign that their new life in Louisville would be happy. But none of the root problems had been addressed. How could the healing come when the infection had never been treated? They had both been manipulated into whitewashing the problem. But maybe a fresh start in a different city would give them a new perspective. She had worked the Bluegrass Room at the Brown Hotel when she'd been booked in there for a week before Bill had ever moved there. She'd loved Kentucky at the time. Perhaps this place would be the answer to their marriage, she thought.

The landing at Standiford Field in Louisville was rough. They kangarooed down the runway and when the engines were reversed the plane seemed to stand on it's nose. Lisa gleefully clapped her hands. Bill leaned across the aisle and told Sandy, "I think our pilot let the stewardess land the plane." As he stood up to deplane, moving Kent to one hip, he exposed a huge apron of a yellow stain on his trousers. Kent's diapers had leaked all over him.

The house on Cornell Place was white stucco with green trim. Had it been a horse, it would have been referred to as "long in the tooth" as its vintage was obvious. Eric and Lisa entertained themselves by running up the front staircase, across the landing and down the backstairs. The fourth bedroom was on the first floor and because Eric was the oldest he got that bedroom. The downstairs bath was also off the back hall. The other three bedrooms and bath were upstairs.

A quick inspection of the basement sent Sandy and kids running back upstairs. The furnace looked like a massive octopus with fat arms stretching in all directions. But that was mild compared to the bubbling, hissing, fire-shooting thing that threatened from the north corner. It was black cast iron, the burner on the bottom had a circle of exposed flames, and it looked like something Benjamin Franklin had whacked together in his own basement. Sandy vowed to give that thing a wide berth and keep the children far away.

As they were inspecting the house, the moving van arrived just as they had scheduled. It was comforting to see their familiar furniture coming into this strange house.

Once settled, Bill and Sandy had to address their lackluster relationship. Now there were no outside distractions to polish the tarnished marriage. After the children were in bed they had to face each other. There was now no excuse for Bill to be gone in the evenings as he'd done in the insurance business. As traffic manager for a large corporation his job was relegated to nine to five.

Sandy was convinced that communication between them was the key; therefore, since they couldn't seem to talk without getting into an argument, she suggested they find a marriage counselor. They looked in the yellow pages and found a Unitarian minister who advertised marriage counseling. After three months of appointments with no results, they stopped going. Several months later the Louisville Courier Journal carried an article that the minister had committed suicide. "We probably sent him over the edge!" Sandy dryly observed.

Bill again seemed to find solace in a case of beer and this always ramped up a biting sarcasm that would then mutate into a verbally combative attitude. Lack of finances added to the rather hopeless and oppressive atmosphere.

Sandy offered to go back to work singing, not on the road again, but only doing club dates around Louisville and surrounding towns. There was a theatrical agency in Louisville and they booked her to promote a movie at Fort Campbell in Hopkinsville, Kentucky. There were several weekend dates in Cincinnati, but other than the Bluegrass Room at the Brown Hotel in Louisville, there were no supper clubs that featured entertainment. And then an opportunity presented itself that seemed to solve their financial dilemma.

There was a country singer by the name of Tommy Downs who had his own band. Tommy had signed a contract for a TV show with a thirteen week option on WLKY-TV. While the country entertainer had a tremendous following between Louisville and Nashville, he had never before been on television. Autorama, a car dealership, was to be the show's sponsor. The theatrical agency who had been booking Sandy recommended her for the purpose of giving Tommy "camera presence". They knew she had appeared on television in various cities around the country as most local TV stations would cameo traveling entertainment on local afternoon shows for promotion purposes.

After an initial meeting with Tommy and the sponsor, Sandy was hired to produce the show and ended up writing the script. She had never worked in the country field before, but adapted quickly to a different genre. Video taping was a new technique and if an error took place within the first twenty minutes the tape could be re-rolled; however, there were no retakes after twenty-one minutes. The show was taped on Thursday night for replay on Saturday and the station receptionist grumbled to Sandy about televising by video tape. It was so new the public didn't understand.

"You don't understand, Sandy," Sue, the station receptionist complained, "I keep getting calls all through the program with fans of Tommy wanting to talk to him. Last Saturday one guy called and rudely said, 'I wanna' talk to Tommy Downs'. I explained that Tommy wasn't in the studio."

"Doncha' give me that, little lady. I'm lookin' at him right now on the tube. Don't you tell me he's not there!"

Several weeks into their 13 week TV contract, Eric came down with the flu, then Lisa and Kurt. Bill and Sandy were the next victims, but Kent was the last of the family to succumb. Whereas it had attacked the rest of the family with three days worth of fever, aches and pains, congestion and coughing, Kent experienced all the same symptoms, but became extremely lethargic. He was only two and one-half and it became readily evident that he was not able to rally from the influenza. Sandy had planned to go to the studio to work on the Tommy Downs script that day, but called the station to tell the receptionist that she wouldn't be in.

"I need to take one of my twins to the doctor, Sue. He's pale and limp from this flu we've all had. In fact, I almost don't want to take him out of the house. It's scary he's so lethargic."

"Our doctor, Keith Hammond, makes house calls, Sandy. Why don't you call him?"

"Great idea... thanks so much. I'll do it."

After explaining to Dr. Hammond's nurse that her young son had chest congestion, Sandy was told that they would need to do a chest X-ray and therefore she would have to bring him into the office.

Dr. Hammond was so thorough that Sandy felt she'd made the right decision to bring Kent there. After a chest X-ray the doctor also decided to draw blood and take a look at his blood counts. With all the routine doctor's visits the twins had gotten in the past, this had never been done before. Kent slept on her lap as they waited for the results. Dr. Hammond read his own X-ray films and his office had their own lab so he was able to quickly review the blood counts.

He finally called them back into his office. A frown creased his forehead. "The lungs are still clear, no pneumonia, but I don't like what I'm seeing with the blood counts. His white count is sky high. Now that could indicate a virulent bacteria infection, but I don't want to take a chance with this. I want you to see a hematologist. If you'll permit me, I'd like to make an appointment for him myself."

Fear threatened to smother Sandy. "Is it that critical?"

"Possibly. May I make the call?"

"Of course, please do, doctor." She sat frozen while Dr. Hammond spoke to a doctor on the other end of the line. Apparently the symptoms were crucial enough that they were to leave this office and go downtown to the specialist's office immediately. "May I call my husband and have him meet us down there?"

Dr. Hammond smiled for the first time as he extended the phone across his desk. She clutched Kent to her and rocked him slightly while explaining to Bill why he needed to meet them at the hematologist's office.

The specialist's office was downtown and Kent slept on the backseat, whimpering slightly, as Sandy raced to get him there. A dark fear hovered over her and the foreboding only increased when the hematologist suggested he be hospitalized immediately for tests. Sandy's eyes met Bill's over top of Kent's blond curls. She looked down to find her fingernails were digging into her wrist in order to keep from crying.

The doctor hurried through the door of the hospital room. Raking fingers through his dark hair, he announced in a flat, coldly impersonal voice, "I'm sorry. You have a very sick son. The bone marrow tests reveal that he has acute lymphocytic leukemia."

Leukemia! Ever since Dr. Hammond had suggested the hospital for tests the word had tried to creep into Sandy's mind, but she'd vigorously resisted it. Now the doctor's words were like a cold slap in the face. She began rocking Kent back and forth in her arms, hot tears cascading down on his head, hearing nothing the doctor was saying about his prognosis as she chanted, "No! God... No!"

Across the room, the color drained from Bill's face. Looking dazed and, obviously stunned, he seemed to be holding himself in check as he listened to the clinical, detached voice droning on about medication and what they were to expect.

"If we're lucky Kent could survive for a year. That's all I can give him at best," the voice was impersonal, but Sandy noticed that the hematologist tightly gripped Kent's medical chart and his eyes kept darting toward the door as though he would rather be anywhere else but in that hospital room. He spoke directly to Bill alone, eyes purposely avoiding Kent and Sandy.

Sandy felt like she was strangling on her own breath—the room telescoped and refocused several times as though looking through a camera lens she couldn't seem to control or adjust. This couldn't be happening!

They drove home from the hospital that night in silence. She couldn't seem to erase the picture of Kent, his little face, so very pale, framed by the metal sides of the hospital crib. He slept with one arm extended from which an IV cord ran to the bottles suspended on a tall metal pole. As they drove down Lexington Road, for the first time, the silence began to scream at Sandy as she realized that even in the face of hearing their son had leukemia, they were grieving separately. Dark thoughts presented themselves accusing that as an ugly cancer of hate had eaten away at their marriage, now a cancer insidiously was attacking their son. Was there a parallel? She was grateful for the silence as frankly, she wanted to be alone with her sorrow.

She hurried to the hospital the following morning---overnight; every moment with Kent had suddenly become precious. Two blood transfusions the day before had worked their magic. There was color again in his face and he had rallied enough to want to be entertained.

"Let's go exploring," she told Kent, lifting him into a small wheelchair. A nurse transferred the IV bottles to a pole with a hook on the back of the chair.

"Let's 'splore", he tried to mimic her word, not fully understanding, but obviously eager to get out of the cage of his hospital bed. He wrinkled his nose and smiled up at his mother. As she pushed the chair up and down the hall of the pediatric floor, she glanced into one of the sterile looking rooms. A woman sat woodenly erect in a chair—the bed was unoccupied. At that precise moment, a voice came over the room's intercom announcing in soothing tones, "Susan is doing just fine, Mrs. Raymond. The tonsillectomy is finished and she is in the recovery room."

Tonsillectomy, Sandy thought bitterly. *And she sits there on the edge of her chair! Big deal!* She would have traded places with her in an instant.

The third day, as Kent napped, she sat by his bed bursting with a love for him even greater than she had had before. She found herself struggling with a swarm of guilty thoughts and harsh recrimination laced with pressing self-examination. She had never really been a mother to this child. She had worked ever since he was born, leaving him and the other three children in the care of a well-qualified housekeeper, but this wasn't his mother. Raw guilt pooled and grew inside her in a throbbing grief. One thought would not go away: *Could Kent's diagnosis be a form of punishment for the self-indulgence of her career?*

With stinging tears of remorse, she slipped out of the room and followed signs that she had seen in the hall marked "Chapel".

Tiptoeing into the quiet of the little sanctuary, she felt a sudden panic as she hadn't prayed or even been in a church in the last few years. In fact, she had begun to doubt that there was anyone "up there" at all, wrapping herself defiantly in existentialism theories that seemed to salve any twinges of conscience and supported her new way of life. *If there really is a God,* she had told herself, *I can't be that much of a hypocrite to go to church for He surely knows what's going on in this marriage.*

Now she knelt in a chapel, seeking an audience with.... Whom? Surprisingly, the words spilled out easily and simply, "God, if this is Your will I accept it, but please don't let him suffer." That was all. But she came away with an impression that maybe for the first time she had been heard. No clouds parted, no voice was heard, but somehow she strongly sensed inwardly that a loving, righteous God would not give Kent leukemia in order to punish her.

As she came back up onto the fourth floor and approached the nurses' station, the head nurse stopped her, "Mrs. Ghost, your doctor is on the phone and wants to talk with you." She extended the receiver across the counter.

Sandy took a deep breath and heard, "Mrs. Ghost, I've taken it upon myself to contact the National Institute of Health--the government research hospital—in Bethesda, Maryland. They've agreed to accept Kent as a patient if you can get him there quickly enough and if you and your husband are willing. Their methods are highly advanced and they are making great strides in the field of leukemia." For the first time his voice held a note of encouragement, "Although a cure has not been effected, this undoubtedly would be the place where the most help for Kent can be secured."

She thanked him profusely and promised to talk it over with Bill that night.

As she handed the telephone back to the nurse and started down the hall toward Kent's room, a question began to insistently push its way to the foreground of her mind... Could this possibly have been an immediate response to her prayer in the Chapel? *Ridiculous,* she decided, *it would have happened anyway.*

That evening Bill and Sandy decided to tell the doctor they wanted to admit

Kent to NIH—they had to do everything possible. The doctor had explained that if they paid for the first airline tickets to DC from that point forward NIH would pick up all the expenses. Sandy would be responsible for her own living expenses while in Bethesda. They made a hasty telephone call to a woman who had babysat for them before, to see if she could come in every morning to get Eric and Lisa off to school and take care of Kurt until Bill would get home from work. Mrs. Ross was pleasant, but Sandy longed for the loving care Brakie had provided.

Two days later, as an early morning snow blanketed Kentucky, Kent was discharged from St. Joseph's Hospital in Louisville and he and Sandy flew to Maryland. He was heavily sedated for the trip and fell asleep immediately. Leukemia had ruthlessly attacked his usual sunny disposition and he had now become cranky and irritable. She covered him with his red snowsuit jacket and hoped the trip would be swift. She was frightened to be solely responsible for him in this condition.

The plane banked sharply and headed east as she looked out the window. For the entire flight the sun shimmered blindingly directly ahead of the plane, as though beckoning it all the way—was this somehow an encouraging portent? Then, a disturbing thought rudely inserted itself—*Yeah... yeah... remember the sun was shining through the window of the plane on the way to Louisville. Look how that's worked out!*

The driver of a government van from NIH met them at the gate as they deplaned at Washington National Airport. He held a sign that asked, "Ghost?"

His sunny smile greeted them. "I was afraid maybe you'd be invisible," he said.

As she carried Kent through the revolving doors of the National Institutes of Health Clinical Center there was a sudden flood of relief. Everything possible would be done here. The receptionist told her they were expected and ushered them into the office of the Administrative Officer of the Day to fill out forms. The room was empty.

Her hands shook as she took off Kent's jacket and lifted him onto one of the two chairs that faced the desk. He rubbed his eyes. "We'll have a nice bed for you soon, sweetheart. Then you can go back to sleep," she promised.

"Well, good morning!" The AOD knelt down in front of Kent. "If I can fit into that snazzy red jacket of yours, can I have it?" He was at least six feet tall.

Kent nodded, "Yes".

"And is this pretty lady your wife, young man?"

This brought a smile and a giggle from Kent—the first in days. With a start Sandy realized that the somber atmosphere around her son since his diagnosis, plus seeing his mother constantly on the verge of tears, must have frightened him too. Even though he understood little of what was happening to him, he undoubtedly was absorbing the fear from the grownups around him. She vowed to take a lesson from this that Kent needed more humor and fun.

Once the paperwork was completed the AOD suggested it was time to "find Kent a bed."

They were escorted up to 2-East, the children's leukemia unit. A sign posted outside the closed, metallic blue door announced:

"Visiting Hours: 11:00A.M.-1:00P.M.

3:00 P.M.-8:00P.M."

The AOD held the door open as Kent and Sandy walked into their new world… Alice-in-Wonderland and Winnie-the-Pooh stared down at them from the walls as they walked toward the nurses' station past a playroom that, at first glance, contained every plaything prop from a Shirley Temple movie. *What an unusual hospital,* she thought.

The head nurse, Mrs. Zealy, kissed Kent on the cheek and took them to a room directly across the hall. It held six beds that were all empty at the time. She handed Sandy a hospital gown covered with smiling blue whales for her new patient. The walls of the room were painted with forest animals. Small groupings of toys and child-size tables and chairs were scattered about. The cheerful room could have been the nursery in some rich estate until Sandy spotted the ominous oxygen and suction valves affixed to the walls at the head of each bed.

"Dr. Gallo will be with you shortly," the head nurse told them.

The doctor swept into the room with all the grace of a bulldozer in a white coat. He smiled rather self-consciously and shook Sandy's hand while pushing heavy horned rimmed glasses back into position on his nose with the other hand. There was a vibrant intensity that seemed to radiate from this tall, handsome, young doctor.

He turned toward Kent who was sitting cross-legged on the bed. "Kent, I've been expecting you. My name is Doctor Gallo." He offered his hand which seemed rather business-like for a two and half year old patient. Sandy was to find later that Gallo had just come from the adult leukemia service. Kent was his first pediatric patient.

Kent shook hands solemnly. "Dr. Jello!" he said.

Gallo's hearty laughter and smile were like watching the sun rise up over a stormy landscape. Still chuckling over Kent's name for him, his slender hands probed his new patient's midsection. "We have a lot of work to do, Kent, to make you feel better." And then directed at Sandy, "We need to do our own bone marrow and do a work up. Why don't you step into the hall while we start an I.V, Mrs. Ghost?" A nurse approached with an arm board and some bottles.

From the hall Sandy could hear a minor wrestling match going on.

Apparently, the doctor was attaching Kent's arm to an arm board after the intravenous was started. The arm board was being affixed to the metal sides of the bed to keep it immobile. She could hear Kent belligerently protesting, "But I wanted that arm, Dr. Jello! I wanted that arm!" as though it had been taken away from him permanently.

Gallo beckoned her back into the room. A disturbed lock of dark hair on his forehead said more about the struggle she had overheard. Undoubtedly the doctor's adult patients had never challenged his medical expertise like this before. He heaved a sigh of relief. "Thank God he has large veins and an even larger spirit. We're going to need both. Still friends Kent?" He wiped a tear off Kent's cheek.

"Dr Jello," he said in answer and smiled, seemingly fascinated by this new doctor's name that he had corrupted. Somehow he appeared to sense that what was being done, though it hurt, was to help him. There was a deep and curious friendship cemented that day between this dedicated doctor and his small patient.

Sandy later learned that all the doctors at NIH were Navy doctors, who usually stayed on each service for a period of six months, then moved on to another service to broaden their field of expertise. Dr. Gallo shared that he had lost his sister to leukemia and that was the catalyst which had set him on the course of study to become a doctor.

Within two weeks Kent's sunny disposition had returned. His face had color again and the chemotherapy had worked a magic sweeping the bone marrow almost clean of the immature lymphocytic cells. At times it was hard to remember he had a terminal disease. The Clinical Center, Building 10 on the NIH campus had fourteen floors, six main elevators and six side elevators in each wing. The top floor was a huge recreational area, movie theater and chapel.

Any motion seemed to calm Kent, whether it was riding up and down in the elevator, or being pushed in a wheelchair. Consequently they spent a great deal of time being whisked by elevator to Occupational Therapy, recreation, or the cafeteria on B-2. Sandy finally began to relax and reflected on the difference between NIH and the atmosphere at St. Joseph's hospital back home. There they were an oddity. She remembered the episode with the mother whose child had had a tonsillectomy—a nice, normal illness. At NIH it was a huge comfort to be with other mothers whose children were all facing the same dreaded prognosis. They seemed to lean heavily on each other for support and Sandy had been warmly welcomed immediately into this tragic sorority.

The medical staff was efficiently superb, while managing to project a genuine caring, mingled with a light-hearted attitude that put everyone at ease. Between the other patients, their families and the staff, Sandy and Kent had begun to feel they'd gained a whole new family. But the day they met Mr. Botts, Sandy didn't know quite what to think about him.

The elevator stopped at 2 East and Sandy managed to get Kent and his wheelchair on board the crowded car. Other patients, visitors, doctors, technicians and nurses squeezed a bit closer together to accommodate them. "Fourteen please," Sandy told the kindly-looking, black elevator operator.

He closed the doors, engaged the switch and bent down toward Kent. "And how's my little man today?" he asked. Kent curiously touched the sleeve of his shiny gray uniform.

"Oh, he's doing great! Just great." Her enthusiasm was genuine.

Mr. Botts stopped the car to discharge some passengers. In a booming resonant voice, that seemed to bounce off the walls of the elevator he said, "Well, we can thank the good Lord for that!"

Sandy's toes seemed to curl up in her high heels; she could feel a cloud of embarrassment rising. There were doctors in the car, stethoscopes hanging from their necks. Not a very appropriate thing to say at a government research hospital, she told herself. She couldn't wait to get to the fourteenth floor.

"You sure are a handsome little man," Mr. Botts ruffled Kent's blond hair. He took his hand in his, "Want to drive the elevator for a minute?"

Kent beamed with pride at the other passengers as he presumably "drove" the car. There were chuckles at the misconception. They stopped at fourteen.

"Now, you take care of your little Mommy, my man!" Mr. Botts called after them as they left the car.

While there were many elevators at NIH it was surprising how many times they seemed to encounter Mr. Botts. Every time they saw him the scenario seemed to follow the same pattern. He would ask, "How's my little man?" And at Sandy's positive reply he would proclaim, "Well, we can thank the good Lord for that!" in a voice that threatened to implode the elevator. While she deeply appreciated his concern, she regarded his remark as surely being more appropriate in a church. He made her uncomfortable.

Kent's love affair with music had started as a baby in his playpen when he would snap his fingers in time to a song on the radio. There was a small stereo in the playroom on 2 East and a vast library of children's records. One morning Sandy put a record of Alvin and the Chipmunks on for Kent. He listened for a minute then wrinkled his nose in disdain, "That's not jazz! That's bunny rabbit jazz," he declared. They couldn't find any records Kent wanted to hear so that afternoon, while he napped, Sandy took a bus to Bethesda and purchased a few Herb Alpert albums and some Miles Davis. Being the child of a jazz singer, Kent had cut his teeth on heavier musicians and refused to be fed a diet of kiddie nursery rhymes.

He was delighted with the new music—and so was the staff. From that point forward it was not unusual to see orderlies boogie down the hall with trays of medication, or nurses swaying in time to "Hang on, Sloopy".

One afternoon Sandy purchased a toy doctor's kit at the gift shop and Kent was delighted to play doctor. He paced up and down the hall outside Dr. Gallo's office door waiting for him to come out. The toy plastic stethoscope hung around his neck and he waved a plastic thermometer in one hand. Gallo opened his office door to find Kent clutching the black, plastic doctor's bag in one hand, thermometer in the other.

"Well, well... what do we have here? Is this Doctor Ghost?" Gallo smiled and bent down to Kent's level.

"I take your temperature, Dr. Jello!" Kent threatened.

"No... no. It's your Mommy that needs her temperature taken," Gallo looked in Sandy's direction and chuckled.

Kent responded by whipping the thermometer up Sandy's skirt. Gallo had forgotten that Kent would relate to the fact that his temperature was always taken rectally. Both Sandy and the doctor were red-faced, but laughing hysterically.

Two weeks later, they were still enchanted by Kent's new temporary home. Despite the hospital's forbidding, impersonal atmosphere and enormous size, they were both enveloped in a genuine warmth and concern on the part of the personnel—extending from the doctors and administrative staff down to the housekeeping department. Later, she was to share her feelings of gratitude toward the staff with a woman who had been a patient for several years. Her reply was, "I leave my family and come here to be admitted for a few weeks each year, but when here I gain a whole new family." Outstanding, even in this atmosphere of sincere concern, was Mr. Botts the elevator operator. He never failed to pay singular attention to Kent.

On the 8th of February, Bill's birthday, after they had been at NIH for nearly two months, Sandy held Kent up to the pay phone outside the solarium so he could wish his daddy "Happy Birthday". A wet snow was falling softly in Maryland, clinging to the telephone wires molding them into swollen white ropes.

After lunch she lifted Kent into his bed and raised the metal sides until they clicked. "Take a good nap, sweetheart, and Mommy will bring you that red truck you wanted in the gift shop." She kissed his cheek and pulled up the covers. His sleepy smile was like a gift.

Parents had to be off the unit from 1:00 PM until 3:00 o'clock to allow the children to nap. They usually convened in the sunny solarium to play cards or just talk out their frustrations.

ıat day it was a game of bridge. Sandy's partner bid a small slam and
...... it. She looked at her watch and realized she could be back on the floor in
fifteen minutes. Excusing herself, she ran down the stairs to the gift shop on
B-2 and purchased the truck.

Back up on the second floor she walked swiftly down the hall with Kent's
reward. As she approached his door, it was strange to see a nurse who blocked the
entrance to his room. She could see past her shoulders that his bed was gone.

"Mrs. Ghost... Kent's not here. Dr. Gallo suspects he's had a cerebral
hemorrhage. It was quite sudden and unexpected. The doctor's performing
an L.P... a spinal tap... right now... in the treatment room to confirm his
diagnosis." Her eyes misted slightly.

Sandy stared at the nurse in disbelief, hardly comprehending.

"Will you please wait here? Dr. Gallo would like to talk with you when he's
finished." There seemed to be a churning apprehension in this young nurse.
She lightly touched Sandy's shoulder.

An icy glaze of fear drained Sandy's coordination... She was actually
shaking and wanted to sit down, but paced the hall. The security—the normalcy
they had experienced was merely a false reality. They'd been betrayed. What
had gone wrong?

After a few minutes, Dr. Gallo exited the treatment room carrying a test
tube filled with a bloody substance. He went into the nurses' station and picked
up the phone. The test tube itself obviously confirmed the worst. She couldn't
hear but instinctively knew it was true. He'd had a stroke.

Through the glass of the nurses' station she could see Gallo hang up the
phone. He came into the hall and motioned her into his office.

She was surprised by the tears that turned the intensity of his flashing
brown eyes to a softness she'd never seen. Finally he said, "It's just a bad break.
Just a bad break!"... And then he added, "We don't know why it's happened,
but Kent's had a cerebral hemorrhage. He's paralyzed and in a coma. There's
little we can do, for if we were to do an angiogram--- that is, injecting dye into
the neck and tracing it, hoping to operate, this might in itself kill him he's so
young. I'm sorry... so very sorry."

She tried to draw on some inner strength to even hear him and respond.
There seemed to be nothing available to her. She sat enveloped in a wound of
numbness that threatened to strangle her voice and so just nodded mutely.

"Mrs. Ghost, this is a research hospital and as there will be many neurologists
working over him, we would suggest that you remain out of the room. There's
not much we can do, but your presence might hinder us."

She mustered every resource to discipline the tone of her voice, "Should I
call my husband in Louisville to come to the hospital?"

"Are you asking me if he is grave?"

She said, "Yes", though she knew Kent was.

His reply was harshly blunt, "He is grave and the call is your responsibility, for I don't know if he will live long enough for your husband to make the trip. I'm so sorry... so sorry. Do you understand?"

She nodded that she did.

Gallo hurried off down the hall to attend to Kent. But she had detected tears now and then in his eyes and she had to check an impulse to comfort him somehow. He had let his clinical mask down and revealed his personal feelings. He really cared...

She stood alone now in the hall, a tumor of fear spreading and gnawing, growing inside of her until she found it difficult to breathe. Frantically, she caught the elevator to the fourteenth floor—the recreation area and also the chapel. This time there was no reticence in being in a chapel. She carpeted the floor with tears and pleaded, "God, at least let me have him as long as the other parents of children with leukemia are allowed to keep theirs. Kent's just been diagnosed... we've only had two months together...two months for me to make up for the two years he had without me. Please God, please..."

There were no other words... Nothing else would come... She felt stymied and totally helpless. She used the pay phone outside the solarium on 2E to call Bill in Louisville. It was grim for him to face this on his birthday. He agreed to catch the first plane he could. Then she began an anxious vigil in the solarium outside the ward. The other mothers, who knew of Kent's condition, rallied around sympathetically offering sandwiches, coffee, support—and most important of all understanding. She realized that no one else in this world could really know her mental anguish except another mother of a child with leukemia. While life had placed them in a macabre club it was based on love and identification. Underlying all the conversation, the song, "Hang On, Sloopy" kept circling in Sandy's mind.

At 7:30 P.M Dr. Gallo suddenly appeared in the doorway. He looked weary and collapsed into a chair. Taking off his glasses, he set them on the table and swiftly rubbed both eyes. Those same eyes seemed to give her no hope.

"There's no change, Mrs. Ghost. Kent's still in a coma. His right side is totally paralyzed. I realize this is rough to hear, but I've got to be honest with you. We've done all we can do, but I've just got to go home now...been here since early this morning. The floor doctor will carefully attend to him."

He pushed back an unruly strand of hair that had fallen onto his forehead, "You may go in and be with him now if you like. He's in an intensive care situation on the unit, apart from the other children. There's a nurse taking vitals every ten minutes. I keep saying it, but I'll tell you again... I'm so terribly sorry..."

Strangely, Sandy couldn't seem to shake a feeling of being sorry for the

, but just thanked him profusely. Then she hurried down the hall to the ive care room and pushed open the heavy door. Even though she had prepared herself, she was shattered by what she saw.

Kent lay on the hospital bed, eyes closed... He looked so small—his face, framed by blond curls was stripped of any color. The fleshly pallor terrified her. He was so still and she was afraid to touch him. Sitting in the solarium visualizing his state and actually being confronted by it were two different things. She sank into a chair by the bed and began to cry. Not until then did she realize she was not alone with Kent. Slightly behind the curtain, on the other side of the bed, a nurse sat in a chair. She was writing on a stack of charts attached to a silver clipboard.

She must have sensed Sandy's surprise at her presence. "Don't be embarrassed, Mrs. Ghost, you can call me Di Gi. I lost my mother and little sister in an automobile accident two months ago. I know exactly what you're feeling." Her words were a tonic.

She looked at her watch. "Dr. Gallo's ordered vital signs taken every ten minutes. This consists of blood pressure, temperature, shining a light in his eyes and trying to ascertain some sign of consciousness by grip or response. It's time." She laced a blood pressure cuff on Kent's small, limp arm. After a moment..."It's still sky high—no change." She made an entry on the chart.

Sandy watched with plunging hope as Di Gi took his temperature and calling his name, tried to get him to grip her hand. There was no response.

She shook her head, "No change at all. It's just rotten luck... I'm sorry." and settled back into her chair. "Why don't you go and get us a cup of coffee," she said with distinct emphasis on the "us". Did she really want a cup of coffee? Or was this a thoughtful ruse to give Kent's mother a few minutes of release from this room?

Sandy gladly took the bait and retreated to the snack bar in the basement. She bought two cups of coffee from the machine, putting lids on them both. Juggling the cups of steaming coffee, she pressed the elevator button to go up. The doors opened and she was surprised to see Mr. Botts on duty at night. He always worked the day shift. The elevator was empty of other passengers. As they started their ascent to the second floor he asked as always "How's my little man?"

She couldn't hold back the tears and struggled to keep from choking on her own words, "He's dying, Mr. Botts. He's had a cerebral hemorrhage and they don't expect him to live through the night."

The car stopped on the second floor.

"He's been in a coma for seven hours now."

"God is able," he said so softly it was almost a whisper.

Sandy took one step off the elevator and turned to look at him. She realized that this caring, humble man had heavenly connections she certainly didn't have. "Will you pray for him?" she asked, surprised at her own words.

"Get back on the elevator," he beckoned to her with one large hand.

Was he going to pray right there? she hesitated.

"Please get back on."

Now she was embarrassed and slowly walked back into the car. He closed the doors. She bowed her head as he did. They were alone in the elevator, which was unusual in itself in this huge hospital,

"Father, in the name of my Lord Jesus, and because I belong to Him, I ask You to heal this child as You healed me." The deep rich bass voice spoke with a familiarity tinged with a surprising authority. "Now, you know, Lord, the doctors said I'd never walk again."

Was this a prayer, she wondered? It sounded more like a conversation with a good friend. The thought briefly crossed her mind that if God disapproved of his familiarity they were both candidates for a lightning bolt. She cringed. Realizing she was desperate she tried to focus on his words....

"And Lord, You know the church prayed and You heard our prayers...You healed me. Now, I'm going to hold You to Your Word...the scripture says that 'God is no respecter of persons' and what You did for me I am asking that You would do for little Kent. Heal him, Lord, and please be with his little Momma here. Give her strength and let her see Your love and Your power. Thank you, Jesus for it's in Your name we pray." He opened the elevator doors and Sandy realized the call bell from another floor hadn't even interrupted them. How odd.

She resisted a sudden urge to hug him, but as she still held two cups of hot coffee she murmured a genuine heartfelt "Thank you so much!" As she walked briskly toward intensive care she realized she'd never in her life heard a prayer like that before. It both amazed and puzzled her. She just thought you said, "Thy Will be done" and that was that. Was it really possible to just come right out and ask for healing? What was it he had said "In Jesus name and because I belong to Him"—was this what made the difference she sensed in him?

She backed into the double door, pushing it open—both hands full with the coffee cups. Kent looked just the same. Di Gi was obviously finishing up another set of vital signs. Looking up, she shook her head gravely--no change. They drank their coffee and the young nurse made an attempt to engage Sandy in conversation to keep her eyes and mind off the frail child who lay paralyzed on the bed. Both of them were painfully aware of the red sweep hand of the clock on the wall that seemed to be ticking off the seconds of Kent's life.

Two more sets of vital signs were taken ten minutes apart. With each set the hopelessness became more vivid. Di Gi began the third set—temperature first. As she held it at an angle to read she almost dropped it, "Temp's

103

down... fast! She quickly pumped up the blood pressure cuff that ɹained on Kent's arm and as she took the reading, "Blood pressure's coming down too... fast!" He seemed to be breathing faster, but was he dying? Di Gi sprinted out of the double doors and could be heard calling for the doctor.

But as Sandy watched life seemed to be ebbing back into Kent's paralyzed body. Slowly he began to stir, his eyes opened and he turned toward his mother. "Mommy, I'm thirsty," he said, just as Di Gi and the doctor ran into the room.

The nurse quickly grabbed a paper cup and filled it with water as Sandy leaned over the bed and gathered Kent into her arms. Tears splashed down on his wrist that the floor doctor held as he took a pulse.

"Daddy's coming, sweetheart. Daddy's coming," Sandy told him. "I love you so much!"

The young, blond doctor kept shaking his head as he did a complete examination recording his findings on the chart Di Gi had placed on the foot of the bed. "Pretty astonishing recovery, Mrs. Ghost. Really remarkable in anybody's book. He's totally stable." He shook his head again as though in disbelief.

Di Gi was ecstatic. It was obvious she struggled to keep her composure, but the minute the doctor left the room, she threw her cap in the air and yelled, "Whoppee!" She hugged them both. From that time on, Kent seemed perfectly normal except for a small trickle of blood that drained from his left ear. It was as though he had just wakened from the afternoon nap when his mother had promised to bring him the truck.

Slowly an idea began to present itself... her mind calculated... two sets of vital signs after Mr. Botts' prayer... that would be only twenty minutes. Could it be possible that's why he recovered the way he did? She quickly dismissed the thought. That kind of thing just didn't happen.

When Bill arrived from the airport, Kent was sitting up in bed, drinking a soft drink, and playing with the promised red truck. It was difficult for Bill to fathom just how critical the situation had been only a few short hours ago. He hugged Kent and announced, "Well, I guess I'd have to say it's been a happy birthday, after all!"

They were permitted to stay all night with Kent as he was still on the critical list. After he had fallen asleep, they pulled two chairs together and talked. It was a new experience as they hadn't communicated well in years. Sandy tried to fill in all the details of exactly what had happened and shared in depth about the elevator operator's unusual prayer just twenty minutes prior to Kent's sudden recovery from the coma and paralysis.

"So, what do you think? Was it the prayer? I wasn't here so I can't really weigh in on this like you can." Bill kept his voice at a whisper so as not to disturb Kent's sleep.

"I honestly don't know. I really felt something... something different in that elevator when he prayed. And Bill, I've never heard anybody pray like that before. It was so... so friendly, you know... like you'd talk to a good friend. It was Almost irreverent in a way."

"Are you saying an irreverent prayer got Kent healed?"

"Well, at first I thought it had to be that. Both the nurse and the doctor were so surprised. It wasn't normal, for sure... I just don't know."

But the real shock came the following morning.

Unlike the majority of hospitals, NIH made every attempt to educate and include patients and parents alike in treatment procedures, test readings and prognosis. In the case of a pediatric patient the parent served as the link between NIH and the home maintenance doctor. Therefore, every attempt was made to educate the parent. In the short length of time Kent had been hospitalized, Sandy had learned to read blood counts and adjust the drips on an IV. The patient's chart was an open book—there were no secrets and nothing withheld.

The following morning, Bill and Sandy sat by Kent's bed as he played with his stuffed animals. The metal bars of the sides of his bed were the "zoo cage" for his stuffed animals. He pretended they were all in the cage together as he was confined to bed rest. After a soft food diet breakfast, Kent begged to go to the playroom. He appeared to be perfectly normal.

The door opened and suddenly a platoon of white-coated doctors filled the room on Grand Rounds. They were apparently in the midst of a heated argument as Bill and Sandy watched and listened, completely ignored as the retinue examined Kent. It was a shock to see such a vigorous debate. The neurologists seemed to be ganging up on Robert Gallo.

"Look, Bob," Sandy recognized one of the neurologists who had attended Kent the day before. He shot the words in Gallo's direction, "I insist Kent couldn't possibly have had a cerebral hemorrhage and stabilized in that fashion. You punctured a vein going in on the lumbar puncture."

Dr. Gallo spread his hands wide in a placating gesture, "Guys... guys... you diagnosed it yesterday as a cerebral hemorrhage too. You worked over him for hours. Look at the chart again. I performed that lumbar puncture and know I absolutely did not puncture a vein. It was a cerebral hemorrhage." he argued firmly. "I stand by the original diagnosis."

"Hi, Doctor Jello," Kent tried to get his attention. "You mad?" This brought laughs and was a moment of comic relief in the seriousness of the doctors' problem.

Though the neurology team had concurred that it had been a brain hemorrhage the day before, apparently they were not to be appeased and were reversing their diagnosis. This was based on a sentence Sandy and Bill heard many times during their argument. "Nobody ever recovers from a cerebral hemorrhage in that manner."

All the doctors began talking at once. The decision was finally reached to perform their own lumbar puncture right away. The stuffed animals were taken out of his bed before Kent was rolled away to the treatment room.

Sandy paced around the room, "I hate it that he has to go through this again... I just hate it, but we've got to know I suppose."

"Poor little guy!" Bill stretched and walked to the window. Neither of them had had much sleep though the nurses had brought lounge chairs into the room for them the night before. "Sure would like to brush my teeth," he said. "I'll go get us some coffee and find a men's room." He rooted in his overnight bag for a tooth brush.

Later, Dr. Gallo and an orderly rolled Kent's bed back into the room. Sandy got the stuffed animals back into the bed and held Kent while wiping away the tears on his cheeks. "I'm sorry," she told him. "I'm so sorry, sweetheart."

Dr. Gallo stood by and watched. He looked triumphant and smiled at Kent's parents. "Well, the second test affirmed that it was, indeed, a cerebral hemorrhage. We think possibly that some leukemia cells invaded the spinal fluid, made their way into the brain and ruptured a blood vessel. We'll have to confirm that conjecture with tests, but I've got to tell you, there seems to be no medical explanation for the way he recovered."

"Do you know Mr. Botts, the elevator operator?" Sandy asked.

"Sure," a slight frown creased his forehead as though questioning what this had to do with anything.

"Well, he brought me up from B-2. I'd gotten coffee for Di Gi and me. I asked him if he would pray for Kent... that he was... dying. He told me to get back on the elevator and we prayed together. Twenty minutes later Kent opened his eyes and said he was thirsty, Dr. Gallo."

He was silent, obviously trying to filter this new information through a lens of medical perspective. At length he smiled, "We prayed a lot for my sister who had leukemia," he said rather wistfully. Then he seemed to snap back into the present, "I'm prescribing radiation on the right side of the brain to deal with any leukemia cells that might still pervade. He'll start a course of radiation tomorrow, okay? By the way, it's been recorded on his chart as an "unexplainable medical recovery." He grinned, "That was the entry recorded by the neurologists."

Bill and Sandy thanked him profusely for all he had done. But Sandy couldn't wait to tell Mr. Botts and introduce Bill to him.

Two days later, as Kent rode the rocking horse in the playroom, and listened to his jazz on the stereo, Mr. Botts came to see him on his break. Just as he picked Kent up and held him, the same retinue of neurologists that had attended Kent now congregated in the doorway. One waved at Sandy and another told Kent hello. Then they watched for a moment in silence until the doctor who had challenged Gallo the most leaned against the door and shook his head. "Would you believe that's Kent Ghost?" he asked the others.

Mr. Botts smiled as though he knew some mysterious secret that neither the doctors nor Sandy and Bill shared.

Before Bill went back to Louisville they had several long conversations to try to sort out just what had happened. They couldn't seem to nail it down. "But neither can the doctors," Bill observed.

"Has to have been a miracle. What else explains it? The first night I thought it would have happened anyway... until the doctors said Kent couldn't possibly recover that way. Even did their own L.P. to prove it was some other diagnosis and..." she twisted the cap off a bottle of Coca Cola, "they were wrong!"

"Well, jury's out for me, but I'm just grateful for what happened."

It was hard to see Bill leave, but after Kent had stabilized he had to fly back home.

The radiation of Kent's head took a balding toll on his blond curly hair and the sustained protocol of POMP (prednisone, vinchristine, 6MP and methotrexate) made his small body swell into obesity. It was heartbreaking to watch, but Sandy realized they were striving for remission at any cost. The dreaded leukemia had to be defeated and the sword was radiation and chemotherapy. Prednisone, however, took his sunny disposition on a roller coaster ride.

One afternoon, when the playroom was crowded with other children, Kent bit a little girl. It was a sudden attack on her hand as she reached for one of his records. Sandy's reaction was a swift swat on Kent's bottom. "Don't you ever do that again!" she told him and apologized profusely to the little girl and her mother. The skin wasn't broken and the mother was gracious about the incident.

Later, Mrs. Thomas, the social worker called Sandy into her office. "I understand you spanked Kent in the playroom, Mrs. Ghost," her eyes accosted from across the desk.

"No... I didn't spank him. I swatted him one time on the bottom because he bit another child."

"Well!" She exhaled deeply and Sandy expected to see steam expelled from her ears. "You wouldn't do that if he had an IV running would you?"

Sandy met her accusing gaze. "If it wasn't running in his bottom I certainly would! As far as I'm concerned discipline is a part of Kent's security. If I stop disciplining him, and you people find the answer to leukemia we're going to have a flock of spoiled brats when they reach maturity. If I stop disciplining Kent it will destroy his security. My job is to keep his life as normal as I possibly can, don't you agree?"

"Well, I guess..." Reason had extinguished the fire of the social worker's huffy self-righteous attack.

Mr. Botts became like close family. He came to see Kent many times on his breaks. Kent had gotten a new instrumental record with a catchy rhythm and one afternoon he attempted to dance to it in the playroom. The poor little guy was so obese now from the drugs that he resembled the Michelin Man. His stomach mainly did the dancing, bobbing up and down as his feet moved in time to the music. "This is my stomach song" he told us. His favorite orderly came into the playroom and added a few moves of his own.

Mr. Botts smiled and laughed at the demonstration.

"You always seem so happy," Sandy remarked. "How do you stay on such an even keel all the time with all this sickness around you?"

His fingers reached out and touched Kent momentarily, "Well... you see man's extremity is God's opportunity. So if you look at it that way, know how much Father loves you... you've just gotta' be happy. Nothing's too big, or too hard for Him."

That night, Sandy lay in bed staring at shadows from the hall that crept across the ceiling of her room. The words Mr. Botts had uttered echoed from the depths of her subconscious: "Man's extremity is God's opportunity." That had to be a key to what had happened in Kent's recovery. The doctors had admitted they were at a blind end to medically help him. They had told her all they could do was observe and record. *That was surely man's extremity*, she tried to sort through what it all meant. *And because Kent was at the end... the extremity of what the doctors could do, God stepped in... took the opportunity to heal him. But it was Mr. Botts, who knew the key... and knew he could ask for it to happen... knew how to ask.*

As she drifted off to sleep it occurred to her to wonder just how Mr. Botts had gotten on such a chummy relationship with God that he could ask something that big and it would happen. She snuggled down between the crisp, cool sheets feeling a bit bewildered, but having the distinctly warm impression that she and Kent were loved. The fear that had clutched her so tightly since the diagnosis of leukemia slowly began to melt a bit that night. But would it last? What would happen when they went home and left the security of NIH, and Mr. Botts' link to God?

Chapter Thirteen

*T*wo months later, they were told Kent was in remission and well enough to be released from the hospital, returning on an out-patient basis every two months. Many hugs and well-wishes from the other parents gave them a hero's send-off. Sandy felt a heart wrench at leaving them behind. However, she really wished she could kidnap Dr. Gallo, just pack him up in their suitcases. She truthfully was extremely afraid to be totally responsible for Kent's care even though he was in remission. But her major worry was in leaving Mr. Botts. She felt she needed his connection to God to protect Kent. He told her she could pray, but she knew he had God's "ear" and felt she wasn't good enough for the Lord to hear her.

They flew back to Louisville and there was a joyous reunion with the rest of the family that seemed to last about a week. Then she and Bill resumed their former roles of mutual unconcern which occasionally flamed into slashing sarcasm. She felt boxed in by Kent's illness—it hadn't brought them any closer together in their marriage. There could be no divorce now and the tension between them mounted.

There were other problems: She watched with horror as Kent lost the last few wisps of his hair, and struggled around in a ballooning body. His temper continued to flare easily as a result of the drug side-effects and he had problems keeping food down from the accompanying nausea.

His twin brother, Kurt, suddenly required more attention than Kent. In the three months Kent and his mother had been in Maryland a frightening change had taken place. At two and one-half Kurt could hardly have been expected to realize the seriousness of his twin's illness. Now it seemed that in his baby-mind he thought his mother had left him—apparently taking Kent (her favorite, it must have seemed) with her. When they returned, they found Kurt had erased them completely from his world. He stonily rejected both of them. For three months all of the toys had been his; whereas, Kent felt he had come home to all *his* toys! They bickered incessantly—fought violently.

Her heart ached for Kurt and therefore she tried to lavish love on him, but he rebuffed and ignored her. Drenched with self-pity, Sandy trudged drearily through household tasks and spent most of her time in the bathroom crying.

One night as they were sitting in the backyard, Bill broke the silence with, "I had the strangest experience today. You remember my talking about a man by the name of Joe Hardy who calls on me?" She nodded recalling he was a salesman with a trucking firm.

"Well, he seemed troubled over something and told me he wasn't there to talk business, but would I have coffee with him. We went across the street and, after we were served, he explained that he and his wife belonged to a prayer group that has been praying for Kent. He asked if we would like to come to a prayer meeting."

Prayer meeting? How caring of them to be praying, she thought. Aloud she agreed to go. "But I want to make it clear," she told him, "I'm only going out of a sense of obligation to these people who seem concerned for Kent."

She really didn't know exactly what to expect—perhaps some old-time religion type of affair. And as they walked down the concrete steps to the auditorium, she was surprised at the location. The Full Gospel Business Men's meeting was being held in a Teamster's Union Hall!

Joe Hardy seemed thrilled that they'd shown up and courteously found them two seats near him and his wife, Leita. Sandy quickly scanned the room. Her previous impression of people she considered "extra-curricular Christians" (those who went to a service or meeting other than on Sunday) was that the women probably dressed in long-sleeved dresses, well below the knee, and wore no make-up. She was pleasantly surprised. Here were well-dressed, contemporary-looking people that totally blew her preconceived biased notion. She'd expected something like her remembrance of the Salvation Army lady with the tambourine who used to come into the bar when Sandy was singing.

The room was bulging with people sitting on folding chairs, and the stir subsided abruptly when a man on the platform called the meeting to order. *It resembles the P.T.A.*, Sandy thought and had to suppress a snicker. There was to be a speaker. That was another surprise as she thought they would just pray.

Bob Engle, a businessman from St. Louis, was a small sensitive-looking man. He began to tell a story about himself—he appeared to be nervous and not accustomed to speaking before a large crowd of people.

"My wife and I were on the verge of divorce," he began. Suddenly, he had Sandy's full attention. "Each time we considered taking legal action to escape our dying marriage we were invariably blocked. We had a small son, Robin, whom we both dearly loved and each of us wanted custody of the child." Bob briefly wiped perspiration from his forehead with a handkerchief. "To compound matters," his voice broke slightly, "we were both alcoholics." A soft, sympathetic murmur briefly sifted through the crowd.

They found that Robin would have to have a simple tonsillectomy operation, but on the operating table he had a cardiac arrest. Sandy found her mind guiltily flashing back to that day at St. Joseph's hospital when she had bitterly overheard and reacted to the woman being told that her child with the tonsillectomy—was alright. She had envied that child's uncomplicated illness. But the speaker's son had experienced severe complications.

Her mind returned to what he was saying, "In the time that Robin was in the recovery room, nobody ever told me about Jesus Christ. Robin... my baby... died. My wife and I stayed together, going from bad to worse. Our marriage continued, not because we loved each other, but because the only person we had ever loved had been taken away from us." And he repeated, "During this time, no one ever told us about Jesus Christ."

The speaker was perspiring more profusely now, and the handkerchief that he used to mop his forehead made furtive dabs at his eyes. He continued, "There followed a period of trying to drown our grief by drinking. Then, one night while sitting in a bar, I abruptly pushed my drink away and not until then did I notice that my wife was not drinking at all. God had begun to deal with us. However, I was consumed with an inner turmoil and contacted my uncle. I confided to him that I had decided to kill myself so I could be with my little boy. He begged me to reconsider and asked me to go to a church service with him. This is where I heard about Jesus Christ."

Here his nervousness seemed to evaporate. There was a fresh luster in his voice as he told the crowd, "Jesus Christ is the Son of God, Who was crucified for us, rose again, and now sits on the right hand of God the Father."

Sandy had personally identified with his story until now. *So what's the big deal?* she thought with total disregard for reverence. She'd heard that in the Episcopal church as a kid and was deflated that this was all that Bob's mystery was about. She'd been sitting on the edge of her chair, awed by the coincidence of being there when their circumstances matched so closely. But now she felt let down as though he'd led her right to the wire and then deceived her with platitudes.

And then Bob added something else she hadn't heard before... or perhaps hadn't been ready to hear it; "It's possible to have an intimate and personal relationship with Jesus if you will ask Him to come into you, turning your life over to Him. You must surrender your will by admitting you're not capable of running your own life without His help."

He closed by saying that, turning this over in his mind, he had gone to Robin's grave and kneeling there, had given himself and all his problems to Christ. He *had* died, in a sense, for he had handed over the old Bob Engle and had been born again. He claimed that Jesus had died in his place so that he would never have to die! Bob's wife made this same surrender of herself. He claimed that the Lord not only healed their lives, but their marriage as well, opening up a completely new world for both of them.

His final words were, "He took my son—but He gave me *His* Son in return."

It was over... Sandy realized with a sense of embarrassment that she'd been crying and made a fumbling attempt to wipe away the evidence of streaked mascara. Bill caught her repairing her makeup and smiled as though he understood. Could it have been more than coincidence for them to be there and hear a story so close to their own? Did Joe Hardy know what Bob Engle was going to say and that's why he'd asked them? She leaned over and whispered to Bill, "Did you tell Joe Hardy our marriage is in trouble?"

"No way. All he knew about was Kent's leukemia. This guy really hit home, didn't he?" Bill shook his head in disbelief.

People were milling about. No one seemed in a hurry to leave and as they had been invited to go to a restaurant for coffee with Joe Hardy and several others, they stood apart surveying the crowd.

Bob Beckett, whom Joe Hardy had introduced to them earlier, was now courteously elbowing his way through clusters of people. He seemed to be headed in their direction. Suddenly they were face-to-face and she was astonished when he confronted them abruptly with, "I understand you have a child with leukemia."

How did he know? Inwardly she balked at his intrusion and fleetingly entertained an impulse to run out the double doors.

Instead, she answered cautiously, "Yes, we do."

"God will heal him, you know." It was an assured, positive statement. She said, "Yes," though she certainly didn't know at all; however, she was reminded of Kent's cerebral hemorrhage. She was fairly convinced God could, if He wanted to... but He certainly wasn't going to do it for her. Bill stood quietly watching their exchange.

"Are you both Christians?" Bob asked.

This whole conversation was taking on a puzzling tone. She said they were. After all, they had a little piece of paper that said they belonged to a Presbyterian Church up north. They'd both been baptized as infants, and they were Americans, for Pete's sake, she reasoned with herself while struggling for composure.

Bob must have sensed her inner conflict, for he said, "Where do you believe you'll go when you die?"

And then the most astonishing thing happened. Words tumbled out of her that she heard as though she were a bystander. Immediately she couldn't believe she had said it. They were: "To hell for all I've sinned."

Bob ushered them aside to a small grouping of chairs and began to show them sentences that he had underlined in a small, black Bible he produced from his hip pocket. Thoughts swirled as apparently all this had something to do with the fact that they weren't Christians. Confusion and embarrassment glazed her sight. She couldn't read the small print and hardly heard a word he said until he skipped to a phrase in the back of the Bible. It was as though something within her snapped and she heard Bob say, "This is Revelation 3:20, Jesus is speaking saying, 'Behold, I stand at the door and knock; if any man hear my voice and open the door, I will come in to him, and will sup with him, and he with me.'" Bob explained that the word "sup" meant fellowship. *Jesus have fellowship with me? Impossible!* she thought.

They knelt together, in a Union Hall, in front of some folding metal chairs, that apparently to Bob was an altar as acceptable to God as Abraham's. Bob explained that if they confessed their sins, He would be faithful and just to forgive their sins. That's when the fellowship would come. She felt the warmth of an arm around her shoulders and realized that a girl she had just met had knelt beside her, was praying with her as she said in a most unflowery prayer, "Jesus, if You are really there like this man says You are, please... come into my life, for I'm up against a brick wall and have nowhere to go. I'm at the end of trying to manage my life. I give up."

They were in the car, headed for home, when she began mentally questioning what they had done. There was the familiar silence between them, but it was different this time, reflecting embarrassment more than antagonism. She certainly didn't feel any different. Thoughts swirled: *Maybe nothing really happened... perhaps I should have waited until I studied up on this thing a little more. Was this what made the difference in Mr. Botts... how he could have such an intimate relationship with God? He had said "my Lord Jesus and because I belong to Him"... Is this what gave him access to God that most people didn't seem to have? Do I have it now?* she wondered.. Thoughts tumbled around threading their way through memories... the note the Salvation Army lady had given her in the bar that said, "Do you know Jesus?" Had God been trying to get her attention way back then? Could all the coincidences have been more than coincidence? Would they live happily ever after now? Sandy was to discover her fumbling prayer had been heard...

End Of Part One

Introduction to Part Two

*W*hen two neighbors who live in Bucksnort, Tennessee unexpectedly meet in New York City they usually say the same thing, "Well, it's a small world!" This seems to be the phrase that always accompanies a remarkable coincidence. But what if it isn't coincidence at all? What if these extreme happenings could be orchestrated by God. to get our attention, to further His plan for our lives, or as some kind of heavenly protection? Have doubts about that? Well, in the next few chapters you will read about one "coincidence" after another all laced together with the love of a heavenly valentine.

You may have heard the story about the little boy in Sunday school who was given crayons and paper. The children were told to draw anything they wanted. Soon the teacher saw little Michael vigorously whipping out different colors, eagerly drawing with a zeal she'd seldom seen him display.

"So... what are you working on, Michael?" she asked.

"I'm drawing a picture of God," he said, never looking up from the paper. She smiled broadly. "But no one knows what God looks like," she told him.

"Well, they will when I get done with this picture!" he said.

My hope is that when you finish with the picture of God I've drawn between these pages you, too, will see what He looks like. And yes, I have written Part One, but there was no possible way I could tell Sandy's story in the first person. That person... the singer was no longer me. My real life began that night in front of a metal folding chair in a union hall.

So... fasten your spiritual seat belt, get prepared for the ups and downs of a heavenly roller coaster ride that will leave you breathless with what the world would deem to be remarkable "coincidences".

Chapter Fourteen

*M*y body always wakened promptly to the alarm clock at 7:00 a.m. every morning. That same body would get breakfast, see the two oldest children off to school and Bill off to work. Then, somewhere around 10:00 a.m. and after four cups of coffee—my mind would wake up.

This was my usual sleepy state on the morning after the prayer meeting at the union hall. I got up and began lethargically struggling with the coffee pot in the kitchen, never remembering the events of the past evening. I helped Eric and Lisa off to school and went back to the kitchen table to give the twins their breakfast.

Bill walked through the kitchen door and I cannot attempt to explain the feeling that came over me—an overwhelming, supernatural love such as I had never felt before was apparently sprinkled down upon me as though with a Divine Hand. No words were spoken between us, but Bill said later he could actually feel this love coursing through me, across the room to him, as positively as if it had been an electrical current.

We had exhausted outside help. We had been to the one Unitarian marriage counselor and two ministers. One of the ministers had washed his hands of us completely, adding firmly we were not to bother him anymore. Over coffee, Bill and I cautiously examined what had happened to us. It was refreshing to be conversing without arguing.

"I'm still kinda' reeling from last night. I've got to sort some things out." I put a Danish on the plate in front of Bill and wiped up orange juice Kent had spilled.

Bill admitted, "It's a sad thing to look back on now that not once did any of our counselors mention Jesus Christ to us, not even the ministers."

I couldn't contain my excitement, "You know what? I think my prayer was heard! Yours too! It's really neat... Jesus is not just up there abstractly floating around like a mythical Santa Claus or merely sitting at the right hand of God. It would seem, He's loving and personally concerned. For the first time since Kent's unexplained healing I have to believe He's anxious to become involved with us and our problems. It has to be more than coincidence... you know, Bob Engle's story so clearly paralleling our own... our just happening to be there that night for his talk." My eyes met Bill's and he was nodding in agreement. From that morning forward there were subtle changes in our marriage. But all of the problems didn't just magically disappear with the wave of a heavenly wand.

A month passed and the promises seemed to fade back into dullness. It had rained continuously for nearly two weeks. I stood looking through the screen door of the kitchen into the relentless afternoon drizzle that continued to drown my backyard. Rivulets of water wound through each mud spattered flower with a moat of rain water. Even the petunias in the window box bent in puckered distress. My dampened mood seemed to match my backyard as I reflected that my outlook in the last few weeks had become as sodden as my petunias.

Leaning my head against the screen, I gave in to the sullen thoughts I'd struggled to push aside. *No use pretending anymore*, I told myself. *Nothing at all happened that night we turned our lives over to Christ... I've just been kidding myself all along. Yes, something unnatural took place between Bill and me the following morning. But maybe it stemmed more from wishful thinking at a subconscious level than from God. Was this Jesus-thing just a myth or a cruel joke?*

There had been a slightly muted change in the discord of our marriage. At least we didn't seem to be arguing as much. But Bill hadn't suddenly become Prince Charming either.

And where was this miracle that was supposed to change me? For a few days after turning myself over to Jesus I seemed to have a new love and patience with the children. But lately, my newly acquired disposition was fading away like the Cheshire Cat in Alice-In-Wonderland, until only the leering smile was left.

Now my smile had vanished too. With a sense of guilt, I realized I was again carping at the children over insignificant things and brooding about my problems.

Nothing had changed... Kurt and Kent were actually worse. Playtime was like World War III between then as they bickered over toys, clashing constantly over everything. The side effects of Kent's drugs seemed to mount dangerously. The hospital had told me to expect toxicity from the high levels of medication he had been given, but even their warning had not prepared me for the alarming changes that were now taking place. His body had suddenly ballooned into an obesity that scarcely allowed him to waddle around the house. Of all four children Kent's disposition had been the most balanced; however, this was distorted by the steroid drugs and each day brought raging temper tantrums and ugliness in personality that matched his new appearance. It was like having a strange child in the house that didn't belong to me. But all the physical changes didn't compare to his constant problem with nausea; he couldn't seem to keep down one solid meal and lately had begun vomiting even small amounts of liquids. How long could he go on this way? I was alarmed by his condition, heartbroken over what he was going through and grieving over the loss of my adorable, bright and loving child. I also had to admit to myself that I had begun to resent having to follow him around with a mop and bowl. How long could I cope with this little person who had been turned into a Mr. Hyde by leukemia drugs?

And then there was Kurt... wounded by what he thought was his mother's abandonment and not coping well with the return of his twin who now seemed like a stranger.

Where was this victorious Jesus who was going to march into my life and change it? Bob Engle had embroidered too rosy a picture the night he had told us about turning our lives over to Christ. Maybe it had worked for *him* and *his* wife, but it certainly wasn't working for Bill and me. I felt cheated... hurt.

A sudden change in the direction of the wind interrupted my belligerent woolgathering. Rain lashed my face, splashing through the screen. I recoiled, startled, as though some bystander had sloshed water in my face to waken me from unconsciousness.

The name "Bob Beckett" softly inserted itself into my mind. What was it he had said to us that night before we left the meeting? Something almost mysterious... I racked my brain to recapture his words.

Suddenly it was as though Bob stood in front of me again. I vividly remembered he had said, "There's more to it than this. There's more, another experience with God—the Baptism in the Holy Spirit." I was amazed I could remember his words so accurately. I could almost feel the warmth of his hand on mine. Was I actually recalling his words or had God backhanded me with the rain to bring me to my senses and given me some kind of answer to my mutinous mutterings?

Closing the back door on the rain, I made a cup of tea and sat down at the kitchen table, grateful for this quiet time alone. Eric and Lisa were in school-- the twins were napping.

Stirring in two teaspoons of sugar, I savored the words "Holy Spirit". That sounded almost spooky. If there really *was* more than just turning your life over to Christ... if there *was* another experience, then maybe that was what was lacking in our lives. Perhaps this was why we'd seen so little change. It was worth investigating. After all, what did we have to lose? I decided to corner Bill after the children were in bed and talk with him about what Bob Beckett had said.

That evening I whisked the children through baths and off to bed in an effort to get some time alone with Bill. They seemed cowed by this sudden spurt of energy and direction in their mother and surprised me by an absence of all the usual prolonged excuses.

I found Bill on the porch swing and without any preface launched into a tirade about my discouragement, the lack of change in our lives and my disappointment in Jesus for not having done anything about our problems. I couldn't see Bill's face as it was dark, but paused to catch his reaction.

I could smell the smoke from his pipe mingling with the dank night air. "Sandy", he said at length, "Are you feeling sorry for the problem, or sorry for yourself?"

He'd hit the nail on the head. "Well, to be honest I guess I'm feeling sorry for *me* and I don't mind admitting it! I know I'm bloated with self pity and it seems like I'm no good to anyone. Kurt needs extra love and attention to compensate for my leaving him to be with Kent at the hospital. And what do I do? Yell and scream at him. Kent's in misery, constantly vomiting up everything from the drugs and yet I resent every mess I clean up. I hate myself... I feel guilty about it, but I'm tired of playing Pollyanna since trying their 'Jesus Formula'. It didn't work. Nothing's changed."

The rhythmic squeak of the porch swing was the only sound for minutes until Bill said quietly, "I wasn't really under the impression that by accepting Jesus everything would change. We're the ones who are supposed to change, aren't we?"

"But that's just the point. My attitude toward everything seemed to be different in the beginning. Now I've just settled back in my old rut; I feel powerless, which brings me to something I thought of this afternoon. Do you remember Bob Beckett saying something about another experience with Christ?"

"Yes, he mentioned the Holy Spirit."

"Well... do you suppose this is what's lacking with us? Bob said to 'go on', that there was more and then he named this additional experience the 'Baptism of the Holy Spirit'. Maybe we need to look into this. Certainly if there's anything to it, I obviously need it; I'm about ready to crack. I hate myself and everything about my life." I waited. There was no response from Bill. "Are you with me to at least find out about it?" I urged.

Bill reached out and took my hand, "Of course I'm with you. I'll call Joe Hardy tomorrow and find out where they hold their weekly prayer meeting."

The following Thursday night, Bill and I found ourselves in the pine-paneled game room of Leola and Walter Carby, friends of Joe and Leita Hardy. A bizarre assortment of chairs from apparently every room in the house formed a large circle around the perimeter of the room. I could smell coffee from a huge urn on a card table in the corner and silently wished for a cup to steady the sudden attack of nervousness I felt.

We were early and timidly sat down in the circle of rapidly filling chairs. Everyone who arrived was greeted by the others with such warmth it almost seemed like a party.

Now the chairs were all filled and some sat on the floor as the room began to overflow with people. Abruptly a spontaneous hush seemed to call a halt to conversation. I was puzzled. No one had called for order. It was uncanny that everyone should sense it was time to begin at the same moment.

I noticed some people slipping to their knees, using the chair seat as an altar. I was relieved that others just bowed their head and closed their eyes. I certainly didn't feel like kneeling. In fact, I didn't feel very reverent at all—just uncomfortable and embarrassed. Struggling to pray silently, all I could do was listen to random voices here and there praying for people I didn't know.

During a long silence a curious thing began to happen to me. Slowly, a feeling of nearness to God began to sweep over me. I felt loved... secure. I began to understand how Mr. Botts talked like he did to Jesus I too, began to feel as if the Lord were right there in the room with us. I realized with a start that this was exactly the same atmosphere that had been in the elevator with Mr. Botts the night he prayed for Kent.

Just as abruptly as the prayer time had begun, it ended. Spotty conversation broke out between little groups of people and some got up and began to move toward the coffee urn. We also migrated toward the urn that was now surrounded by people laughing and talking. There I recognized Bob Beckett, the Baptist seminary student who had led us in prayer at the Full Gospel Business Men's meeting the night we turned our lives over to Christ.

Bob appeared to be in his early thirties. His blond closely clipped hair stood in undisciplined right angles to his head. He was not tall, but his big-boned frame seemed to tower over those standing around him. He wheeled around and crunched my hand in a knuckle-breaking handshake, "Well, how are you, sister!" his cultured voice was rich and deep.

I winced. Not only from the pain in my hand, but from the term, "sister".

"Fine, thank you." His twinkling, gray-blue eyes seemed to penetrate my being and I had the uncomfortable feeling he knew I wasn't "fine".

"How do you two feel about your new relationship with Christ?" Bob handed us each a cup of coffee and motioned us over to a couch in the corner.

I hoped Bill would answer his direct question, but when he didn't I offered, "Okay, I guess."

A slow, boyish grin spread across Bob's face. He waited for me to go on. Why did I have the feeling he knew what was going on inside of me? It was maddening.

In a sudden spurt it all rushed out. I told him of my disappointment that nothing had changed, the problems we were facing at home, that frankly I thought Jesus had let us down. Bill sat silently listening. *Am I embarrassing him*, I wondered fleetingly?

Bob quietly nodded his head now and then, but I could feel a current of understanding passing between us. I felt he really cared and this seemed to wash away my first rude impression as the conversation continued.

"Sandy," he said softly, "I have the feeling you thought by turning your life over to Christ all of your problems would just dissolve and everything would be rosy. That's not how God works. You gave your life to Him and His part of the bargain is to walk through it with you, helping you to be victorious in the midst of your problems."

I took a big gulp of coffee to help fight back the tears that threatened. "Victorious! That means I should change. And believe me, I've been trying the past few weeks, but I just can't do it."

"Now you've hit on the real problem," Bob explained. "All the other things you've been telling me about are just surface obstacles."

"You mean I'm the real problem?"

"No, I mean you're trying to change yourself because you think that's what's expected of you now that you're a Christian. You can't do it, and the frustration of your own inadequacy is driving you up a wall. Perhaps that's what God wants."

"Well, what kind of a cruel God is that?" The familiar self-pity welled up in me again. Apparently, even God was against me.

Bob smiled again, "Let me explain. You've been trying to do it on your own. You can't, Sandy. Maybe the Lord has allowed things to even become worse in order for you to see that you can't meet these problems in your own strength—they have to be met in His power… His power in you."

"Now you've lost me again. I don't have any power."

"Precisely. But the Lord has provided power for you through His Holy Spirit. Even the disciples were pretty powerless until the Holy Spirit was given at Pentecost. I don't know how much you know about the Bible…"

"Next to nothing," I interrupted, "I've just started reading the Bible, " I admitted. "I've never been able to understand it before, but now it seems to make sense."

Bob threw his head back and laughed heartily. "Well, after you get into it, you'll see that even Peter turned into a quivering coward and denied Christ before he received the Holy Spirit. Jesus told the disciples, just before he ascended, to go forth and teach all nations, but not until they received power from on high."

He paused to take a swig of coffee and continued, "In other words, Sandy, they weren't to undertake Christianity in their own power, but they were to wait until they received the Baptism of the Holy Spirit on the day of Pentecost. When they did, they turned the world upside down."

"So how does that apply to my problems?"

"What I'm trying to tell you is that the same experience the disciples had with the Holy Spirit is available to you... and the same power."

I began to feel an excitement I couldn't explain. "You mean that God's sort of been waiting for me to see I need His power to change? It's funny, but the other day when I was the lowest, grumbling to myself about my problems, I suddenly remembered Bob Engle had told us something about the Holy Spirit. But... but *me* with the same power the disciples had? Wow!"

Bill, who had been listening to our entire exchange now added, "In fact, that's really why we've come—to find out more about this Baptism in the Holy Spirit."

But I hardly heard him. Had it been coincidence that rainy afternoon as I poured out my troubles and swam in self pity that the cold rain in my face had acted like a first-aid slap to counter hysteria? Directly afterward, the same answer had come that Bob Beckett had just given us. "Bob, could it be the Lord Himself was trying to give me the answer when I was reminded so suddenly of your words to us about another experience?"

"It's certainly possible."

"Well then, where do we go to get it?"

Bob leaned forward, clasping his hands around his knees. He grinned slightly, "Not 'it', sister—Him."

Bob had so completely won me over that now "sister" seemed like a compliment. "You mean the Holy Spirit is a *person*? I thought it was something like heavenly electricity... you know, God's power."

Patiently Bob explained, "The Holy Spirit is the third person of the trinity. Jesus told the disciples that He must go that the Holy Spirit might come—His Spirit. The trinity isn't an easy thing to understand, but to bring it to the level of our understanding; we too are three in one -- body, soul and spirit. The baptism of the Holy Spirit is simply the Holy Spirit filling us."

"I feel like a dunce, but you haven't told us how this is supposed to happen, Bob."

Bill pointed out objectively, "Most churches teach that you received the Holy Spirit when you received Christ. If it's Jesus' spirit, as you just said, then maybe we've already experienced it."

Many of the people were leaving now and Bob waved goodbye to a group still talking by the stairs before answering.

"No one can come to receive Christ, Bill, without the Holy Spirit drawing him. But the Baptism of the Holy Spirit is being filled with the Spirit. If you'll read through the book of Acts with this in mind I think you'll see that there's another experience involved. I have no doubt that there may be some people who have received Christ and the Baptism at the some time, but there's another way to tell."

He opened the leather Bible in his hand. "In I Corinthians, Chapter 12 there are gifts of the Spirit listed: wisdom, knowledge, healing, working of miracles, prophecy and tongues, just to name a few. If these gifts are operating in your life then you can be sure you've experienced the Baptism or infilling."

"That lets me out!" Bill said dryly, shrugging his shoulders. "Working of miracles, prophecy..."

But I pounced on tongues. "What do you mean by 'tongues'? Was that the strange language I heard tonight?"

"Exactly, Sandy. What you heard was a message in tongues and the interpretation, which is another gift of the Holy Spirit; however, most who have received the Holy Spirit are given a whole new prayer language. This is a manifestation of the Spirit and not to be confused with the gift of speaking in tongues."

He set his coffee cup on the small table beside the couch. "Paul said, 'I will pray with the Spirit, I will pray with the understanding also,' meaning he could pray in tongues and likewise he could pray with his own understanding."

It was getting late and we had a sitter, but this subject fascinated me. "Well, the tongues, or whatever it was really broke the spell with me. Up until then I had begun to really feel like Jesus was right in the room with us. But that's a real turn off with me. We're Presbyterians you know, Bob."

Bob struggled into a tweed sport coat and picked up his Bible. "Think you'll be back?" He grinned.

Bill and I both assured him we would as we climbed the basement stairs together. But as we drove away I told Bill, "I don't know if you're as confused by all this as I am, but that meeting was something else! "

The darkness hid Bill's expression, but he spoke thoughtfully, "They certainly are enthusiastic."

"I will say, Bob Beckett got through to me. Everything he said seemed to make sense except the part about tongues. That gives me goose-bumps."

For the next two weeks our evenings seemed to follow a specific pattern. Any outsider would have thought we were two students cramming for an exam. Television was forgotten as Bill and I sat on the couch reading, surrounded by books on the Holy Spirit. Occasionally one of us would grab the Bible and look up a certain passage to read a few sentences aloud, while trying to bypass a mouthful of potato chips.

At one point we admitted to each other that the Baptism in the Holy Spirit was real and we were excited about it. As a result the thought occurred to me that in many years of marriage we were finally doing something together. But when we ran out of reading material the unity ended abruptly.

Succeeding evenings I desperately wished that Bill would turn off the television, take my hand and say, "Let's pray to receive the Holy Spirit together.

Let's do it now." And then in some silly fairy tale way I believed we'd live happily ever after. But Bill made no move. It was almost as if now that we'd investigated God's power and found out it was real, it was all over.

One afternoon as the twins napped I decided to spiritually take things in my own hands. I just couldn't wait for Bill any longer. I picked the walk-in linen closet off the bathroom to pray. Closing the bathroom door, and closet door, I buried my head in a pile of towels. "Lord," I began. "I guess this experience with the Holy Spirit is real and You know how badly I need this power to change my life. It would be nice if Bill and I could have this experience at home, alone...together. But, Lord I can't wait any longer—I want this." Then almost as an addenda, "And could you please leave off the tongues? I know that it's supposed to accompany the Holy Spirit... but God—I'm a Presbyterian."

Absolutely nothing happened... or so I thought!

I said nothing of my prayer to Bill, especially since nothing happened anyway. But two nights later, after we had gone to bed I became strangely restless and couldn't sleep. A buoyant feeling of expectancy began to fill me hinting that something was going to happen.

It was a hot summer night and I got up to check the window fans. Was the Lord trying to tell me to stay awake because a fan might catch fire? That seemed silly so I carefully analyzed my feelings and found it was more an underlying expectancy of good not bad.

I wandered aimlessly through the house in the dark, peering out the windows at the yard washed in summer moonlight. Caught up in this strange sense I found myself saying with a new abandon, "thank you, Lord, for my husband---this house--my children." Finally I was able to drift off to sleep toward morning, still aware that something big was about to happen.

The alarm rang at 7:30 a.m. I was surprised to find that the bubbly expectancy hadn't left and the feeling remained with me through all the household routine as the day progressed. The small prayer group met that night and Bill said he didn't particularly want to go.

This time I felt at home. Perhaps I was less inhibited because of Bill's absence. At one point, I surprised myself by speaking up and suggesting that instead of asking the Lord for things we simply praise Him—an idea founded by the involuntary praise I'd known the night before. To my amazement they took me up on it. The balance of the evening was spent in prayers of praise. For the first time I felt a part of the group. Was this the reason for all the excitement I had felt, I wondered? But taking my emotional temperature I realized the expectancy still simmered.

It was over. Driving home I suddenly had an eerie feeling. I was not alone in the car. It was as though Jesus was my passenger! A pulsing Love seemed to fill the entire car and at that moment I felt as though hot oil were being poured down upon me, bathing my head first and then my whole body. I pulled off onto the side of the road and sat there in awe of the supernatural feeling that now enveloped me. This had to be it... the Baptism of the Holy Spirit!

Bill was asleep when I got home. I decided not to waken him. I'd tell him about it in the morning. A brief check on the children told me they were all covered and sleeping. I snapped a leash on our Collie, Laddie, and decided to take a walk hoping to savor this feeling that enfolded me.

The trees whispering secrets in the night breeze, the streetlights, the shadows—everything looked new and clean. Or maybe my eyes were new... God was real. He loved me. Everything would be alright. I knew with a clear inner certainty that the Lord would take care of Kent. How strange, this sensation of hot oil upon me, clothing me in a mantle of protection—protection against the world—my problems.

Abruptly I realized I did not have tongues. *Wasn't that downright polite of the Lord to honor my prayer asking that I not have tongues?* I thought. *He must realize that I'm just too sophisticated for such gibberish.* (Jesus, who was the One to give the Baptism must have winced, but smiled patronizingly and, in retrospect, I can imagine Him saying in a Jewish accent, "Have I got a surprise for you, little girl!")

The glow of God's presence surrounded me for over a week. There were days when I would stand at the backdoor and actually know Jesus was standing there beside me. One side of my body would feel heat. At the same time, a loud thought would surface in my mind as though from a source outside myself. Each time it would be teaching about scripture—in simple form which almost resembled parables.

Bill thought I had gone crazy. One evening at the dinner table I decided to broach the subject and include him in the day I'd spent with the Lord. I began, "I had the most beautiful day today," and promptly burst into tears.

Bill shoved his chair back impatiently and looked at me as if I were a stranger bound for an asylum. "Then what the devil are you crying about?"

I ladled out corn soufflé onto the twins' plates and sniffed, "If you're going to take that attitude I won't even tell you about it. You just don't understand because you haven't received the Holy Spirit," I said spitefully, smug in my new relationship with God. However, as soon as the words were out of my mouth a creeping uneasiness filled me. Was this experience a new thing to separate Bill and me? Was I wrong? Maybe I hadn't really received the Holy Spirit in the car that night. After all, I didn't have any tongues. I had to know.

Late that night I again crept into the linen closet, making certain that everyone was asleep. There was one small window without a curtain. Shafts of moonlight flooded the tiny room, frosting the stacks of sheets and towels with an imposing stateliness. Silently I prayed, "Lord, I guess I do want those tongues after all. I want everything You have for me... so much so that I'm going to just make up words until You give me the real thing."

Deliberately I began to whisper strange words thinking I was making them up, waiting for the real thing. It was easy; much like when I was a little girl and would pretend I was speaking a foreign language.

After a time a loud thought introduced itself as though from an outside source. This happened in the same manner I had come to recognize as the Lord's voice speaking to me. I *heard* more than thought: "You see, they've been there all along. This *is* the real thing. It's just that easy."

I couldn't believe it. I had been expecting some overpowering force to take hold of my tongue and make me blurt out foreign words.

Then I *had really* received the Holy Spirit in the car that night. That had been an overwhelming experience. Tonight there was no accompanying feeling at all. Therefore, I reasoned, if the tongues had been there all the time, then they must have been latent or dormant. Perhaps this had something to do with a blockage at a subconscious level. I hadn't really wanted a prayer language before. Tonight had my will to have them been the lever to release the tongues?

Almost conversationally, the loud thought of an answer came, "Just as your own will divided you from the tongues that you already had, your will is dividing you from Bill—not the Holy Spirit. A good relationship is yours; it is a matter of the will."

But I only toyed with this new instruction hardly digesting it. Perhaps I didn't want to hear. Preoccupation with my new prayer language turned my thoughts again to tongues.

God must have a sense of humor, I thought, *or He is certainly being extremely patient and indulgent with me. I should have been zapped with lightning for thinking I was too sophisticated for tongues,* foolishly remembering how delighted I had been that He had not given a Presbyterian "such gibberish". Or was it that He knew sooner or later I would be willing to fling away dictatorial conditions?

However, the longer I stayed in the closet the harder my own logic began to assault me, trying to erase any supernatural aspect of this new language, I was making it up... just making it up, pure and simple.

I wanted to believe this was the scriptural evidence of having received the Holy Spirit, but my own mind wouldn't let me. Finally I confessed, "Lord, I've got to settle this doubt, forgive me," and began to pray in my new language rapidly, accelerating to such speed that I had to admit my conscious mind could not be making up the words. In fact, the words seemed to be bypassing my mind completely. With relief I realized I'd settled it; I was convinced but now wondered skeptically, "So I really have tongues. But what good are they?"

A chain of circumstances dramatically answered my question within one week.

The following Tuesday night Jerry Davis, another Baptist minister in the prayer group, called proposing we explore a different prayer meeting with him and his wife, Carol, in Clarksville, Indiana. It was to be a special meeting, Jerry said. A Canadian Episcopalian Archbishop was to speak. Bill accepted the invitation.

Jerry said he'd pick us up and as I hurriedly dressed and rounded up a sitter I wondered if Bill would receive the Holy Spirit that night. Lately I had begun to whip up schemes, plotting just how God and I were going to get Bill into this experience. But the evening was for me.

The meeting was held in the red, brick, colonial home of Mitzi and Jack Hammon. As we climbed the steps from the hall to their living room I caught sight of the now familiar circle of chairs. Apparently this staging was universal for home prayer meetings—silver coffee urn glistening at the ready on the dining table. Even the warmth of the people seemed the same and had I been blindfolded, I would have thought I was in one of the meetings back in Louisville.

I expressed this to Jerry and his answer made sense, "Sandy," he said, "there's only one Holy Spirit and He's the common denominator. Of course, it's reasonable that He'll teach and guide everyone the same way in all locations."

Through the fast-growing crowd my attention focused on a small, gray-haired man in a black suit. A white clerical collar pronounced that he belonged to some religious order. This must be Archbishop Pattison, but why did I feel I knew him? I turned to Bill, "That must be the speaker over there. Somehow I have the feeling we've met before," I told him.

Bill drenched my fantasy. "It could very well be you feel that way because he looks just like Barry Fitzgerald in 'Going My Way'." he pointed out dryly.

It was true. George Pattison was almost the exact counterpart of Barry Fitzgerald in his priestly role—but Archbishop George Pattison was very real.

When the room became quiet, he began to unfold how he had received the Baptism of the Holy Spirit while still Dean of Queen Anne's Cathedral in Canada. A thick brogue and sly sparkles of humor laced his story with a refreshing charm. He was so candid and unassuming that I had a difficult time keeping up with the details of his story because of my wash of admiration, until he began to pinpoint one incident:

"It was late one night," he told us, "and I was praying in tongues before the altar in the cathedral. Abruptly a drunken sailor burst through the unlocked doors. He was dressed in the uniform of the Norwegian Navy. To my surprise he reeled down the aisle, grabbed me by the collar fairly lifting me off the floor."

"Why did you call me?" he demanded.

"But I didn't call you," I stammered.

"Oh yes, you did. You said in Norwegian, 'Olaf, come in here and accept Jesus Christ as your personal Lord and Savior.'"

"But I don't even speak Norwegian," George Pattison told the sailor. "My statement trailed off," he added, "as I suddenly realized God must have called him using what I'd thought was a prayer in tongues."

I couldn't believe my ears. But I did believe this fatherly, sincere priest who had endeared himself to me in such a few short minutes. My mind whirled with a new evaluation of tongues. If he was praying in tongues and said *that*… maybe my own tongues were important.

Archbishop Pattison was finished and I had to repress an urge to rush up and hug him. I wondered fleetingly if all females wanted to invite him home to dinner and smother him in Brussels sprouts and fried chicken for the honor of his presence.

The group took a coffee break on the invitation of our host, Jack Hammon. As we migrated toward the large urn in the corner, we learned that there was another Archbishop present—Archbishop Christopher Stanley of the Greek Orthodox Church in Louisville. I was eager to see this other priest as I was told he had come to hear about the Baptism in the Holy Spirit. We were told he wanted to investigate the validity of the experience. Bill and I slowly made our way toward the coffee oasis. Jerry spotted Christopher Stanley talking with a group of people. He had obviously shed his priestly garments for "civies" so most weren't aware of who he was.

My first impression was astonishment. The man had cauliflower ears! Mentally I pictured maybe he'd engaged in Golden Glove fights before he turned to ministry. When we were within earshot his conversation erased my image. He was extremely articulate.

The archbishop was saying, "I've always served Jesus to the best of my ability; therefore, I feel it's my duty to examine this Baptism of the Holy Spirit." His manner seemed to be defensive. "Frankly it's new to me. Not new to me in scripture, but I've never considered the possibility of experiencing it myself. I'll be honest. The aspect of tongues leaves me extremely skeptical."

"But the same experience that the disciples had is available to us today," a stocky man offered from the crowd fringing Christopher Stanley.

Suddenly my attention switched from Archbishop Stanley to a woman who stood directly next to me in the coffee line. She had opened her Bible at random as I watched and nudged the girl standing on the other side of her.

"Look what I opened to." I heard her say. "See here in Act 21:37 it says 'Do you know Greek?' I wonder if my tongue is Greek?" She giggled and pointed to the sentence in the Bible.

There was a silence in Christopher Stanley's conversation and he obviously overheard the woman. "Madam," he began formally, "if you would be willing to say a few words in your tongue, I could tell you if it is Greek or not as I'm a Greek Orthodox priest."

The woman was obviously embarrassed. Apparently she had meant it as a joke and Archbishop Stanley had put her on the spot. The crowd around them both became silent.

The woman bowed her head, putting a hand over her mouth and began mumbling words in a language that sounded not unlike my own. Abruptly her tone and language changed markedly. She said one sentence in a loud clear voice.

Not only our little group, but the entire room became silent. The articulate archbishop seemed speechless, visibly shaken. Slowly and with great deliberation he seemed to force out the words, "I cannot believe this! The tongue you have spoken in is not Greek, but classical Latin. You have told me in this language that the trip I am planning to take is in God's Will for me."

The woman seemed to be as staggered by the incident as the archbishop.

"Surely this is of God… this Baptism of the Holy Spirit and tongues, for no one knew of my plans except God Himself. This has to be of God." he repeated shaking his head.

The meeting was over. The room remained hushed as the people left and I perceived there had been a supernatural curtain to this meeting. Few spiritual encores could surpass what we had just witnessed.

Later, getting ready for bed, my mind sifted back over the events of the evening. I sensed that perhaps I'd not been at the Hammon's by chance. Because of both archbishops I had a rapid-fire answer to my question, "What good are these tongues I have?"

Slowly a comparison began to take shape in my mind. I remembered the first day when Kent and I had walked through the door of NIH. We had entered a whole new world. Now that my doubts about the infilling of the Holy Spirit were settled and I'd personally tasted it, I realized I had walked through a second doorway—this time into a supernatural world. I was to find that as I began to take baby steps, the door of the past creaked slowly shut behind me and miracles began to happen.

Chapter Fifteen

*T*he flight attendant handed us our breakfast trays: fluffy scrambled eggs, tiny crisp sausages, an exotic arrangement of orange slices mingled with blueberries on mint leaves, and steaming coffee. I checked to be sure Kent's tray held a glass of milk and tied the napkin around his neck bib-fashion. As I offered the first forkful of eggs he pushed my hand away.

"I can't, Mommy."

"Kent, just one bite," I coaxed. Perhaps I was pushing my luck. This was no ordinary case of airsickness. I had to talk with the doctor about his constant nausea just as soon as we got into NIH for his monthly checkup.

"Please, honey, one bite." Obediently Kent took the offered mouthful and gagged.

I reached into the pocket of the forward seat and grabbed the air-sickness container, ringing for the trays to be taken away. The food suddenly looked unappetizing. How could I possible enjoy a meal when my child couldn't even force it down because of the leukemia drugs he was getting?

Kent leaned his head on the cool window and went to sleep. With a start I realized I no longer resented the constant cleaning up after Kent's nausea bouts. All I felt was compassion. I hadn't even resented sending back the lovely tray. How long had I been free of this? A day? A week? Maybe something was changing me for my resentment had just dissolved without my even being aware of it until this episode with the trays.

Summer rain pounded the runways as our plane landed at National Airport in Washington and nosed into the gate. Trustingly, Kent took my hand, unaware of the painful check-up that awaited him at NIH.

I had seen a "bone marrow" once before. This test, though extremely uncomfortable was the only way to determine the extent of the leukemia. It had been explained to me that the blood cells are made in the marrow of the bone. In order to tell what is medically going on inside, a large needle is inserted into the bone of the sacrum or lower part of the back. A syringe is attached and marrow is sucked or aspirated out into the syringe for testing. There is no anesthetic other than the local numbing of a Novocaine derivative.

I shuddered knowing what I was leading Kent into, but it had to be done. It had to be viewed from the standpoint of helping him I resolved. However, Kent had a unique problem. Dr. Gallo had explained when he discharged Kent and allowed him to come home that Kent had fibrosis of the bone marrow. This meant the marrow had become filled with scar tissue, probably due to the drugs that he had been given, the doctor explained. In fact, it had become impossible to get any marrow out for an examination.

Before his discharge the problem had become so perplexing that Kent was sent to Georgetown Hospital by NIH for a bone marrow scan. A doctor there had developed a technique to photograph the marrow and NIH wanted to see if he had any sites of good marrow left. They found a few, but Kent had to endure endless bone marrow tests in unusual places such as the knee or hip with no results. Now months had passed without being able to determine the extent of his disease. This frightened me. I'd been taught by NIH how important this procedure was.

The Out Patient waiting room was choked with children and parents. There was a spirit of family reunion as we checked on the condition of each other's children and drank coffee from the cart pushed by a Red Cross volunteer. We rejoiced together over the patients who were doing well and shared our grief over those who hadn't. There seemed to be a mother's grapevine. Through it we learned what children were "on the floor" upstairs and not doing as well as those in Clinic who were allowed to go home.

In the midst of so much shared love and concern I was smacked by comparison. There was a spirit of family reunion because we actually *were* a family. This was the same brand of warmth and caring that I had experienced in the prayer groups. Perhaps these people were not all Christians, but because of our mutual adversity we had caught a special current of God's Love operating among us.

"Kent is next, Mrs. Ghost," interrupted my thoughts.

Kent smiled broadly at Dr. Gallo. Even at the age of three, he seemed to sense that the doctor was helping him even though it hurt. He stretched his arms upward and Dr. "Jello" carried him into the treatment room for his bone marrow.

Later after Kent had undergone all the sophisticated testing, Dr. Gallo called me into his office for a consultation. "Good to see you, Mrs. Ghost. How's he been?" He laid heavy horn-rimmed glasses on the desk.

Was it my imagination, or had our doctor aged a bit since we had last seen him? I thought I detected new lines in his face and more than the sprinkling of gray hair he had had just a few short months ago. I wondered how any doctor, dedicated to save lives, could walk through this experience with these children and not feel a measure of defeat. My new faith champed at the bit to tell him about the Lord.

But I said, "He's vomiting constantly. That's our only complaint."

He nodded his head. "That's par for the course with the treatment he's getting, but we ought to be able to control it better. Have you tried suppositories and the prescription I gave you?"

I told him I'd exhausted everything, nothing worked. He seemed concerned and scratched another prescription onto a small pad in front of him. "Let's try this. Now, Kent's situation remains the same. We had another unsuccessful bone marrow--a dry tap--that, as you know, means we're unable to tell just what the leukemia percentage is."

He frowned and swiveled to face me. "I wish I could give you more to go on, but as long as this situation exists we'll just have to rely on his general condition and blood counts. Those are good. On this basis I've discharged him for another two months, but I want you to get blood counts in Louisville so we can stay on top of the situation."

We shook hands. A wave of gratitude welled up within me for this dedicated man and what he was trying to do for my son and all the others. But there were no words to tell him. I formally thanked him and collected a tearful Kent in the waiting room. The doctors always seemed to prefer talking with parents without the patient's presence.

After we had erased the tears with cookies and a coke, Kent begged to go up to the playroom on the second floor to ride the rocking horse. We had three hours to kill before we had to leave for the airport so I agreed. Kent greeted the wooden horse like an old friend.

As I sat in one of the small chairs I marveled again at the spirit of these hospitalized children. A boy of about five ran down the hall at top speed while pushing an IV pole. The IV needle was inserted into a vein in his arm, the cord stretching to the bottle of medicine above. Even at such breakneck speed he guarded the bottle that dripped into the cord as he ran.

A delicate little blonde of about three sat across the room at a child-size table, laboring over a piece of modeling clay. As one of the children sat down next to her she warned, "Watch out for my IV" moving the tubing out of the way of the other child. Even the younger children seemed to sense the importance of protecting the flow of the drugs they were getting intravenously. They knew from experience that if it infiltrated, a new vein-site would have to be found, and introducing the needle into small veins could be painful. In this world of leukemia even the smallest tyke learned to acclimate to the constant presence of an IV running when they had to be hospitalized. They seemed to accept it with a grace that astonished me. They were special children—all of them.

I heard running footsteps in the hall. Stepping out of the playroom quickly, I looked toward the nurse's station. Something was wrong.

Gene Palmer, Kim's father, ran down the hall. His eyes broadcast fear and I sensed he was close to tears. As he neared, I intercepted him.

"Gene, what's happened? You look awful."

"Kim's had a cerebral hemorrhage. We had a police motorcycle escort from

D.C. and the Maryland police picked us up as we crossed the district line. Don't think we got him here in time." He fumbled for a cigarette with shaking hands, then shoved it back in the pack, obviously realizing he couldn't smoke it here. "Doctor says he may not live."

In a flash it all came back... Kent's cerebral hemorrhage.

"I don't know the circumstances," I tried to comfort him, "but Kent had a cerebral hemorrhage—they didn't think he would live either, and two days later he was riding that rocking horse over there, completely alright, Gene."

He blinked, looking like I'd thrown him a lifeline. "You've got to talk to my wife." He grabbed me by the hand, fairly dragging me down the hall.

I had never met Laura Palmer. In fact, I'd only seen Gene once before, and a flood of misgivings swamped me. How could I meet her this way? What could I possibly say to her?

Gene yanked open the door to the doctor's office, holding it for me to step inside and shut the door from the outside. To make matters worse, I suddenly realized he hadn't come in with me. We were alone.

Three desks positioned at different angles were covered by microscopes, other equipment and random papers. Chairs were the only other furniture in the room. At one of those desks a stunning, dark-haired woman sat crying, her head rested on arms that nested in a stack of papers.

With a start the past came back to me. I had sat at that same desk when I was told Kent would probably not live... for the same reason. Though we'd never met, a deep sense of identification moved me to a boldness that surprised me.

I pulled up a chair beside her. "Laura, I'm Sandra Ghost. I have a son with leukemia too."

The woman raised her head from the desk and looked at me in surprise. I had never seen such beautiful eyes. They were dark wells of sorrow begging for help.

I took a deep breath and began, "I've got to tell you about my son, Kent. He had a cerebral hemorrhage too... just like Kim."

Laura listened intently as I told her the entire story of Kent's cerebral hemorrhage, stressing the point that just like in Kim's case, the doctors had felt Kent could not possibly live. I ended by pointing out what we felt had been God's intervention, through the elevator operator's prayer, as Kent's recovery had been unexplainable medically.

She said nothing, but I could tell there was an electric intelligence beyond those dark eyes that sparked occasionally in response to different points in the story.

There was a long silence and I finally stammered, "Laura, have you prayed for Kim?"

She fidgeted in the chair and finally confessed, "You may think this strange, especially since I'm Catholic, but I haven't been able to pray for Kim since I found out he has leukemia." A heavy southern accent clothed the halting words.

Only because I'd gone through it myself, I could clearly identify with what Laura must be feeling. Suddenly it was clear that the resentment toward God I had felt in the beginning must be consuming her too.

I said, "Have you ever felt that God was punishing you with Kim's disease? When Kent was first diagnosed I felt like shaking a fist at God and shouting, 'How can You do this to me?' Have you felt like this too?"

Tears welled up in Laura's eyes again, "Yes, and I know there's a God somewhere… but maybe not for me. Frankly, what I feel now is bitterness—just bitterness."

Hearing my reply to her almost as a bystander, I was astonished as I found myself saying, "Laura, the Lord didn't give Kim leukemia and I don't believe He wants him to have it any more than you do."

"I don't know what you mean." The soft southern accent was now a whisper.

"Well, if you, who are obviously a loving parent, would never give your child a disease, then surely a loving, heavenly Father wouldn't. Can you believe that?"

Laura nodded "yes".

Encouraged by her response I went on, "Everywhere that Jesus met sickness or disease He said it was not from the Father; it was from the devil."

I'd reached her! I could tell. But just as this realization broke through I sensed deeply that it hadn't been by my own effort. The Holy Spirit must have had a heavy hand in our conversation putting words in my mouth that I hadn't even thought through, but words that made sense.

"Laura, let's invite God into this situation through prayer, for He's not in it now." There it was again, a boldness not my own. "I would get Mr. Botts to pray with us if I could but when I inquired about him they said he'd retired. But we can do this together, okay?"

Eagerly Laura bowed her head and we prayed for Kim.

Later we bracketed our prayer time at approximately 4:00 p.m. Kim's hemorrhage had occurred at 3:00 p.m. Later Laura learned from the doctor that sometime during this hour, Kim's heart and breathing stopped. He died. Kim dramatically was revived somewhere around 4:00 p.m. but was then comatose.

Can there be allowance for coincidence with the Lord? Or are all things part of a gigantic plan? There were three doctors who attended the juvenile leukemia patients, each doctor having specific patients. I found out later that both Kent and Kim had drawn the same doctor—Dr. Gallo.

The next time I saw Laura was two months later. She described what had happened to Kim that day after I had left her to catch the plane back to Louisville.

In her own words: "I sat endless hours in the solarium as Kim lay in a coma. Doctor Gallo came in later that night and painted a gloomy picture of his condition. I sat through the night waiting for them to come and tell me it was all over. Dr. Gallo had told Gene and me that even if Kim made it, there was a likelihood that there would be brain damage as his heart and respiration had stopped for a time after we got him to the hospital. It was a hideous night... we counted the hours... Kim lay in a coma, paralyzed for fourteen hours."

"At 10:00 o'clock the next morning Dr. Gallo burst through the door. His first words were: 'Kim's going to be alright, Mrs. Palmer! He stabilized quite suddenly and there seems to be no brain damage or paralysis of any kind!'"

"I wanted to hug him and stammered gratefully, 'Thank you, doctor, for saving my child!'"

"Mrs. Palmer," he said soberly, "a greater power than me saved Kim. Your child was dead. At one point Kim had no pulse and no respiration."

"He turned and walked out of the room. Gene and I just stared at each other in disbelief. Kim's recovery was identical in pattern to Kent's—it had to be God. I think he sent you to us that day."

A cerebral hemorrhage is uncommon in leukemia. There are other enemies. Wasn't it strange that both Kent and Kim had stabilized in exactly the same fashion? A margin of coincidence had given them the same doctor—our Dr. Gallo. I remembered my urge to tell this kind, sensitive man about the Lord. But had the double experience of living through Kent and Kim's remarkable recoveries said more to this doctor than any religious platitudes I could have thrown at him, I wondered?

Was Laura right? Had the Holy Spirit planned for us to be there on 2 East at that point in time? What if Kent hadn't asked to ride the rocking horse? What if we'd gone to the cafeteria or Occupational Therapy instead? Certainly I had been reinforced by His presence when I talked to Laura. I just didn't possess that kind of boldness or articulation on a subject that was still brand new to me.

In point of fact, shortly after I'd become a new Christian one of the women who regularly attended the prayer meetings had given me a gold lapel pin shaped like a fish hook. It was rather large, very handsome, and Betty said it would initiate and spark conversation that might lead to my being able to testify. I decided to wear it on the lapel of my champagne wool suit the next time Kent and I went to NIH

We were in the office of the Administrative Officer of the Day picking up our tickets to fly home when he commented, "Well, I see you like to fish, Mrs. Ghost," he handed me a large envelope.

Ah ha... the pin's giving me an opening, I thought and took a deep breath. "I'm a fisher of men," I smugly told him.

His eyebrows raised in a Groucho Marx leer. He smiled broadly and nodded.

"I mean... for Christ... for Christ..." I sputtered. "I'm a fisher of men for Christ." I grabbed Kent's hand and couldn't get out of his office fast enough!

Reflecting on this past embarrassment, I decided to shy away from manipulating openings. It was better to let the Holy Spirit manage the circumstances.

Back at home, two weeks passed in the bliss of a normal household routine. That Tuesday it was my turn to host the women's weekly prayer meeting. Each of us eagerly looked forward to this intimate weekly housecleaning of our souls together. There seemed to be an unseen cord of closeness that bound us together and because of this we were in one accord—the one factor stressed in the Bible as present when the Holy Spirit fell at Pentecost. This total accord that ebbed beneath the surface of all our meetings seemed to get many prayer jobs done. In the few short months we had been meeting we had seen some pretty powerful prayer results.

I had just passed around a tray of donuts when the telephone rang. It was Loretta Hopper. Breathlessly she explained that she and Doris Roan were leaving for the meeting when Doris had fallen in the driveway. She had broken her leg—a horrible fracture as the bone was protruding through the skin. Loretta said she had just called an ambulance to take Doris to Baptist Hospital and would I get the women who were there to pray.

Before I went back into the living room to tell the girls, I called several of the men activating the prayer chain. There was no prayer meeting in my home that day. It moved to Baptist Hospital.

Beads of perspiration covered Doris' upper lip as she lay in the hospital bed. She was obviously trying to be brave, but seemed to be in torturous pain. We tiptoed into the hall as an orthopedic surgeon made the examination.

Exasperation filled me. Where was God? Here were all these people praying for Doris and nothing was happening. The surgeon came out of the door. His swift pace never broke cadence as he tossed our way, "We'll have to operate immediately. It's a compound-fracture." He disappeared around the corner.

Bud Roan, Doris' husband, joined us in the hall and explained that Doris was being prepped for surgery. We moved the prayer meeting to the waiting room and Carter Foster joined our small group there. Apparently the prayer chain was at work sending out the call for help as others arrived at the hospital.

Carter, like Bob Beckett, was a Baptist Seminary student. He smiled warmly, confidently at us. "Let's join hands in a circle while we pray for Doris. This will be an active expression of our agreement for this healing," he suggested.

But it's already too late, I pouted mentally. *God's missed His chance!* However, I placed my hand in Loretta's on one side—Bud Roan's on the other.

Joe Hardy appeared at the door. He must have heard too and gotten off from work, I thought. The circle broke momentarily to include him.

We prayed silently. There were other people in the room. *They must think this is the prelude to a square dance with all of us joining hands in a circle,* I thought, slightly embarrassed to be a part of any spiritual demonstration.

At that moment the surgeon who had examined Doris poked his head in the door. His gaze swept the circle. Spotting Bud Roan, he motioned him into the hall.

We heard clearly, "Mr. Roan, we're not going to have to operate on your wife." There was a pause. "I can't understand this. I know I examined her thoroughly before arranging for surgery—the bone was protruding through the skin. The fracture showed on X-ray. She was prepped and taken to the operating room." He seemed to be recounting it step-by-step for his own benefit.

"Strangely, once she was on the table..." His voice trailed off. "Well Mr. Roan... what I'm trying to say is... that leg's already been set!"

Bud walked back into the waiting room with hands clasped over his head in the classic prize fighter victory sign. "Jesus did it again," he announced triumphantly.

Our little group stood woodenly still in a mutual silence of dismay. Finally, Carter quipped, "My, what a coincidence!"

Grateful laughter filled the small room. I couldn't help noticing the faces of the other people in the waiting room. From their expressions they seemed to be impressed by the results of what had happened... of something they could not understand, but they witnessed the prayers.

That night, after the children were tucked in, I eagerly told Bill about Doris' healing. I'd saved it for a time when we could discuss it alone.

"That's fantastic," Bill agreed. "How could anyone not believe in healing after seeing a miracle like that?"

"It set me thinking. Well, not just this particular incident, but Kim's remarkable recovery and Kent's healing twice... now this."

"I think I know what you're going to say, but go on." Bill seemed to sense my personal application to all this.

"Okay. If God is real, if He still heals like we've just had proof of, maybe we're supposed to take Kent out of NIH... just trust the Lord for his healing."

Bill frowned slightly. Crossing his arms, he stared into space. "Do you realize the responsibility involved in making a decision to pull him out of NIH?"

"Yes, of course I've thought of it. If anything went wrong. But if we were really being led by the Lord to do it, nothing would."

Bill turned and faced me. "Sandy, I realize that. But we can't even consider this based on other people's experience. God deals differently with different people. We can't even base our decision on scripture without the Holy Spirit leading us to do it. You agree?"

I shook my head "yes".

"Then let's put it to the Lord. Ask for direct guidance—now."

Bill reached out for my hand and we knelt together in front of the living room couch. At length he said aloud, "Father, in Jesus name, we thank You for this new life with You. You've gone out of Your way to prove to us that You can heal. How does this apply to Kent? Please show us."

"Lord, do You want us to take him out of NIH," I added more specifically. "Or do You want us to stay there, not give him any medicine, load a suitcase with the pills he should have taken after six years and present them to the doctors? He might even be healed now for all we know—they can't get any marrow out of him with the fibrosis he has. How can we tell whether or not he is healed? Kent belongs to You. We're just babysitting him for You. Show us what You would have us do."

The answer came at the end of two months.

Chapter Sixteen

---◦✦◦---

Kent and I traveled to NIH for his bone marrow checkup and chemo. Afterward, Kent's new doctor called me into his office. The beloved "Doctor Jello" had moved on and an entirely new team now attended the juvenile leukemia patients. The typical white coat on this new doctor covered a loud Hawaiian shirt embellished with a necklace of strange beads. The rather hippy-type outfit was punctuated with sandal clad feet. He had the slight appearance of having just gotten off a surf board, but I was to find he was most professional. He greeted me with, "Good news! We were able to get marrow out this time. The fibrosis seems to be gone."

"Gone?" I echoed. "How can scar tissue just disappear?"

"You've got me on that one," he confessed. "There's no reasonable explanation I can give you, Mrs. Ghost."

He seemed to dismiss the subject with a shrug of his shoulders. "However," he warned, "there are slightly less than five percent leukemic cells showing in the marrow. I strongly suggest you maintain strict faithfulness to the pills Kent is to take at home. Let's get his IV started now."

I had time to ponder this on the plane back to Louisville as Kent slept. Secretly I hated the pills that were part of Kent's treatment. I knew that they were the agents of the extreme nausea which still plagued him, separating my child from a normal intake of food. But Bill and I had asked for guidance. One specific part of that prayer had suggested we would never know if the Lord had healed him or not because of the bone marrow fibrosis. Now suddenly, unexplainably, it was gone.

By this time I felt I had seen the Lord in action enough to know that if He hadn't allowed the small percentage of leukemia to be there we might have thought he was healed. Why were they there? Had the Lord healed the fibrosis to show us positively that there was still leukemia in Kent's system? Then maybe He was telling us to stick with NIH and their treatment. I decided to rest a conclusion until I talked with Bill and see how he felt.

That night I told him exactly what had happened stressing that it had to be a small miracle for the fibrosis to mysteriously disappear after six months.

With a methodical precision Bill reviewed the facts: "We asked for guidance concerning NIH. Your one specific question, Sandy, inquired if Kent was healed or not and this was unknown because of the presence of the fibrosis. Now... today, we've had two equally specific answers covering both questions."

"We've got to regard it as some kind of answer because of the timing involved," I agreed.

"If we believe God can heal," he said thoughtfully weighing each word, "then we'd have to say He could have taken away that small percentage... after all, we asked."

I nodded in agreement.

"Then the fibrosis could have been healed to show it to us."

I nodded again.

"At this point, even though we know it's God's will to heal, I feel we'd be outside His guidance to pull Kent out of NIH, Sandy."

I had never felt so close to Bill. He seemed like a spiritual knight in shining armor at the moment. "That's exactly the conclusion I reached on the way home. If our lives are in God's hands and if our prayers are heard, how can we dismiss this as being anything but guidance?"

But the school of the Holy Spirit now dished out an accelerated program to help Kent.

The following morning Kent wakened me at 5:00 a.m. Pathetically he vomited time-after-time—the results of his IV at NIH the day before. Were we wrong in our analysis of what we thought had been our guidance?

It was Sunday. Like most families we went to church, had a large roast for Sunday dinner and tried to plan a day of relaxation. It was a sunny, summer day and Bill suggested that afternoon we pack a picnic lunch and drive south to a park on the river near Fort Knox. The children squeezed into the back of our small Dodge Dart, flattened together by two safety belts, like sticks in a pack of chewing gum.

"Is this really your idea of a restful day?" I shot the question sarcastically at Bill trying to be heard over the chorus of "Move over, Lisa"

"Don't stick you're elbow in my ribs!"

"Kurt kicked me!"

We headed out Dixie Highway with a picnic basket and a backseat full of wrangling, squirming children. But when we got to our destination the mood changed. The park presided on a cliff high above the river—the view was splendid. Stately oaks towered above us, lending their shadows for a breath of cool air.

The children invented a game. Whoever gathered the most acorns would get a prize. The award was a coke and Kent won. I watched with misgivings as he gulped the entire contents of the bottle with pride. Surely he couldn't keep it down.

It was time to start for home. We rounded up the children and began to drive up the bumpy, dirt road that led to the main highway. Just before we turned onto the main route to Louisville, Kent vomited all over himself, the backseat and the floor carpeting.

Bill pulled into the first gas station on the main highway. I carried Kent into the Ladies room, and stripped him of all his clothes. Setting him on the closed toilet seat, I washed off the sour smelling results of his nausea.

"Stay right there, honey. I'll be right back," I told him and went out to the car, handing the soiled clothes to Bill to stow in the trunk.

As I re-entered the restroom I was suddenly filled with an unexplainable rage at this "thing" that was doing this to Kent. I had no idea what I was doing, but I began to literally stalk Kent—not Kent himself, but what was causing this constant battle between him and food.

My child watched wide-eyed as I advanced toward him.

To my own surprise, I clamped one hand on his head and commanded, "Come out of him in Jesus name!" The fury in my own voice frightened me. What had made me act this way?

Kent began to laugh, an odd and eerie type of laughter, almost like a release. At first I thought it was because his mother was acting like a crazy woman. But he kept up this odd laughter all the way from Fort Knox to Louisville… twenty-five miles.

He sat in front with us now and Bill and I looked at each other across him.

"What's eating him?" Bill questioned. "What the heck went on in there?"

I told him in clothed language so the older children wouldn't be frightened. Bill seemed as puzzled as I was about what had actually happened.

The minute we walked in the house Kent asked for food. This was unusual. It was the first time in months he had displayed an interest in food. I got the leftover roast out of the refrigerator with some misgivings, afraid it would all come back up again.

As fast as I could slice it Kent wolfed it down. Bill stood by and watched with me in amazement as Kent ate nearly one-half of a three pound roast beef and six slices of bread.

We waited for the onslaught of nausea. It never came. Afterward, as the weeks stretched on, Kent's nausea never returned again!

We were to find out later exactly what had taken place spiritually to release Kent from his torturous attacks of drug side-effects. But at the time Bill and I were content to just view the marvelous results of what seemed like a moment's madness in a gas station.

Kent's bone marrow fibrosis was gone; within a week, six months of drastic nausea disappeared in a split second. It was almost as though by discovering that God wanted us to leave Kent in the hands of NIH, heavenly doorways of protection had now opened to wipe away the discomfort caused by the leukemia drugs.

If the Holy Spirit became our Teacher as it was promised in the Bible, then it seemed we were in a crash course to learn and again He used the weekly prayer meeting to stress a spiritual point in our lessons. That night we were late and as we slipped into the room Bob Beckett seemed to be telling the group a story.

We settled into our chairs while he was saying: "I can't tell you the name of this fellow for obvious reasons, but he's a seminary student too. He called and asked if I'd see him. Said he had a problem. I picked him up and we drove around Cherokee Park while he talked. Seems the Lord gave (I'll call him Ed) a dream showing him that he had three demons. Ed claimed that in the dream they were represented by balloons with the names imprinted on them. He saw Jesus pop two of them, but the third was left. Ed confessed to me the names on the balloons were uncontrollable vices in his life that he had always tried to hide. He felt Jesus had delivered him from two of the demons, but left the last one to be cast out."

Bob squinted, surveying his audience. He rubbed big, bony hands together and boomed, "Glory! I sure wished he hadn't picked on me to do the job!"

Laughter filled the room and some nodded knowingly. *Had Bill and I arrived at the tail-end of some joke?* My mind whirled. *Surely Bob couldn't be serious. If poor Ed-what-ever-his-name-was thought he had demons he must have been a candidate for the funny farm!*

Bob squirmed in his seat and grinned sheepishly. "I'd never handled anything like this before. I knew demons were scriptural—I believe in them—but I'd never prayed for deliverance, so as Ed talked I began to pray in tongues.

"We got out of the car and walked to a picnic table in the park. As Ed sat down on the table he suddenly seemed to have a seizure, falling onto the ground. As he writhed and twitched at my feet I was terrified."

The group sat in hushed suspense.

"I knew Ed wasn't epileptic. He was going through all the scriptural appearances of deliverance and believe me, I was scared! I paced back and forth helplessly praying in tongues and the thoughts raced through my head, 'What if this thing goes into me? What if Ed stays this way, he'll die before an ambulance can get here? What if a car comes by and someone sees us?' Suddenly I felt a surging power come into my hands. I had a decided leading to put those hands on him. I yelled, 'Come out of him in Jesus' name,' and as I did this, Ed jumped to his feet, completely normal and praising the Lord."

Bob's words yanked at my memory. That was precisely what I'd said and done that day in the gas station when I had been infuriated by Kent's constant nausea. It had been the turning point for the attacks hadn't returned, but was I casting out a demon that day? How could I do that when I didn't even believe in evil spirits?

I watched in wide-eyed astonishment as the room erupted with cheers of "Hallelujah" and "Praise the Lord". Were all these people crazy? Did they actually believe Bob Beckett's story? I trusted him to tell the truth, but I thought believing in demons went out with the Dark Ages.

Bob seemed to sense my reservations from across the room. "You look like you've seen a ghost, Sandy." He grinned. "No pun intended. You don't believe my testimony?"

I fumbled with embarrassment as I suddenly became the focus of attention. "Not that I don't believe you," I stammered, "Well... I'm having trouble adjusting to the idea of demons. But I'll bet Edgar Allen Poe would be proud of you."

There was scattered laughter again, but I felt the group was laughing with me, not at me and my embarrassment eased.

"But the evidence of an evil spirit actually taking possession of an individual is scriptural, Sandy," Bob said. His tone was kindly.

There was much head-nodding around the circle in support of Bob's statement. Did all these people have such medieval beliefs, I wondered? I looked toward Bill for reinforcement. His expression suggested perhaps I'd put my foot in it by voicing my views.

I hoped my tone sounded intellectual. "Don't you people believe that Jesus just used the term 'demon' to explain what we now know are psychological difficulties? After all, civilization then was not as advanced as it is now. It was a different type of culture."

Bob seemed to enjoy the challenge of my arguments. "Sandy, the field of psychology is just beginning to admit the possibilities of possession. In fact, the Psychology Department of one large university down south has made some remarkable experiments and studies on this. I know of one positive study that involved a woman pronounced incurably insane. Several ministries approached the university asking permission to pray for deliverance for the patient.

"This was done under strict clinical conditions, with doctors present, as the ministers cast out the demons in Jesus' name. At the end of the session the patient was pronounced completely normal... by her own attending psychiatrists."

"That's incredible!" I shivered lightly. "But it still sounds like voodoo or black magic to me."

"Maybe we need to do a little Bible researching on the subject tonight," Bob suggested and reached for his large black leather Bible. "Let's turn to the fifth chapter of Mark."

The balance of the meeting was spent in a systematic search through scripture. I was surprised to find that not only did Jesus have the power to cast out evil spirits, but the disciples practiced this as well. In fact, a passing parade of demons threaded their way through the New Testament, in each instance leaving their victims when commanded to do so by Jesus or the disciples in His Name.

Still hanging onto my intellectual theory, at one point I asked, "Couldn't it be that just by a word from Jesus the person's problem left? That wouldn't necessarily have to mean it was an entity or a spirit."

Bob cocked his head to one side, almost as though he were listening for some type of guidance to answer me. No one else in the room offered comment.

After a time he said, "We just read about the man with a legion of demons that Jesus cast into the swine, right? I have a theory that perhaps the Lord allowed the demons to go into the swine for a purpose. If you had been there, Sandy, and actually seen the man change before your eyes, and then immediately a nearby herd of swine stampede, throwing themselves off a cliff, wouldn't it have been visible proof that a transformation of some kind had taken place?"

"I guess so," I said, trapped be the admission.

"Well, it's just a personal theory, but perhaps there were people there that day who didn't believe in demons either. The Lord gave them visible proof."

"You've got me there… but it's still hard for me to believe." I held stubbornly to my own opinion.

"I'll say 'amen' to that!" Bill sided with me.

As we left the meeting later, one woman lovingly patted me on the shoulder. "Don't wrestle around with this," she suggested. "Just set it on a shelf for now. Tell the Lord to show you what He wants you to learn about it, in His way and in His timing."

I promised I would, not realizing that the Lord was proving a point I needed to know.

Sunday morning was a rat race. Just getting a family our size ready for church on time challenged my Christianity. We hurried through breakfast and I scrambled the twins into their clothes while rooting through the closet for my own dress.

"Calm down!" Bill called out from the bathroom, attacking his morning stubble with a razor. "Some philosopher once said, 'A rat race is only won by rats.' By the way, I don't have any clean socks."

"We're going to be late for church," I threatened, heading for the dryer to search for socks.

"You want to be on time and break with family tradition?"

I herded everyone to the car wondering if we were all clothed properly underneath. Bill and I were attending the largest Presbyterian church in Kentucky with a lengthy name to match its size—Harvey Browne Memorial Presbyterian Church.

The adult Sunday school class was conducted by an outstanding minister who was semi-retired. Bill and I had decided that if the Lord had favorites among His servants, Murray Peegram must have headed the list. Gray haired, distinguished Mr. Peegram taught the Bible to his class with a gifted knack of projecting us as students right into the text as though we were shaking hands with Moses, John, or Paul.

`As usual, we were late and slipped into the stiff-backed chairs just as Mr. Peegram opened his notes on the lectern. He smiled at the class.

"Do you believe in demons?" He asked, cocking his head to one side.

There was no response.

Smile wrinkles creased around his eyes which twinkled teasingly. "Jesus did," he said softly.

I turned toward Bill in astonishment and whispered behind my hand, "Here it is again! Does the comfortable old Presbyterian church accept this?"

For the balance of the hour, Mr. Peegram skillfully wove in and out of scripture, lacing episodes concerning evil spirits together to convince us they existed. Discussion time was a free-for-all. Apparently the majority seemed to side with my former opinion. But now I yearned to tell them what had happened with Kent in the gas station.

Bill must have sensed my churning desire to blurt out the whole story as he leaned over and cautioned kiddingly, "You keep your mouth shut, young lady. Nobody's going to believe that story anyway."

He was right, but I had a hunch that Mr. Peegram would have believed.

That night as we readied for bed I asked Bill, "Don't you think it's rather odd that all this business about demons seems to me coming at us all at once? In fact, it was just the beginning of the week when we heard Bob Beckett's story about casting out a demon… and now today, we walk into Sunday School and bingo—demons again."

"Sandy, you have a knack for reading something into everything." Bill balled his tee shirt up and scored two points by tossing it into the laundry basket.

I folded my arms, planting myself in front of him. "Okay, I want to know just where you stand on this."

"You mean do I believe in evil spirits?" He looked at me questioningly. "If you'd asked me last week I would have said 'no', but after the cram course in demonology we've had….." His voice trailed off.

"I'm fairly convinced, Bill, that what happened in the gas station with Kent that day---when I said... well, no, I actually *yelled* at something in Kent to 'come out of him in Jesus' name' I was casting out a demon. It worked, you know."

Bill raised his eyebrows in obvious skepticism.

"Maybe it worked before I believed in demons because it wasn't me doing it—it was the Holy Spirit in me doing it." I felt like I had to defend what I'd done.

"Let's see how long it works."

Would it really hold I wondered? Would Kent be able to eat normally now even with monthly chemotherapy?

Chapter Seventeen

*W*inter pounced on Louisville that year like a snarling polar bear. Snow swirled outside in small white tornadoes that danced down Cornell Place. Kent and Kurt raced small scooter cars round and round the dining room table in their own version of the Indianapolis 500. Freezing rain spattered against the dining room window, reminding me that I was imprisoned with two energetic three year olds. I reflected that in the months that had passed, Kent had never suffered a return of nausea. I was so grateful to the Lord for what had happened that day in the gas station. Surely it had been a deliverance from a spirit that had insinuated itself into Kent's situation on the invitation of the drug side effects. Bill and I had to agree that this put an entirely different perspective on chemotherapy side effects.

Plastic wheels ground against the bare hardwood floor, punctuated by enthusiastic screams of delight each time a corner was rounded. The noise was deafening. "It would be just my luck to have the landlord drop by," I muttered to myself and crossed through the living room to make sure the floor was not being gouged by their wheels.

The miracle of plastic had spared it scratches. I stood looking at the floor, wishing it were carpeted. We could only afford carpet for the living room. It was an old house and gaping cracks ran like canyons between each board in the hardwood. I was probably the only woman in Louisville who could sweep her floor and have no dirt left to put in the dustpan. It all filtered down into the basement.

But the basement was where my worst enemy lurked—the hot water heater. On the day we moved in, our landlord had given me a guided tour of the house. As we reached the basement he pointed to a squat, black, pot-bellied object in the corner.

"They just don't make 'em like that anymore." He gestured proudly.

"I'm sure they don't," I said apprehensively. "What is it?"

"The hot water heater!" His tone reminded me of a used car salesman. "Instantaneous heat from the coils. They cost so much back then the company had to go out of business."

As it hissed a threat, a ring of blue flame shot out of it menacingly. I gave it a wide berth and headed for the stairs. It resembled an evil alien from another planet that had landed.

From that day forward the hot water heater and I were on hostile terms. It scalded me with hot water when I did the dishes, or refused to cooperate with anything but a lukewarm offering for baths.

Each time I did the laundry, it belched and bubbled and hissed from its corner threateningly. I lived with the expectancy that one day it would blow up, taking me with it in a final mushroom cloud of revenge.

As Kent careened around the table my attention returned to the dining room. Dark green wallpaper covered the walls—a hideous background for the pattern of enormous flowers and vines which turned the room into a garish jungle. Suspended above the table, like a huge spider, was a chandelier that had been converted from gas to electricity.

I shuddered and went back to the couch in the living room. *"I hate this house,"* I thought. As I picked up my magazine a small voice within me said, "Will you praise Me for this house?"

I wanted to evade the question but thought, *"Lord, if this is You speaking to me, how can You ask that of me? I'd be a hypocrite to praise You for a house I loathe."*

"Make a list." It was a positive statement.

What in the world could this mean? Make a list of the good things about our home? There were a few.

In obedience to what I felt the Lord was telling me to do I rummaged around in the buffet for a pencil and paper. After much thought I began:

1. *In this house I have discovered that God is real and loves us.*
2. *In this house we have begun a spiritual adventure—the adventure of being led by God in all things.*

There were the obvious things. We had a home large enough to house all six of us, Kent was in remission, and our marital problems weren't quite as bad as they'd been. But suddenly I realized with an impact that the first two written statements scored higher with me than a list of eighty points toward a "House Beautiful".

With genuine sincerity I was able to say, "Lord, I *do*... I really do praise You for this house." But I really didn't understand why the Lord would require praise for it.

That night I flipped through my Bible before going upstairs to bed. To my astonishment I opened to the words, "At all times and for everything give thanks in the name of our Lord Jesus Christ to God the Father."

I sat back down on the couch. Could this be coincidence or another lesson? Give thanks in everything? Then that had to mean for the bad circumstances in our lives as well as the good. That afternoon my hatred for the house had surfaced. As a woman, my whole being rebelled at this antique barn with no personality. But the Lord had suggested that I praise Him for it in the midst of my grudge.

The list had helped me to a reappraisal and with newfound sincerity I found I really could praise Him for it. Now I knew the reason. We were to praise for the bad things as well as the good. Through the list I'd found just cause.

I climbed into bed with the same warm feelings of security which I had experienced in the beginning. If this was where God wanted me, then that was where I wanted to be also. I fell asleep wrapped in a blanket of contentment.

Through a blur of sleep, I suddenly became awaked by a wall of heat in the room. I felt like I was smothering. Was I dreaming or was I lying in a burning pool of water? Fear swept away the cobwebs of sleep. I was lying in a river of my own perspiration. Something was desperately wrong.

As I sat up I realized the heat in the room was so intense I couldn't breathe.

I shook Bill screaming, "The furnace... Something's wrong with the furnace!"

Bill scrambled out of bed heading for the basement. I wakened the children and herded them outside, but as I grazed the stair wall with my elbow I was burned. If the house was not on fire, it soon would be, I thought, as I guided the children to safety.

"Jesus, please help us. Get Bill out of there in time and show him what to do," I pleaded. The children and I watched from the street scanning the darkened house for flames which seemed inevitable.

After a time, Bill joined us. "I got the furnace shut off." He was breathing heavily. "Apparently the thing overheated. The thermostat registered over 100^0. Can you believe that?"

I shook my head. "And, no fire? That's a miracle. Angels must have been working overtime to protect us."

Together we put the children back to bed with extra covers as now there would be no heat until a service man could get to us in the morning.

I climbed into bed for a second time. "I praise You, Lord, for protecting us," I said wearily. And then added, "If we're to praise You in all things, I thank You that this has happened. I don't know why, but I praise You for it."

The next morning the service man arrived and after much clanging and puttering in the basement he came upstairs and declared, "The safety valve on the furnace stuck that's why the temperature just continued to climb. You're lucky you woke up in time to prevent a fire."

"Safety valves like that I don't need," I said sarcastically. "Put another one on that knows its job, will you?"

Five months passed and during this time I had the unmistakable feeling that we were supposed to move. I didn't want to mention this to Bill because I felt he would attribute it to the near-fire. Before this I had nagged to find another house, but since the making of the list I had a measure of contentment about our home. Lately, however, there seemed to be an underlying suggestion that we should move. The prayer meetings were now exclusively being held in our home and as more miracles happened—more people showed up. The walls of our house were bulging.

One evening, as Bill and I sat drinking our coffee over the debris of dinner dishes he announced," I think we're supposed to buy a house."

My cup was half-raised and I set it down sloshing coffee all over the saucer and the table. "Buy a house! But we don't even have one penny for a down payment."

"Nevertheless, I think we're supposed to start looking for a house to buy."

My thoughts swirled. Bill had always seemed to be staunchly mortared together with a conservatism that scraped across my rash impetuosity like fingernails across a blackboard. And here he was proposing that we buy a house when even my spend-thrift nature told me it was impossible.

Somehow I felt the lesson in praise was involved. The Lord had taught me to thank Him for something I hated and perhaps He had used it. Ironically, the night I learned the lesson the furnace had threatened us with fire.

Aloud I admitted to Bill that lately I had felt we were to move too, but it never occurred to me that we might buy a house.

"It might just be my own wild idea, Sandy. We'd better pray about it."

He sat his coffee cup down, closed his eyes and asked simply, "Lord, we want to be exactly where You want us to be. If You want us to move across the river into Indiana or to another suburb, the choice is Yours. Maybe this is my own idea and not Yours, but it seems You've hinted it to Sandy too. We put this in Your hands."

Bill instructed me to call a real estate agent and make an appointment to see some houses the following evening. As I cleared the dirty dishes from the table, I leaned over and impulsively brushed his cheek lightly with a kiss. It was hard to believe this new attitude of his. It was unlike him to even consider buying a house with no money for a down payment. I shook my head concluding the Lord must have been behind his decision to pry loose such a monumental amount of faith on Bill's part. And remembering how he proceeded without me to buy the house in Greenville, this was a pleasant new twist to be included. We searched fruitlessly for a month. Many of the houses we saw pleased us, but in discussing each one afterward we agreed that there was no sign from the Lord about any of them.

One Sunday night, as we drove back from another disappointing excursion with our agent, I suddenly blurted out," I want to live within walking distance of the church and the school."

Immediately I was shocked I had said it. Hadn't I really put the location of this house in the Lord's hands?

Bill's reply mirrored my own thoughts. "Hey, I thought we were going to leave all that up to our Heavenly Real Estate Agent!"

"I don't know what made me say that," I confessed. "Strange. It just sort of popped out of my mouth."

As soon as we got home Bill began to search through the classified ads in the paper. It had never occurred to us to do this before as we had been relying on the listings of the realtor's agency.

"Listen to this." Bill sounded excited as he read, "'For Sale by owner, 3932 Nanz Ave., four bedroom Cape Cod, dining room, large family room with fireplace."

"That can't be far from here," I said catching his excitement.

"Why don't you call this telephone number tomorrow and make an appointment? I've got a funny feeling about this ad."

From the time I arranged for an appointment with the owner the next day, the words, "This is it. This is it." became a mental undercurrent.

The following evening we got a sitter for the children. We found Nanz Avenue was several blocks west of our house. We slowly drove down Nanz Avenue and as the numbers indicated we were nearing 3932, one house stood out from all the others. It was constructed of stone and an unusual pale pink siding. Warm yellow light beckoned hospitably through the small panes of a large picture window. An immense cottonwood tree the circumference of a baby redwood towered beside the front door.

"I wish that could be it," I said wistfully, pointing toward the storybook house on our right. "But it won't be. It's probably that ramshackle place at the end of the block."

But, as we looked more closely the number above the door announced: "3932".

We stood on the front porch and rang the bell. Short gusts of a breeze rustled through thick ivy leaves that clung to the stone. As we waited for someone to answer, my attention focused on the door itself. "Bill, it's a double Dutch door! Ever since I was a little girl I've wanted a house with a double Dutch door."

Bill stepped down the two steps from the porch and lovingly patted the huge trunk of the cottonwood that seemed to guard the house like a sentry. "Can you imagine owning this tree? If this is the house we're to have it's yours... but this tree will be mine. My tree!"

Just then the door opened and we were greeted by an attractive middle-aged couple, who introduced themselves as Bob and Jane Schneider, the owners.

Although in ten years of marriage Bill and I had never been able to satisfy

152

our own tastes, we leaned heavily toward Early American period influences: colonial fireplaces; small paned windows; pegged floors.

As the Schneider's ushered us into the living room, Bill and I exchanged a look of disbelief. One entire wall of carved paneling surrounded a gracious colonial fireplace. Soft green carpeting exposed large areas of the most beautiful Early American random width pegged flooring I had ever seen.

Jane Schneider followed my gaze. "The carpeting goes with the house," she said.

It was too good to be true. I remembered my barren floors at home that occasionally attacked the children's socked feet with splinters. At our house, splinters were a common hazard on bare footed trips to the bathroom.

As we toured the house, we discovered a spacious paneled family room in the basement. A brick fireplace with raised hearth casually rambled across one corner of the room.

"Sandy, this would be perfect for prayer meetings. Look, it even has an outside entrance." Bill poked his head through an outside door and discovered steps leading upward to a patio.

"We've been holding prayer meetings in our home," I explained to Bob Schneider. "At the rate the group has been growing, our house now can't accommodate everyone. Some nights we've had as many as fifty people and when the living room and dining room fill up we've had to seat people on the stairs. We've come to refer to the stair sitters as the 'peanut gallery.'"

Bob laughed and offered, "This room would certainly fill the bill for that purpose."

I shook my head in disbelief. "I feel like I've stepped out of reality and into my own personal version of House and Garden."

Our previous month with the real estate agent had taught us the proper buyer's approach. When viewing a house apparently it was an unspoken code to wander sourly from room-to-room pointing at a plaster crack, or chipped paint, meanwhile verbalizing all the visible faults in an attempt to discourage the owner into lowering the price. Apparently this little psychological game was played everywhere. However, Bill and I now trampled rough-shod over the code, exclaiming and praising delightedly like small children as we discovered each facet of this house to be just what we'd always dreamed of owning someday.

The backyard was like a miniature park, sheltered protectively by massive, magnificent trees. To our surprise, we found by going out the back gate and through the adjoining yard, we arrived directly in front of the grade school Eric and Lisa were already attending.

"Bill! There's the school... And we're three blocks from the church. You don't suppose, I mean, when I said 'I want to live within walking distance' and it just popped out of my mouth last night… could the Lord have put those words in my mind so we'd recognize this tonight?"

As we walked back toward the house, Bill asked the question I had fearfully been trying to shove into the background. "What's the price Bob?"

"Well, we just put it on the market three days ago. We don't really know ourselves. I'm not evading you, but it would depend on what financing route you intend. We need $18,500 clear out of it. If you're a G.I. the points would have to be figured in on top of what we need."

As we parked in front of our rented house on Cornell Place it looked shabbier than ever. The children had gone right to sleep, the sitter informed us.

The next morning presented a particularly hectic scheduling to get Lisa and Eric off to school, the twins dressed and fed by the time Bill was ready to leave. We were to ride to work with him so that I could keep the car and take Kent for blood counts.

I belted the twins into the back seat and we started down Lexington Avenue toward downtown Louisville. We had driven for five blocks in silence when quite unexpectedly Kurt announced from the backseat, "I want to live in the pink house, Mommy."

Bill swerved to miss a telephone pole. In his surprise at Kurt's statement he had looked into the back seat losing control of the car. He and I exchanged a look of mutual bewilderment. We knew we had not mentioned the house—the pink house—to any of the children.

I jerked my head around and tried to appraise Kurt's statement by his expression. He seemed completely detached from what he's said.

"Why?" I asked.

"I don't know. I just want to live in the pink house."

I lowered my voice. "Bill, do you suppose we passed a pink house a few blocks back? It seems uncanny he'd say that. Pink houses might be the rage in Florida, but not here!"

He turned left off our regular route. "Let's see. I'll circle back to where we got on Lexington."

"If there's not a pink house," (I secretly hoped there wouldn't be), "then we're going to have to consider that maybe it's guidance for us about the pink house we saw last night."

There were no pink houses on Lexington Avenue.

After the twins were bedded down for their naps, I remembered Bill had told me to call the Veterans Administration. They informed me that the points varied from one mortgage company to another. "Call a mortgage company… any mortgage company," I was told.

I hung up. An ad on the back of a Louisville Real Estate catalog that lay on the kitchen table caught my eye. The first thing I saw was an ad for Louisville Mortgage Company. "Why not?" I thought as I dialed the number in the ad.

The switchboard operator answered nasally, "Louisville Mortgage."

I explained what information I wanted and was transferred to some mysterious department. They didn't have the information and got the operator back on the line suggesting I be transferred elsewhere. After the third transfer a sympathetic employee emerged on the line. Her name was Miss Bennett. After ten minutes of having my simple question shuffled from pillar to post I was exasperated.

"Can you *please* tell me what the current V.A. points are?" I didn't try to hide my impatience at what I thought was inefficiency. But little did I know I was dealing with the Lord's precise timing and placement of my call.

"It's five and one half percent, Mrs. Ghost." Miss Bennett's tone was pleasant despite my rudeness.

"Could you tell me possibly, just what would your company lend toward an $18,500 property, plus this five and one-half percent?" I asked feeling foolish.

"It would depend upon the appraisal," she said crisply.

"Well, the owners said that they were having one made."

"Mrs. Ghost... where is this property?"

"3932 Nanz Ave."

There was a sudden gasp and intake of breath from the other end of the line.

"Miss Bennett... what's wrong?" By her reaction I was afraid some emergency had erupted on the other end.

"It's just that... well, I have those very appraisal papers right here in front of me. Of all the mortgage companies in Louisville you might have called! And of all the employees in this company you might have reached... to think that you got me and I had the papers on my desk..." Her statement trailed off in bewilderment.

I tried to think past my own shock. I had been impatient at being referred from one employee to the other. If the Lord was in this coincidence, as He certainly seemed to be, then my impatience was not only unjustified-- it was unforgivable. And I'd called Louisville Mortgage just because I caught a glimpse of their ad on my kitchen table. Had it been lying where I'd see it on purpose?

I called Bill at work and recounted my conversation with Miss Bennett. Surprisingly, he seemed to be convinced that this incident coupled with Kurt's random statement had happened above coincidence.

The next day Miss Bennett called to say that the company had fixed the amount of down payment--$550.00 I relayed the bad news to Bill that night. It might just as well have been $5,000. We didn't have it.

His reaction surprised me again. He seemed undaunted. This was so unnatural for his conservative nature that I was awed by his reservoir of faith in this matter. After the children were in bed he suggested we pray about the financial aspect specifically.

With a measure of pride in Bill's initiative spiritually, I remembered my past longing that he would take my hand and pray to receive the Holy Spirit together. That hadn't happened. But here he was now stroking many lengths past me in faith.

We knelt by the couch and asked," Lord, is this really You causing all these things to happen? It would seem You are pointing a finger at this house. But, now we're down to the moment of truth. The down payment is $550 and as You well know, we don't have it. If all this is Your will, we trust You to provide the money."

"Or," I interrupted Bill, "show us where we have it already and perhaps don't know it."

I opened my eyes and Bill was staring at me in surprise.

"That's a new thought," I said in astonishment. "It came out just like when I told you I wanted to live within walking distance of the school."

"Do you suppose we really do have something of value we don't know about?"

Suddenly I looked down at the ring on my right hand. "Bill, that's it! The diamond ring my grandmother gave me. I have no idea what its worth, but wouldn't it be another coincidence of it was just the right amount for the down payment?"

A quick trip to the jewelers the following day revealed an appraisal of $450. Just $100 short of the money we would need. Bill and I agreed that the balance could be scraped together somewhere if we could find a buyer for the ring. I decided there wasn't enough time to advertise and deeply felt that if we were in the Lord's will, some jewelry store might buy the ring.

Fourth Street in Louisville is the mecca for stores of this nature. The following afternoon I set out to storm the jewelry merchants. Starting at the foot of the street, I glibly pushed through the heavy glass door of the first store. A bell attached to the door tinkled my arrival to the salesman behind the counter.

"May I help you?" he asked courteously.

"Yes. Do you buy diamonds?"

The hint of a smirk crossed his face. "No, lady. We sell them." He turned his back on me and began rummaging in the display case.

I tiptoed out of the store feeling like a fool, did the clerk think I was a fence trying to get rid of a hot piece of jewelry?

I criss-crossed back and forth across Fourth Street. Each jeweler seemed to have the same reaction to my question as the first. As my embarrassment mounted, I began to wonder whether I had gotten my signals crossed. Perhaps this was a wild goose chase after all. Maybe the Lord hadn't given me this guidance.

My feet hurt and I decided to try one more store and then give up. Will Sales Jewelry seemed to be the last one in sight on my itinerary.

I was met with the same disappointing answer. But just as I started out the door the clerk yelled, "Hey wait a minute! I just happened to think. There's a guy upstairs who buys diamonds sometimes. Second floor, third door on the left."

My heart began to beat rapidly. I could scarcely thank the man. It was an old building and as I climbed the worn stairs I wondered what kind of office I'd find. The hall was dark and dirty. I walked past exposed steam pipes which clanked and rattled; peeling paint shredded off the walls. The third door on the left was open.

It appeared to be a machine shop. A workbench covered the waist high area of one wall and at it stood a small man, wearing a hat with a visor. He was using some type of power tool. Sparks cascaded from it like a Fourth of July sparkler.

Noticing me in the doorway, he pushed back the visor and asked, "Can I help you?"

"I must be in the wrong place," I stammered. "A clerk downstairs in the jewelry store directed me up here. He said I might find someone who buys diamonds." I felt more foolish than ever.

"What have you got?"

His question took me by surprise and wordlessly I took off my ring and handed it to him.

In one swift movement he whipped a jeweler's eyepiece out of his pocket and holding it up to the light, peered at the ring.

"What do you want for it?"

I gulped and in a hoarse whisper ventured, "$450?"

I'll take it," he said matter-of-factly.

My head spun. "I think I need to sit down," I said easing into a wooden chair nearby.

It had been almost too simple. "By the way," I managed, "Just what type of business is this?"

The man smiled and extended his hand, "I'm Herbert Norris, an engraver.

Sometimes I have time to handcraft jewelry and that's what I'll do with your ring—pull the stones and remount it in a modern setting."

I took his hand, "I'm Mrs. Ghost and I'm just sitting here wondering how in the world I ever would have found you otherwise… an engraver! I'd never have thought to try that."

Mr. Norris toyed with the ring in his hand, "Just coincidence I guess," he said.

I wanted to tell him the whole story, but checked myself. He might think I was some kind of freak and back out of the deal.

He set the ring down on his desk. "I can only pay you $60 today, Mrs. Ghost, and the balance in fifteen days. Is that alright?"

Because of the shabby surroundings I might not have been as quick to trust this man, but circumstances seemed to indicate that the Lord had been in on this deal.

"That's just fine," I told him with confidence.

I could feel myself bursting at the seams to tell Bill as I drove home. We had our down payment and it had been provided in exactly the manner we had believed we were being instructed to pursue. Not another coincidence!

Triumphantly I waved the $60 under Bill's nose and described in detail how I had been led to Herbert Norris.

Bill shook his head from side-to-side and grinned like a small schoolboy. "Wow! That is fantastic--simply fantastic. It's ours. The pink house is ours!" He threw his newspaper up in the air like a monstrous wad of confetti and rushed to the telephone to tell the Schneider's we would put a contract on the house.

One week later our bubble broke. From Bill's expression I could tell something was wrong from the moment he came in from work. Tossing the paper on the chair by the door, he motioned for me to come and sit down.

"Louisville Mortgage called me at work today."

"So?"

"They made a mistake in figuring the down payment. The guy was extremely apologetic about it. He explained that a VA-FHA mortgage is brand new. In fact, we're the first they've had to figure."

Even though Bill seemed to be trying to cushion his words I steeled myself for some disappointment.

"They missed it by a mile, Sandy. The down payment is not $550—it's $1050."

"$1050! But that's impossible. There's no way we could raise that. The money from the ring was our only chance."

"I know. We need to do some serious questioning about whether we've been mistaken in the Lord's guidance. Maybe we've fantasized this whole affair."

"I just don't understand," I pouted. "What about all the signs we've had— coincidence piled on coincidence?"

Bill shrugged his shoulders.

I folded my arms and said childishly," If the Lord wants us to have this house He will just pour the money down out of a hole in the ceiling. We'll wait and see."

Two weeks passed and no money fell out of the sky. Meanwhile the Schneider's had two other prospective buyers warming up in the bull pen. Talking it over, Bill and I decided it was unjust to keep the owners dangling any longer. We would have to lose the house.

But before we called the Schneider's our deep disappointment suggested we pray again. "Lord, forgive us for presuming on Your will," Bill began. "Apparently this was not Your will from the beginning. We don't want it anyway if You don't want us to have it."

There was pronounced sincerity in Bill's tone. I examined myself wondering if I too could relinquish this house as easily. On this basis I added, "And please don't let us be disappointed."

I chewed my lower lip to keep back tears as Bill called the Schneider's. How could we have been so misled?

The doorbell rang just as Bill hung up the phone. Carter and Ann Foster had come to visit with us. It was unusual timing that they should come just when we needed cheering. They had never paid a call to our home before. Their companionship altered our disappointment, easing the sting of losing the house.

But the following four days proved to be an even greater surprise in curbing our doldrums. It all began when a neighbor whom I scarcely knew appeared at my door with a cake.

"Just thought you might like to try my family recipe for German Chocolate," she explained.

The advent of the cake was followed by a steady stream of visits paid by neighbors, friends and members of the prayer group. Though no one knew of our recent letdown, Bill and I became the wide-eyed recipients of love lavished upon us in an avalanche of pies, cakes and visits.

There seemed to be some unmistakable design in all this attention. The people could not have known they were being used as instruments to show God's concern and love for us. This timely shower of thoughtfulness had to have been master-minded by the Lord we concluded.

The fifth gift of pastry on the fourth day finally ruptured any remaining reservations I had. Standing by my kitchen sink the tears finally came. But they were not tears of disappointment; they were tears of appreciation.

"Lord Jesus, I finally see what You're saying. That house isn't important at all. It's Your people who really count. I gladly give up my own will in it. I can tell You now with genuine sincerity that I really don't want it if You don't want us to have it."

Immediately the reply of a loud thought suggested, "Will you praise Me for not getting the house?"

How could I have been so stupid? Initially, I had been taught the lesson of praising for the bad things as well as the good. My hate for the old house and the near fire had been the vehicle for my lesson. But when the chips were sown with the pink house, I had forgotten to apply it. The spiritual lesson had come full circle.

"Father, forgive me. You have a retarded child," I said aloud. "Of course I praise You for losing the house." And I deeply meant it.

That night I confided in Bill that I had experienced a turning point with regard to giving up the house. As I reported what I felt I had discovered God was trying to say to us almost in the form of a lesson, Bill agreed. We concluded that apparently in all things we were expected to relinquish our own will and then that surrender could serve as a stepping stone to genuine praise.

No one came the next day. No one called. The offerings of pastries were a thing of the past. But the point had been made-- we didn't need to lean on them anymore.

Two weeks passed and on a Thursday night Jane Schneider telephoned. Her first words ignited a strange excitement in me.

"Mrs. Ghost, I'll get right to the point. Quite mysteriously both of our buyers backed out. In fact, one party showed up for the closing appointment, cash in hand. At the last minute they decided not to sign the papers and walked out of settlement!"

I didn't know what to say to her.

"Bob and I have decided you and Bill are supposed to have the house. We would agree to pay the closing costs if you still want it."

"Can I call you right back after Bill and I talk this over?" I asked eagerly. "I want you to know... that is, I can't thank you enough." I hoped my gratitude had registered over the telephone line as I hung up.

Bill was stunned by their proposal. Both of us had completely washed the house off the slate, and now here it was laid lovingly back at our feet. This turn of events called for a re-evaluation on our guidance.

"Could it be that we were not misled by all the signs that had pointed to the house in the beginning?" I wondered aloud. "What if the Lord was in all of that and just wanted us to come to a point of surrender of our own wills in it—then He gave it back?"

"If the Schneider's pay the closing costs, there is a balance to make up." Bill calculated. "But I think we are supposed to take it. This has got to be a green light to go ahead, and if that's so the difference will come somehow."

We were to find that our heavenly Real Estate Agent held all the trump cards. More than fifteen days had passed and no check from Herbert Norris had appeared. In the disappointment of losing the house we had never pressed him for the balance he owed.

Now, to our amazement, the very day the F.H.A. was to investigate our bank balance to see if we had the proper amount of down payment, Herbert Norris' check arrived.

Also, in the same morning mail, we received a check from the government— our income tax refund. But Bill had miss-figured our return in their favor. The error was corrected on the check. To our astonishment, when we added Herbert Norris' check to our income tax refund it was the exact amount of the down payment—to the penny!

We made a beeline to the bank to make the deposit, jubilantly agreeing that this had to be the grandfather of all coincidences. Not only were we awed by the prospect of the new house, but the thrill of seeing the Lord move so overtly actually upstaged the house itself.

The day of our closing appointment at Louisville Mortgage another unexpected check arrived in the mail—a Veteran's Administration insurance dividend for $22. These were usually issued much later in the year.

"I wonder if that's for something connected with the house," I said, having become suspect of all sudden twists.

"We'll deposit it on our way down there. Come on, let's go. We'll be late." Bill struggled into his coat.

We met with the Schneider's at a long conference table in the office of the attorney for the mortgage company. After all of the formalities of the deed and closing statement, Bill made out the check for the down payment and all inclusive fees.

As I glanced over his shoulder I gasped at the figure. When the subtraction was made on the check stub there was a balance of $2.00 left in the bank. Without the extra $22.00 that morning we would have been overdrawn!

Chapter Eighteen

*G*olden sunshine bathed the humid summer Louisville morning. Puffy clouds dotted the sky like huge chunks of frothy cotton candy. The prayer group planned on helping us move into the "pink house" three days after Kent and I returned from his appointment at NIH, so we struggled toward the front door with the suitcase through rows of packed boxes that lined our path through the living room.

Once outside in the car, I belted Kent into the backseat. He smiled and asked, "Can I drive the plane this time? Ple-e-e-e-eeeese?"

He seemed so serious about it I had to suppress my laughter. He was becoming a sophisticated flyer with all our trips. "I think you'd better get a license first," I told him.

"Sidney's dog's got a license. Can I use that?" The china-blue eyes begged for permission.

"Don't think that would work, sweetheart. You have to go to school to fly a plane." We had an uneventful flight to DC and wonderful news awaited us.

Kent was finally in remission and we didn't have to return to the hospital for two months. His protocol now called for five days of chemotherapy and then two months' resting period. It was like being on parole, but the freedom it afforded was fresh air to the soul.

Once we had settled into the "pink house", Eric built his own ham radio, became licensed and now the sounds of "CQ....CQ...CQ" echoed down the stairs from his bedroom like some mystical chant. I tried to keep from interfering in the jungle of his bedroom that was laced with wires to an outside antenna and serious projects that protruded from drawers and shelves.

His live project, "Curious", his beloved hamster resided on top of a bookcase. His exercise wheel had to be removed from the cage at night as his nocturnal gymnastics threatened to parallel the noise of metal rasping and grating of the night shift at a steel mill. After enduring nights of sleeplessness, I had imposed a ban on the wheel before moving to the "pink house". Eric had cared for his buddy, Curious, for almost three years when the little creature "gave up the Ghosts". We had no idea of his age when he came to us. The entire family grieved with Eric, who solemnly lined a cigar box with blue velvet, gently laid the body of his little friend on the sidewalk in the backyard and prepared to dig a grave with a garden trowel. I watched from the kitchen door as Kent stood by, eyeing the efforts of his big brother.

After a time he came in and climbed onto the bench of the kitchen table.

"How's about a glass of milk and some chocolate chip cookies?" I tried to lighten the mood of the grave-digging going on in the backyard.

He shook his head, "no" and I could tell he was processing what he'd seen. He looked through the kitchen window and saw Kurt helping Eric dig now. "Can I pat Curious?" he asked.

It was as though I felt my heart try to climb up into my throat. How could I explain death to my son who might have to face it himself soon? *Oh, Father, please tell me what to say... help me!* I prayed, never even thinking that the Lord was perfectly capable of by-passing me completely and explaining it to Kent Himself.

Suddenly Kent's eyes widened; he looked like a light bulb had come on over his head. "Oh... oh," he said and smiled. "I don't have to pat *that*. That's only *half* of Curious!" He jumped up from the table and ran back outside leaving me in absolute astonishment at what had just happened.

But this tender taste of death that had just been introduced into the family caused me to reflect on Kent's future. With all the healings that we were now being introduced to could it be that Kent would just be completely healed by the Lord? I realized that every time there was answered prayer I was grateful for the recipient, however, I always seemed to analyze it with reference to Kent. Would the Lord ultimately heal him and we'd all live happily ever after?

Kent's checkup was two months later. Because of my continuing experiment to see if certain people were brought to my attention at NIH, I decided to remain watchful for some type of guidance again. Would this trip bring someone else? This time, I told myself, I would be extremely careful that nothing I said or did could initiate it.

Kent passed his admission examination with flying colors and the A.O.D. made reservations for us in the nearby Governor's House Motel where many of the outpatients stayed. Three days of chemotherapy, visiting with other parents and Occupational Therapy passed in the usual hospital protocol. I kept my spiritual antenna up, but nobody was brought to my attention as the focus of attention.

On the fourth day, Kent and I went down to the cafeteria for lunch. Long lines of hungry laboratory workers, doctors, nurses, patients and their families passed by the steam tables. People carrying trays milled through the seething crowd trying to find tables. The food was excellent, but it was like attempting to down a meal in the middle of Grand Central Station. Suddenly, I heard my name above the clatter of dishes and conversation. As I turned around, I saw Laura Palmer, Kim Grigg's mother, pushing her way toward me. "Sandy!" She threw her arms around me and began to cry. "It's Kim... he's terminal. I'm sorry for this blubbering but I..." she wiped her eyes with her fingertips.

"What do you mean terminal? Come and sit down."

"He's dying. Every organ in his body is shutting down. He's only got a matter of time to live. Just before lunch our doctor told me his kidneys had shut down." She searched frantically through her purse for a handkerchief. "He can't live long now no matter what they do."

I handed her my paper napkin for her eyes. "Laura, I just can't believe this. I don't know what to say." I shot a look toward Kent, wanting to protect him from Laura's words.

"There isn't anything you can say that will change things. But I feel better now that you're here." The huge sorrowful brown eyes begged, "Will you pray for him? Like we did the last time... will you pray for him?"

My knees began to tremble beneath the lunch table. Somehow it was different this time. The last time Kim had been dying of the same symptoms Kent had been healed from. This was different. Leukemia usually ended this way. Could the Lord pull Kim back from death again?

I pretended an assurance I didn't feel. "Of course, we'll pray for him, Laura. Is he conscious?"

"Oh yes, I've never seen anyone so brave."

"Then let's go right now." I picked up our trays and deposited them on the tiered receptacle for dirty dishes.

"First, I want to take Kent to Occupational Therapy. I don't want him to see Kim this way."

Everything went wrong. Nurses scurried in and out of Kim's hospital room, an x-ray technician rumbled his portable unit up to the bed to get additional diagnostic films, and several specialists appeared on the scene. How could anyone pray in such bedlam?

I apologized to Laura and told her I'd call her from the motel that night. She agreed we should give up our idea to pray that day.

That evening, after Kent was bathed and in bed for the night, Laura and I talked for several hours. It seemed to help her to pour it all out into the thread of the telephone line which ran between us.

As she told me in detail about the horrors of the past few weeks and confessed her fear of what even the next hours might bring, my concern for her mounted. How would she take Kim's death if it came? Could she accept it? Could I?

With this in mind I wondered if I ought to talk to her about turning her own life over to Christ. He could bring her the help she would need if death came. Would it be stepping on her toes to mention it? Would she feel at this

164

point that a move on her part toward God might be bargaining with Him for her child's life?

Finally, as I listened to Laura's desperation it resolved in my mind. I couldn't help her, but I knew Someone who could. Did I dare withhold this help from her? It would be on my conscious if I didn't at least mention her own relationship with Jesus Christ.

Timidly I inserted into a pause, "Laura, have you given any thought to turning yourself over to Christ?"

There was silence on the other end of the line. *Now you've done it,* I thought. *You've broken the rapport you have with her.*

"What I mean to say is…" I stammered, "I can't help you, Laura. God knows I wish I could just reach through this telephone and wipe it all away, but I can't. But I know Someone who can help. It may sound corny, but that someone is Jesus."

Still silence on the other end of the phone.

Feeling fearfully that I was digging myself into a deeper hole I continued, "We know He can heal. He healed Kim before, you've admitted that."

There was a faint "Yes" through the receiver.

"And He may again. But somehow I have the feeling He's yearning to reach out and help you too, Laura. He's the only one who can see into the future… the only one who can take away your fear no matter what happens."

Laura's voice sounded weary. "Okay. Something inside me says you're right. I'm ready."

We talked about how to receive Christ and prayed together on the telephone. As we were about to hang up she admitted, "To tell you the truth, I feel better already. Nothing's really changed, but I feel like a load's been lifted off me." The soft, southern drawl pronounced it like a benediction.

"I know what you mean. The load's still there, but you've given it to Him to carry."

"Will you still promise me you'll pray for Kim tomorrow?"

"Of course I will, but I think you should be there too."

"Before 10:00 o'clock in the morning would probably be the best time. I just can't make it that early. I've been at the hospital night and day for the last two weeks. Tomorrow morning I've got to go to work and get the payroll out at least, or nobody in the company will get paid."

"Okay. I'll try to get in the room at 10:00, but I wish you could be there too. I just have this feeling you should be with me," I said. Did my feelings stem from guidance or from cowardice, I wondered?

After we hung up I paced the motel room. If my faith counted in praying for Kim it would be better to disappoint Laura and not show up. With the end so near for him medically, I was honestly afraid to pray. What if nothing happened? Selfishly I knew it would shake my own faith for Kent.

What a hypocrite I am, I told myself. *What's wrong with me? I've seen God step in before... even with Kim on the brink of death for a different reason. Don't I believe the Lord can do it when it pertains to leukemia? Is this the real reason for my reticence?* My own questions came at me like a machine gun volley of accusations.

My pacing took me past the mirror over the desk. I turned and faced my bath robed image, "Sandy Ghost you're a fool," I lashed out at my counterpart. "You preened your spiritual wings and asked the Lord to let you be a channel for Him at this hospital. On this trip you even vowed you'd wait for someone to be led to you. Laura falls into your arms in the cafeteria and you want to run away. You dissolve into jelly and resent being put in a bind to pray for Kim because it's leukemia this time. Either God is God or He isn't! The trouble is... you think it depends on you!"

That was it! My own tongue lashing had severed through to the meat of the problem. Somehow I had gotten the warped idea that I was to wait for God's guidance in focusing in on people and then just plunge in with prayers for healing or mealy-mouthed platitudes after God said, "Go!"

How could I have forgotten Bill's words when I had decided to experiment with guidance on our trips to NIH? He had reminded me that when the Lord healed He did it in different ways; different circumstances were involved. How could I have neglected the lesson of the woman's prayer meeting that morning when we learned we were to always "seek His face and call upon His name before any prayer action was taken?" That day we learned to ask the Lord to show us how to pray on a specific basis.

I'd been experimenting with guidance, but I hadn't gone far enough. If I really wanted to be a channel it meant more than just waiting for Jesus to shove the right person under my nose at the right time. It also meant waiting for the mind of the Lord in order to pray once the person got to me. Nothing depended on me! My part was to keep a listening ear turned heavenward for instructions.

What a relief, I told myself. If I follow those guidelines my responsibility isn't heavy. Laura's recent words came back to me. "I feel like a load's been lifted off me." So did I. And now I shivered at my presumptuousness in telling her I knew what she meant. She had given her load to Him, while I was still carrying the load for the responsibility of prayer results as though it depended on me.

With this resolved I knelt by my bed, "Father, I must be a real insult to You at times. You've heard my argument with myself just now. Forgive me for taking over what are Your responsibilities. I've promised Laura I'll pray for Kim tomorrow. Open my mind to how You would have me pray for him. Please show me Your perfect will in this."

I waited. After a time I grew restless at the silence. Nothing came back in return. But slowly a scene began to unfold in my imagination. It was as though I were holding an imaginary conversation with Kim. Was this just what I wished would happen or were these my instructions, I wondered?

Sentence after sentence filtered into my thoughts. Some startled me at the simplicity of the examples I could give him. But I'd asked for guidance with the perfect prayer for Kim; however, what came to mind was a conversation. Was this what I was to say to him once I got in the room?

Just as a secretary takes dictation, I carefully set what had come to mind on paper trying to commit it to memory. Could I be brave enough to repeat those words to Kim the next morning I wondered as I turned out the light and left a call at the desk for 7:30 AM?

At 9:45 I went to 2 East. My entry to Kim's room was barred by a throng of doctors gathered in the hall outside his door. Grand rounds were being held by the staff.

I left word at the nurses' station that I wanted to see Kim whenever it was convenient and for the rest of the morning I watched from my sentry post in the hall. A steady stream of doctors, nurses and complicated-looking equipment rushed in and out of his room. Again I marveled at our good fortune to be at NIH as the staff pulled out all the stops to save this precious child.

But why couldn't the Lord maneuver a pause in all this actiivty so I could keep my promise to Laura? Perhaps I'd been wrong in thinking I was to talk to Kim at all. Immediately I chided myself for thinking my promise to Laura meant more than the help Kim was receiving medically. It was noon and I took Kent down to the cafeteria for lunch.

At 1:00 o'clock we went back up to solarium on 2 East. I was beginning to panic. Time was running out. Kent and I had to catch a 3:15 PM airport limousine.

Leaving Kent to entertain himself with the television in the lounge, I tiptoed up the hall to the nurses' station again. The head nurse, Mrs. Zealy, recognized me.

"We haven't forgotten you, Mrs. Ghost," she said apologetically. "I know you're aware that Kim's critical. There just hasn't been a moment we could let you in."

"I understand," I told her.

"Why don't you wait in the solarium and I'll call you on the intercom if there's a breathing space between doctors."

Back in the solarium, I plunged myself dejectedly into one of the leather recliners chairs. "Why was I so tied to this commitment to Laura?" I sulked. Obviously I just wasn't supposed to pray for Kim. What was wrong? Were all

167

those sentences I'd put on paper last night nothing except exaggerated fantasy? But I was to find out I'd forgotten one important factor--the Lord's timing.

At exactly five minutes of 3:00 Mrs. Zealy's voice came over the intercom. "You may see Kim Griggs now, Mrs. Ghost."

I rushed down the hall and through the door which had been closed to me for five hours. Just as I entered the room, I heard the clicking of high heels in a fast pace behind me. It was Laura Palmer.

"You mean you just got in here now?" she asked breathlessly.

"They've been working with him constantly," I explained.

"Well, now I know why I got here when I did. Sandy, about twenty minutes ago the girl who works at the desk just opposite mine suddenly said, 'Laura, come on. I'm going to take you out to NIH' I insisted I planned to leave in an hour, but she was adamant we go right that minute. She practically dragged me out the office door."

"I told you I had a feeling you should be here when we prayed. I have a hunch maybe this is why I couldn't even have fought my way in here until now."

I was shocked by Kim's appearance. His tragically thin arms and legs were covered with ugly purple bruises. The dark, sensitive eyes, so like his mother's, were sunken hollows in his face. But his smile as he recognized me forced me to a cheerfulness I didn't feel.

"*Oh Father, help me to remember what I'm to say,*" I pleaded mentally.

"Kim... how would you like to go home, back to school, and not be sick anymore?" I repeated from memory, but the words sounded wretchedly deceiving when I looked at this eleven-year-old child wasting to nothing. Did I have any right to give him false hope?

"Sure!" Kim's eyes widened. His enthusiastic reply shouldn't have surprised me. I felt quite certain no one had said anything like that to him.

"If the doctor were to walk in here and tell you he had done something to make you all better, you'd believe him, wouldn't you?" The words I'd written the night before began to roll out of me.

"Yes."

"But if Jesus were to walk in here and tell you He had done something to make you better, you'd believe Him even more than you would believe the doctor, wouldn't you?"

The small boy in the bed now frowned and grew very serious. Thoughtfully he said, "Yes."

"Kim," I said, "I know an exciting secret. God doesn't mean for it to be a secret, for it's right in His Word, the Bible, but if you don't know it's in there, how can you know what the secret is?"

He shook his head in understanding and smiled.

168

"God's Bible is like a love letter He's written to us. Now... let's suppose you were in Atlanta visiting your grandmother, and your mother wrote you a letter saying that she'd bought you a new bicycle at home. Let's suppose you never opened that letter. You wouldn't know you had a bicycle, would you?"

"No ma'am. I guess I couldn't know it if I didn't read the letter."

"Exactly. And it's just the same with God's letter to us--the Bible. If you don't know all that's in there for you, how can it be yours?"

A broad smile of understanding crossed Kim's face.

"Now... here's the secret! You know Jesus died for your sins, right?"
He nodded.

"But did you also know that He died for your sicknesses?"
The small face on the pillow hinted at his surprise.

"Kim, God's letter to us says in the book of 1ˢᵗPeter that, 'By His stripes we were healed' and that means that when they whipped Jesus, He took it that we might be healed. And in the eighth chapter of Matthew it says that Jesus took our infirmities (that's our weakness) and bore our sickness. Did you know that?"

"No, ma'am."

"You've heard your mother say, and I've heard her too, 'If I could only have this leukemia in Kim's place'. Well, we both know that she can't, but Jesus could... and He did. Can you accept this?"

"I see what you mean. Just like a substitute comes in and does the job in place of my teacher."

"You've got it! Jesus was your substitute for your sins and your sickness."

"Boy! That's great."

"Kim, have you ever turned your life over to Jesus and asked Him to come into you?"

He looked puzzled and shook his head indicating he hadn't.

"Would you like to and receive all He wants so badly to give you?"

There was an enthusiasm in Kim's "yes" which matched his tone when I had initially asked him if he wanted to go home and not be sick anymore.

Laura, Kim, and I prayed together as he stumblingly, but with clear sincerity asked Jesus to come into him. Together we thanked Jesus for having taken Kim's leukemia in his place.

I hurriedly started out of the room to catch the limousine, but paused long enough to tell Laura, "Begin thanking the Lord for what He's done for Kim... even if you don't see any change at first. If we believe what we've just talked about, Jesus didn't do it today, Laura. He did it 2,000 years ago. I think as we begin to thank Him it will actually take place."

"I don't understand. Say thank you now?"

As I hurriedly buttoned Kent into his jacket, I told her, "Try thinking of it this way. If I were to call you from Louisville and say I had a new lizard purse for you, what would you say?"

She shrugged her shoulders. "Thank you."

"You mean you'd say it *before* you saw the purse?"

"Well, yes... if you said you had it for me."

"It's the same thing with God," I told her. "He says He has it for Kim in His Word."

As Kent and I raced toward National Airport in the limousine, I wondered at my last words to Laura about the lizard purse. That example hadn't been written on my paper that I felt had been dictated to me the night before. Had I just pulled the example out of a hat on the spur of the moment or had that been guidance too? I remembered the first time we'd met and Kim was then dying of a cerebral hemorrhage. God had given me words to say to her beyond my own knowledge. Had the Holy Spirit given me the right words again?

As Kent and I climbed the steep metal stairs to board the plane I realized I was leaving part of myself behind in that small hospital room. But the outcome was the Lord's responsibility I reminded myself.

Two months passed. I continued to praise and thank the Lord for "having" healed Kim. But my own prayers began to waver as I grew edgy and fearful hearing nothing from Laura's end at all; this fear grew as the time came for Kent's checkup again. We went back to Maryland.

I heaved a sigh of relief after Kent's bone marrow testing indicated his condition was excellent. No one in the Outpatients Clinic knew anything about Kim Griggs. My suspense mounted as we boarded the elevator for 2 East. Would the nurses' station tell me that he had died?

The elevator doors opened on the first floor to admit more passengers. To my surprise, Mrs. Zealy, the head nurse on 2 East got on.

I sidled over to her and apprehensively asked the question which I had been harboring for two months. "Can you... can you tell me anything about Kim Griggs?"

She turned toward me and her smile was radiant. "Do you know, a miracle happened with that child! Why, he's at home and in school!"

I couldn't believe it. "At home and in school" the very words, my first words to Kim that day... the day we prayed. "How would you like to go home, back to school and not be sick anymore?"

No, not "my" words, I reminded myself. Jesus' words. No wonder there had been a miracle. I wondered why Laura hadn't let me know.

That night I telephoned her from the motel. She gave me the impression she might leap through the receiver at any minute and hug me.

"Isn't it fantastic? Kim's just great. He began to improve gradually. Just like you said he would."

"But Laura, why didn't you let me know? I've been biting my nails off in Kentucky these past two months wondering."

There was a long silence. Laura sounded puzzled. "I was going to call you, but my mother said I didn't need to. She said you had enough faith to know Kim was healed."

I felt like crawling into the woodwork. "There's something I must confess to you, Laura. While I was praying for Kim the night before I finally got into his hospital room, certain words and sentences just seemed to sift into my mind concerning him... just as though a voice were dictating them. That day... in his room, I just repeated what I had been given to say the night before... all the examples about the letter and the bicycle... Not that I didn't believe what I was saying. I did. But on that basis, can you forgive me for being human enough afterward to let some doubt creep in?"

"You mean you believe that Jesus gave you a speaking part in His plan for Kim? Is that what you're trying to say?"

"That puts it well. You're right on the button."

"Then if that was the case," Laura seemed to be trying to put her own thoughts together, "the whole thing was planned, even down to my split second arrival to pray with you."

"I suspect it was. But the mechanics aren't nearly as important as the fact that Kim is well now. I'm so happy for you."

We agreed to meet for lunch in the hospital cafeteria the next day before Kent and I had to go back to Kentucky. The next morning at the Outpatients Clinic Kent climbed up on the bed eagerly, rolling up the sleeve of his left arm. He bounced on the bed while waiting for them to start his IV. "I'm going home today!" He loudly announced to the other kids stretched out on the beds who were receiving their chemotherapy. I silently marveled at his sunny attitude and bravery with all he had to endure.

At that moment, a Marine in full dress uniform entered the IV room carrying a young boy of about three. The nurse pointed to one empty bed and he gently lowered the youngster onto the bed. They were obviously new to NIH One of the doctors was starting an IV on a child in the next bed. The Marine straightened up, watched the procedure for a moment, blood seemed to drain from his face and he began to faint. As he started sinking, the doctor grabbed his belt and kept the Marine from hitting the floor. One of the nurses hastily snapped a vial of smelling salts, holding it under his nose. He sat on the floor and coughed, looked around the room and broke into a sheepish smile.

"Kinda' rough duty these kids have here," he told the grownups.

After treatment, Kent and I set our trays on one of the formica topped tables. I looked at the cafeteria clock—12:30 PM. At that moment Laura and Kim walked through the double doors. I wouldn't have recognized Kim.

This couldn't be the same shell of a child I'd seen two months before. Plump, sturdy arms, free of any bruises protruded from his short sleeved, plaid shirt. The hollows in his face had filled out. He walked across the cafeteria toward us with the swagger of a miniature athlete.

While we ate our lunch he told us about school and his classmates. At one point, he reached into his hip pocket producing a small, black Bible and held it up for me to see.

His dark eyes danced, "You know, I almost died," he told me, "but, Jesus healed me."

"I do know, Kimberly." I smiled on the outside, but I felt like someone had poured liquid sunshine into my insides.

He pointed toward the small book in his hand. "I'm reading this. I want to know what's in here now. Thanks for telling me the secret."

His words followed me to a height of 30,000 feet in altitude as our jet majestically bore us home to Kentucky.... "Thanks for telling me the secret," he'd said.

But I had learned a secret from Kim Griggs—the secret of waiting on God for His guidance, His Words, His timing, His way to meet each individual situation. Bill had been right. I couldn't just run rampant through the hospital praying for everyone and expect results. The secret was in listening, waiting, for some guidance to point not only the direction, but the way.

As we made the approach to Louisville our pilot announced, "This is your Captain. There is heavy ground fog and we are maintaining our pattern, circling the field. As soon as we receive a word from the control tower we'll proceed."

I almost laughed out loud. That was it! My instructions too. Most of the time my life might be in a fog spiritually, but my responsibility to Jesus was to maintain my pattern, circle the field, and wait for a word from the heavenly Control Tower.

I was to find out that those very words were portent, prophecy—a forecast of an experience to come with two Eastern Airlines flight attendants and an empty airplane.

To be returned to: Sandra B. Ghost
                           11320 Connecticut Ave.
                           Kensington, Md. 20795

With this statement I give permission for my son Kimberly Griggs
to appear in the book on N.I.H. by Sandra Ghost and attest
that all references to the subject above are reported
accurately in the material.

                   Signed: _____

With this statement I give permission for reprint of a
testimonial to Kimberly Griggs written by me, understanding
it is to be published in a book by Sandra Ghost.

                   Signed: _____

Chapter Nineteen

I was to have greater proof to nail down my hunch about God's exquisite timing on our next flight home from NIH. We spent the usual five days in Maryland. Not one patient was put in my path to pray for, but this time there was a break in our long-established travel pattern. When Kent and I picked up our tickets at NIH's Patient Travel Services, we found we were to return home on an Eastern Airlines flight originating at Dulles Airport instead of the familiar Washington National.

Perhaps this, in itself, should have raised my spiritual antenna to an attitude of attention. But as we checked in, I just considered it to be a mistake in the arrangements made by the hospital.

However, I felt a nameless alerting from the moment Kent and I entered the airport... as though something unusual was about to happen. To my surprise, after handing our tickets to the gate attendant, I found we were expected to board a lounge-bus to take us to the plane. At Dulles, aircraft left from the middle of the field instead of the terminal.

Trying to muster an attitude of sophistication I didn't feel, I told myself, "I'll just step right on this thing like I do it all the time." But aboard the bus, I found my mental rehearsal for the benefit of my fellow passengers was unnecessary. Kent and I were the only ones there! As the driver roared the motors to life, I realized with a jolt that no one else was coming. *Where was everybody? Had the shuttle already made one trip with the rest of the people?*

To my amazement, as we boarded the plane itself, the flight attendants greeted us with, "I can't believe this! You're our only passengers... an eighty-eight passenger Jet Electra all to yourselves!"

Not only was I shaken, my trumped-up façade of sophistication was shattered. They continued to rave that nothing like this had ever happened to them before, as they steered us past our tourist class seating toward the first class lounge in the rear.

I learned that Sandy Abbenante, the senior flight attendant, had been on that particular run for eight months; Vivian Smith, her co-hostess, for six. Both made it a point to emphasize they had never had less than thirty passengers on that scheduled flight.

Remembering my strange anticipation from the time I had entered the airport with Kent, the thought began to surface within me that maybe this situation was no coincidence. Somehow the Lord might be in all this. I knew I needed to keep a listening ear heavenward to find out.

As the girls went to fix coffee and get Kent some juice, I tried to stifle my bewilderment by looking out the window. My imagination comforted me by suggesting swarms of guardian angels in flight formation with us. I whispered, "Father, I think You're in this. Please show me what I'm to do."

Kent's eyes quizzed me. "Mommy's praying?" So many times my five and one-half year old son's sensitivity was a surprise.

"Praying for the ladies, sweetheart," I whispered, not wanting him to think I was concerned about our safety.

The only obvious explanation for the empty plane seemed to be that I was supposed to talk to both girls about the Lord. They were a captive audience. Even one more passenger might have divided their attention.

Once we were airborne a voice came over the intercom. "This is the Captain. It's against FAA regulations, but come on up. It's your plane!"

Sandy and Vivian led us up to the cockpit. The first officer hoisted Kent into his lap and proceeded to show him all the controls. He activated a "quacking" fire alarm on the ceiling to the delight of my son. My thought flitted back to Kent's declaration that he wanted to "fly the plane". In essence, I realized he was getting his wish.

"Highly unusual that you two 'own' this plane," the handsome Captain observed as he put his cap on Kent's head. "Never in six years have I had anything like this happen before... usually about thirty people minimum on this flight and more like sixty to seventy."

A rising fear began to wedge its way into my mind. *What if the plane was going to crash? What if we were going down like a rock?*

At that moment the Captain told Kent, "These are the four jet engines. And this is the way we turn one off, little buddy." He reached toward one of the four levers near the floor.

"Wait! Stop!" I said. "You're scaring Mommy half to death. If it's supposed to be on leave it on, please!" Everybody laughed, but I was dead serious.

If the plane were to go down I knew where Kent and I were going, but not the crew. Huge, fleecy white clouds caressed the glass of the cockpit and it was as though I heard a voice say, "Why are you afraid? Those are your Father's clouds." I silently prayed for the crew and felt my fear lift like an untethered helium balloon.

Back in the lounge after Kent's flying lesson, I made the mistake of following my own logic rather than any direct guidance. Vivian served me coffee and gave Kent a large glass of orange juice. Both girls sat at the lounge table with us. I took one sip and immediately launched into the story of Kent's cerebral hemorrhage. But the girls didn't seem to be hearing me at all. Their attention drifted and it was awkward. The pilots piped a broadcast of Grand Old Opry music over the speaker system. I was baffled, but in obedience to what I thought I was now being told to do I stopped—as abruptly as I'd begun. Perhaps I'd been dead wrong in suspecting this situation had been set up by the Lord. Or was I out of step with His timing?

Later, as the plane made its approach for the landing, I asked the girls, "How often do you two fly this route?"

"Well, our schedule currently takes us into Louisville about twice a week," Sandy offered.

"How about staying overnight with us sometime you have a layover? We only live twenty minutes from the airport," I invited.

Finding some scratch paper, I scrawled out our address and telephone number as our wheels touched down on the runway. With a promise to call us soon, Sandy and Vivian said "goodbye".

As we made our way down the stairs, the ground crew, knowing there were only two passengers on the plane, applauded our arrival hooting upward through cupped hands, "Howard Hughes never had it so good!"

For days afterward, I puzzled about the unusual circumstances. If the Lord had arranged all that what was the point? Nothing much had seemed to come of it… for Him. Finally I reached the conclusion that if I really did believe it had been planned, then I should pray for both girls. Maybe that was my part. At the Wednesday prayer meeting I told the group about our strange experience, asked for prayer for the flight attendants and said I strongly felt the Lord's Hand was in the empty plane. But where?

The following Sunday afternoon we received a long-distance call from Alexandria, Virginia. It was Vivian Smith. She and Sandy were arriving in Louisville at 9:05 PM Tuesday night and wondered if the invitation still stood. That night I excitedly drove to the airport to meet them. On the way I prayed, "Father, show me if this is the right time to tell them what You've done for us. And if it isn't, please stick a sock in my mouth to help me keep it shut. Let something come from them to let me know it's the right timing."

When I arrived home with the girls Bill straightened his tie and told me impishly, "You bring home the nicest things!"

Sandy and Vivian were a study in contrasts: Sandy—a dark-haired, beauty with flashing black eyes, warmly vivacious; Vivian—a gorgeous, willowy blonde with a soft southern drawl. Both changed into casual clothes and the evening passed with snacks, music and light conversation.

Around 1:00 a.m. Bill excused himself to go to bed, and as he left the room, I was given an unmistakable "go-signal" through a question asked by Sandy. She had brought up the subject of God herself.

"Didn't you say something during our flight together about God healing your son?"

"Yes," I said haltingly, wondering if I should go on.

"How is he now?" Vivian asked.

"Well, he's still a leukemia patient," I told them. "But after he was first diagnosed he had a bad cerebral hemorrhage…" This time, as I told them the story, I couldn't help noticing the timing seemed to be right. Sandy and Vivian sat listening attentively, urging me on by their attention.

"At that time, my relationship with God wasn't very good."

"What do you mean?" Sandy asked.

"Well, I went to church once in awhile, but God seemed way off somewhere… impersonal. And Jesus was like a historical figure to me—sort of an imaginary being--like Santa Claus."

That brought smiles.

"I know what you mean," Vivian added.

"Oh, I prayed for Kent during the time he laid there in a coma… earnestly, but it didn't seem like my prayers were going any higher than the ceiling."

"I know that feeling myself," Sandy said.

I continued telling them about Mr. Botts's prayer in the elevator, Kent's recovery and the bafflement of the doctors. Both Vivian and Sandy sat suspended—wide eyed.

"Kent's still a leukemia patient, but because Bill and I found out that Jesus is real, we've turned our lives over to Him and have seen some pretty startling answers to prayer ourselves, since then."

Both girls were silent, but there were tears in Sandy's eyes. "You don't know what this means to me," she said. "I've been praying for my parents for weeks. They're getting a divorce. But I've never turned *myself* over to Christ."

"Neither have I," Vivian chimed in. "And since I saw you last week, my fiancé and I've broken up. I've been praying about that, but with the same feeling you had. My prayers seemed to stick around the ceiling."

She pushed back the long honey-colored hair from her face. "Wow! If miracles still happen today… if Jesus is that real. Well… that kind of changes everything."

Sandy seemed to be deep in thought. "You think that makes the difference in prayer? I mean the elevator operator had turned himself over to Christ and therefore he knew Him… you didn't then?"

"It seems that way. I've found out since the Bible says no man can come to the Father except through the Son. Well wait a minute, I can describe that better. I read in a book called, *Prayer The Mightiest Force In The World* that prayer is like this: You can walk into a room that has a lamp sitting on a table and turn the switch to get it to come on. You can turn it repeatedly, but if the lamp's not plugged in, the light won't come on. Receiving Christ is what plugs us in to God--connects us up to the Father."

"Can I do this… now? I mean show us how. If Jesus is that real…" Sandy's voice trailed off.

"I need to too!" Vivian added eagerly.

After we had prayed together, Sandy suddenly began to cry again, "That's why that plane was empty except for you and Kent—God meant for this to happen! He knew we both had needs and were praying, but didn't know how to...get through."

"You know," I told the girls, "I thought maybe God was in it as soon as we boarded the plane and found we were the only ones on it. If you remember, I tried to tell you both the same thing I said tonight, but the timing didn't seem right."

Vivian gasped. "I know why," she said," it wasn't until the day *after* the flight together that I started praying about my fiancé!"

As we put our dirty dishes in the kitchen sink, Sandy grabbed Vivian by the shoulders and exclaimed, "Look at the additional timing in this, Viv! You know I've strictly held my father responsible for the divorce." She turned toward me, "I've refused to see him, but he still lives in Syracuse, New York. He knows the flight we take tomorrow terminates in Syracuse and he constantly calls me to see if I'll have dinner with him. I always tell him, 'I have nothing to say to you' and slam down the phone. Yesterday, for absolutely no real reason when he called I told him I'd meet him. When I got off the phone I told Vivian I couldn't imagine why I'd accepted. Now I know... I believe God emptied out that plane so you could bring the message of Jesus to us. Now, I have something to say to my father. I think I'm to take this message on to him!" Vivian hugged her and dabbed at tears in her own eyes.

Several weeks later I received a letter from Sandy Abbbenante saying she had met with her father and it was a time of reconciliation. She found her father was not solely responsible for the failing marriage. Just as she was to leave to fly back to Washington she told him the story of the empty plane. Then she added that when she and Vivian returned to Washington they checked with Eastern Operations, still convinced the Lord had something to do with the empty plane, they searched for proof. What we had only suspected before was now spectacularly confirmed by Eastern's operation records. Twenty-eight reservations had been made for that particular flight to Louisville. There had been no cancellations, but Kent and I were the only ones to check in for the flight. Twenty-six people had to have had a flat tire, missed the airport limo or been mysteriously blocked by some delay or they would have cancelled!

The empty plane seemed to point up an almost computerized split-second timing was involved in witnessing and getting results.

I could envision the Holy Spirit behind the scenes, scurrying around busily preparing the hearts and circumstances in the lives of others. Then, at just the precise moment a wave of His hand might bring the person He has chosen to come on stage, fulfilling the role of saying the right words about Jesus. Our job seemed to be to stand in the wings, ready for His cue.

As the testimony of the empty plane spread by people in the prayer group, more and more new people began attending our Wednesday night group. Those I hardly knew just began popping in anytime it pleased them to ask questions and "chat" about the Lord. It became overwhelming. At first it was flattering. I began to feel like some kind of spiritual celebrity until I found myself the recipient of an admonishing Word from the Holy Spirit.

I was getting ready to go out to dinner with Bill, needed the hair spray and realized Lisa must have borrowed it leaving it in her room. I ran upstairs and hastily grabbed the can in the dark, spraying in large arcs around my head. Not until that moment did I actually look at the can—it was Pledge furniture polish!

I ran downstairs wailing, "I Pledged my hair! I Pledged my hair!" Looking in the bathroom mirror my image looked back resembling the mythical Medusa and her head of snakes! Children and a befuddled Bill appeared from all corners of the house and began collapsing in gales of laughter.

"It's not funny!" I brooded. "I can't go now. I'll have to wash my hair."

"Just put your hand over your heart and pledge allegiance to the United States of America," Bill tried to salve the situation with his dry humor, but this brought on a new wave of giggles and pointing by the children.

"It's not funny!" I repeated and slammed the bathroom door cutting off the laughter. I looked in the mirror again, where was that glamorous singer? What had happened to my former glitzy life? *It's okay, God's using me mightily* I told myself. I stepped into the shower, and letting the hot water bathe away my indignity, I lathered my hair with a lavender shampoo. As the bubbles cascaded toward the drain, soft words invaded my mind. I had come to recognize the soft voice of the Holy Spirit Who now seemed to whisper the words, "Spirit of vanity."

"Spirit of vanity? Spirit of vanity...me?" I repeated aloud. "Are you saying I've gotten too spiritually proud over the things that have happened to me?"

"Spirit of vanity", He said again. There was no sense of accusation in the words... no scolding or berating. The words came as a statement of fact alone.

"Oh, my gosh... oh, no!" I saw it immediately. I had allowed a spirit of vanity to perniciously creep into my attitude. I had begun acting like I was God's favorite daughter or something. "Forgive me, Father, in Jesus name," I asked. "I rebuke this spirit—pride was Satan's sin and I don't want anything to do with it! I rebuke this spirit in Jesus name. Help me, Lord!"

Chapter Twenty

The large prayer group had continued to swell in size over the last two years, since we had moved to the pink house. Christians begat other Christians and our basement room became jammed with swarms of people on Wednesday nights.

I reflected on some of the subtle miracles we'd witnessed: Richard, the homeless, warmhearted alcoholic who'd been brought to us. He had lived with us for three months while Jesus slowly transformed his life and eventually reconciled him with his family—we'd shared in that joy. I was reminded of the Smith's who had also been reconciled to their married son by the help of the prayer groups' counsel and prayer; the wives who felt free to drop by and share intimate facts about their troubled marriages, knowing I was still walking that path too. The deep scars in our own marriage had not completely healed yet.

The Kentucky humidity that August was like trying to breathe under water. The huge air conditioning unit in our dining room picture window snored loudly and spat streams of water onto the patio stones outside. Lisa bounced in the back door, giggling happily. "Can we have Kool Aid, Mom?" Perspiration glazed her forehead and the long blonde hair threatened to weave itself into tight curls. She seemed to wage war with her hair on a daily basis, resenting any intrusion of waves. I became alarmed one day when I found her, head cocked, long hair spread into a fan on the ironing board. She was ironing her hair! At age eleven, she was becoming so beautiful, and exceptionally smart. Several weeks before she had come to Jesus and been born again. As I poured the cherry-red liquid I began to reflect on how each of the children now seemed to be richly blessed. I reflected on the miracles we were seeing now in lives around us.

With all the healings I had been honored to witness, I had to admit each one held promise for Kent. He most assuredly had been healed of the terrible side effects of the chemotherapy. And while his protocol still dictated that he have chemo, was the remission he was now enjoying just a reprieve from the disease, or was it a permanent healing?

Several nights later I had a nightmare. Even as I experienced the horror, I knew it was just a dream. I was walking down the aisle of a huge warehouse, carrying Kent. Mountains of cardboard boxes were stacked to the ceiling, but huge mechanical toys were stationed at certain points in our journey. They were like vending machines.

I stopped at the first to show Kent how it worked. As I pushed the button a large mechanical cow leaped high in an arc over the moon. Kent was delighted until two large robot-like arms reached out to choke him.

I screamed and then yelled, "In the name of Jesus!" The arms retracted and we continued down the aisle. As we turned the corner, a bright red and yellow Humpty-Dumpty machine stood at rest against the concrete-block wall. Kent begged to see it perform. I pushed the button and Humpty-Dumpty fell from the wall, cracking in two. As the action of the machine finished, two robot-like arms shot out reaching for Kent's throat. And again I screamed, "Jesus! In the name of Jesus." The arms subsided at the words.

It seemed as though we walked for miles. The toy machines continued to clutch at Kent, but each time responded when I used the name of Jesus.

About midway down the main aisle toward the exit door, we passed one of the toys already in motion. It was a horrifying tableau. A large roller coaster car zoomed around a curve with a replica of Kent in it. At the very crest of the curve Kent was thrown out of the car.

I was repulsed, but not actually frightened knowing I had the real Kent still in my arms as I continued to trudge toward the door carrying him. But the scene had frightened Kent and he now began to cry.

I was becoming increasingly weary in the dream. It was only with tremendous effort that I could lift one foot and put it down in front of the other. As the toys continued to attack Kent I could scarcely say the name of Jesus any longer to ward them off. My mouth seemed to be filled with cotton. It took every last ounce of strength to force each word.

The door was in sight! Our escape—the end of the journey was near as I dragged each foot, trying not to drop Kent. Just as we were within ten feet of the exit a huge, dark, stick figure form ran through the door toward me. I was too exhausted to sidestep its rush toward me and as we collided, it merged into my whole being.

I screamed, "Jesus! Help! Jesus!", and wakened in the darkened bedroom sobbing.

Bill sat straight up in bed. "San, what's wrong?"

"It was a nightmare—the worst I've ever had." I described it to him, hoping my panic would subside by putting it into words. I shivered with fright.

When I finished Bill looked grave. "Do you suppose it's a warning of some kind about Kent?"

"I don't know if it's even of the Lord. Would He give me a dream that is fear inspiring? I don't know if He even speaks to us in dreams for sure. I know it's scriptural but.... Can we trust a dream to be used for instruction or guidance?"

"I don't know. But if I were you I'd just try to forget it and get back to sleep."

He punched the pillow to plump it up. Lying back down he mumbled sleepily, "That was macabre. Try to erase it from your mind and get some sleep."

But I couldn't. The dream was with me for weeks and I had to have it settled. Was it from God or from Satan? Or was it just a production number caused by the spaghetti I'd eaten for dinner that night? I began to pray about it. Bill seemed to feel my probing into the area of the subconscious might be forbidden ground to a Christian.

Laughingly he told me, "Sandy, you're going to wear God out with all your constant questioning. "Why Daddy, why?"

He chanted teasingly, "Yours is not to do or die. Yours is but to reason *why!*"

I squirmed a bit. "You and I've said before that everything in the life of a Christian is a lesson. If that's so, then I think God will honor the 'whys'. Maybe not all of them... but the important ones."

When I made that statement I had no idea that in this lesson God would provide a textbook. Carol Davis from the prayer group telephoned one morning. "Sandy, I've just read the yummiest book. Agnes Sanford's, *The Healing Gifts Of The Spirit*—it deals with the subconscious mind in the life of a Christian."

I couldn't wait to borrow it. Carol Davis' timing in suggesting it to me hinted that perhaps the Holy Spirit, as my tutor, had whispered something of my questioning in her ear.

The main thrust of the book seemed to be that even though the Christian has been born again--the slate of the past wiped clean--our subconscious is like a computerized memory bank, still storing incidents from our non-Christian past. Sometimes these memories need the surgery of prayer for removal. The book suggested that our deep mind that never sleeps can also be a point of contact for the Lord to instruct us through dreams. I read and re-read the book, sifting through and savoring the deep wisdom from God.

About 7:00 o'clock one evening I got a telephone call from Maureen. (Name changed.) She was a young, pretty girl of about twenty—Spirit-filled and vivacious, with a sparkling sense of humor. She and her parents regularly attended the weekly prayer meetings.

"Sandy, I've got a problem," she told me. "Could I slip over this evening for a little prayer together?"

She arrived about 8:00 o'clock and we went down to the family room to be alone. Maureen looked worried as she lounged on the studio couch and I curled up in a chair. Examining her hands she seemed to be rather surprised, "I'm biting my nails again."

I laughed out loud, "Come now! Is *that* your problem?"

She giggled. "Heck no, but I guess my nervousness is a result of my problem.

I keep having a problem with jealousy and..." she squirmed self-consciously, "I think I might be oppressed by a demon." She started to bite the nail on her pinky finger, realized what she was doing and abruptly stopped.

"You think this is a demon of jealousy? For Pete's sake why, Maureen?" Surely she couldn't be serious, I thought. The young woman had everything, looks, clothes, a great walk with Christ...

"Well, it doesn't make any sense. Every time my best friend, Candy, walks into a room this unreasonable jealousy rises up in me. I know I have a better job than Candy does, nicer clothes, a much newer car and just being honest, I know I'm prettier than she is, but I can't control this thing that comes over me. I want you to pray with me to get rid of it, okay?"

"Okay," I responded, but wasn't really sold on the idea that this was a demon, however, since that's what Maureen expected we went to prayer. I took authority over a spirit of jealousy that was oppressing, not possessing, Maureen and commanded that it be gone in the name of Jesus Christ. Nothing outwardly happened and soon she got back onto the couch after kneeling in front of it.

"I haven't told you yet about my real problem, Sandy." The slight dusting of freckles became more pronounced when she smiled. "You see, I have this re-occurring nightmare."

I almost fell off my chair. "A dream? Your big problem's a dream? I can't believe this."

She looked at me as though she thought I was making fun of her, so I quickly amended, "You can't believe the timing in this. I had a dream... a nightmare, really... and I began praying about God speaking to us in dreams. It seems like the Holy Spirit has decided to throw me some kind of spiritual textbook on dreams and I've been taking a crash course on the subject. I met a girl who'd tried to commit suicide, but was praying for help. She kept having a dream about Christ. When we realized that's who was in her dream, she turned her life over to Him."

Maureen blinked in astonishment. "You're kidding. I've had this thing hanging around my neck for at least two years now. Lately it's gotten much worse. Just yesterday I was strongly impressed I should get together with you about it."

"Would you believe, just yesterday I finished a book on the subconscious mind of Christians! Let's hear about this dream of yours." I realized in my excitement I was sitting on the edge of my chair now.

Maureen nibbled on a fingernail. "It sounds silly talking about it but... in the dream I'm a little girl. I'm standing on a porch of sorts. Suddenly I look up and overhead, fastened and hanging upside down from the porch ceiling, are thousands of green turtles with wings. I can feel panic practically choking me as I discover them. And then as I cover my head and run, they fly after me."

She took a deep breath and turned to face me. "At this point I always wake up screaming and my parents run into my bedroom to see what's wrong. But Sandy, my heart is pounding, my palms are sweating and I can't get back to sleep."

"That's pretty grotesque," I sympathized.

"I've tried praying about it, taking authority over the devil in it and nothing seems to work. I have the thing every night. In fact, I've gotten to the point where I'm afraid to go to bed, knowing the nightmare's going to come again."

"I don't blame you. The one I had was a one-time-thing but if I thought I'd have to face it every night I think I'd give up sleeping." I told her. "You know Maureen, that's what started me investigating dreams in the first place. I've uncovered a little bit about the spiritual aspect. Let me share it with you."

I was certainly no authority on the subject. How to put it so I wouldn't sound like a know-it-all, I wondered? "The author of this book seems to feel that many times Christians have a tendency to attribute a dream as a suggestion from the past which floats to the surface as being from Satan. In good faith, we rebuke the devil, not realizing that perhaps this is something the Lord wants lifted out of the subconscious and cleansed. By standing against it we shove it right back down into the deep mind again to fester and seethe."

She nodded indicating she understood.

"Instead, the Lord wants us to offer it up to Him in prayer. Although we're born again with our past erased, many times painful memories that are stored in the warehouse of our subconscious can be clogging up the work of the Spirit… holding us back in our walk with Christ."

"That makes sense."

"Well, it did to me. Why don't we follow the author's suggestions in prayer asking the Lord to walk back through your subconscious mind, showing us what's causing this dream?"

"I'd give anything to bury this thing. Let's try it."

We bowed our heads, still sitting in our chairs. After a time, following closely the suggestion in the book to be highly descriptive in prayer I asked, "Father, You made Maureen's mind… the conscious and the subconscious. We ask now that Jesus would walk back through the room where all her memories are stored. Reach into the file drawer where each incident is kept and pull out the experience which is now causing her so much fear in the dream. Please show us, Lord."

We waited. Suddenly there was a quick intake of breath from Maureen. Her eyes were still closed but she gasped, "I'm sure I saw a picture. Actually *saw* it… like a vision, I guess. In it I was a little girl, standing on my grandmother's back porch. I was waiting for my father to drive in the driveway from work. It was dusk. Just as the car pulled in I ran across the yard to meet him. But as I did a bat swooped between him and me. I covered my head and screamed."

She opened her eyes and turned to face me with a dazed look. "Sandy," she said slowly, "that really did happen! I couldn't have been more than three or four at the time. I've completely forgotten about that. Could that be what caused my dream?"

"Well, we asked the Lord and that's what we got in return. It makes sense really. The turtles with wings, hanging upside down like bats do. They swooped at you. You covered your head. It all seems to fit, doesn't it?"

"It really does. Just to think, so tiny an incident lying around in my subconscious, brooding until it surfaced in the proportions it did. You know, probably a psychiatrist could have probed for months and unearthed it, but Jesus did it in five minutes."

"There's a lot to be said for psychiatrists," I agreed. "The principle seems to be the same as what we just saw take place. Get it up out of the subconscious and when the person takes a good long look at the memory and sees what a trivial thing it was in the light of adulthood, they can deal with it.

"But the Christian way is certainly speedier," Maureen bubbled, her vivacious-self again. Suddenly her mood changed again. "There's one more thing…"

"Yes?" I sensed she was about to tell me something big.

"Sandy, I feel silly in even talking about this… like I ought to lie down on your couch, like we're playing psychiatry now." She giggled, but it was like a self-conscious effort to cover embarrassment, "But I've just got to tell someone about this."

Obviously this was something very painful from the way she was acting.

"It's just that… well you know, I'm reasonably popular. I have dates and they're mostly Christian boys." She took a deep breath and paused.

"But even if I get really interested in one, to the point where I more than like him, I just can't let him kiss me goodnight. Do you think that's normal?"

I held back a laugh and substituted it with a smile. "No, I certainly do not," I told her.

"I'm dating a guy now that I just adore. I really like it if he holds my hand when we're walking down the street, or if he puts his arm around me in the movies." Tears began to well up in her eyes now. "But something's terribly wrong with me, I can't let him kiss me goodnight and feel like I can't breathe if he tries."

"You think it might be something in your past that's causing this wall in your emotions?" I asked softly.

"I don't know what's doing it to me. Maybe the Lord wants me to be a nun!" Her lower lip quivered.

"Maureen, we've just had such spectacular prayer results. Let's take this to the Lord in the same way."

Maureen slipped off the couch onto her knees in answer and I knelt by my chair. I again prayed pictorially as the book had instructed, "Lord, please walk into the room where Maureen's memories are stored in her subconscious. Walk over to the windows, lift the blinds, let Your light come into this room. Walk over to the filing cabinet where this memory is stored, open the correct drawer, take out the file, open it and show it to her."

This time we were not silent for very long when a low moan escaped from Maureen as though someone had injured her. She began to sob.

Not knowing what was going on, I was afraid to go to her, afraid to speak for fear I would interfere. At length, after many tears she told me.

"It was like a picture in my mind again. Apparently this was a memory that was so painful to my conscious mind that I completely blotted this out of my life, Sandy, until now." She was shaking. I went and put my arm around her.

"But the picture was again something that happened when I was a little girl," she continued. "I have no actual remembrance of it, but when I saw the picture... I knew it really happened."

What Maureen "saw" was a scene that happened when she couldn't have been more than six or seven at the time. One Sunday morning her parents, who both taught Sunday school, arrived very early to prepare their lessons and dropped Maureen off at her classroom. The little girl found that none of the other children had arrived yet. It was there...alone, that one of the deacons found her—and molested her. Though nothing of any consequence happened, the little girl was terrified by the experience and in the scene that unfolded through prayer, she had pushed and pushed hard repeatedly to keep him away. Maureen had mentally blocked the incident from her mind, remembering nothing of it until our prayers unearthed the scene.

I had the distinct feeling there was healing in the flood of tears that now issued from Maureen--the child, and Maureen--the adult. "So now we know," I said softly. "Can you forgive him?"

She looked at me through startled eyes, "Forgive him? You must be crazy! How can I possibly forgive him... he's probably ruined my life. How will I ever get married now?"

"But it's imperative you do forgive. Otherwise your own prayer life will be blocked, hon," I reminded her softly. "It's forgive us our trespasses as we forgive those who trespass against us, right?"

The beautiful blue, rather water-logged eyes regarded me with dismay. "You mean God expects me to forgive that horrible man, and a deacon like a wolf in sheep's clothing?"

"You're a Christian now; you're grown up physically and spiritually." Suddenly the Holy Spirit gave me the answer to help her forgive him. "You came here tonight, Maureen, asking for prayer because you felt you had a spirit of jealousy oppressing you. You couldn't control your jealousy because of it. This surely must have been a spirit of lust controlling this man. On that basis, can you forgive the man himself?"

Maureen put her head in her hands. "'Forgive us our trespasses as we forgive our trespassers...'" she mumbled and was silent for a time.

"On that basis, I guess I can." As I watched, she slipped to her knees. "Oh, Father, I *do* forgive him and pray for him wherever he is today. And as he is freed from this, I ask You to free me from this past experience. Heal my emotions...please. I know deep inside that this is what has caused this blockage I feel toward any nice boy I date."

I thought, more than prayed from my chair silently, "Lord, I've seen You perform two miracles here tonight. We are really on hallowed ground!"

"Sandy!" Maureen almost yelled from her kneeling position in front of the studio couch. "I'm having another vision... It's a burning bush like Moses saw. There are words that seem to go with it. They are: 'Take the shoes off thy feet for you are on hallowed ground'"

For the second time that night I almost fell off my chair. My prayer about hallowed ground had been a silent one. Maureen could have had no way of knowing. Was the Lord troubling to let me know He'd heard me by giving *her* a vision?

Her tone became tinged with reverence. "Now the picture's changing. I see a prison door with a tiny, high window. Through the window I can see Paul manacled to the wall, in chains. Wait! There's a shaft of light piercing through the window. His chains are dropping off. Oh! I can even hear them clank to the floor."

She was silent for a time. "There seem to be words with this picture too. They are: 'As the chains dropped from Paul, the chains of your past have dropped from you this night, my child.'"

After a time, Maureen got up and sat on the couch. She stared at me with a dazed look. "What does that mean? That my bad memories have been healed?"

"I would guess so," I ventured. "It seems like a word from the Lord reassuring you that the bad memories of your past will no longer have any hold on you. But I've got a question. How did you know it was Paul in the vision? Peter was in prison too."

She shrugged her shoulders, "I don't know. Something just told me it was Paul." She looked at the clock hanging on the wall by the stairs. "Good heavens, it's twelve o'clock! I've got to go. Thank you so much for listening, Sandy, and all the prayer help."

"Believe me, it was some kind of fantastic experience for me too!" I told her.

Maureen had had her last vision approximately seconds before midnight. She called me the next afternoon, breathless with excitement. "For the first night in months I slept the night through! The nightmare didn't come back and I've got the feeling it's over for good.

"And do you know, I've had about three people at work today tell me, 'Maureen, what's different about you? You look different today—just radiant.'"

"I'm so happy for you," I told her.

"But I've saved the best part until last. The Lord really confirmed to me that those pictures I saw in my mind last night were really visions."

"How?" I asked, catching her spirit of excitement.

"Well, your question to me about how I knew that it was Paul sent me Bible searching when I got home. Remember what time it was when I had that last vision?"

"Yes, exactly midnight, because you looked at the clock and said you'd have to go."

"You'll never guess what I found... In Acts 16:25 it starts out 'But about midnight'... and goes on to say that this was when Paul and Silas were released from prison."

My arms broke out in a rash of goose pimples. "Wow! I don't think there's a doubt in the world something really spiritual happened here last night to free you from your past. Only time will tell the tale in proving it, Maureen."

I'd asked the Lord a question about His communication with us through dreams. I was willing to rule out coincidence that shortly thereafter my path had crossed that of two girls, Carol who had just read a book about dreams, and Maureen, the recipient of a dream that were surely from God. But how did this apply to my dream of Kent in the warehouse? The only common denominator seemed to be instruction.

I decided it was high time that I did some research in scripture. To my surprise I found; God expressly forbids anyone to consult soothsayers, enchanters or diviners to interpret dreams as Nebuchadnezzar did before he sought out Daniel who was a man of God (Daniel 2). Daniel prayed for the answer and received it from God. And as he related the interpretation to Nebuchadnezzar, the king just seemed to know deeply within his spirit that this was the correct explanation (just as Carol had known).

God spoke in a dream to so many of His people my head began to swim at the list: Abimelech, Jacob, Laban, Solomon, Joseph, Paul....

But I discovered that apparently the relationship between Moses and the Lord excluded dreams. In Numbers 12 I found:

5. "The Lord came down in a pillar of cloud, and stood at the tent door, and called Aaron and Miriam, and they came forward.
6. And He said, Hear now MY words: If there is a prophet among you, I the Lord make Myself known to him in a vision, and speak to him in a dream.
7. But not so with My servant Moses; he is entrusted and faithful in all My house.
8. With him I speak mouth to mouth (directly) clearly and not in dark speeches; and he beholds the form of the Lord."

Lucky Moses! What a tender and loving compliment he'd received from the Lord. My spading and raking through scripture had proven to my mind that God does speak through dreams. But I had also unearthed a warning that they must be tested prayerfully in the laboratory of the Holy Spirit before determining whether the source is God or the pickles we've eaten for dinner. The Bible also points out logically that if the dream comes true it is from the Lord.

In my dream-hunt through the Old and New Testaments, I had skirted one scripture in Job. My neglect had been purposeful. I just had no desire to dig into Job's dreams, figuring Satan's scapegoat could produce nothing but full-blown nightmares in vivid color and stereophonic sound.

But when I finally made myself look it up I knew it was for me. As I read, that certain little leap of spirit within said, "Pay attention!"

Job 33:15-16 "(One may hear God's voice) in a dream, in a vision of the night, when deep sleep falls on men, while slumbering upon the bed; Then He opens the ears of men, and seals their instruction (terrifying them with warnings)

Now I had my answer. I knew my nightmare had not been from Satan. I had questioned if God would give me a dream that inspired fear. But it had been a warning posted on the gates of my soul to not get spiritually tired in our walk with Kent.

There would be attacks upon him down the long aisles of leukemia that seemed to be our path. But we were to stand against them in the Name of Jesus and NOT GET TIRED of using that Name... guarding against Satan wearing us out physically and spiritually when we were buffeted by attacks. I sensed, as I read the scriptures that day that my dream had been a warning from God Himself, but what I didn't know was that it would come true. Only then, did I heed its instruction.

Chapter Twenty-One

*I*t was a heart-tug watching Kent and Kurt start kindergarten that fall. The proximity of the "pink house" to Greathouse School made it a short walk across the alley in the back, but it seemed to me like a thousand miles that Monday in September. A conference with the teacher had been necessary to establish Kent's schedule at NIH that would dictate absences and makeup work.

A few weeks into the school year, Eric brought home an extraordinary friend. One afternoon, I looked out the backdoor and saw him in the backyard talking to a very large, very black crow that sat in the tree by the garage. Their exchange had an enchanted quality. Eric would say a few words and the crow would respond with loud caws, garbles and squawking, meanwhile strutting up and down the branch. To my astonishment (and maybe Eric's too) the huge bird flew down, sat on Eric's shoulder and then, as my son lifted his arm, the crow perched on it like he had on the tree branch. Eric walked slowly toward the back porch and proclaimed with the pride of the father of a newborn, "I'm going to call him 'Isaac', Mom!"

"I'm going to call him out of bounds in the house, son." I stopped them at the door. "He's tame, isn't he? Must belong to someone."

"Nope! I don't think so. He just followed me home from school. I was walking along and he adopted me."

"Well, sweetheart, you can't possibly adopt a wild bird. He stays outside, okay?" From that point forward, Isaac followed Eric to school every morning and home every night. The children adored him and apparently miffed at being left outside of the school, Isaac located Eric's classroom and would perch on the window ledge. Occasionally the teacher would open the window and Isaac would fly in and get an education. He became the mascot of the children. Finally word reached the Louisville Courier Journal newspaper who sent a reporter to cover such a human interest story.

Eric had gotten a used Nikon camera for Christmas that year, had become extremely talented at taking photos and had his own darkroom in the basement. His pictures of Isaac were so outstanding that the newspaper used those for their article.

Isaac the crow became a celebrity in St. Matthews and surrounding suburbs of Louisville and to prove his ecumenical love of children he also became a regular at the Catholic parochial school. He became adept at knowing the varying dismissal times of the different schools and would always show up like clockwork.

"I sure don't believe in the saying "bird brain" anymore to describe somebody who's not very bright," I told Bill. "You know all kinds of extraordinary things have begun to happen to Eric ever since he accepted Jesus as his Lord and has become filled with the Holy Spirit."

"Sure seems that way. Can't be coincidence."

My thoughts spun back to the night it had all begun:

"Mommy, the devil bugs me" Eric had flung the words in the air casually, but there were tears in his eyes. At the time he had been just ten years old and was seldom this serious. I had come into Eric's bedroom to tuck him into bed and hear his prayers.

"Why, honey?" I sat down on the side of his bed and smoothed the hair from his forehead.

"Well, every time I go to say my prayers," he swiped at one eye with his pajama sleeve, "swear words come into my mind. A whole bunch of them."

I smiled at his wisdom. I think you've hit the problem on the nose. You're right, that is the devil and you don't have to put up with that."

He looked relieved. "I don't?"

"Jesus' death on the cross defeated Old Public Enemy Number One." I told him. "We don't have to put up with pranks like that from the enemy. There's a place in the Bible that says, 'For this purpose was the Son of God made manifest, to destroy the works of the devil'. With Jesus in us, we have the power to tell him to scat."

His eyes grew wide. One hand flew up to his mouth to cover an embarrassed grin. "We do?"

"Would you like me to pray with you about it?" I suggested.

"Sure!" He grew serious again. "Could you pray with me to receive the Holy Spirit too?"

He had turned his life over to Jesus about a month before after one of the prayer meetings in our home, but we hadn't pushed about receiving the fullness of the Holy Spirit trusting the Lord to initiate that in His timing. My eyes scanned the obstacle course of model airplanes, race car tracks, and the assorted boy-litter that was sprinkled all over his bedroom floor as Eric slipped out of bed and onto his knees by the bed. I knelt next to him.

"Lord, we thank You for this night," I said aloud. "We ask that Eric might be emptied that he might be completely filled with your Holy Spirit."

A curious thing began to happen within me. Slowly, I became engulfed in an awareness of God's love for my son that seemed to superimpose itself over my own mother-love.

I continued, "Using the weapons You've provided us with, the Holy Spirit and Your Name, we command this spirit of obscenity to leave Eric in the Name of Jesus."

I placed my hands on his head. "You know, Lord, this child has turned his life over to You. We now ask that Jesus would baptize him with the Holy Spirit,"

Eric seemed to shiver slightly under my hands. After a time, when it seemed obvious nothing more was going to happen, I suggested he climb into bed.

"You've asked son," I told him. "And now, to show the Lord you've accepted in faith that He's done it, just begin to thank Him for *having* filled you with His Spirit."

I kissed him gently, turned out the light, and left the room. The kitchen was just across the back hallway from Eric's room and I realized I had left half the dinner dishes undone. I had just run fresh hot water in the sink and laced it with dishwashing soap when I heard Eric yelling.

"Mom! Mom! Come in here."

I hurried down the hall to his bedroom. As my hand fumbled for the light switch, Eric cautioned, "Don't turn on the light! I can see a light the size of a man by my bookcase. Can you see it too?"

I started for the bed and in the reflected glow of the hall-light I could see Eric sitting up in bed, wide-eyed, but seemingly not frightened. He was staring in the direction of his bookcase by the door. "There it is again. Do you see it? Do you see it?"

I sat down on the bed—a puzzled spectator, perhaps a little frightened by what seemed to be a hallucination my son was having. "What's it look like?" I asked.

"Just a huge light which goes from the floor clear up to that top shelf. About as tall as a man."

With those words Eric swung his head around and stared in the direction of the closet. "And, there's a small ball of fire hanging in the air over there! It's traveling toward me!"

There still seemed to be no fear in what he was experiencing—just curiosity. However, I was shaken.

"Can't you see it, Mom? The ball of fire... it's traveling all over me." At that moment Eric began to speak in tongues.

Relief flooded over me. It hadn't been a hallucination. It was God, proving to a small boy the reality of His presence, lending dramatic signs to show He had heard our prayers.

"Honey," I told him, "I think maybe I have some understanding of what you're seeing. Jesus said,' I am the light of the world'. I think the light in the corner was your Lord, letting you know He's here with you. And sweetheart, the Baptism of the Holy Spirit is mentioned in the Bible as the 'Baptism of Fire'. That could explain the small ball of fire you saw. It was right after that when God gave you your new prayer language, son. Boy, do you ever have proof that you got the Holy Spirit when you prayed for Him." I kissed him on the cheek.

"Now I can say 'thank you' and really mean it." Eric grinned. "When you left the room the first time I just kept thanking Him over and over and suddenly that light came on in the corner. You really couldn't see it too?"

"No, dear. This was your experience—not mine. I think the Lord meant it for your eyes alone. Try to get some sleep now."

Afterward, when we were settled in front of the television, I told Bill "Wasn't that precious of the Lord to allow me to be with him so he wasn't frightened by what he saw?"

Bill shook his head from side-to-side. "Come to think of it, anybody who is skeptical about the validity of the Baptism of the Holy Spirit should have been in that room from what you tell me. That child had no idea of the biblical significance of either the light or fire... yet you're saying that's what he saw. There's no doubt in my mind he really saw a vision."

"I wish the Lord would give me one too," I admitted.

Three nights later as I got into bed I said aloud, "Father, maybe I'm just not good enough to have a vision." But deep inside I knew our goodness had nothing to do with it when it came to God's grace.

Suddenly the wall opposite the bed lit up! In full color, the size of a huge movie screen, an enormous image of our dehumidifier in the basement appeared. There were words that seemed to accompany it: "You left it on, now go turn it off."

I laughed until I cried at God's sense of humor, and scampered down the basement stairs. Sure enough, the machine was humming nosily when it should have been off.

I climbed back into bed, hugging myself joyously, but not over having the vision. As mundane a picture as it had been, nevertheless I was convinced it had been a vision. But the joy seemed to come from the inner certainty that the Lord had bothered to prove a point with me. I now knew that if He had something to tell me, He would. I didn't have to try to pull it down from heaven. That night I promised Him that in the future I would seek Jesus and not the experiences He could give me. The humor of giving me a vision of something so un-spiritual was not lost on me.

Several weeks later, as Kent and I checked into the Eastern Airlines desk at the Louisville airport for our scheduled trip to Bethesda, a dark cloud of foreboding seemed to fall on my shoulders like a heavy shawl. As we boarded the plane the feeling grew heavier and I felt a great need to pray. I tried to shake the feeling as the tinkling sounds of "Baby Elephant Walk" played through the plane's intercom. *Was the plane going to crash? Were we in danger? Had Kent relapsed? What was it that was threatening?* But I knew without a shred of doubt that the Holy Spirit was instructing me to pray. I tried to hide my anxiety from Kent and silently prayed in tongues trusting that the Holy Spirit would make "intercession when I knew not what to pray". As the flight headed east, high above snow frosted fields below, the feeling continued to grow in intensity. Kent busied himself with a puzzle as I continued to ponder what dilemma awaited us once we got to NIH.

The feeling continued to increase in intensity while Kent had his bone marrow extracted and I couldn't even talk with anyone casually I was so busy silently praying. The doctors had changed again on the service and Dr. Salem, our new doctor, seemed very pleased with Kent's condition after his exam. I felt like I was in a breath-holding parenthesis waiting for the bone marrow test to come back from the lab. The prayer urging never let up as we waited and I was fearful that he might be in relapse; however, the doctor proudly proclaimed him still in remission.

"Let's get your chemotherapy over with now," he beamed at Kent and led the way back to a small three bed room with IV poles bristling in stainless steel brilliance from the headboard of each bed. This was across the hall from the usual, large ward-type room for Out Patient chemo. "I do things a little differently," he told Kent. "I'll start your IV, we'll hang the D5W... get it going, and then I like to inject the chemotherapy drugs directly into the IV cord. That okay with you, sport?"

"Sure!" Kent eagerly hopped up onto the bed. He'd become an old pro and seemed to know this procedure had to be borne in order to keep the leukemia away.

The nurse readied the bag of D5W on the pole, stretching the cord onto the bed. She opened a packet of alcohol pads and scrubbed at the crook of Kent's arm. Dr. Salem removed the IV needle from its sterile packet and said, "Just a little stick, Kent." Once inserted into the vein, the doctor hooked it up to the IV cord and adjusted the flow of the D5W.

I had seen this procedure a myriad of times, but I couldn't shrug off the intense foreboding that now oppressed me like a dark cloud. I couldn't keep from pacing the room as I silently prayed.

Kent winced slightly and looked at me, "Why do they always say, 'Just a little stick', Mom?"

The doctor and nurse both laughed and Dr. Salem said, "I guess we learn it in medical school, Kent," and still chuckling he went into the adjoining room where there was a sink and counter. He picked up a large hypodermic needle and I could see him filling it from a small pharmacy bottle. He held the syringe up to the light momentarily flicking air bubbles from it with his thumb and forefinger, then replaced a heavy plastic bubble-type protective covering over the needle itself.

He now positioned himself on one side of the bed, the nurse on the other preparing to shoot the drugs into the IV cord. I felt like my prayer language was going to explode out of me! The nurse reached over to remove the large plastic encasement around the needle and the entire needle fell apart—drugs spilled out all over the bed.

"Oh! I'm so sorry, doctor... so sorry," she exclaimed. They both seemed bewildered and Kent started to giggle at his impromptu bath.

"I've never seen anything like that happen before... not your fault," Dr. Salem muttered. "No matter... I'll just fill another syringe," he tossed in our direction as he went back into the adjoining lab room and took another syringe out of a drawer. As he went to fill the needle this time apparently his eye caught the lettering on the bottle.

"My God! My God! My God!" he screamed. People came running down the hall, poking their heads in the door. "If I'd given him that it would have killed him! Would have **killed him**! The pharmacy sent the wrong dosage. What if that syringe hadn't broken? What if...?" He abruptly sat down on one of the bedside chairs.

The nurse appeared to still be in shock and slowly shook her head from side-to-side. But I knew exactly what had happened. It couldn't have been an accident to spill the medicine on the bed. That was precisely why I had been so intensely alerted by the Holy Spirit to pray. I had no idea what deadly misfortune could have awaited us, but He knew! I couldn't see the intricate happenings behind the scenes that permitted this prayer to be answered, but the Holy Spirit had to have had a hand in breaking that needle and not permitting the deadly drugs to enter my son!

As we waited for the pharmacy to send down the correct dosage, I felt led to tell both Dr. Salem and the nurse of my experience upon boarding the plane to come to Bethesda. "Had to have been some kind of heavenly intervention," he responded still seeming stunned. I actually felt sorry for him. It surely wasn't his fault. (But not his real name used.)

Kent summed it up, "The Holy Spirit sent my guardian angel to break the needle, Mom, didn't He?"

I took his other hand that wasn't engaged by the IV and kissed the fingers. An overwhelming relief, gratitude and joy rose up in me, replacing the intense urgency to pray that I'd felt before. "Yes, sweetheart, you have the Lord's protection, for sure."

"For sure," echoed Dr. Salem as he introduced the proper dosage into the IV cord.

As we flew back home, I silently thanked the Lord over and over again. *What do people do who don't have the fullness of the Holy Spirit to guide them, protect and forewarn them, Lord? I can't imagine. When Your word says that "the Holy Spirit makes intercession for us when we know not what to pray"... what a gift! If we pray in our prayer language this is the perfect prayer to accomplish whatever we need to protect us from happenings we can't see that might threaten us.*

As I looked out the window of the plane, small wispy clouds drifted past. **Suddenly I was reminded of my dream!** It was as though the dream scrolled before me again in warning... I had carried Kent through the warehouse and toys reached out to him threateningly. Surely Kent's close call with death today had been the first attack.

Would there be more?

Chapter Twenty-Two

*T*wo months later, as Kent and I prepared to fly back to Maryland, we entered the Eastern Airlines entrance for Standiford Field. Our tickets were always waiting for us, courtesy of the government, and I wondered fleetingly how our family could ever pay back the blessing of finding such fabulous medical help in the shadow of catastrophic illness.

Kent spotted him first. A tall figure dressed in a white suit walked toward us across the concourse. The black string tie, cane and white goatee spoke of the graciousness of the old South. A white Palm Beach hat completed the picture.

"Colonel Sanders," Kent breathed the words with reverence.

I immediately realized that Louisville was the home of the Kentucky Fried Chicken corporation and wondered if we'd be sharing a flight with the celebrated Colonel. An aide lifted his luggage up to be tagged and checked.

"Well, and who may ah' have the pleasure of meeting," he drawled bending down toward Kent.

"I'm Kent Ghost, sir," Kent squared his shoulders and offered his hand.

"And is this lovely southin' belle your wife, young man?"

Kent giggled and put a hand to his mouth. "She's my mother, sir!"

The Colonel leaned on his cane, obviously enjoying the conversation. "And are you both going to grandma's house?"

Kent looked up at me briefly as if to see if I wanted to answer. When I just smiled he offered, "I'm a research patient at the National Institutes of Health in Bethesda, Maryland, Colonel." To my surprise he said it proudly as though at his young age of seven somehow he realized his case was a contribution to curing the disease.

"That's admirable, son! Simply admirable! How often do you travel?"

The two of them walked ahead of me and I felt I should stay in the background as there seemed to be bonding going on.

"It depends on my protocol," Kent told him. (I didn't even know he knew that word!)

"Well, I'm going to be doing a good bit of traveling to DC and Virginia now, Kent," his new friend told him. "Maybe we can get to be friends, okay Champ?"

"Sure!" Kent smiled and squirmed with pleasure.

As we boarded, Colonel Sanders was seated in first class. We went beyond the curtain to tourist class and the two waved at each other.

Once we were in the air the flight attendants began serving drinks and lunch. Shortly thereafter, the first class flight attendant came to our seat and said, "Colonel Sanders has requested the pleasure of Kent's company in first class. Is that okay with you, Mom?"

"Oh can I? Can I please... please?" Kent begged.

"It's okay," I told them as the flight attendant took his hand. I set aside his luncheon hamburger and salad for when he came back.

Almost an hour passed. Trays were cleared away and the compartment had settled down to reading magazines and quiet conversation when Kent appeared through the curtain. He closed it behind him and jerked a thumb back toward first class announcing to one and all in a loud, rather indignant stage voice, "They are eating *steak* up there!" Spontaneous laughter filled the cabin.

So began the friendship between Colonel Sanders and Kent. The friendship extended to our entire family as we were invited to new store openings and other events. I was to find out later that Colonel Sanders was a Christian and we had the honor and pleasure of hearing him speak at Evangel Tabernacle in Louisville. His testimony was touching and our children were impressed. Kent leaned over and whispered, "He looks like an angel up there all dressed in white!" But his story was anything but angelic for like the rest of us he'd made a lot of mistakes and was a sinner saved by grace. At the end of his testimony I wanted to run up and hug him.

As the friendship of the Colonel and Kent continued through many trips and invitations, I marveled at how this elderly, southern gentleman treated a little seven-year- old as an equal. Other than his huge commercial success, for which he had become a symbol, he had learned to truly put into practice that we are "one" in the Spirit when we are in Christ—age and station in life are irrelevant.

Although NIH continued to reassure us Kent's health was excellent, I felt there might come a time when we would need the resources of any spiritual lessons learned about healing. Little did I know that I was in for a rude shock to add to my textbook on healing. In fact, the Lord shook me by the shoulders of my understanding.

As Christmas approached, our house buzzed with activity. Pungent green wreaths with crisp red bows proclaimed to passersby on Nanz Avenue that the Ghost household was ready for Christmas. All of the treasured decorations were lovingly put in their familiar holiday places. Gold tinsel looped its way across the mantel as a festoon for the fireplace. A bunch of mistletoe flirted from the archway between the living room and dining room.

It was our family tradition to set aside the night before Christmas Eve to make cookies and a birthday cake (angel food, of course) for Jesus with one candle for each year our family had known Him. Each child had his own function greasing cookie sheets, cutting dough, or decorating the cookies with sprinkles of red and green sugar. Lisa actually took charge as she was the baker in the family. It was legendary that "Mom can't bake." The other family legend was told by the children that "if you lost Mother in the grocery store, you had to stop and think what color her hair was *that week!*"

Just as I had sifted the flour into a huge wooden bowl, the telephone rang. I could tell it was long-distance by the hollow sound on the line.

"Sandy," I recognized the southern drawl. It was Laura Palmer, Kim's mother from NIH. There was a long pause, then... "Kim's gone."

"Gone? Gone? But that's impossible... oh, God!" I felt tears rising up to choke me and slid into a sitting position on a kitchen bench. I waved for Lisa to take the twins out of the room. She immediately seemed to perceive the twins should be shielded from whatever was happening and said, "Come on, guys! Let's leave Mom alone for a minute." She shepherded them out of the room.

"He died about 3:30 this afternoon. I felt you should know." Her tone was flat, her voice weary.

I felt as though someone had punched me in the stomach. It was hard to breathe. "Oh, Laura, I'm so sorry," I finally managed. "I didn't even know he was sick. Why didn't you let me know he was bad?"

There was no answer from the other end of the line.

"The last time Kim was critical Jesus healed him." I was crying now. "Laura why didn't you let me know? We could at least have been praying." *Would Kim have lived under those circumstances,* I wondered?

"Sandy, I prayed. I prayed for the Lord to take him at the last. He didn't seem to have any pain, but he was so tired... just so tired. I know I should have let you know, but it all happened so fast."

Laura began to relate the nightmare of circumstances that led to Kim's death. On November 26th, the day after Kim's birthday that fell on Thanksgiving that year, he began running a fever of 107°. They were in Atlanta, Laura's family home, for the holiday. She called NIH and the doctor told her to make a run for Maryland as quickly as possible—there would be a bed ready for Kim at the hospital at any hour she got in.

It was impossible to picture the frenzy of mental anguish she must have experienced trying to take care of her child while driving at top speeds the 740 miles from Atlanta to Bethesda, Maryland.

They reached the hospital shortly after noon. NIH again pulled out all the medical stops at their command. A battery of tests was run to find the cause of the fever. The diagnosis was grim. Bacteria had gained the upper-hand in Kim's body—the deadly enemy of every leukemia patient.

The following Monday he had four seizures and internal hemorrhaging. Many units of blood and chemotherapy drugs had to be given intravenously to set up a wall of defense against the leukemia that was taking over Kim's entire system. His condition began to stabilize; however, he was now becoming immune to the chemotherapy—the only weapon left. And, because it had become necessary to keep an IV running constantly, changing vein sites as his little veins collapsed, there were now no sites left to introduce the IV A "cut-down" was the only resort to keep the IV flowing—the source of his life.

I shuddered as Laura explained to me what a "cut-down" was. The main artery in the shoulder had to be cut and the IV tubing run directly into the artery itself. *What a horror for a child,* I thought.

It was done at 3:00 PM in the afternoon. Kim told his mother he would only have to have it in for five days. Each morning she said, he would hold up the amount of fingers to indicate how many more days were left before the cut-down would be removed. Laura distinctly remembered that the doctor had not promised Kim how long it would have to be in—but Kim had insisted five days. It was removed at 3:45 PM the afternoon of the fifth day. Kim was dead.

"Sandy, I had him baptized by one of the hospital chaplain's five days before he went… with water from Lourdes. He was so brave. He cared so much about the other children, worried about them and about me."

"You know," I told her, "I'll never forget when he had to be hospitalized before, he always went around taking care of the other children."

"It was the same way this time, until he had to be in bed all the time. Then his concern was for me. He was so brave."

What could I say to comfort her I wondered? Kim was such a sensitive, unusual, loving child. And now he was gone from us. "We know *where* he is, Laura. Still very much alive. This was one child who was walking in his resurrected life long before he ever crossed over to the other side."

"I know. There's no doubt in my mind he's in heaven. No more needles. Thank God for that. We had a Christmas tree in his room… gave him his presents early. He wanted a set of drums. They're still in the boxes. I think we'll leave them for the leukemia patients… the other children he loved so much."

I fought back tears again. Kim had left the gift of a shiny set of drums to the children on the leukemia unit. But his true legacy to NIH had been the gift of a loving and brave spirit to anyone his life had touched.

After we'd hung up it was hard to resume the jolly cookie baking atmosphere. The children hadn't comprehended our conversation, I felt sure. I decided to tell Bill later and not ruin their fun. Trying to roll up my sleeves and plunge back into the festivities, I found that bittersweet thoughts kept pulling at me.

Kim, sitting across the lunch table in the cafeteria, his dark brown eyes flashing happily. "I almost died, but Jesus healed me," he had told me pulling the tiny Bible out of his hip pocket.

Would things have been different if we'd been there to pray for him again? It was an audacious thought, but I couldn't help speculating.

How could the Lord let him die? He'd become a Christian. What could be more cruel than the timing in his death? Christmas! I felt guilty surrounded by my own family. What a bleak Christmas it would be for Laura. How could the Lord do that to her? What had gone awry spiritually?

I had to resist an urge to gather my own brood protectively into my flour covered arms—especially Kent.

Later that evening, after the cookies had been carefully stacked in tins, the angel food cake frosted, I put the twins to bed. After hearing their prayers I knew I could expect a certain amount of stalling. Therefore, I didn't pay much attention to Kurt's question until he repeated it more forcefully. "Mommy, why doesn't Jesus get any presents for His birthday?"

I floundered for an answer, but before I could think of anything Kurt's eyes suddenly widened with understanding.

"Oh, I know," he proclaimed. "Because the *people* are His presents."

His words rang in my ears while I ran water for my bath. "The people are His presents..." It wasn't in the same words, but some familiar strand of scripture pushed to the surface of my mind asking to be compared. I turned off the water and sat down on the side of the bed, hastily leafing through the Bible.

I was stunned by the deep wisdom of Kurt's answer to his own question. It was almost as though an angel had whispered in his ear. And then I found the comparison my mind had been trying to make.

> John 10:27: "My sheep hear my voice, and I know them,
> and they follow me; And I give unto them eternal life;
> and they shall never perish neither shall any man pluck
> them out of my hand. My Father which gave them to me
> is greater than all."

Afterward I sat in the bathtub brooding. Kim had belonged to Jesus. I knew he had eternal life, but why had he been allowed to die? The "what ifs" attacked me.

What if his parents had been filled with the Holy Spirit? Would that have made a difference? Or, what if we had been there to pray for him in person? Jesus had healed him twice before under those conditions. What had gone wrong? I was determined to wring the answer from God and carried a chip on my shoulder for several months after that, licking my spiritual wounds. In the four years Kent had been a patient at NIH I'd known other children who had died. But we'd not been as close to them as we were to Kim. Although these deaths hurt me terribly I mentally made excuses: The parents weren't spirit-filled; the home was out of order; there was doubt present, or the faith of those surrounding the child had not been strong enough. Everything I'd ever learned about healing now had to be crumpled up and thrown in the wastebasket. There were no formulas.

To say that death is sometimes an answer to prayer seemed like a cop-out for the spirit-filled Christian. The organized church has assumed this position for years claiming that sometimes God heals through death. Yet, the Holy Spirit movement has put more of an emphasis on healing miracles and claiming the promises. I'd been a first-hand witness to spiritual healing. Now I felt stretched like a rubber band between the two positions. I had believed our Spirit-filled status gave us privilege somehow. Kim's death seemed to sink my spiritual life raft for Kent—until God threw me a lifeline through experience of another child.

Gay Payne, mother of Larry Payne, an eleven-year-old boy who had relapsed and was hospitalized had also become a dear friend at NIH. Relapse is when the leukemia is no longer under control. Usually, at this point the patient is put in the hospital and high induction drugs are given again in an effort to gain another remission.

Gay was a woman in her late thirties, soft spoken, with the eyes of a Madonna. Larry was a handsome young boy with certain qualities that reminded me of Kim, particularly his concern for the other children on the floor and his devotion for his mother. I was not surprised to learn that both Gay and Larry were Spirit-filled Christians.

Two months after Kim's death, Kent and I returned to NIH for Kent's bone marrow. Afterward, we raced for 2 East to see Larry and Gay again. But his room was empty.

"Maybe he's gone home, honey." I took Kent by the hand and we stopped at the nurses' station.

I poked my head in the door. Several nurses were flipping through charts on a metal rack. One arranged plastic pill glasses on a tray.

"Can anyone tell me anything about Larry Payne?" I asked.

All activity stopped. I could tell by their expressions. Mrs. Zealy shook her head sadly from side to side. There was grief in her eyes. No one seemed to want to put it into words in front of Kent.

I took him by the hand again and we walked slowly down the hall. "Did Larry go home, Mommy?" Kent asked.

"Yes dear." I fought the tears which burned my eyes. "He went home." I closed the unit door behind us.

It wasn't exactly a lie. I knew Larry Payne was in his real home. I felt I had to protect Kent from the knowledge that another close friend had died. Of course, in the span of four years there had been others. But patients were on different schedules in clinic. If Kent didn't see a friend he assumed they were at home. He never questioned and I saw no reason to burden my seven-year-old with the knowledge that his hospital friends were passing away all around him.

In answer to his question I told him, "Remember, *you* almost died once too."

That seemed to satisfy him.

Now I bit my lip and decided to try to protect him from Larry's death. Both deaths might worry him about his own condition. He knew they had leukemia.

That night, in the motel room, after I made certain he was sleeping, I called Gay Payne who lived in Gaithersburg, Maryland not far from NIH.

"Gay," I began. "I'm so sorry about Larry. I just found out today when we got in. What can I say?"

"Oh, I'm so glad you called." There was genuine warmth in her voice. "I've got something to tell you about Larry's crossing to the other side… something you should know. It was a real victory."

"Victory?" I repeated hollowly.

"Yes. It really was. You must believe me, Sandy."

I detected the same quality of peace in Gay's voice that had been in Laura's.

"Can you talk about it?" I didn't want to upset her.

"Oh, I've been anxious to tell you. Larry's Aunt Alice, my sister, and I were with him the day he crossed over to his real home."

She'd used the words "real home". It was like a comforting pat on the back that my judgment in not telling Kent was alright with the Lord.

"His little mouth was so dry. I kept going out and getting ice for him to hold in his mouth—he wasn't allowed any liquids. Every time I would leave the room, Alice said Larry would start to say the same sentence, "Tell my Mommy…" But he wasn't able to finish it. Alice said it seemed to her Larry knew he was dying and his concern was for me."

I was thankful Gay couldn't see me wiping tears.

"About 8:00 o'clock that morning I sat down beside Larry on the bed. We didn't say much. I put my arms around him. He was sitting up, Sandy, on the side of the bed. Suddenly he smiled radiantly. It illuminated his whole face, but he wasn't looking at me. He was smiling at someone else—someone he seemed to recognize. Someone I couldn't see."

"I don't understand," I said.

"At the precise moment Larry smiled, he fell into my arms. His heart stopped."

"Oh Gay, how awful for you!"

"But you don't understand. It wasn't. I guess it might have been if Larry hadn't smiled in recognition. You see, Sandy, I know—just as surely as I'm talking with you—that Larry saw Jesus."

I was stunned. Suddenly, the little speech I had planned to try to comfort Gay seemed hollow. I didn't know what to say.

"But that's not really what I wanted to tell you, Sandy. Alice's daughter Debby, Larry's cousin who is thirteen, just couldn't accept the death. We couldn't find any way to console her. Maybe if she'd been in the room with us… seen his joyful smile as death came, perhaps then she could have accepted it as her mother and I did."

"But to be in the same room…" My voice trailed off.

"The funeral was in Green Cove, Virginia. Alice and Debby were staying in a motel the night before Larry's body was to be buried. Sandy, what I'm going to tell you may be hard for you to accept, but Alice and Debby's account is identical. At exactly 3:00 AM in the morning they were wakened by the sound of a mighty rushing wind. The windows of their motel room were closed. They both sat up in bed. At that moment they saw what looked to be like a light—in the shape of a dove—that flitted from corner to corner of the room."

I felt chills begin to travel up and down my arms.

"The light lasted for scarcely a minute or two when they distinctly heard Larry's voice. 'Tell Mommy,' he said. 'Tell my Mommy, I'm happy,' he said. 'Tell my Mommy, I'm happy.' From that time on Debby was never sad again."

"Oh, Gay." I didn't care whether she knew I was crying now or not. "How beautiful! Those were the same words… the same sentence he never got to finish before he died."

"That's right." Gay's voice seemed to exude a quality of tranquility. "I believe Jesus allowed him to finish the sentence, so we'd know first-hand he'd made an entrance into his new life."

My mind raced ahead probing. "But why do you think Larry wasn't allowed to tell you personally?"

"I guess because the Lord knew I'd witnessed the joy on his face when he crossed over. It was Debby who needed to be consoled."

"Yes, that makes sense," I told her.

"Debby's outlook on her cousin's death was totally different after that."

"Gay, you just don't know what this has done for *me*. I've held such a grudge against God for taking these children we've prayed for at NIH. This experience of yours opens a whole new door of my understanding of death."

Her words were gentle. "I know you've had a struggle in this area too."

"Struggle's not quite the word—'arguement' would be a little more like it."

"Larry was spirit-filled," Gay told me.

"I hadn't thought of that! I remember now. Well, Gay all my theories are out the window. One of the mothers maintained that when you pray for healing and death comes we have to accept this as an answer to prayer too."

"I certainly agree with that," she said softly.

"I'm going to have to come over to that side of the fence too. After what happened with Larry, I've got to believe it's true."

"It's the Lord's prerogative just how that healing takes place. Sometimes it's physical... sometimes its total healing of body, soul, and spirit."

"You don't know how much you've helped me," I told her. We promised to see each other on our future trips to NIH and hung up.

I got up from the desk in the motel room and paced back and forth in the narrow aisle at the foot of the beds. Suddenly I was transported back in time. I remembered the night I had paced the same floor plan when Laura had asked me to pray for Kim. He'd had forty-eight hours to live then the doctors had figured. Our prayers reversed his condition. There had been a miracle. But then he had died.

My spiritual disappointment with God had begun at this point. I was so sure something had gone wrong—that we had failed Him somehow on a spiritual basis. But if I now accepted what Gay believed on a very real and firsthand basis, then Kim's death was not accidental. Nor was it due to any spiritual shortcomings. Quite simply, God *had* healed him—completely—totally. Not just temporarily or fractionally as He had in response to our prayers that had strictly bought time on this planet. Perhaps Laura's prayer for God to take him had helped release Kim into his new life. And because God loved her, He waited until she was ready.

I crossed over to the luggage stand and opened my suitcase. A small index card was tucked in the side pocket. It had been given to me months before by Laura, Kim's mother. On it, Gene Palmer, Kim's stepfather had written:

"The day that Kimberly was taken into the National Institutes of Health he began a journey of endurance that was to test the very limits of his soul. His only companion was pain; his only solace a deep well-spring of courage and inner strength.

Behind the final cure for cancer—when that moment arrives, will stand an army of volunteers like Kimberly, whose sacrifice is a debt their fellow men can never repay. Someday, somewhere, a program of treatment will be outlined for a new patient, another cherished and unique life. If, miraculously, this life can be saved, who could deny that a share of the success belonged to Kim and the children who joined him?"

Only then did I remember something else Laura had told me about Kim's death. She had said, "For five days before he died he kept talking about the children in his room. 'Tell them not to touch the Christmas tree, Mother,' he'd say."

"But there are no children in the room, baby." I told him.

"Yes there are. They're all over the room playing. And they keep pulling at me to come play with them."

"He was on no pain-killing drugs and he wasn't hallucinating. I talked about it with the doctor," Laura told me.

For five days, Kim insisted the children no one else could see played in his room, tugging at him to come with them and play, while he was imprisoned in bed tethered to IV cords, cut-downs and pain. It was then I remembered Laura had said, "I even asked the doctors if perhaps these were the children with leukemia who had died before him, helping Kim to cross over to the other side."

To be returned to: Sandra B. Ghost
                     11320 Connecticut Ave.
                     Kensington, Md. 20795

With this statement I give permission for Larry Payne
to appear in the book by Sandra Ghost on N.I.H. and attest
that all references to the subject above are reported accurately
in the material.

                              Signed: _Mrs. Kermit B. Payne_

Chapter Twenty-Three

———— ◌↬ ————

*D*espite the wrenchingly sad, but breathtaking beauty of some of the answers to my questions on spiritual healing, I constantly kept trying to apply what I was learning to my own son. Much as I cared deeply for the children and families at NIH, though selfish, Kent was the bottom line and I found myself back to square one after so many precious children had not made it. I kept analyzing everybody else's experiences through the lens of viewing Kent's healing. And just when I had begun to reconcile myself to the fact that perhaps healing wouldn't take place, I was staggered by a divine appointment that spun my thinking back to a totally opposite direction.

I had been asked to speak in a small Baptist church in Louisville. And now, as I stood in front of a curious congregation I wondered what I could tell them. What encouragement could I offer? When I'd spoken in other churches before, my subject was always God's healing power based on our experience with Kent's cerebral hemorrhage. The theme had always been "God heals today." I wrestled with my new knowledge that sometimes it is through death. How could I tell them that?

I stood in front of the congregation with knocking knees, grateful for the wooden lectern that hid me from the waist down. I had the momentary thought that if I asked for a time of silent prayer, while heads were bowed I might be able to escape down the aisle of crimson carpet to the door. I wasn't sure whether it was my own thought or not, but I felt I heard, "Leave your confusion in the pew you just sat in. Just tell of your own experience—that's not being a hypocrite."

I took a deep breath and launched into the story of Kent's near-approach to death and our introduction to the Lord through the prayer of Mr. Botts. When I was finished I stepped down... back into the front pew where I had left my spiritual confusion swirling. The pastor walked forward and asked for those who wanted to accept Jesus Christ as their Lord and Savior to come to the altar. Several people filed toward the front of the church. However, one woman came and sat next to me. She was short, robust, and middle-aged. Glasses framed eyes that sparkled with excitement.

"I knew I was supposed to come tonight," she said, smiling warmly and settling herself on the pew beside me. "And I just knew I was supposed to give you this." She pulled a folded paper from her purse handing it to me. It looked like a letter that stated a medical summary. The letterhead read:

"Dr. O.J. Hayes
Medical Towers Building

Louisville, KY"
It was dated December 16.1966, four years prior. It began:
"The following is a summary of my office records on Mrs.
Joseph Blanford as requested by the patient."

My eyes scanned down the page, wading through medical jargon that
seemed to indicate on June 29, 1959 Mrs. Blanford was examined by Dr. Hayes
and diagnosed with cancer—"epidermoid carcinoma of the cervix."
The summary continued: "On September 29, 1959 this
patient was operated upon. The entire lower abdomen and pelvis
was filled with a malignant tumor mass which extended up the
left side to the basification aorta indicating a very wide spread of
her malignant disease. These masses were biopsied at surgery
and the diagnosis was confirmed of threat of metastatic cancer..."
She was seen again in April, 1960. The patient had
developed severe swelling of her left leg. She was unable to
get around very well and was requiring narcotics for the relief
of this very severe pain. The entire mass was still palpable on
examination extending out throughout the entire pelvis and
it was felt at this time that this patient was definitely terminal
and probably would not survive."

"But I don't understand why you've given me this," I said, turning the page.
"Who is Mrs. Blanford?"
A broad smile lit up the face of the red-haired woman who sat next to me.
"I am, honey," she said softly.
"This is *your* medical summary?" I sputtered, staring incredulously at the
healthy-looking woman who sat smiling at me. "Dated *four* years ago?"
"Just read the next page," she patted my hand, "then maybe you'll
understand."
I picked up the paper again.
"In June of 1960, this patient was started on external
irradiation therapy, which she did not complete, due to the
marked pain and discomfort and difficulty in getting around.
I believe she had approximately three courses of X-ray, which
certainly was well below what would be required for any
effect.
Contact was lost with Mrs. Blanford at this time, and
I assumed that this patient had expired. In May of 1962,
she appeared at my office. She was two and one-half years
following her operation and her last X-ray had been in July of

1960. The swelling of her leg had gone. She had full use of her leg. She had no symptoms whatsoever and on examination, I was unable to ascertain whether any cancer was left or not.

She was seen again on November 5, 1962, at which time, her examination was completely negative and no evidence of cancerous disease could be found.

She has been seen periodically since that time for routine examinations. She has been in the hospital on several occasions for X-ray studies, all of which have been termed as normal. At one time the left kidney was non-functioning, and on re-check, it has now returned to normal and functions satisfactorily.

She was last seen by me on September 28, 1966. She is absolutely asymptomatic. No bleeding; no discharge and no evidence from examination of any cancerous condition.

This case is most unusual in that this woman had proven, far advanced, metastatic cancer of the cervix and there should have been no hope whatsoever for her survival. She did not complete her X-ray treatment, due to her illness and she had a minimal amount of X-ray, not enough to bring the cancerous condition under control, but, as best as can be determined, at this point in 1966, following her original disease in 1959, this patient is well, healthy, and no evidence of cancerous disease can be found."

It was signed: "O.J. Hayes, M.D."

"You've been completely healed of cancer for years, Mrs. Blanford... with no medical help?" I asked in astonishment. I could scarcely believe the paper I held in my hands.

She smiled warmly, folded her hands in her lap. "Just call me Maude, honey. Yes, the Lord healed me in 1960." She stated it matter-of-factly as though miracles of that magnitude happened all the time.

"Your medical summary is an answer to my prayers," I told her excitedly. I've been asking God to give me a medically documented healing of some terminal disease. I know miracles can happen, but sometimes Christians can be pretty vague about the details in a healing. Your evidence is solid--can't be disputed."

"Dr. Hayes keeps checking me periodically. I've even been hospitalized for studies. I guess the doctors can still hardly believe it. But Jesus still heals. He's the 'same yesterday, today, and forever.'"

I shook my head in wonder as my eyes traveled slowly over Maude Blanford's healthy-looking body. Had this medical summary just fallen in my lap? Or had the Holy Spirit gently guided Mrs. Blanford by the elbow to my side to show me the other side of the coin—that God can heal cancer physically, not always just through death?

I suddenly realized we were the only people left in the church. The minister was turning out the lights in the side rooms and a dark-haired woman stood waiting to take Mrs. Blanford home.

"I've just got to talk with you again. I want to find out what happened during those two years you lost contact with the doctor," I told her. "Could we get together tomorrow? I don't have the car, but could you come to my house?"

"I don't drive and I live way out in the West End, but I'm eager to tell you about it."

"I'll call you then, Maude—tomorrow."

She scribbled her telephone number on a church bulletin and hugged me in a motherly fashion. "I have the feeling the Lord's brought us together," she told me.

If you could only guess my underlying confusion about healing, I thought, *you could see how badly I needed a real-live miracle, Maude Blanford.*

But aloud I told her, "I sure think so too."

I couldn't wait to telephone her the next morning. I dumped breakfast dishes in the sink and shooed the children off to school a little earlier than usual. Collecting my cup of coffee and a note pad, I sat at the kitchen table and dialed.

Once Mrs. Blanford was on the line I asked," Is this too early for you, Maude? I could call back later."

"Good heavens, child, I've been up since 6:00 AM. All my housework is done. I'm so glad you called."

This woman who had been dying of cancer seemed to be a veritable dynamo of energy. I eyed the stacks of dirty breakfast dishes on my own kitchen counter and in the sink.

"You're way ahead of me," I laughed. "Now, tell me, what happened during those two years the doctor lost track of you thinking you had died?"

"Honey," her voice was deep, throaty. "The Lord Jesus did it all. I know that now. But in the beginning, when I was diagnosed—when the tumor I had was the size of a football, there was nothing to trust in but what the doctors could do."

"I can understand that," I murmured in agreement.

"They operated on me on the 29th of September and just did exploratory surgery. Three days later I talked to the doctor. He told me there was nothing they could do. It had gone too far. Then the first week of January, I had a cerebral hemorrhage."

"Just like Kent."

"That's one of the reasons I knew I had to talk to you. When you told your story last night I just had to show you my medical summary."

"I didn't mean to interrupt. Please go on."

"I was at home when it happened. The pain was unbearable while I waited for the ambulance to come. I remember crying out, 'Father, hast thou forsaken me?' Sandy, you may not believe this, but I heard an audible Voice that said distinctly, 'Lie down, my child' and as I heard this, my pain left immediately and a calm came over me."

"I believe you, Maude," I told her.

"I lapsed into a coma which was to last for twelve days. During that time, my husband Joe was told again that there was no hope. Even if I regained consciousness, I would probably be nothing but a vegetable."

"We were told that was a possibility for Kent too."

"But I came out of it on the twelfth day—went home on the fourteenth day. At the time I really didn't realize the Lord had worked a miracle."

I smiled. "We went through that too."

"About this time I began having horrible pain from the cancer and my surgeon referred me to Dr. Farnsley at St. Joseph's Hospital for mild cobalt treatments. They told me it would not help much, but should cut down on the pain."

"How many courses did you have?"

"Well, I was supposed to have twenty, but after the third one—that was on July 1st 1960—I decided not to come back. Sandy, the pain was unbearable and as I left the doctor's office that day I couldn't control my tears. I began sobbing. I remember leaning my head back on the seat of the car and saying through my tears, 'Lord, take me as I am. I don't know anything about You. I don't know how to pray, but Lord, have Thy way in my heart'."

I shook my head in sympathy. This woman had had to endure so much.

"Up until this time," she went on, "I thought I was a Christian, but now I suddenly realized I had never really given myself to Jesus Christ totally. I didn't really know how to pray."

"Do you think this was a turning point for you?" I asked.

"Definitely. Two days later on a Sunday afternoon, my husband carried me out into the yard. It was so hot that day and we didn't have air conditioning. He made me as comfortable as possible on a cot under the trees. I had just gotten settled and was beginning to enjoy the slight breeze when suddenly a scripture verse from the Bible came to my mind. Now, this might seem rather normal to you, but I'd never read the Bible before!"

"Then how did you know it was scripture?"

"Just by the sound of it—it didn't sound like ordinary English. It was: 'Is not this the fast that I have chosen? To loose the bands of wickedness, to undo the heavy burdens, and to let the oppressed go free, and that you break every yoke… then shalt thou call, and the Lord shall answer; thou shalt cry, and he shall say, Here I am… And the Lord shall guide thee continually, and satisfy thy soul in drought, and make fat thy bones…' Honey, I weighed ninety pounds at the time. I just knew I'd heard the Lord."

"Did you ever find out if it really was scripture?"

"Oh, yes. As soon as the sentences came to me I thought, *Is that in the Bible?* Right away the words came back: *Isaiah 58!* I didn't even know there was a book called 'Isaiah' in the Bible."

"I believe you, Maude," I told her. "I've had an experience like that myself."

"Well, I got Joe to go in the house and get a Bible. I hunted and hunted and finally I found the part called 'Isaiah'. I turned the pages eagerly toward the fifty-eighth chapter and when I got to the verse, there it was! Exactly the sentences I had heard. Sandy, I know I had heard the Lord and felt He was promising me healing."

"That's beautiful, Maude!"

"Believe me, I began reading the Bible constantly then, sometimes until 2:00 or 3:00 AM and discovered all the miracles. They began to come alive for me."

"I know what you mean," I told her.

"On the fifth of July, I decided I wanted to go fishing. Everyone thought I was crazy, because I could scarcely walk. But they finally agreed. I was sick from radiation and still taking narcotics, but it felt so good to be outside and close to the Lord by that lake. I started going twice a week."

"You were so brave," I said, my admiration continued to leap higher for this woman as her story unfolded.

"Not really. I just felt much closer to the Lord there. In fact, I can remember saying to Him, 'If I have to suffer, can I please have some enjoyment with it?' This prayer was answered. In two months time, I could walk the 300 feet from the car to the lake. When my fishing trips first began, my leg was bloated and swollen—there was no feeling from the knee down. But by the second month my leg was much better and my symptoms just began fading away. I was stronger."

"That's remarkable. But didn't you wonder at any time if it was due to the radiation?"

There was a long pause. It seemed Mrs. Blanford was reflecting seriously on what I had asked her. "No, I can truthfully say I didn't. I guess mainly because the doctors had told me it wouldn't help the cancer—just the pain."

"When did the total healing come, Maude?"

"Now, you have to understand it didn't happen all at once. It was gradual. But it seemed to speed up after one particular Saturday night. I had gone to bed and suddenly all the pain in my stomach returned. I prayed and almost in answer a scripture popped into my mind, 'All things are possible to those who believe.'"

But what about the NIH children? My mind interjected, *we believed for them.* I quickly rebuked my thought and returned my attention to the voice on the other end of the line.

"I drifted happily off to sleep. At about 2:00 AM I wakened. I know it wasn't a dream, but I felt as though I were being carried to heaven. I suddenly realized I was dying! I could feel my spirit separate from my body."

The same creepy chills began traveling over my arms that I always seemed to have when someone told of something highly supernatural.

"It seemed as though someone was on each side of me carrying me, lifting me, racing with me toward heaven. I couldn't see who or what was carrying me."

"It might have been angels. Were you afraid?"

"Not at all. It was a beautiful feeling. There seemed to be thousands of voices rejoicing in the distance. I couldn't wait to get there, but then I heard it! From far out in space I heard the Lord's voice saying, 'My child, your work is not finished. You will go back.' It was repeated slowly, majestically, three times."

I was glad Mrs. Blanford couldn't see me wiping at my eyes with a crumpled paper napkin.

"I began praising the Lord and was filled with a happiness I'd never known before. I stayed awake, but in bed for the rest of the night. When Joe wakened about 8:00 AM the next morning I told him, 'Honey, Jesus healed me last night.'"

His mouth flew open and he just stared at me like I was crazy. It was then I realized what he was staring at--the swelling of the tumor the size of a football… it was still there. Of course he didn't believe me."

"You mean you had the faith to make a statement like that even though all your symptoms were still apparent?"

"I still had the pain too, but I knew in my heart that what had happened to me in the night was real. God had sent me back and that must have meant He had healed me. Joe had always carried me up and down stairs. Now, I learned to walk up and down stairs and with every step I said, 'Thank You for my health. It's You I want to please, Jesus.' And I got stronger."

"That's just incredible! How long would you say it took for the healing to be completed?"

"About nine months for my leg, almost two years for all signs of the cancer. I kept thanking Him for it and the symptoms just gradually melted away. It wasn't pretty. It was like having a miscarriage as all the cancerous tissue and mucus passed from me.

In the beginning, I had to sit in a chair to scrub my kitchen floor. I'd have my bucket in front of me, mop a small area of the black and white squares, and say 'thank you, Jesus' for each square I'd scrub. Then, I'd scoot the chair along slowly. After a time, I could do all my own housework again."

"Your bravery and your stamina… all the faith involved sets my head spinning, Maude."

"But don't you see, honey, I didn't have a thing to do with it. It's not hard to have faith over something the Lord has clearly and personally told you He's going to do."

"Well, what happened when you walked into Dr. Hayes office after two years?"

Deep hearty laughter came over the line. "He thought he was looking at a ghost! He just kept walking around me calling me his 'miracle girl'. He figured I was dead by that time."

"Did you tell him the Lord has healed you?"

"I certainly did and you know, I think he believed me. He called in every doctor who had attended my surgery and they all examined me. Their verdict was that there was no evidence of cancer left. That was in May of 1962. In November they wanted to do a complete examination. I agreed to be admitted to the hospital and they went over me with a fine tooth comb. I guess they still just couldn't believe it."

"And they still couldn't find anything?"

"Nothing at all. It wasn't until 1966 that I asked Dr. Hayes if he would mind writing a medical summary on my case that I could have."

"And for all these years you've remained completely healthy?"

"That's right. And I haven't had my medical summary out of the drawer for a long time, but I just felt the Lord telling me to put it in my purse and take it to church last night. When I heard the story about your little boy I knew I was to give it to you."

"Maude, you seem to have such a direct line to the Lord. Would you answer a question for me? You seemed so sure you were to bring your medical summary to church last night. Now, you seem sure you were to give it to me. Would you say the Holy Spirit was leading you to do this?"

"If there were any doubts in my mind they were erased when I heard you telling about Kent's cerebral hemorrhage. Yes, I certainly think the Holy Spirit was directing me."

"I'll tell you why I asked. I've been going through some very real spiritual confusion about healing. Some of the children from NIH who have been prayed for have died. It shattered me until I finally learned that sometimes death is answer to prayer and actually is healing. Now it would seem that the Holy Spirit purposely guided you to me to show me the other side of the coin."

"The other side of the coin… I don't understand?"

"Well, that sometimes Jesus does heal cancer and not always with death. What I don't understand is that you stood on the promises for healing in the Bible. We did that for those children too—but they died."

"But honey," Maude said softly, "I didn't do that until *after* the Lord had told me He would heal me. If you remember, I asked the Lord to take me… I wanted to go, was prepared to die. It was only after I saw His will in the matter that I began to stand on what He'd told me."

A glimmer of an answer began to spark inside me. "I think I get it! What you're saying is that you feel we should lay down our own wills, relinquish them utterly, then wait to catch the mind of the Lord. When that's made clear to us, then we're to pray it through accordingly."

"Sandy, I think relinquishment is the most important factor. Then when guidance comes, put a prayer shoulder to it and claim what Jesus has told you to claim."

"I see."

"If you remember I told you earlier, it's not hard to have faith over something the Lord has clearly and personally told you He's going to do."

"Maude, you've taught me perhaps the most important lesson regarding healing that I'll ever learn. I can't thank you enough for your time and help. Let's get together for coffee some time soon. As Dr. Hayes said, you really are a 'miracle girl'!"

I hated to hang up the telephone. I'd just talked to a walking miracle. Surely she was right—the Holy Spirit must have led her to the drawer where her medical summary had laid fallow for several years.

If I accepted that we had not stumbled into each other by mere chance or providence of coincidence then what was I to learn from this? God had let me in on an extraordinary miracle, but for what purpose?

"Relinquishment." I rolled the word around on my tongue. *This had been the key to the Lord giving us the Pink House. Was this also what the Lord expected of Bill and me with regard to Kent,* I wondered?

To be returned to: Sandra B. Ghost
11320 Connecticut Ave.
Kensington, Md. 20795

With this statement I give permission for reprint of the
medical summary of Mrs. Joseph Blanford. I attest that
all references to me and my diagnosis of Mrs. Blanford
are accurately reported in the text and give permission
for publication in a book by Sandra Ghost.

Signed: _____

Chapter Twenty-Four

*T*iny fingers of apprehension began tugging at me in the spring of 1970. Kent had almost reached his fifth year of complete leukemia remission—his health was excellent and we had been told by the hospital that if the five-year mark were passed, chances for a normal future would widen.

However, the week before he and I were to go to NIH for his monthly bone marrow, a strange feeling became my shadow—a feeling I couldn't seem to lay aside. I would pass his school picture on the wall of our bedroom and suddenly become engulfed in a wave of sadness. Underlying currents of anxiety for Kent would creep up on me while I did the dishes or cleaned the house.

I told myself it was silly. I tried putting the blame on the devil and rebuking each thought as a dart from the enemy, but I couldn't seem to shake this new fear.

As I packed our suitcase the night before our flight to Maryland my anxiety erupted into a flood of tears. I knelt beside our double bed and asked, "Lord, is this feeling from You or the enemy? Please lift this from me if it is not of You, in Jesus Name."

Slowly a comforting warmth began spreading over me as though a large hand had been laid upon my shoulders. I felt the new strength of a spiritual transfusion and yet the apprehension still remained.

I spotted my Amplified Version of the Bible lying on the headboard of the bed and with my usual impatience of waiting for heavenly answers, I flipped it open at random saying, "Please Lord, tell me *something*. You know I'm frantic."

The first verse my eyes touched down on was Ecclesiastes 12:6:
"Remember your Creator earnestly now, before the silver cord of life is snapped apart, or the golden bowl is broken, or the pitcher is broken at the cistern" (and the whole circulatory system of the blood ceases to function).

I gasped and the Bible fell out of my hands onto the floor! Sinking back onto the bed dazed, it suddenly became crystal clear that my anxiety for Kent had been prompted by the Holy Spirit. *He must be in relapse,* I thought, *and my heavenly Father has told me first to curb the shock of hearing it from the lips of a doctor.* I decided not to tell Bill until it was confirmed.

The next morning the heaviness of my apprehension was gone. Through the night it had been mysteriously replaced with the strength I had felt fleetingly the night before. In fact, I began to wonder if I had just been overwrought until our airport limousine slowly rounded the circle toward the entrance of the Clinical Center.

My mind was occupied with counting out change for the driver's tip when suddenly a scripture verse I had never used or thought much about over-powered my mind in a crashing thought. "God is our refuge and strength, a very present help in trouble." The thought came so loudly, was so strong, that I dropped the change.

As Kent and I walked through the revolving doors and down the long hall toward the Out Patient's Department I knew... knew with certainty what the testing would show. But God had troubled to tell me and seemed to be promising help.

"Mrs. Ghost, may I see you alone in my office." Dr. Seigel beckoned to me from the door. I handed Kent a coloring book and crayons to keep him occupied in the waiting room.

The doctor motioned toward the chair beside his desk and sat down. He folded his hands on top of Kent's large chart which lay open before him.

"I've got bad news. I'm so sorry. Kent's relapsed." The words seemed to churn out of him steeped in genuine sympathy.

The cloud of strength I had felt the night before settled upon me like a blanket. "Just how bad is it, Dr. Seigel?"

He shook his head slowly. "The worst it can be—100 percent—total relapse."

"I see," I said calmly, amazed at the current of tranquility that buoyed me above the doctor's words.

"I don't think you do, Mrs. Ghost." He seemed to be studying my face. "This is pretty serious—100 percent. That means he is probably facing a much harder climb toward another remission. It's possible we may not be able to get him back in."

"I see," I said again.

Dr. Seigel seemed puzzled by my reaction. The dread word "relapse" to the parent of a leukemia patient can mean death is around the corner.

"There's one thing in Kent's favor though. In four and one-half years he's responded well to the POMP medication. We still have a battery of other drugs that he should respond to as he's never been exposed to them."

I nodded my head affirmatively. "Will he have to go in the hospital?"

Please... oh please, Lord, let me keep him with me. It will frighten him to go on the ward, I prayed silently.

Dr. Seigel frowned and studied the wall appearing to weigh the factors. "No, he can stay in the motel with you unless he gets an infection of some kind."

I breathed a sigh of relief.

"We'll start a protocol tomorrow. In the meantime," he hung a stethoscope around his neck, "I'd better do a general exam and tell him. Do you want to call Kent in now?"

I went out to the waiting room and ushered Kent into the office with one hand on his shoulder.

"How's first grade agreeing with you?" Dr. Seigel swiveled around in his chair smiling broadly.

"Just fine."

"Kent, I have something to tell you. I'm sorry, but your bone marrow was not good. You've relapsed."

"Yes, sir." Kent stood tall in his yellow plaid sport jacket.

"Do you understand what that means?"

"Yes, sir."

"You may have to stay here for a long time. And it may mean a lot more IV's."

"Yes, sir." Kent answered bravely.

"Wait here. I want to check on your blood counts before we start the exam." Dr. Seigel hurried out the door shutting it behind him.

With the slam of the door, Kent's shoulders visibly sagged. He burst into tears.

I ran to him, surrounding him with my arms. "Don't cry, honey... don't cry. I'm so proud of how brave you were with the doctor."

I fumbled through my purse for a Kleenex. Kent wiped his eyes and I began to ask for some heavenly help mentally.

"Sweetheart, we belong to Jesus, right?"

He nodded affirmatively, still blinking back tears.

"Well, Jesus never promised that we wouldn't have any problems come up in our lives. But what He did promise was that He would walk through them with us. He's here... in this office with us now. Can you be brave for Him?"

"I'll try." He bit his quivering lower lip and the little shoulders under his sport coat straightened as he took a deep breath.

Dr. Seigel appeared at the door. "The blood counts aren't too bad," he said. "But we'll have to transfuse him with platelets."

"Platelets?" I asked.

"The component of the blood that keeps the patient from hemorrhaging."

I shuddered at the word "hemorrhage" vividly remembering Kent's cerebral hemorrhage. Would we have to face that again?

When we were finished we stopped back in the waiting room to retrieve

Kent's crayons. I recognized Charlie O'Bryan, Yvonne's father. They were also from Louisville and Yvonne had been hospitalized for a long period of time.

"How's she doing?" I asked.

He brushed back a lock of hair from his forehead and smiled, "Better, I guess. You know this disease is like a roller coaster—up and down."

His voice was not abnormally loud, but the words hit me with impact, almost as though he were shouting.

The shrapnel of some painful memory coaxed me to remember. And then it suddenly came to me--the dream about Kent on the roller coaster! My mind sifted back through the details: I had been carrying Kent through a warehouse. Huge toys threatened to wrench him from me, but at my command, "In the Name of Jesus," they would subside. I remembered now, we had passed a replica of Kent on a roller coaster. As it passed a high curve, a replica of Kent had been thrown off. It frightened him badly and he began to cry. But at the same time, he and I both knew I was still carrying the *real* Kent.

Could this dream have been a portent, a stern warning? The roller coaster could have symbolically stood for Kent's relapse. At the time, I felt the dream had been prompted by the Lord. If this were so, I now concluded that we should consider the relapse as phony as the roller coaster in the dream. The *real* Kent was still with us and as the dream had instructed, we should stand against each symptom using the Name of Jesus.

I called Bill in Louisville that night and broke the news of Kent's relapse as gently as I could. There was a long silence on the other end of the line, then Bill's voice was strong, "I can't be with you, but the Lord's there with you both."

"I know. But I wish you were here too. I need you." I told him.

I realized that for the first time in my life, I felt a desperate need for my husband's strength. I couldn't help mentally comparing the difference almost five years and the events packed into them had made. I hadn't needed or wanted Bill's help and support when we had first come to NIH. Kent was in the same condition as he had been originally—but things had changed... radically. Now I needed Bill to lean on. For the first time I realized I was half a person and that brought new meaning to the phrase the "two shall become one". And the biggest difference was that Jesus now walked the halls of the hospital with us.

The next two days were crowded with testing and chemotherapy. I watched with deep sadness as Kent's usual bright personality became clouded; he withdrew into himself. None of my efforts to snap him out of it worked. I tried to interest him in the recreational activities of the hospital, but he just sat glumly watching the other children.

And then on the third day, a curious thing began to happen. It was a beautiful spring day, and as we had to spend most of the time in the hospital, I decided we should take a walk.

Kent walked slowly, disinterestedly, his hand in mine for a time. We hiked silently down a blacktop path which wound through the well-manicured grounds of NIH into a small thicket of trees across the street from the Clinical Center.

Suddenly, hidden from view, a bird burst into song. Kent stopped abruptly and listened. His blue eyes widened as though he had never heard a bird before.

"Listen, Mommy, listen!" he said excitedly.

We walked slowly on down the path. There were shiny red and orange tulips blooming around the next curve. We stopped and he ran his hand gingerly over each blossom.

"They look like they're made out of wax," he said delightedly.

A squirrel darted up a nearby tree, scolding and chattering, shaking his tail at us impishly to remind us of our intrusion into his woods. Kent giggled at his antics—the first time he had laughed in over three days.

For the next hour as we walked, an amazing change seemed to come over Kent, lifting the mood of despair that had hovered over him. It was as though he had his ear to God's earth and the life he found there encouraged his spirit.

We had spent three straight days in the hospital and the motel room. Had the change come because I had gotten him outdoors where the Lord could get his attention, I wondered? I was afraid the bubble might burst when we were confined again in the motel for the night. But I was wrong. After a bath and vigorous tooth brushing, Kent bounced up and down on his bed happily for a few minutes. He folded his legs Indian-fashion under his body and hugged his knees.

"Mommy," he said, growing suddenly thoughtful, "tell me the story again about how Eric received the Holy Spirit."

The abruptness of his statement caught me off-guard. What had caused him to pluck that subject out of the air? "Alright," I told him, sitting down on the twin bed across from his. I went back over the details of my laying hands on Eric and praying for him.

"Nothing seemed to happen right then, but later your brother yelled for me to come back into the room. He had seen a light the size of a man over by his bookcase. We felt Jesus was telling him He was really there. Then, remember, he saw a ball of fire that slowly traveled across the room toward him."

Kent cocked his head quizzically to one side, his expression serious for a seven year old. "Why did you ask God to give him the Holy Spirit, and it was *Jesus* who showed up?"

I couldn't help laughing. "Honey, Jesus is God and when He came down to earth He was God in the body of a man. And it's Jesus who baptizes with the Holy Spirit because it's His Spirit."

"Oh, I get it!" The dawn of new wisdom seemed to break behind his eyes.

"You told us once—Kurt and me—we're really three people in one because we have a body, a soul, and a spirit. So does God! Jesus is the body and the Holy Spirit is His spirit."

The depth of his statement surprised me. Surely a seven year old couldn't have figured that out on his own. Was the Lord doing the prompting in this whole conversation I wondered? And if so, did I have some part to play?

"Kent," I moved over to his bed and put my arm around him, "would you want to turn yourself over to Jesus completely? Ask Him to come into your heart and baptize you in the Holy Spirit?"

A broad smile threatened to split his face in two. "I sure do!" Kent knelt eagerly by the bed without my suggesting it.

"You pray silently, sweetheart, asking Jesus to come into your heart." I stood above him with hands laid upon his curly blond hair. As I touched him there seemed to be an electric current in my hands, heat surged through them. It wasn't my imagination as evidenced by what Kent said next.

"Mommy, I feel like my head has fire on it," he said excitedly.

"Did you just ask Jesus to baptize you in the Holy Spirit?"

"Uh-huh."

"Well darling, He is! Remember Eric saw fire? You're feeling it." I told him.

At that moment Kent spoke in tongues—a jolting, brusque Oriental-sounding language burst from him, flowing freely for minutes. After a time, he lifted his head smiling radiantly.

"I do have the Holy Spirit, don't I?"

"Yes, dear," I said softly, trying to hide my tears from him.

God had given him the power of the Holy Spirit to meet the trial of the painful days ahead. He would need strength so badly.

Kent became a changed person over night. There was a new sparkle in his personality. Our enforced hospital experience transformed into an adventure for him—a treasure hunt for new friends to pray for.

And so it was that little Susie came into our lives.

Kent and I had gone up to the ward for him to see Donnie, a solid tumor patient from West Virginia. Donnie had to remain in bed. The boys played cars, plumping up the sheets as imaginary mountains for their roads while I talked with Jean Herndon, Donnie's mother. When it was time to leave, Kent suggested we pray for Donnie. Just then Russ Willard leaned in the door. He sold laboratory equipment to NIH and was a Christian friend of some of the parents.

"Just thought I'd like to pray for Donnie before I left the building for my next call," he told us.

Jean, who looked like a small, dark-haired child herself, smiled at Russ. "That's funny, we were just getting ready to pray when you walked in."

We gathered around the bed, but as I started to close my eyes, I caught a glimpse of a petite, beautiful little red-haired girl of about five standing in the doorway watching us. She remained there through the entire prayer, but as we told the Herndon's goodbye, I could hear her sobbing in the next room.

"Mommy, why are they all in there praying for Donnie and nobody's praying for me?" We could all hear the child's cries.

Kent's eyes met mine over the bed. Russ had apparently been aware of the child in the doorway and now her voice from the next room was loud enough for all of us to hear. He signaled for us to follow him. We moved out into the hall and into the girl's room next door.

Little Susie Schnick lay face down on her bed. A tall, stunning young woman, in jeans with blonde shag-cut hair, stood over her, apparently trying to be of some comfort. She laid a beaded shoulder strap bag on the foot of the bed and put her arms around the child. "Susie! Susie, what's wrong? What's the matter?" her voice trembled with bewilderment.

"I think I know," Russ offered. "We were in Donnie's room praying for him and Susie feels left out." He sat down on the side of the bed. "Come on, little lady. Dry those eyes."

Susie sat up in bed. I had had only a hazy glimpse of this child before, but as I got a full look, her beauty astonished me. A tiny spattering of freckles bridged a perfect nose and trickled across perfectly molded cheekbones. Her blue eyes were enormous. She couldn't have been more than five, but there was an aura of sophistication that surrounded her.

"Are you going to pray for me too?" she asked.

"If you want us to, dear," I offered, sensing a slight bristling in the mother at our intrusion.

"Nobody prays for me." Susie's eyes swept our faces imploringly.

"Well, we will," Russ said firmly.

"I think I'll go out in the solarium for a cigarette while this is going on." The mother, who had said her name was Joanne, picked up her purse from the foot of the bed and left the room.

After we had prayed for healing and claimed heavenly help, Russ asked Susie if she knew Jesus. Her eyes lit up. "Yes, I know Him." She nodded her head enthusiastically.

"Have you ever turned your life over to Him, Susie?" he asked gently.

"No..." She looked at all of us thoughtfully. "But I want to!" Her blue eyes looked like those in paintings by the Dutch masters. "He loves me. And I love Him!" She hugged herself in enthusiasm. Kent beamed and nodded at her statement.

"Did your Mommy tell you He loves you?" Jean asked.

"No. Nobody told me. I just know He does."

I was reminded of Helen Keller's childhood who, though deaf and blind, when her teacher for the first time spelled the word God on her hand in sign language, spelled back, "I know Him... I just didn't know His name."

After our prayer with Susie, Russ and I made it a point to drop by the solarium to see the mother. Her attitude toward us seemed to have mellowed some we found, for she chatted freely about Susie's condition. We learned that she was a solid tumor cancer patient. Joanne was shouldering the hardship of Susie's illness alone, as she and her husband were divorced . There was an appealing quality about her. She seemed to be a lovely free spirited half-woman, half-child herself wrapped in a cosmopolitan package.

Russ gently moved the conversation toward our prayer for Susie and the step she had just taken in becoming a Christian.

Joanne brushed a stray blonde bang from her eyes and said firmly, "I'll respect what Susie has done, but I want no part of this for myself."

"Even if it would be an additional way to gain spiritual help for Susie?" I asked gently.

"Yes, but you see," she smiled at me, "I don't believe it will. Nor do I want to be preached to." It was a bland statement of fact with no seeming malice.

I laughed. "You're right, we were getting a little 'preachy'. Let's all go down to the cafeteria and get some coffee."

On the day little Susie Schnick formalized her love affair with Jesus, another love affair began with Kent. The two became inseparable and when Susie was finally released from the hospital to live in the motel where we were quartered, Kent was ecstatic.

Joanne was able to talk the desk clerk into giving them a room just across the hall from ours. The doors remained open most of the time and we considered the hall as part of our "suite". To make the atmosphere more like home we brought a record player from the hospital, scotch-taped drawings made in occupational therapy on the walls. Both rooms bulged with toys and projects to hand-craft.

As Joanne and I drew closer together because of our children, my admiration for her grew. She had a zest for life I envied and was constantly thinking up new things to do—adventures that would make our transplanted home seem more exciting for the children.

She stood, hands-on-hips one afternoon surveying our suite and announced, "You know what we need? We need a dog!"

I nearly fainted. "You're crazy. How can we keep an animal cooped up in here all day while we're at the hospital?"

225

"We need a dog with a good bladder," she said firmly, and picking up her car keys, left the room.

Some time later she and Susie returned, being led more than leading, a shaggy, black, bow-legged poodle that panted and slobbered his way into the room. Joanne collapsed in the nearest chair while Susie and Kent patted this new member of our family and fussed over him.

"Neurotic dog with bad breath, but he'll do," she said. "The owner of the kennel assured me he's housebroken. Got a heck of a bladder!" She waved proudly in the dog's direction.

Joanne proved to be right. Her uncanny sense of what would appeal to children had brought us all a new interest. Susie made love beads in therapy for "Barnaby Bix", as she had christened the dog.

"A rhinestone collar would never suit that beast," Joanne explained.

On free afternoons we walked Barnaby in the huge field next to the motel that was a part of the National Medical Library grounds. She bribed the motel cook into packing picnic lunches for us so we could sit on the carpet of pine needles in the thickest of trees and eat our lunch.

It was a new experience for me to extract a Club sandwich, complete with brightly colored fancy toothpicks, from a plain brown paper bag!

Our evenings were spent watching television as Kent, Susie and Barnaby raced back and forth between the two rooms happily playing with a tennis ball. On other evenings, Kent and Susie would have a "date".

There was a seafood restaurant within walking distance, where our meal tickets were honored. Occasionally, Kent would telephone Susie if the doors happened to be closed between our two motel rooms.

"Would you like to have a date for dinner this evening?" he would ask.

Joanne and I let them make all the arrangements. Kent would carefully pick out a sport coat and consult me about color combinations. Susie had a wardrobe of "party dresses", but she inevitably would choose a flowered organdy with puff sleeves that made her look like a miniature Scarlet O'Hara.

When it was time for dinner they would walk down Wisconsin Avenue far ahead of us, holding hands, so it seemed like they were alone.

"Table for four," Kent would tell the hostess and then make quite a fetish out of seating his "date".

One evening, however, Susie had a kidney infection. Just after we'd been served the salad she leaned over and whispered in her mother's ear.

"Powder room," Joanne told me.

Kent sprang to his feet and pulled back Susie's chair. When they returned he stood and seated her again.

The main course was served and again Susie had to take a trip. Kent jumped up, still trying to be a gentleman... up again when she came back.

After the fourth trip he said disgustedly, "How long do I gotta keep this up?"

And yet the morning Susie was to receive Donomyacin, Kent hovered over her like an anxious father. Donomyacin is a drug, given intravenously, which can have dangerous side-effects, yet is extremely effective in treating solid tumor cancer. A cardiogram must be done first to insure that the heart is strong and extra precaution taken to carefully insert the needle intravenously. Donomyacin can burn up a vein in seconds.

Kent finished his IV in another room. "Let's go on over to the motel and take Barnaby for a walk," I suggested.

"No." He frowned. "I want to wait for Susie."

"But Kent, it will be hours before she's done here."

"I don't care. I still want to stay." He wandered into the other IV room and pulled out a chair beside Susie's bed.

Not until the last drop of red fluid slid down the tubing into her arm could I budge him.

These two small children became prayer warriors for the ones who had to be hospitalized, using our room in the motel as their nightly chapel. Joanne never participated, but I began to notice a perceptible change in her attitude. She had remained true to her first declaration that she respected Susie's faith and would do nothing to hinder it. But in the two months our lives were knitted together, Joanne seemed to waver in her own convictions about the absence of a personal God. She began to ask questions, and while I didn't have all the answers to her intellectual approach, our discussions sometimes lasted far past midnight.

Kent's condition steadily improved as did Susie's. One warm, sunny day the last week in May, Dr. Seigel announced that we could go home. While these were the words we had been waiting to hear, it was heart breaking to leave Joanne and Susie behind. We were to return in two weeks and this knowledge took the sting out of our parting.

It was delicious to be back home. Eric, Lisa, Kurt and Bill had cleaned the house until it shined as a welcome home present to me. I felt like a stranger in my own kitchen, trying to cope with the task of cooking again.

On the next trip back to the hospital, our prayers were answered! Kent was found to be in remission and his treatment went back onto a once-a month basis. Susie's condition was better and she was allowed to go home. However, we met again in the summer and for the five days we stayed in the motel it was like old times. Susie and Kent renewed their dates. Barnaby Bix, who had gone to Joanne and Susie's home in Baltimore with them, now slobbered over us lovingly. We kept in touch by telephone after going back to Kentucky.

Late one evening in June of 1971, Bill called me to the telephone. "It's Joanne Schnick," he said, handing me the receiver.

I hardly recognized her voice. She was crying. "Sandy, I'm calling from the phone in the hospital playroom. Susie's hospitalized. Her tumor just suddenly went rampant."

"Oh, Joanne!" I felt like the words had hit me in the stomach.

"She's having trouble breathing. X-ray shows the deadly tumor's surrounding her heart."

"Oh... no! This just can't happen. Joanne, we won't be in there for another week yet. If you ever needed the fullness of the Holy Spirit it's *now*. I know you don't understand everything there is to know about this, but for Susie's sake... turn your life over to Jesus and ask Him to fill you with the Holy Spirit."

"Sandy," she said softly, "I turned my life over to Jesus a few days ago. It was Susie who showed me how."

"That precious child..." I couldn't keep back the tears. "Joanne, I'm so glad you did. You know Kent and I will be praying. I'll get the church here to pray. But now, ask Jesus to fill you with His Holy Spirit and then lay hands on her. You know, you've seen us do it before."

"I will... I'll do it as soon as we hang up," she promised.

I got another telephone call that night. It was Joanne again.

"Sandy," she sounded excited. "I went back into Susie's room after we talked and stood in the dark praying. She was asleep. After a time, I held out both of my hands and asked for the Holy Spirit."

There was a short silence. It seemed Joanne was trying to get control of herself before she went on. "And Sandy... I actually felt Jesus take my hands in His!"

Oh...thank you, Lord! I sent the words heavenward mentally. She had disbelieved so strongly before and needed strong proof.

"I took my hands then and laid them on Susie. She woke up and asked what I was doing and I told her, 'I'm laying hands on you like Sandy does and praying for you. Susie, I just received the Holy Spirit and I know you have Him too.'"

"Oh, that's so wonderful," I told her and I was suddenly reminded of that day when Susie had first stepped daintily into our lives. "Nobody prays for me," she had said. Now she had her mother.

"I've got a feeling everything's going to be alright, Joanne."

"I do too," she told me.

The week passed quickly and when we got back to NIH Joanne and Susie were back in the motel. She had made a remarkable recovery, "response to the drugs" the hospital called it. And though she was still weak, she and Kent and Barnaby Bix romped through the halls of the motel once more.

However, two days later Susie had to be hospitalized again. She just couldn't seem to breathe properly and had fainted coming out of the hospital cafeteria where we had had lunch together. Kent was stricken with anxiety when a bed was readied for her on 2 East. She was too weak to be taken to X-ray on the sixth floor. A mobile X-ray unit had to be sent down. The verdict from the reading was terrifying.

The tumor in Susie's chest had now engulfed both lungs and surrounded her heart. It was literally choking the life from her. Kent, Joanne and I laid hands on her again and prayed. Our only hope was that Jesus would intervene again.

Kent and I went back to the motel that seemed so empty without Susie and Joanne. Susie had been put on the critical list and Joanne would be allowed to remain on the floor with her that night. Her bed would be a chair. Barnaby Bix waited by the door for his mistress to come back, but finally around midnight, curled up at the foot of Kent's bed. I couldn't sleep.

Kent and I were just crossing the lobby the next morning on our way over to the hospital when the switchboard operator called to me.

"Mrs. Ghost, I've got a call for you. You can take it on one of the house phones."

It was Joanne. "You'd better sit down," she said. The excitement in her voice traveled electrically through the receiver.

"You want me to sit on the floor, silly? I'm in the middle of the lobby!" I told her.

"Sandy, the doctor just appeared in Susie's room a few minutes ago. They took a new set of X-rays this morning.

There's no tumor showing up at all... just since yesterday it's disappeared!"

"Praise the Lord!" I shouted. The bellboy standing by the desk and the switchboard operator swung their heads around in my direction, staring at me like I was a freak in a circus.

"There's proof positive beside the X-rays. Susie couldn't breathe well enough to go upstairs to X-ray yesterday. Today she's running up and down the halls."

"What was the doctor's reaction?"

"He's absolutely perplexed."

"Jesus did it again, Joanne."

"You'd better believe I know it... and so does Susie."

"See you as soon as Kent has his treatment." I told her.

As soon as we got up to the room, Susie threw her arms around me and planted a kiss on my check. Kent hugged her gently. Sad eyes spoke of his heart tug as he told her, "We're packed to go home, Susie. I don't want to leave you. I don't want to go home."

"Let's go up to the chapel and pray for the other children," Susie suggested to him.

She had an IV running so we had to put her in a wheelchair, fastening the bottles to the small IV pole on the back of the chair. Kent pushed her down the long hall toward the elevators. We had brought her a child's version of the New Testament that she held on her lap. Joanne had spent much time reading from it to her and confessed to me that it was the first time she had ever read the Bible herself.

After our prayer time in the chapel, Kent and I left for the airport. I realized with a twinge that part of our hearts would always remain in Maryland with Susie and Joanne. Kent was unusually quiet on the trip back and I wondered if he was feeling what I did. We wouldn't see them again until the middle of July.

We were due back at NIH on July 21st. As I was packing the evening of the 20th, Joanne called from the hospital. Suddenly the tumor had come back. Susie was on oxygen, hospitalized again.

"Hang on," I encouraged her. "We'll be in tomorrow."

But underneath I was frightened.

I had packed the last article and squeezed the lid of the suitcase shut when an odd feeling began as though I might be forgetting something. I felt drawn to my jewelry box and stood dumbly staring at the tangle of rings and chains inside. Suddenly my eye caught a necklace my parents had given me, a tiny mustard seed encased in a small bubble of glass.

It seemed as though the Lord instructed me, "Take this to Susie," and as the thought came, I remembered Jesus has said, "If you have faith as a grain of mustard seed, you shall say to this mountain, move from here to yonder place; and it shall move; and nothing shall be impossible unto you."

I reached down into the box and extracted the necklace, putting it in my purse.

The trip to Maryland seemed endless. The airport limousine seemed to be sluggishly moving under water. "Hurry up, hurry up," I muttered under my breath. I didn't want to tell him, but had decided I absolutely had to tell Kent Susie was sick again the night before we left. He had vigorously prayed for her when he said his bedtime prayers. Now, he seemed worried too.

Joanne met us outside. She must have been pacing the sidewalk waiting for our limousine to arrive. Dark circles under her eyes told me Susie had had a bad night. She threw her arms around me, clinging for a moment as though hoping strength might pass between us. "She's just awful," she said, "Please, don't even see Kent's doctor or start treatment until you've been up on the floor."

I promised her we'd go right up. I really had hoped to leave Kent in clinic and go up to 2 East without him. I just didn't want my son to see her in any kind of a terminal condition. I had fought with myself for the entire flight, but knew I couldn't deny Kent the opportunity to be with her. He'd never forgive me if I deceived him and then whisked him away. After all, they were prayer partners and Susie needed his prayers probably more than mine I realized. We opened the door of the room.

Susie's appearance shattered me. I felt Kent's grip on my hand tighten as we approached the bed. An oxygen mask completely covered her mouth and nose. The large sky blue eyes above it were bloodshot. Her skin seemed transparent and tinged with blue. The enlarged chest heaved with each breath. One small, spindly arm lay exposed on the sheet.

I tried to force the words past the lump in my throat, "We've brought you something, honey... a present." I dug through my purse for the necklace and held it up to the light from the window for her to see. "See that tiny speck in the center?"

She nodded her head affirmatively.

"Susie, that's a mustard seed. Jesus said that if we have faith as a grain of mustard seed nothing will be impossible to us. You know why He used the mustard seed as an example? Because it's the smallest seed in the whole world."

Her eyes smiled at me over the mask.

"Now, you know you and Kent, your Mommy and I have *that* much faith."

She shook her head again.

"We're going to ask Jesus to take this tumor away once and for all." I placed the mustard seed necklace in her hand, folding the tiny fingers over it.

"There's no magic in the necklace. I've just brought it to you to teach you what Jesus had to say about faith. And you know we've got more than that tiny speck between all of us."

Kent looked as though he were about to burst into tears, but lowered his head and laid his hand on her thin little arm. Joanne moved to the other side of the bed and laid one hand on her daughter's forehead. I placed mine on her distended chest.

"Father, once again we come to You in Jesus name for Susie. Lord, we stand on Your Word that if we have faith as small as a grain of mustard seed nothing will be impossible to us. We ask that You would take this tumor away as in the past. And we praise and thank You for it, before we see the evidence."

We stayed for a short time after that. Susie seemed to be in some pain and our presence obviously tired her. We went downstairs to the Clinic. Kent had his checkup and bone marrow. While we were grateful to learn he was still in a good remission, both of us were terribly disheartened by Susie's condition. We were free to leave for the day. "Want to go up to the chapel and pray, Kent?" I took his hand in mine.

He just shook his head "no". I silently begged the Lord to show me how to comfort him, but nothing came. We took a government contract cab back to the Governor's House to check in.

The desk clerk at the motel welcomed us as though we were family. He accommodated us by giving us a room that adjoined Joanne's and sent a bellboy up to unlock the connecting door in between. It seemed strange to be in a motel room without Barnaby. Joanne had made the decision the month prior to send him back to Kentucky with us because Susie was spending more time hospitalized.

We decided to have room service bring up dinner. Kent restlessly paced the room, obviously worried, and I deeply regretted my decision to allow him to see Susie in her present state. As I tucked him in bed for the night he asked, "Mommy, what if the Lord heals Susie like He did Kim?"

I was stunned and groped for an answer. I smoothed hair back from his forehead. "He might, Kent. His will is always healing. We really don't know *how* He's going to do it."

My concern mounted for my own child. "How would you feel about it if He did decide to take Susie to be with Him?"

There was a long silence and I could see he was weighing his feelings.

Finally he smiled at me. "It would be better, wouldn't it? She hurts so much... and she can't breathe. I mean... if the tumor won't stay away for good."

"Honey, we just don't know," I told him. "Jesus has taken it away before. He may again."

"I just don't want her to hurt and be in the hospital all the time." Tears sprang up in his eyes.

"I don't either, dear. Joanne doesn't, the doctors don't, and I'm sure Jesus doesn't more than all of us."

He seemed at peace with my answer, said his prayers and soon drifted off to sleep. I tried to keep my mind on a television program, but went to bed too around 11:30 PM.

Suddenly I was awakened by the sound of the connecting door being eased open. Joanne stood in the doorway, the light from her room shining behind her. She motioned for me to come. I got out of bed and followed her into the other room. Only then was I able to see her tear stained face.

She fell into my arms moaning, "Susie's gone. She's gone!"

"Oh no, God, no!" Even though I had considered the possibility, now that it was reality I couldn't face it.

"She just quietly lapsed into a coma. I sat on the bed and kept pleading,

'Come on, Susie, fight! You can make it! But she never woke up... And now she's gone! I can't believe it." She picked up Susie's Raggedy Ann doll off the bed and crushing it in her arms cradled it against her chest. She began to rock back and forth sobbing softly.

I was crying myself. What help could I possibly be to her I wondered? My mind sifted back over the details as though trying to stabilize itself. God was good. He had allowed us to be here just in time with Joanne when it happened. Surely He had arranged for the connecting rooms. We had never had them before. I doubted if Joanne would have pounded on an outside door at 4:00 AM in the morning. But what about the mustard seed necklace? Had I been so misguided to bring it to Susie?

As if she had read my thoughts Joanne looked up and said, "Do you know, Susie clutched that necklace you brought her tightly in her hand through it all. She wouldn't let a doctor or nurse remove it. It was still in her hand when she died."

This brought a fresh wave of tears I couldn't fight off. How could I help Joanne when I couldn't help myself?

"And now she's gone..." She ran her hands forlornly over the stuffed animals and dolls on Susie's bed.

"You know she's not *gone*, Joanne."

"I know she's still alive. But I want her with *me*."

"Even if she would have to suffer worse than she did? Wouldn't that be selfish on your part?" The words sounded cruel as they left my lips.

She looked like a little girl herself, sitting cross-legged on the bed amidst the toys, her shiny blonde head bent over them. But when she looked up, the eyes were those of a deeply grief-stricken woman.

"I wouldn't want her to suffer anymore. But why did she have to suffer in the first place?"

"That's something I just can't answer," I told her. My thoughts returned to the mustard seed necklace. Had I been mistaken about feeling I had God's guidance to bring it to Susie? But if the Lord *had* instructed me to give it to her then had He deceived all of us about faith moving mountains? I shivered at such an outrageous blasphemous thought.

There just didn't seem to be any answers. And even though Joanne and I sat up the rest of the night, stunned by our grief, I had nothing to offer her. I prayed for the Holy Spirit, the Comforter, to operate through me—but no words of comfort came. My arms around her and copious shared tears were the only tattered shreds of miserable ministry I could seem to muster as my own heart was broken.

I dreaded having to tell Kent, but at 8:00 AM I left Joanne in her room, closing the connecting door in between, and wakened him. He smiled broadly and stretched.

"Mommy, I had the most wonderful dream," he rubbed sleep from his eyes. "Susie went to heaven. She had a long white robe and golden crown on her head. And she was smiling and playing with the other children. She's so beautiful."

I nodded.

"She looked like a princess!"

Breath caught in my throat and I fought back more tears. God was so good. He had prepared Kent for what I had to tell him. "Sweetheart, it wasn't just a dream. I think the Lord was trying to tell you something while you slept. Last night, Susie *did* go to heaven. She's with Jesus whom she loves so much."

Kent's eyes widened momentarily. He blinked back tears for one brief second and then smiled again. "If you could just have seen her, Mommy. She was so much happier!"

"I'm sure she is."

"And, you know what? You know her hair had fallen out from the drugs? Well, when I saw her, her red hair was long and thick—just like it was when we first met her."

My mind began to give Kent's dream greater credence than I had originally. I knew that Kent was certainly not acquainted with the book of Revelation in the Bible. And yet gold crowns were promised as the heavenly apparel of one who overcomes. Surely his dream had been prompted by the Holy Spirit. With this thought a new feeling of comfort began to steal over me. My grief began to ebb.

"Perhaps you should tell Joanne about your dream, dear. She's very sad and it might help her see Susie as you did. She's in the next room."

He struggled into his bathrobe and padded through the door in bare feet. Joanne was lying on the bed, one arm covered her face, but at the sound of the door opening she looked up.

"Come here, Love." She patted the bed beside her and sat up.

Kent sat next to her in the spot she had indicated. He put one small arm around her protectively.

"Your Mommy told you?" Joanne dabbed her eyes with a shredded ball of Kleenex.

"Yes. She did, but Jesus told me first."

"How?" Joanne threw the crumpled tissue in the waste basket and drew another sheet from the box on the bedside table.

Kent described his dream in detail and as he did a strange thing began to happen. The savage grief that had engulfed Joanne seemed to lift visibly from her face. When he was finished I offered, "You know, I believe it was much more than just a dream, Joanne. I think Kent actually *saw* Susie. The Bible describes just what she had on in the dream in the book of Revelation as what our heavenly attire will be like when we get there. Kent had no idea that was even in the Bible."

"But why did she have to die?" Fresh tears sprang up in Joanne's eyes.

"Because her work on earth was finished," Kent said. "Just like Jesus, He didn't stay here 'til He was an old man. When his work was finished He went to heaven."

Both Joanne and I stared at him in disbelief. Was the Holy Spirit speaking through my small son I wondered?

"What work, Kent?" Joanne stammered.

"I think God sent Susie to you so you would accept Jesus as your Lord. Maybe He knew that no one else here on earth could have made you see Jesus was real."

I was rocked by this new thought. "Joanne! I think he's right! Jesus healed her physically, dramatically, just enough times that you knew He was real and turned your life over to Him."

"I was a real rebel, for sure." She shook her head and smiled. "And when I did finally yield to Him—Susie was the one to show me how." Joanne seemed to be considering that we had hit on a new truth.

"You know, this life is so short in comparison to all eternity that you now have to be with the Lord, and Susie too." I told her.

"You children absolutely seem to have a direct line to God." She hugged Kent, then took a deep breath. "Come on, Love, help me pack. Can you scramble under the bed and get my tenni-pumps?" Joanne wiggled her bare toes at him playfully.

The funeral was to be in Baltimore and Joanne asked if I would get in touch with the minister there. "You can tell him more about Susie's spiritual life than I can," she explained. "And I want you to pick out the scriptures for him to use."

We had to fly back to Kentucky the day of the funeral so we couldn't attend; however, I was secretly grateful that Kent wouldn't have to be put through this added strain. Yet he seemed to be completely happy in the knowledge that Susie was living joyously in her new life.

I sat at the desk in our motel room prayerfully asking for help in the selection of the scriptures to be used. I knew I had to call the minister before it got much later in the evening.

Taking my small black Bible out of my purse I asked for help and opened it at random, much in the same way I had done when asking for an answer about Kent's relapse. The tiny print was hard to read, but suddenly the words "mustard seed" leapt up at me off the page. I couldn't believe it! Slowly I read: "The Kingdom of heaven is like a grain of mustard seed, which a man took, and sowed in his field; Which, indeed, is the least of all seeds; but when it is grown, it is the greatest among herbs, and becometh a tree, so that the birds of the air come and lodge in the branches of it."

The kingdom of heaven! Then I had been guided by the Holy Spirit to bring the mustard seed necklace to Susie! I had never thought of the parable of the mustard seed—just the reference Jesus had made to the seed with regard to faith. Perhaps if I had been better attuned to the Holy Spirit I would have known the Lord meant to take Susie. I had applied the wrong scripture verse to His guidance.

But had I? Hadn't Susie's seed faith in Jesus dying for her been the agent which rooted her in her new life in heaven? And the mountain of her tumor had moved hence to yonder place. I hadn't been wrong. I just hadn't been allowed to see the whole picture.

"Her work on earth was finished," Kent had said. Perhaps the purpose of her entire life had been to bring her mother to the Lord. My mind whirled back over the past five and one-half years. Would we have ever known the reality, the power and the presence of God had Kent never been diagnosed with leukemia?

I opened the Bible again. My eyes fell on: 2 Timothy 2:12. "If we suffer, we shall also reign with him; if we deny him, he also will deny us."

I wondered about the other parents who have faced tragedy with a child. If these circumstances hadn't acquainted them with the Lord, would anything else in their lives?

I looked at Kent sleeping, his blond curls tousled, a half-smile upon his face. Somewhere from the recesses of my mind came the sentence, "And a little child shall lead them…"

Before Joanne knew we had to fly back to Kentucky the same day of the funeral she had asked me to sing the song "Bridge Over Troubled Water" at Susie's funeral. "She loved that song and told me that Jesus was her 'bridge over troubled water'," the tears bubbled up again as she remembered.

"That's a Simon and Garfunkel song. I used to do it when I was singing professionally, Joanne. I'd give anything if I could, but the government's already made reservations for us back to Louisville that day. No way to change that. I'm so, so sorry, hon. I'd have been privileged to have sung it for her. I never knew she liked that song. And how spiritually astute to have equated Jesus with her 'bridge over troubled water'. Wow! I've got to savor that for awhile."

Our "goodbyes" were stabbingly painful. "Give Barnaby Bix two pats for me and three hugs for Susie," she told us.

"He still wears his love beads that she made for him,"
Kent ran to her and his hugs threatened to not allow her to leave.

Five days later, after Kent had completed his protocol we boarded the plane to go back home at the precise time of Susie's funeral in Baltimore. Once we took off, Kent dozed off and I couldn't seem to concentrate on a magazine the flight attendant had given me. I prayed for strength and comfort for Joanne through the funeral and wondered if she had been able to get someone to sing "Bridge Over Troubled Water". The minister had been strong spiritually plus extremely helpful and understanding with regard to the scriptures we agreed to use. He seemed struck with awe over little Susie's relationship with Christ and I knew it would be a beautiful service worthy of her life.

I released the lever on my seat, pushed back closing my eyes and tried to remember the lyrics of "Bridge Over Troubled Water" as Susie had said Jesus was her "bridge". The words came back in tumbling lyrics filled with comfort, tenderness and caring to the point where it was clear Jesus held her at the end and laid down His life for her. I gasped and remembered,

When darkness comes
And pain is all around,
Like a bridge over troubled water
I will lay me down.....

As the words scrolled through my mind I fought to keep from sobbing. Making certain that Kent still slept, I made my way to the lavatory, closed the door, slotted the "occupied" sign and collapsed into tears.

Once confronted with the words, I now knew I could never have gotten through singing it without breaking down. It was more spiritual, more personal, more loving than any hymn and I could picture Jesus holding little Susie in His arms while singing it to her as she had endured her suffering. Small wonder it was her favorite song....

Chapter Twenty-Five

———— ⌇ ————

*B*arnaby Bix had settled into being a regular member of the family when we'd flown him to Kentucky several months prior. Lisa and the twins usually fought over who would get to feed him. Now, on our return from NIH after Susie's death, as I fixed dinner, Kent took Barnaby out onto the back porch. They sat side-by-side on the concrete step and I overheard Kent explaining to him that Susie had gone to heaven. He had an arm around the dog's shoulders as if in protection, like two pals facing the backyard. With one hand he caressed the love beads that encircled Barnaby's neck—a collar Susie had made for him.

"I know you loved her very much and I did too. But if you could have seen her in my dream you'd know how happy she is, Bix. It's really beautiful up there in heaven, you know... well, maybe you don't, but we'll see her again."

Was he thinking about his own death? My racing thoughts threatened to choke me. I chided myself for eavesdropping as it was a totally private conversation and could surely be an opportunity to provide healing for any grief Kent might be suffering. I quietly closed the back door so that they might be alone, but the image of the scene was seared into my soul.

Several weeks later, at about 9:30 PM I got a prayer chain telephone call. It was a request for prayer for a man who was in the hospital dying of cirrhosis of the liver. The children were in bed, Bill was bowling and I just sat at the kitchen table, where I had answered the phone, bowed my head and began to pray. I didn't know the man so within a short length of time I had prayed everything I possibly could for him—"Lord, if he doesn't know You, draw him to Jesus Christ by the power of the Holy Spirit. I ask you to heal him according to Your word that, 'By your stripes he is healed' and that 'I am the Lord thy God that healeth thee'." Having said all I knew to say, I began to pray in tongues in order for the Holy Spirit to make intercession for him. And as I did, the strangest thing began to happen. I began to weep as though this person was the most precious one I had ever known. I felt genuine love for him as I prayed in my prayer language and couldn't seem to turn off the tears. I frankly attributed it to still being emotional over Susie's death.

When Bill got home I suggested we pray together and as we did, once I lapsed into my prayer language the same thing happened again. I began to cry so hard I couldn't catch my breath.

Bill lifted his head and looked at me like I was crazy. "You don't know this guy, do you?"

I couldn't manage to answer and just shook my head.

"You may need to get some help, San. You're crying a whole bunch lately," he observed.

I shrugged my shoulders. "I don't get this... doesn't make sense."

The following morning promised to be a sticky, hot and humid day. Ominous, dark clouds pompously scuttled across the horizon and thunder grumbled in the distance. I felt sorry for the mailman as he shouldered his brown leather mailbag and wiped perspiration from his forehead with a swipe of one arm. The mail plopping on the floor through the slot in the door was an obvious enemy attack in the mind of Barnaby Bix, who immediately bushwacked the envelopes and catalogs.

When we had lived together with him in the motel he had always been extremely well-mannered. His only breach of etiquette was to attack his mortal enemy—the vacuum cleaner. The battle plan was always the same. He would retreat to a foxhole under the desk. Then, as the maid vacuumed, he would seize just the proper moment to emerge triumphantly from his lair, bark twice to announce the battle cry, rush his enemy, bite the vicious vacuum cleaner twice and retreat back to the foxhole. The battle plan never varied much to the delight of anyone in the motel room and the maids who had come to love him too. Bix, now transplanted to Kentucky, (and most likely surprised that this place also had a vacuum cleaner) had modified his military plan to also include mail invading the house through the slot in the front door. I rescued the stack of envelopes and explained to Barnaby Bix that they were retreating to the kitchen table.

Weeding through the junk mail, I spotted a letter from my sister, Chelie, in California. It was unusual in that we customarily kept in touch by telephone. I ripped it open and read:

> "Dearest Sandy,
>
> Daddy has asked me to write this letter as he can't do it. Mother is in the hospital with cirrhosis of the liver and is not expected to live past a week or two. Neither of us can bring ourselves to talk about it, so please forgive this short note, but we wanted you to know."
>
> Love,
>
> Chelie"

I read the words with a strange detachment. I couldn't believe that such a dire pronouncement would leave me so emotionally devoid. I even felt guilty that I wasn't weeping over my mother's illness and impending death. After the children had had their lunch, I slipped downstairs to the family room where the prayer group always met. I didn't turn on any lights, but welcomed the darkness to help me pray for my mother. Our relationship had greatly warmed since I'd become a Christian and I found myself admiring her incredible sense of decorating, her delicious gift of description in letters between us. While she and Daddy had only been able to make three trips back east to visit, there was now a love that easily flowed between us. As Chelie had grown, attended college, and married, their relationship too had seemed to improve.

Now, as I knelt in front of a chair to pray for my mother I found I was still without tears. "Our Father", I began..."

The still, small voice of the Holy Spirit interrupted, "But you have already prayed for your mother," He said. "You prayed for her last night when you prayed for the man who had cirrhosis of the liver. You let Me pray through you in using your prayer language. And while you didn't know your mother had cirrhosis... I did! All of your tears were shed for your mother, not the man you didn't know."

I could scarcely breathe. *So this is what it means when the Word says, "the Holy Spirit will make intercession for us when we know not what to pray." I hadn't known until today that mother had cirrhosis, but by the limitless power of tongues I was praying for something I desperately needed to be imploring heaven for when I didn't have any fore knowledge of it.* "Thank you, thank you, Lord. I praise You and from now on I will have a greater reverence for the gift of this prayer language." It seemed like that was the only prayer necessary.

However, if I had thought this lesson in praying in tongues was the final curtain I was dead wrong. Not a week passed when Chelie called. "Sandy, the most incredible... well... the most, I guess you'd say it was a miracle... well..."

"What? What? Spit it out, hon, what happened?"

"It's mother! She's home from the hospital and the cirrhosis is completely healed. The doctors were just baffled that it just... it just... went away."

"Can you put mother on the phone, Chelie, and you stay on an extension? I want to tell you what happened to me here on this end."

After we had hung up, I sifted through the lessons in this. I had begun an emergency quest to learn about spiritual healing after Kent had been healed of the cerebral hemorrhage. I had learned that letting the Holy Spirit pray through me had most likely saved his life when the needle broke spilling a deadly dosage of chemotherapy drugs. The Holy Spirit had known what was going to happen, knew it could be prevented by prayer. The Holy Spirit knew my mother needed prayer for healing when I didn't and by allowing Him to pray through me she was healed. I concluded that this precious gift of praying in tongues was one of the biggest weapons against leukemia we could have.

I also reminded myself that it had absolutely nothing to do with me! I was only the instrument to let the Holy Spirit verbalize the prayer. While many loyal

Christians felt that tongues had ceased with the death of the disciples, these two episodes had surely proven that this was still a valid prayer tool. Someone in the prayer group mentioned that they had been challenged by another Christian about tongues. The other person had tossed out a verbal jab that they thought they were better because they had the gift of tongues. "No, tongues don't make me a better Christian than you," he had said. "They just make me a better Christian than I was before."

I concluded that I dared never neglect this in my prayer life as in doing so I would be praying God's perfect Will whatever it might be in a particular situation. I vowed to file this lesson at the very top of my list of ammunition to fight Kent's leukemia. However, at present on our next trip to Bethesda, Dr. Seigel was extremely pleased with Kent's bone marrow that showed a solid remission. I tried to keep Kent distracted with Occupational Therapy and trips to the record shop downtown in an attempt to wipe away thoughts of little Susie, Kim and all his friends who had walked those halls in times past. Soon it was time to go back home.

Kent and I leaned into the window as the plane lifted off. The spire of the Washington monument pointed toward heaven as our plane banked sharply and followed the Potomac River out of the DC congestion. Climbing to cruising altitude our plane crossed the Blue Ridge Mountains and the Allegheny chain as our flight headed toward Kentucky. We had been contacted by Eastern Airlines almost two months prior. They had become aware of all the air miles that Kent had logged with them at such a young age. Eastern's corporate offices had apparently been informed by some of the flight attendants of his diagnosis and continuing treatment at the National Institutes of Health. Their Communications Department asked for permission to do an article on Kent to appear in their own house organ newspaper. After some prayer and discussion, Bill and I felt it would not be in Kent's best interest, nor would it be spiritually ethical for his diagnosis to be used for any type of notoriety. We therefore thanked Eastern for the opportunity, but declined the idea.

Apparently the Lord had plans of His own, however, to use the story of the empty Eastern Airlines plane where Kent and I were the only passengers. It all began so innocently...

Lynda Eline and I were sitting at my kitchen table having coffee. She and her husband, Sidney, had been the very first couple to join us when we first decided to hold the prayer meetings in our home. We had vowed that if nobody else ever showed up we'd honor the Lord by meeting. They had shared in the same meetings and Holy Spirit experiences that Bill and I had. Subsequently, of course, the more we prayed the more people came: bouquets of Presbyterians, Lutherans, Baptists, Methodists, Catholics (even including two precious nuns), and a bunch of budding non-believers. Now the original prayer meetings had blossomed into a church. Lynda had always been a dedicated Christian and described her additional experience in receiving the fullness of the Holy Spirit as, "I just kinda' waded out into the water and sat down." Her sparkling sense of humor and bubbly personality magnetically drew people to her.

Lynda's flair for decorating had just blessed my kitchen with several pairs of curtains she had sewn. "They look smashing! Changes the whole look of the kitchen... wish we could do something to revitalize my looks, Lynda," I told her wistfully. "Sometimes I look back on my former life when I was singing and wish I could wave a magic wand over my image now."

"What are you talking about? That's crazy. You look great!"

"Well, it really propped me up when you frosted my hair...that was a big improvement. I came out of the womb wearing makeup so that hasn't changed. But things were so glamorous back then. Now my perfume smells like bug spray and the only way I can get a new pair of panty hose to fit properly would be to go and jump on a horse!" I filled Lynda's cup again.

"Get outta' here! You look great." She started to giggle. "I remember when Barbara Rodgers and Delphine Board said they made the trip up to the State Park where you, Bill and the kids were camping to see if you would be wearing eye makeup in the woods—you were!"

"Yup! Baptized in Maybelline!"

Lynda stirred a small amount of cream into her cup. "Get serious a moment. I've got an idea I want to run by you. Have you thought about maybe giving Maude Blanford's testimony further exposure about her total healing from cancer?"

"I'd like to, but I just don't know where to go with it. It's so solid factually from a medical standpoint. It surely deserves publication. The world should know how valid spiritual healing is. Got any ideas?"

Lynda squinted thoughtfully and stared out the kitchen window as if to pluck an answer off my butterfly bush in the backyard. "Well, the most famous Christian writer is Catherine Marshall who wrote *A Man Called Peter, Mister Jones Meet The Master, Christy, Beyond Ourselves...*"

"I've devoured everything she's written and *Beyond Ourselves* laid a rich foundation for my own born again experience, Lynda. But... how in the world would I ever get in touch with her?"

Lynda leaned backward in her chair, crossed her arms and a knowing smile hinted at an answer. "I know where she is. She lives in Boynton Beach, Florida and is now married to Len LeSourd, who is the Editor in Chief of Guideposts Magazine. Why don't we pray about it and you can just call her?"

I found myself stammering. "Lynda... that's like calling God. I'd feel so intimidated."

Her ever present granite-solid common sense surfaced, "Sandy, don't you 'call' God every day?" She grinned again.

"Well... yes." I found myself scuffing my tennis shoes under the table.

She grabbed the wall phone off the hook next to her. "The area code's the same as my mother's. Let's see if there's a listing in Boynton Beach."

There was. Subsequently after much prayer, two days later, I called and talked with Jeanne Sevnigy, Catherine Marshall's secretary, and told her Maude Blanford's testimony, about Dr. Oscar Hayes' letter and the medical files that backed up this extraordinarily well-documented healing of cancer. I could tell Jeanne was taking notes as we spoke. She said she would report all this in detail to Catherine. Less than an hour later Catherine Marshall called me back.

Her voice was crisp, yet it was wrapped in the softness of tissue paper. I couldn't believe I was actually talking with such a spiritual giant and found myself clearing my throat repeatedly as I filled in details in response to her questions.

"This exciting story is indeed so well-documented it can't be denied, Sandy. What a find! Could you arrange an interview with Maude for me? I intend to talk with Len about flying to Louisville."

"Oh, I'll call her, but I'm sure she'd love to meet with you." (And *me too*, I thought, resisting an urge to hug myself).

"Well, I'll call you after I talk with Len and we see about reservations. Thank you so much for this extraordinary lead. Talk with you later..." The phone clicked off without my saying goodbye. I was to learn that this was so typical of Catherine Marshall's disciplined, no-nonsense devotion to her craft.

Two weeks later I was thrilled to be able to pick up Catherine and Len LeSourd at Standiford Airport and take them to their hotel. We'd arranged a meeting with Maude Blanford for the following morning and dinner at the Ghost home that evening. I got out my grandmother's crystal goblets, the Battenberg lace tablecloth she had given me and sharpened up the children's table manners while imploring, "Lord, please don't let me incinerate the roast this time... no burnt offerings!"

Catherine was as articulate in conversation as she was in print and Len's casual, relaxed manner and sparkling sense of humor soon put us all at ease. I silently marveled at how the Lord smoothly made a level playing field among His children where any wrinkles of age or station in life seemed to be swiftly ironed out by the Holy Spirit.

Children had been excused from the table; I had served coffee and cake when I began to tell them about Kent's cerebral hemorrhage in answer to their question about how Bill and I had come to know the Lord. The sun was setting outside the picture window in the dining room and Catherine's muted auburn hair glinted in the reflection as she kept turning her head toward her husband. There seemed to be some unspoken language going on between them as I told the story. Bill added a few details now and then from his perspective.

There was a long pause as I reached the end. Catherine took a dainty sip of water from the crystal goblet. Her vibrant blue eyes seemed to be looking down into my soul. "Sandy, you have been given a rare gift of describing this and I seem to be getting confirmation of this from Len." He nodded his head in affirmation. "Let me suggest that you enter the Guideposts Magazine Writers Contest. We'll give you the rules before we leave. After our interview with Maude tomorrow, I hope to gain an interview with Dr. Hayes and also try to obtain a release of her medical records from St. Joseph's hospital. We'll be here for several days, dear, and will have more time to explore your prayer meetings if we may."

I was overjoyed and a bit intimidated at the same time. They wanted me to enter a writing contest? I'd never even written a note to the milkman back when they used to deliver it!

The prayer group was thrilled to have two spiritual celebrities in our midst. Catherine expressed high interest in the miracle of leg lengthening and we prayed for her. There was a remarkable evidence of difference between her two legs and that was healed to the witness of many standing and watching. The following morning as I took Catherine and Len to the airport she remarked that her "legs kept tingling" to the point where she hadn't slept much the night before. "But I know it was witness to the healing I had," she smiled and shook her head in wonderment.

Len stuck their tickets in the breast pocket of his tan suit. "I want you to understand, Sandy, that neither Catherine nor I have anything to do with the Guideposts contest itself. We don't judge it; but the winners have the opportunity to fly to Rye, New York... fellowship with the others and spend a week learning from speakers like Norman Vincent Peale, his wife, Ruth, Jamie Buckingham, John and Tibby Sherrill, Catherine and me plus others. Guideposts would pay all expenses inclusive of your airfare."

"You told us the story about the flight attendants and the empty airplane," Catherine patted my hand. "That might be an exciting entry to submit."

"I'll start to work on it immediately." I told them. "I can't tell you how grateful I am that you suggested this to me. Don't know if I can write it or not, but I'll try."

"No... ask the Holy Spirit to write *through* you, Sandy. Don't try to do it on your own. Pray and then consider yourself a scribe." Those piercing blue eyes added punctuation to the fervor of her statement.

I savored those words as I watched their plane grow smaller after takeoff. When it had shrunken to the size of a toy, I finally walked across the parking lot to the car. I drove home wrapped in a mental prayer shawl of praise for all that was happening to me. Even if I didn't win the contest, I was in awe of the privilege of meeting Catherine and Len. It was like I'd stepped into somebody else's life.

It was as though the Holy Spirit took those words and began to teach me about my new life and a part of this new lesson was instruction about burying my "old man". And, as usual, nothing ever seemed to happen to me in an orthodox way.

I had begun to write the account of the empty plane and in my "quiet time" in the morning with the Lord I was led to re-read the book of Acts. I wondered if it was just my imagination or perhaps emphasis by the Holy Spirit that water baptism kept jumping off the page at me. When Bill and I had first become Christians our Baptist friends had begun to chide us about water baptism. But after I had received the baptism of the Holy Spirit I told them, "Wait a minute! The Lord must have honored my sprinkling as a baby because He's filled me with the Holy Spirit. Don't need to do that." I told them.

"That was dedication," they told me. "A baby can't make a decision to accept Jesus Christ as Lord and Savior."

That statement introduced a huge question mark in my mind. But I turned that question mark upside down into a hook that I had suspended any action on. However lately it seemed like baptism kept presenting itself in everything I read. And then the morning came when I turned the page and there it was—Acts 10:44 where Peter had gone to the Gentiles and as he was speaking the Holy Spirit fell on them and they spoke with other tongues and magnified God. Then, in verse 47, Peter said, "Can any man forbid water that these should not be baptized, which have received the Holy Ghost as well as we." Whoops! Just the reverse order... just the order that it had happened to me. I started to become convicted that I should be water baptized. I reasoned I wanted to tidy up my obedience and not leave anything unturned. Two days later, after I had determined I needed to do this, I received a mysterious telephone call.

"Is this Sandra Ghost?" an unfamiliar woman's voice asked.

"Yes, it is. I'm sorry... who is this?" I inquired.

"That doesn't matter," the voice was pleasant, but terse. "Are you considering being water baptized?"

This was getting really weird! I hadn't mentioned it to anyone, even Bill. "Yes... I am... how did you know?" I could hear my heart beat in my ears. That happened sometimes when I was anxious.

"I was praying this morning and the Lord gave me your name. He said you were going to be water baptized and I should call you with teaching."

"'Teaching'?"

"Yes. I'm sure you know you're burying your old man under that water, rising to newness of life, right?"

"Right... I just found the scripture that supports doing it in reverse order from being water baptized first and then receiving the Holy Spirit. That's what convicted me."

"Well... what I called to tell you is this: have you wondered at the scripture where after Jesus had risen He told the disciples in Matthew 38, verse 19, 'Go ye therefore, and teach all nations, baptizing them in the name of the Father, and of the Son, and of the Holy Ghost.' But then they went out and baptized in the name of the Lord Jesus Christ. Ever wonder about that inconsistency?"

"Actually I have and it's confusing."

"That's why I called. To baptize in the *name* of the Father, and of the Son, and of the Holy Ghost are not names—they're titles."

I swiftly wondered if she could see me scratching my head!

"If you wanted to write your son a check for $10.00 and you signed it 'mother' instead of with your name, would it be negotiable?"

"No... not at all." I was beginning to see there wasn't an inconsistency in the scripture.

"So, if we are to baptize in the *name* of the Father, Son, Holy Ghost, what *is* the name? It's Lord—Father, Son—Jesus, Christ—Holy Spirit. Lord Jesus Christ! And that's how they baptized."

"Amazing... oh thank you! That's simply awesome and I know this is truth. Thank you so very much, but tell me... who are you?"

There was a smile in her voice. "That's not important. Just say I'm your sister in Christ." And she hung up leaving me breathlessly listening to a dial tone. I sat down abruptly on a kitchen chair and sifted through the conversation again. Had I been talking to an angel?

My thoughts spun back to Mr. Sorbo's telephone call to me. He hadn't known me at all either, but had been in prayer for the woman in his office who had tried to commit suicide the night before. He said the Lord had told him to call me. I concluded that the Holy Spirit had wanted me to have this teaching and had alerted His obedient servant who picked up the phone and called. What an exciting new world this was! I just hadn't counted on trying to convince the Baptists of what I thought the Lord wanted for my water baptism. I had to convince everybody that this new curve to what they believed wasn't akin to asking for blood sacrifice.

I asked Jerry Davis to do the honors. Jerry had been a Southern Baptist seminary student along with others who were in our church now. When I explained to him about the Spirit-led telephone call I had gotten and what the stranger had conveyed to me he was less than enthusiastic. "And she didn't say who she was, or what church she goes to?"

"No, but Jerry there's not a way in this world she would have known I wanted, or was even considering to be baptized. It had to have been the Lord that had her call."

"But Sandy, Jesus was known by many names: Lily of the valley; the Prince of Peace; Rabboni; Master. If I get you in the water and run through all those names you'll drown!"

"But I really feel I wouldn't be obedient to be water baptized any other way." I didn't want to be obstinate, but I was totally convinced that there was cohesion between the two instructions from Jesus in the Bible—and this was the answer.

"Okay...let's compromise," Jerry said... "I'll say, 'I baptize you in the name of the Father, Son, Holy Ghost...Lord, Jesus, Christ."

"Perfect," I told him. "It'll be next Sunday after church. We'll all go out to Christine and George Ellsworth's farm and I'll be baptized in their pond, okay? I've already checked it out with them."

"Sounds good to me!" He unwound his tall frame from my kitchen chair. "Got to pray over this new interpretation of scripture...do my homework."

At church on Sunday it was announced that I was going to be water baptized at Ellsworth's and that those who wanted to celebrate this with me should line their cars up with headlights on as this was a "funeral procession". Carter Foster announced that, "we are going to bury Sandy Ghost's old man". I felt shivers go up and down my arms. I had thoroughly explained to the children what was about to happen and why I was doing this so as Bill drove, we all started singing praise songs. Most of the church turned out and as Jerry and I waded into the water I asked him, "Can I hold my nose?"

He laughed. "Because your 'old man' stinks?"

"Well, I'm sure that's right, but because I don't want pond scum up my nose, okay?"

"Absolutely kosher. Let's pray."

We stood facing each other as we bowed our heads and asked for the Holy Spirit to circumcise my heart as scripture explained that whereas Abraham had the circumcision of the flesh as an outward sign of his covenant relationship with God, we now had circumcision through water baptism. I felt as though hot oil was pouring over me, even though the water was a bit chilly.

"And now," Jerry said, "I baptize you in the name of...the Lord Jesus Christ!" and under the water I went.

He was as surprised as I when I came up out of the water and said he had firmly intended to say "Father, Son, and Holy Ghost" first, but he felt the anointing of the Holy Spirit had come upon him and 'Lord Jesus Christ' is all that came out.

Several weeks went by and every time we were in church Kent kept asking to be water baptized. Carter and I talked about it and I told him I wasn't too sure that this wasn't just a natural reaction to his mother having that experience.

I didn't want him to be water baptized until he absolutely knew what he was doing and why.

"But he has had the experience of the infilling of the Holy Spirit, hasn't he?"

"Oh, yes."

"Well then, how can we deny him being water baptized?" Carter's response made sense.

After talking it over with Bill we decided to tell Kent he could be water baptized the following Sunday. I was still worried, however, that my teaching him about it wouldn't be a good enough explanation for him to know exactly what it was he was doing. As usual, I didn't anticipate the Hand of the Lord to emphatically make it clear.

On Sunday morning the sun had just begun to peep through the blinds of our bedroom when Kent came running into the bedroom shouting, "This is the day I'm going to be baptized! This is the day I'm going to be baptized!"

I buried my head under the covers, "Sweetheart, it's too early! This isn't Christmas morning." Bill's snoring stopped abruptly. But there was no way to put a damper on our son's enthusiasm.

"The Lord gave me a dream about my water baptism, Mommy."

I surfaced from under the covers. "He did? What was it, honey?" I patted the bed beside me and Kent sat down.

His eyes shone with excitement. "Well, I died in the dream. And they nailed me right over top of Jesus on the cross. My feet were nailed to His feet and my hands had the nails going through them and into Jesus' hands."

I felt hot tears sting my eyes.

"And we both died together. They took us down off the cross and put us into a rock cave. A beautiful angel came and we both came back to life."

The lump in my throat was so large I could scarcely talk. "Kent, do you understand this is what your going under the water today represents?"

"Oh sure!" He couldn't contain his excitement and began bouncing on the bed as he talked. "I should have died on the cross because of my sins. But Jesus did it for me—in my place, Mom."

The bouncing had wakened Bill who now smiled broadly and said to me, "So much for your being worried he wouldn't understand! Guess the Lord solved that problem."

After church as the caravan of our "funeral procession" wound it's way through the countryside with headlights blazing, I had a fleeting thought-- would we someday be in an actual funeral procession for Kent? I immediately rebuked such a thought, but it continued to loom in front of me as I watched my small son go under the water in obedience to proclaim his covenant relationship with his Lord.

Chapter Twenty-Six

With trembling fingers, I inserted the finished Guideposts contest entry into the brown manila envelope. I had tried to follow Catherine Marshall's suggestion to pray, let the Holy Spirit write through me and just be a "scribe". But when I finished typing it up, "The Empty Plane" didn't seem very professional to me—surely not the caliber of Catherine's writing. My remedy was to read it to Bill, Carol, Lynda, the next door neighbor, members of the women's prayer group and just about anyone standing still and breathing. I was looking for critical input, but I finally realized it got to the point where people saw me coming and practically dove into ditches and hid in closets to fend off my reading it to them. I frankly had plenty of confidence in God—but not in my ability to write.

About two months passed and the telephone rang early one morning. Without any preliminaries a male voice asked, "How do you feel about winning the Guideposts magazine writer's contest?"

"Well, I don't know that I have," I told him. "Who is this?"

"I'm a reporter with the Associated Press," he said. "You haven't been notified yet?"

Now I felt my pulse begin to race. My mouth went dry. "No... not at all."

"Well, let me assure you, you're one of the winners and I'd like to use a headline, 'She's a Self-Writing Ghost Writer' with a name like you have. Congratulations! This will be in newspapers all over the country."

Shortly after his interview, I received a call from Guideposts magazine itself. It was true. I was one of the winners and would be flown to New York with all expenses paid. They would call back with my reservations and I was to be the guest of the magazine in a mansion in Rye, New York for a week of seminars with famous Christian writers such as Norman Vincent Peale, his wife, Ruth Stafford Peale, Elizabeth and John Sherrill, Catherine Marshall, Len LeSourd, Jamie Buckingham, Richard Schneider and many others. I felt like I'd died and gone to heaven already!

There were preparations to be made as I'd be gone for over a week. A call to my parents in California brought the praise from my mother that I craved so badly. They immediately sent a set of very sophisticated luggage as a gift. Just seeing it sit in a corner of the bedroom, awaiting the clothes I'd pack, propped up my wavering self-esteem. There were many preparations with sitters and the children, plus friends who offered to pitch in while I was gone. The AP feature appeared in the Louisville Courier Journal. I carefully cut it out as though it were a valentine from the Lord and placed it in my Bible.

When the day finally came, my flight to New York was one of the most frightening I had ever encountered. We hit a vicious storm just prior to the plane's descent that made us the target of lightning strikes and violent air turbulence. I began praying as we jolted and jounced up and down. I'd been told that Van Varner, one of the editors would be personally waiting for me in the baggage area. He would take me on to Rye, New York from the airport.

Not wanting to arrive looking like a disheveled hick, I fished the compact out of my purse and attempted to powder my nose while the plane bounced and shuddered like a bucking bronco. My blouse looked like I'd just floured a fish filet. I managed to get the top off the lipstick tube and holding it aloft I tried to target in on my mouth. A bolt of lightening shot by the plane. The bouncing continued as I waited for enough calm to apply it without ending up looking like Clarabelle the Clown. I brushed a bit of blush on either cheek, then checked in the compact mirror. I looked like my face had been smashed between two bricks so I hastily massaged it in. Having no seatmate, I felt free to murmur a prayer. "Lord, help me...this is not vanity. Actually, Lord, it's faith...faith that I'm going to get onto the ground and somebody will actually *see me alive!*" We finally touched down. I had bitten my tongue twice and the passengers burst into spontaneous applause out of sheer relief to be taxiing to the gate.

Van Varner was waiting in baggage with a sign that said, "Ghost?" He was a very sophisticated gentleman, great conversationalist and I had an almost subliminal impression that had he been born earlier he would have worn spats.

As we pulled up to the mansion where the seminars were to be held and where the contest winners were to be guests, the breath caught in my throat. A huge imposing French chateau welcomed us. The impressive stone architecture was sited on stunningly manicured grounds with a backdrop of sparkling waters and marshland.

It was wonderful (and comforting) to see Catherine Marshall and Len LeSourd again at dinner. To my surprise I was seated near them and felt honored. My mind whirled at meeting Norman Vincent Peale and his gracious wife, Ruth. There were approximately eighteen of us winners from all over the United States representing a wide range of ages and a fairly even gender mix. We met in the library for our first "get acquainted" session after dinner. This was hosted by Norman Vincent Peale himself and I found myself clinging to every word. His book, *The Power of Positive Thinking* had been a stepping stone for me personally into reaching out for something more when I was on the road and singing. I never dreamed at that time that I would ever meet the author himself.

At the end of our first evening session, I mentally kept repeating one thing he had said. The impact of the words was indelible. They were: "Change your thoughts and your life will change." While I had digested *The Power of Positive Thinking* in one huge gulp, that simple sentence seemed to condense the entire "take away". I was to hear those two words time and again in the next few days. We learned the take away was to be the predominant thrust for each work—what lasting lesson or impression would we leave with the reader.

I received my first actual assignment for Guideposts and was asked to write it while I was there. I had shared a testimony with Catherine and Len when they were in Louisville about a corporate fast our prayer group had experienced. The magazine was looking for an article on fasting and Catherine had suggested I had some solid experience on the subject.

As I labored through the article in addition to attending all the wonderful sessions, Tibby and John Sherrill took me under their wing assisting with plentiful constructive editing help. I was in awe of meeting them. They had written *The Cross and the Switchblade* with David Wilkerson and John had richly laid a firm foundation for my infilling with the Holy Spirit in his book, *They Speak With Other Tongues*. Both were roving reporters for Guideposts and their sparkling sense of humor and lack of pretense put me at ease immediately.

It all ended too quickly. The dream come true for so many of us ended in bittersweet hugs and promises to write to each other. We each carried home the gift of a rare experience to be tenderly pulled from a special subconscious velvet box of memories at some time in the future. Lessons learned would filter back in tugging us toward a better mastery of the craft of writing. I knew I would always hear the voice of Tibby Sherrill if I attempted to use a cliche'. "Find a better way," she'd say. I knew in the future common catch phrases were as unacceptable as slurping soup. I sifted through each day's memories hugging them to me through the flight home.

Back to the real world, the house was still standing when I returned to Nanz Avenue. I was grateful to be home, had missed Bill and the children and played catch up with all the things that had happened to them through the week. But when kids were in bed and after I'd bent Bill's ear for hours at all that I'd experienced in New York, I had to admit I felt slightly like Dorothy must have felt after being returned to a bland Kansas since experiencing the glamour of Oz.

While Bill listened politely, seemed to be proud of the fact that I had been offered an assignment with *Guideposts* in addition to having won the writer's award, I never could seem to feel a loving acceptance from him. Would our marriage ever take on the depth, the closeness, it should have? Sometimes I felt we were just walking through the motions that were expected of us with none of the accompanying love to motivate it. Surely I had a right to expect Jesus to heal our relationship, but I couldn't seem to dredge up the true emotion of love when there seemed to be little reciprocity. I realized the consequences of harboring unforgiveness—this could create a spiritual dam holding back God's grace and healing. I tried to put a microscope of truthfulness on my inner thoughts. The finger of my conscience flicked another question in my direction: *What about your mother? Have you forgiven her?* I was picking daffodils in the backyard when the question came. I sat down abruptly on the back steps to ponder this additional self-examination. *Had I?*

Our relationship had gradually improved over the years and her letters from California were a delightful smorgasbord of her unique observations on experiences. No one could describe a situation or opinion with the vibrant flair that she could. But upon reflection, I allowed my mind to sift back over my childhood and a kaleidoscope of positive memories presented themselves: Mother sitting at the piano, with me on the bench beside her. I couldn't have been more than six years old. She had purchased children's books of favorite operas with splashes of colorful pictures, the story line music for piano told the stories of Carmen, Aida and Pagliacci. She made it come alive for a child with her passion for the music. Distasteful memories of when I was a teenager had now been blotted out. Yes, I knew without a doubt I had forgiven my mother... but it was only with the help of the Holy Spirit.

The angel dust of my *Guideposts* experience quickly blew off my shoulders in the swirl of the twins' birthday and Easter approaching. Kent and I made our scheduled pilgrimage to NIH and received a terrible and completely unexpected shock—Kent was in relapse again after a two year remission. Whereas the Lord had prepared me... warned me the last time, this news came unvarnished with no warning. His health seemed excellent. There was not a trace or hint of relapse. Had I missed the Lord's voice, had He tried to warn and I'd been too preoccupied to hear? I asked for forgiveness. Kent was put on a different protocol of a change of drugs and perhaps because he seemed to be in such extraordinarily good health, he took the news of relapse totally in stride.

"We'll bring you back in shortly to see Kent's progress," the new doctor told us. "You realize, Mrs. Ghost, as this is his second relapse you will most likely be spending more and more time at the Clinical Center?" His eyes sent me a message I refused to receive. "As you know, your family has all been tested for being a donor for a bone marrow transplant. There was no match so we don't have that option. Going to have to rely on strictly a drug protocol to get him back into remission."

I nodded my affirmation and hoped that most of our conversation was going over Kent's head. I truthfully wasn't too concerned because we had a secret weapon above and beyond the drugs—Doctor Jesus!

Bill met us at the airport. I had called him with the news of Kent's relapse so I realized his morose expression wasn't because of Kent's condition. The children were in bed before he would talk about it.

We sat at the kitchen table. "Okay, what's up? Something's definitely wrong, you've been positively dour, Bill."

"I've lost my job," he said.

I stared at him. "You can't be serious. They let you go?"

"Not a matter to kid about. I knew it when we talked on the phone, but I didn't want to worry you while you were still at NIH," he passed a hand over his forehead. "Downsizing."

"Well, Corhart isn't our provider—God is, Bill. We'll get by. Don't worry."

But when I went to bed that night I added up the score: Kent had relapsed; my father had just been diagnosed with cancer; Bill had lost his job. Where in the world was Jesus?

Chapter Twenty-Seven

*T*wo months scrolled into a blazing humid summer. Kent and I spent an increasing amount of time at NIH as his doctors changed protocol on his behalf. One dose of the new drug alone cost $48,000. The price tag filled me with new gratitude for the exceptional care he was being given, but meanwhile I was increasingly aware that his friends were being whittled down to a slender few. I struggled to protect him from the knowledge that they had passed on; therefore, we spent most of our time at the motel swimming or taking the bus down to the record store in Bethesda. His love of music seemed to be the strong thread that buoyed his spirits... leveled his life. We always signed out a record player from occupational therapy to take to the Governor's House.

Meanwhile, as our children at home were out of school and Bill was out of work, he became "Mr. Mom". When Kent and I were at home, it saddened me to see him constantly sitting in his chair, circling available jobs in the newspaper. Though we prayed, that door seemed to be firmly closed for some reason. The answer always seemed to be the same—"You're overqualified."

An idea began to softly stir my spirit and as I prayed, it tugged on my sleeve like an insistent child. The more I prayed, the more it tried to burst forth until I knew I had to share it with Bill. He had just shut off the "Tonight Show" after the news and with all the grace of throwing a grenade onto the coffee table I blurted, "Bill, I've been praying about this for awhile... Kent and I are spending more and more time in Maryland. The doors seem to be shut for you to find a job here in Louisville. What would you think about moving to Maryland so I could be a full time mother to the other children as well as Kent?"

"Moving? Sell the pink house?"

I looked around at my dream house and tried to keep back tears. "If that's what the Lord wants us to do... yes!"

He sat down abruptly, frowned and thoughtfully pulled on his left ear lobe. "Kent's protocol now does seem to indicate you're spending more time up there." He stared into a distorted image of the living room in the convex Bulls Eye mirror over the fireplace. "Wonder what the job situation is there... I could get a Washington Post and start looking at the classifieds... get a handle on it," he mused more to himself than to me.

"Maybe that's the direction we're being 'told' to go in, Bill. The door here just seems to be easing shut. Gonna' really be hard to leave the church, but if that's what we're to do, there'll be one there that's just right."

"Guess so. Next trip in why don't you nose around and see what the rental situation is there."

Kent's excitement at the prospect that we might live in Maryland seemed to reinforce the idea to move. On our next trip to the hospital we borrowed a car from friends in the area to check out rentals.

I turned onto Connecticut Avenue in Kensington, Maryland, pulled over and looked at the directions I had written down from the newspaper rental ad. There were townhouses for rent about ten minutes from NIH The pavement shimmered from the summer rain as dark clouds scuttled overhead. Suddenly the sun pierced through the clouds and glittering shafts shot to the ground in four magnificent steaming pillars.

There was a gasp from Kent. "Oh! Look, Mom! God's power!" The words were said in excitement, but wrapped in a reverence I had never heard him express before.

"You're right, sweetheart. That's just what it looks like." I wanted to hug him, but had to turn into the brick gates of the townhouse complex. I parked the Volkswagen in front of the building that had a sign announcing "Office". The two of us stared in silence at the awesome display in the sky before getting out of the car.

"Makes me feel super small, Mom, but I know His power protects me."

I stopped on the sidewalk and stared in disbelief at the spiritual insight of my small son. At eight years old the baptism of the Holy Spirit and his "direct line" to heaven had apparently given him wisdom far beyond his years. I reached down and swept him into my arms. His lilting laughter was like a precious reward.

The brick townhouses were new and beautifully built. Each building housed six three story units, each with a handsomely fenced front patio. The buildings were sited around a small park and from the gates the complex huddled in a circle suggesting covered wagons circled to ward off the outside world from Connecticut Avenue. Four bedrooms plus three and ½ baths would accommodate us nicely.

Kent, who had decided he wanted to be an architect when he grew up, was ecstatic. He constantly drew pictures of houses with double front doors and sketched rough blueprints of the imaginary homes in his mind. Surprisingly, I found that when I tried to keep him entertained when at the hospital, after we ran out of record stores, his next favorite place to go was Levitz—the furniture store, to pick out furniture for his imaginary houses. Now, he was deliriously happy skipping from room-to-room in this beautiful town home.

"This could be Kurt's room and mine. And here's Lisa's room, Mom. Eric could have his own room on the lower level. Wow!" He whirled around in circles, arms extended wide in the family room.

The elderly manager smiled warmly. "You're gonna' take off like a helicopter, son."

"Don't get too excited. We have to run this by Daddy, Kent. He's the one who makes the decisions for this outfit."

"Yes... but God's power was right out front!"

George, the manager, raised his eyebrows.

"The sun broke through the clouds," I made a rather lame attempt at explanation. "Son, that was over all Bethesda... and Kensington... all Maryland, sweetheart. Not just here."

"But we saw it *here,* Mom," he insisted.

I told the manager that I would call him from Louisville, that we hadn't sold our home yet, but that if my husband would be in agreement we would mail the security deposit. Back in the car, I had to admit to Kent that it certainly did seem like the Lord was pointing in this direction. "We'll have to pray about it though, sweetheart. Even when all signs seem to point to God's guidance we still need to pray about it to make sure."

"Okay," he nodded. "I'll pray too."

"But don't just ask Him for this particular townhouse... ask the Lord for *His* will. He just wants us to acknowledge His will is better than ours in all things. He wants the best for us, and we don't know what that is, but He does!"

"I get it. Okay, I'll pray for His will."

But apparently Kent's guidance was right on target. It all happened with the speed of a whirlwind. Bill was in agreement; the house sold immediately when we put it on the market and we packed up getting ready to move directly after Christmas. While the rent was $500 a month for the townhouse, we felt we could live off the proceeds of the sale of the pink house until Bill found another job.

While it was a massive heart tug for me to give up the pink house, I felt more empathy for Lisa and particularly Eric in leaving their friends behind. Eric was in high school and it would not be an easy transition for him. Lisa seemed to take it more in stride. Her sunny disposition and growing walk with the Lord always made it seem like she was standing on tip toe, peering with excitement at what wonderful surprise package life was about to bring her.

The hardest part was in leaving the members of the church. Some felt we were making a terrible mistake by not just "trusting the Lord for Kent's healing, staying in Louisville", but we explained that we had already settled that with the Lord years ago and gotten a clear, strong answer to continue with the NIH protocol. There was more understanding when I explained that after almost seven years it was time for me to be a full time mother to not just Kent, but the other three children as well. I felt like I was at a friendship funeral at the service where we tearfully said "goodbye". Everyone promised to write, but we somehow seemed to sense God was closing this chapter in our lives.

When the house was emptied I walked from room-to-room choking back tears. I caressed the beautiful pale green colonial mantle over the fireplace and imaginary echoes of laughter suggested the Christmas stockings that had hung there. In the family room downstairs, I was reminded of all the prayers of the saints that had gone up like a sweet smelling savor before the Lord. "Thank You, thank You, Lord for this house. Thank You for all the miracles You performed in this place. I praise You for giving it to us and please help me release it back to You... take away my sadness." I softly closed the double Dutch front door and whispered, "Good bye, old friend," to the magnificent cottonwood tree that stood guard just off the porch. By late afternoon of the following day, we crossed over into Maryland. As we entered the gates of the townhouses, I had the distinct impression that we were embarking on a new chapter in our lives that would surpass all the miracles we had been privileged to see in the past. It was as though the Lord whispered future promises in my ear. *Is this where Kent will be healed of leukemia?* My mind dared to probe the feeling I was having as I rubbed my arms. They were covered with goose pimples—but not from the cold...

The Christmas vacation was nearly at an end and therefore I had to get all the children enrolled in school. The grade school, where Kurt and Kent would attend third grade, was close by. We discovered a blacktop path that meandered out the back of the townhouses and up the hill to the school. I enrolled Lisa in the second semester of seventh grade at Newport Junior High School next door to Eric, who was enrolled at Albert Einstein High School.

As soon as we were settled we made another discovery. The blacktop path out back that led to the grade school branched off to the right, climbed a steep hill and dead-ended at a small, brick church. We didn't know much about the Church of the Brethren denomination, but because we considered our family had been strategically planted in this location, we felt we'd better explore the church. Al Houston, the pastor and Maggie his wife welcomed us like old friends. There was an active teen group for Lisa and Eric, Sunday School for the twins and also adults. The Holy Spirit seemed to be strongly stirring the congregation with an excitement and hunger for more of Jesus The people in this church certainly seemed to be one very genuine family in the Lord and they welcomed us with open arms.

As spring began to peek its head around the corner from winter the famous Japanese cherry blossoms budded around the Jefferson Memorial in DC and Kensington, Maryland became a fairy land of colored blossoms. It was a delightful surprise to see blazing fuchsia, demure pink, dazzling white and lavender azalea bushes everywhere. We hadn't known that Kensington was known as the "Azalea Capital". From a distance the residential area of Connecticut Avenue appeared to be festooned with parade bunting.

Late one afternoon before the children got home from school, I began to have strong inner urgings to call my mother. I was in the middle of a writing project and kept setting the idea aside until it came so loudly I suddenly grasped it was from the Lord. I dialed my parent's number in California and it rang a number of times before my mother finally picked up. I could tell something was seriously wrong from her voice.

"Tell me what's wrong, Mother... I really felt the Lord urging me to telephone you, sweetheart."

Dead silence.

"Mother... please... speak to me. Tell me what's wrong."

She could scarcely talk. "I drank lye... Drano... kill myself... wanna' kill myself."

"Oh, Mother... no... no! We love you! I love you!" My heart started to race. I was frantic. "I'm calling Daddy. I have to hang up! Have to hang up so I can call. Help's coming!" I couldn't just call 911... he'd have to call.

Fortunately my father was in his office.

"It's Sandy. Mother's tried to commit suicide. She drank lye—Drano! God told me to call her!"

"Oh, my God! She's upset with your sister. I'll call 911... get an ambulance on its way."

I could hear him dialing 911 on another line and giving them directions, plus what she had taken. He came back on the line with me. "Call you, honey, soon as I get home and get her hospitalized. Thank God you 'listened' and called her."

"I'll be praying, Daddy." The tears came flooding as we hung up. I slipped to my knees on the cold kitchen floor.

Several hours later my father called from the hospital. Despite the lye they had been able to treat her successfully. The doctor had said it was "extremely fortuitous" that I had called when I did. She was comatose when they took her to the hospital and therefore they were apprised of what she had taken. The inside of her mouth and esophagus were badly burned but would heal. I reflected this was not the first time she had tried to commit suicide. Recalling when Chelie had been just two years old she had attempted suicide by taking phenobarbital pills. I had held Chelie on my lap loudly reading a book to cover the noise of the ambulance workers taking her out on a stretcher.

"Why? Why does she do this, Daddy? Why would she want to end her life? Is it the drinking?"

He sounded so weary. "I have no idea, Princess... no idea. She's so smart, so talented, but there are times she just... just goes off the deep end. Usually it's when she doesn't get her own way and prior times she's always telegraphed her intent."

"So she can be rescued?"

"Exactly. Like taking pills in front of us, but not this time. Good grief, lye of all things! So painful and there was nobody there to intervene."

"Nobody but God, Daddy," I said softly. "He absolutely had me call."

"Yes, He did. No doubt in my mind," he said. "I love you, Sandy."

"Love you too, Daddy. Please call when she can come back home and I can talk to her, okay?"

"You betcha'. Kiss the kids for me."

As we hung up I was struck by an overwhelming wave of love for him--sympathy, love and pity for my mother.

Five days passed. Mother was stabilized and well enough to come home from the hospital. Her throat was still blistered, but she seemed to want to talk to me on the telephone. We talked about our trips on the train together to New York when I was little. She had gone to University at the Sorbonne in Paris. When her parents sent her money to come back home she had used it instead to sail to New York from France and become a model. New York City had always remained her second home.

Recounting our memories, I was suddenly overwhelmed by all the culture she had introduced me to: opera; New York shows; music; Greek and Roman architecture; the French language; proper table etiquette; classical books. It was as though a window to the past creaked open allowing me to see past all our arguments—the ups and downs of our relationship through the years. Now all I could vividly remember were exciting fun and loving times.

The conversation grew more serious. "San, thank you for saving me from the Drano." Her tone suddenly grew somber.

"I didn't do it, Mother. The Holy Spirit, Jesus' Spirit, kept prodding me to call you. Remember several years ago, when you had cirrhosis of the liver and were dying in the hospital?"

"Boy, do I remember!"

"And remember I told you about the fact that the Holy Spirit had me pray in tongues for you when I didn't even know you were in the hospital...didn't know you were dying and showed me the scripture that the 'Holy Spirit will make intercession for us when we know not how to pray'?"

"I remember the Lord healed me... had to be Him because the doctors said I'd die."

"Jesus loves you so much, Mother. We all love you so much. Why would you try to take your own life, sweetheart?"

There was a long silence. Then finally, "I know the Lord loves me... puts up with me. But sometimes there are strong thoughts suggesting your father doesn't love me, Chelie doesn't love me now that she's married."

I wanted to crawl through the telephone line and put my arms around her. "Sweetheart, it's possible those 'strong thoughts' are coming from one of the nasty minions of the devil whispering in your ear. The Bible says that the devil is a liar. His game plan is to 'rob, steal and destroy' and maybe you've been a victim to his propaganda scheme."

Silence again. "Could be. I go along just fine for awhile and then all of a sudden a crushing mountain of depression hits me."

"Have you talked to your doctor about it?" *At least she was willing to talk to me about it. She never had opened up like this before.*

"We don't have medical insurance, remember? We're still paying off my hospital stay back when I was diagnosed with cirrhosis. That brings me to something else, San. Daddy and I think we can cut back expenses if we move. I'm going to ship our dining room furniture to you. We won't need it... won't be entertaining any more."

The breath caught in my throat. "Oh... thank you... thank you! We've got a beautiful dining room, but our old furniture was so crappy we didn't load it on the van when we moved to Maryland. I'll take really good care of it."

At the time I had no idea this would be my inheritance. But had Mother known somehow?

Eleven days later a large Mayflower moving van pulled up out front. The driver and his helper graciously carried the furniture into the dining room and positioned it where I indicated. Mother had also sent a flowered slipper chair for the living room that was an additional surprise. The dining table and sideboard were solid pecan wood; the chairs had tall cane backs with seats upholstered in a gold damask. The furniture gave the empty room instant elegance. I called Mother to thank her the moment the moving van lumbered back up the hill and through the gates.

"You're so welcome, dear. I hope you enjoy them as much as I have." Her tone seemed wistful—sad.

"But where are you moving?" I asked.

"We're not sure yet." I could hear her take a long drag on a cigarette. There was a slight whistle as she exhaled.

"But you're sure you won't have a dining room?" Something seemed wrong somehow.

"We need to downsize. Let me ask you a question, San. Why aren't you singing anymore? "

I had the distinct feeling she was purposely changing the subject. "Well, I quit after I became born again."

260

Her tone was slightly sarcastic, "You think God doesn't like nightclub entertainers?"

"No, that's not it at all." I couldn't suppress a giggle. "He loves everybody. It was just that I worried my 'old man', that I buried in baptism, would rise up again. I really felt my old ego might try to take over and I didn't want to have to beat it to death with a stick."

"Even if you sang gospel?"

"Yeah... even if I sang gospel, or sang in the church. Don't want to take that chance. I don't want to resurrect that person. I only performed one time after I was born again. It was a colossal disaster so I figured I was being warned not to go back into that."

"I love you, San." She punctuated her statement with a low laugh.

My throat constricted as hot tears brimmed. All the years of hurt and rejection by her in my adult years melted away. "I love you so much, Mother. You mean more to me than you'll ever know. Please... please... never try to take your life again. I couldn't bear it if that happened. "

"I promise, sweetheart. I love you."

Those were the last words I ever heard her say. Two days later Daddy called. Through sobs he told me he had found her that morning. Apparently she had gotten up in the middle of the night, as she often did when sleep wouldn't come. He explained she must have been listening to the short wave radio on headphones. When he discovered her she had been dead for quite some time. Efforts of the rescue squad to revive her were fruitless and while an autopsy was planned, the doctor suspected Mother had had a cerebral hemorrhage.

I yearned to comfort him, but couldn't--I was crying uncontrollably. She and I had finally reconciled our relationship and now she was gone! Neither of us could stop crying—it was a short telephone call and he promised to call back with more details.

Hanging up the wall phone in the kitchen, I collapsed onto one of the benches at the kitchen table and tried to catch my breath between sobs. I *had* to know if she was with the Lord. "Father, in Jesus name, in Your mercy You took her without it being by her own hand. Please forgive her for trying to commit suicide. And Lord, I know she needed deliverance from something. Sometimes she just became a 'different person', got horribly depressed, drank too much to deal with her demons. But Father, I have to know she's with You. She was really so fantastic when she wasn't under the influence of that outside force. Please... please tell me something... send the Holy Spirit, the Comforter, to tell me something." I laid my head down on the kitchen table and waited.

Shortly the still, small voice came and I "heard" rather than thought, "*I am convinced that neither death nor life, neither angels nor demons, neither the present nor the future, nor any powers, neither height nor depth, nor anything else in all creation, will be able to separate us from the love of God that is in Christ Jesus our Lord."*

This flooded me with reassurance and gratitude. I *knew* with every fiber of my being that she was in heaven. I went and got my concordance .There it was in the Bible! I found what I had "heard" was word-for-word in Romans 8:38. I sat at the table and reflected: when I'd stolen money out of my father's wallet when I was thirteen, she'd given me scriptures to read about stealing; she had always been the one to see that we'd gone to church. Once she had called me and started singing, "Were You There When They Crucified My Lord?"—she'd been drinking. While her experience with God had been different than mine, apparently it was acceptable to Jesus.

Suddenly I remembered another time we'd parted. I had put her on the plane to go back to California from Kentucky. As I'd waited to see if she'd wave from a window of the plane, a white cross had appeared in one of the small windows—and I knew it was her way of letting me know she'd be safe on the flight. She had hated to fly. Now, it was as though a cross had appeared in another window—a window to another world.

Two days later, Kent and I had just gotten back from his appointment at NIH and there was a large box by the front door. The two of us struggled it into the hall. I was shocked to find Mother's handwriting on the return address. "It's from Grandma Boyce," I told him.

"But... she's in heaven."

"I know, sweetheart. She must have fixed this box just before she went to be with Jesus." Once open, it revealed a large oval antique tray, an entire set of imported English Ironstone Old Staffordshire china for eight, and an elegant gold Mediterranean swag lamp. There was a note that read: "I love you, San." I sat cross-legged on the hall floor and started to cry.

Kent came and put his arms around me. He held me tightly without a word and just let me cry.

I wondered, *Did she have fore-knowledge that she was going to die and arranged to personally see to my inheritance from her? Had she just made it up that they were going to move? Or had the Lord put it in her heart that she really was going to move... from earth to heaven? The timing of this package, after she had died, was almost like a message from the other side—"I love you, San."*

Through all this I realized I had mistakenly packaged up salvation as a step one, step two, step three process: step one—repentance; step two—salvation; step three—in-filling of the Holy Spirit. I was guilty of making it so complicated when God was so much more loving, forgiving, and caring than I had ascribed to Him. After all, I was reminded the Bible said, "Whosoever shall call upon the name of the Lord shall be saved." I had doubted that Mother had met the criteria and the Lord, in His love, had set me straight.

Kent took his fingers and wiped away my tears. "When we lived in Kentucky I told my first grade teacher that my Mommy only cried when she was happy or when she talked about Jesus," he said.

"I am happy, sweetheart... very happy, happier than I've been in a long time and I know we'll see Grandma again when we get to the other side."

Two days later Daddy called again with the results of the autopsy. It had indeed been a cerebral hemorrhage and while her attempt at suicide earlier had undoubtedly weakened her body, she had not died by her own hand. He and Chelie planned a private Episcopalian ceremony and cremation. There was no way I could afford to fly out there.

I had talked at length with Bill about Daddy coming to live with us. He had retired, his prostate cancer had spread to the bone and he needed someone to look after him now. Bill was in total agreement that we could use the family room on the lower level as his bedroom. He said he'd close up the apartment and stay with Chelie and her husband while considering it. I told him I would cherish the opportunity for the children to get to know him better. "I just can't make any hard and fast decisions right now, honey," he said. "I'm sure you understand."

Kent finally went into remission again for the third time that autumn. My relief temporarily blew away the clouds of doubt as our entire family celebrated together. Nippy weather coaxed the small orange Pyracantha blossoms on the plants in front of the fence to come out and play. They bloomed like tiny pigmy pumpkins proclaiming their own time of harvest. And one crisp day in October my father finally came to live with us.

We anxiously waited for his plane to land at Dulles International Airport. He was one of the last to exit at the gate and was being pushed in a wheelchair by an airline attendant. I was struck by how much smaller and slight of frame he seemed. His gray goatee had turned white, the hair on his head was thinner and deep wrinkles gave a new signature to his face. But the bright blue eyes behind the heavy-framed glasses still sparkled with a delightful mischievous humor. He wore a large turquoise cross on a silver chain around his neck.

The children ran to him shouting. "Grandpa" seemed to lap up the attention with obvious thirst. As I hugged him close, the familiar odor of Old Spice after shave tenderly took me back to my childhood. I had the thought, *Thank you, Lord, that the children will now have a chance to know the delightful person their grandfather is.* Aloud I told him, "Daddy, there's no way you can possibly know how thrilled we are that you've come to us!"

He repositioned the cane on his knees and shifted in the wheelchair, "Little one, I'm so glad to be here too. Let's get this show on the road, gang!" He waved the cane above his head like rounding up the herd and heading them out. Bill pushed the chair as we started toward Baggage Claim. We would now have two "Bills" in the house. (He had always claimed his parents named him "Bill" because he came on the first of the month!)

His furniture had been delivered by another Mayflower van the week prior. The only possessions remaining of his past life were: a green leather recliner chair; single mahogany bed; two matching nightstands and a highboy chest; plus the most important companion to my father—his large console television set. We were soon to find that his favorite past time was sitting, decked out in pajamas and robe, in the recliner, smoking Pall Mall cigarettes and watching T.V. The children adored him, Bill and I delighted in the salty presence he brought into our lives... always a joke, he brought lilting laughter to us spicing up each day. But I now had two beloved family members in chemotherapy treatment.

When we had first moved to Kensington I 'd been in touch with Catherine Marshall whom I hadn't seen since winning the Guidepost's writers award. Her northern home was Evergreen Farm in Lincoln, Virginia, not far from D C. We had met for lunch several times and I had been out to the farm. While every book Catherine had ever written was a best seller, she had also published a novel—*Christy,* inspired by the life of her mother. I had the privilege of meeting the real life Christy and found myself admiringly charmed. Catherine, and her husband, Len LeSourd, who was Editor in Chief of Guidepost's, had begun a new publishing firm, Chosen Books Publishing—the inception of the offices were skillfully folded into the activity of the farm. It was a lush and restful haven, sited in the rolling hills of Virginia. The beautiful, historic farmhouse had spread her wings lovingly toward gardens of flowers and boxwoods like a gracious matron with open arms.

Because of Catherine I was invited to be a luncheon speaker at the very posh Army & Navy Club in Washington, DC. While I had spoken in several churches, I'd never been in such an elegant atmosphere before except when I'd sung in the Petroleum Club in Tulsa, Oklahoma. That seemed like it had been a hundred years ago—a different lifetime.

I wondered if I could do it? I surely didn't want to embarrass the Lord. But in His love He knew there would be a humorous surprise to put me at ease.

Chapter Twenty-Eight

I expected stogy, but the ambience was so stunning, so elegant, it took my breath away as I entered the historic Army and Navy Club. The ceilings appeared to stretch into heavens that were studded with ornate chandeliers. It was a predominately older collection of officers' wives that I would be speaking to and they were having sherry when I arrived. I resisted the urge to belt one down myself to settle a sudden case of stage fright. The majestically appointed room appeared to be set up for approximately one hundred and fifty places. Starched, white damask table cloths held regal china, glistening crystal goblets and a battery of weighted silver knives, forks and spoons lined up on either side of each plate like military hardware. I had mental flashes of gratitude for my mother who had instructed me as a teenager in proper table etiquette (exercises that I rebelliously thought were absurd at the time).

Soon ice water was poured into the goblets and molded salads were stationed at each place setting. Gleaming silver trays of rolls were placed within reach of all and the majority of the women had now found their places. Most of them looked stunning and I only hoped I could carry myself with such grace when I reached their ages. The officers of the Women's Club were seated at the speakers table where they had put me and to my left there was a minister who was to open the meeting and lead us in the blessing. He was a distinguished looking man, most likely in his late sixties, with salt and pepper hair and dapper moustache. The President of the Women's Club stood and daintily tapped on the rim of her water goblet until conversation finally ceased. She introduced the minister to my left who stood.

"Ladies," he said. And as he said "ladies" his false teeth flew out of his mouth and landed in the salad!

I had to bite my tongue to keep from laughing. Gazing quickly around the room I saw women were lifting napkins to their mouths to cover laughter, some sat wide-eyed just staring at the dentures. There was an embarrassed hush as collectively we waited to see how he would recover.

To his credit he laughed, reached down and grabbed up his false teeth jamming them back into his mouth. "Those darn things just *love* Jello!" he told us. Hysterical laughter broke the stilted silence. Once we had settled down he added, "Let us pray"....

After the courses had been served and I stood to speak, I felt completely relaxed. Delicious humor from a silly incident had united us all and there was a definite atmosphere of camaraderie. After I had finished sharing with them about Kent's healing, Maude Blanford's miraculous healing of cancer and others at NIH, many women came up asking if I would pray with them. It was an afternoon of privilege, a deep honor for me.

As I parked the station wagon in front of the town house, a quick glance skyward revealed huge, gray clouds scuttling overhead, appearing to be swollen with snow which threatened to dump. Hurrying into the kitchen to start dinner, I could hear Kent playing his record of Sammy Davis singing "Candy Man". It was the perfect rhythm for his new bongo drums. He was most likely the biggest fan of the television program "Soul Train". Whenever the program aired, Kent could be seen sprawled like a frog in front of the television snapping his fingers to all the Motown music and watching the dancers. He was double-jointed and when lying on the floor his legs splayed outward in frog-like fashion. The Jackson Five and especially Michael Jackson were at the top of his list. I continually marveled at how music helped him deal with illness. It seemed to be the lifeline that kept him tethered when the seas of chemotherapy got rough. Kurt liked music, but wasn't devoted to it like his twin. He was very popular with a lot of friends and while both were outgoing, Kurt attracted other kids.

As I set the table the telephone interrupted. It was Ruth Shigley inviting us to Sunday dinner after church. We had gotten to be close friends with the Shigleys, meeting them at Good Shepherd Church of the Brethren. Russ had his own business of recovering silver from X-ray film. He traveled all over the state picking up films and extracting the metal. They owned a beautiful home and I can remember feeling like a real country bumpkin as Ruth showed me the first electric crock pot I'd ever seen. Their son, David was a little older than the twins, but they had fun together. Russ and Bill were like Abbott and Costello when they got together, playing off each other comically. Part of their fun consisted of perpetually making up country songs that had to contain the ingredients of: rain; a train; a hound dog; mama; a broken love; a pickup truck, cheating, etc., etc. The children usually stuck fingers in their ears. Ruth and I agreed their attempts at harmony would peel the enamel off your teeth.

The dark clouds made their threat good that Friday night with a deluge of snow that began around midnight.

That icy cold Saturday morning we wakened to about six inches of snow. A storm had blanketed the trees with mantles like white ermine shawls.

That night there was a spontaneous sled riding party. The German Embassy families who lived there brought their quaint curved front wooden sleds out first. The teenagers stayed out long after the adults and younger children had given up, gone in to thaw out. I was fixing hot chocolate for Kurt and Kent when Lisa burst into the house crying, "My cross! I've lost my cross!"

she cried. I knew instantly that she meant the petrified wood cross necklace I had brought back to her from one of my singing trips out West. She never took it off, had had it for years and even wore it in the shower.

I enfolded her in my arms. "Nothing is ever lost to the Lord, sweetheart. He knows where it is." I wiped the tears from her cheeks.

"But, Mom, all that snow. We'll never find it," Tears welled up again in her beautiful hazel eyes.

"We don't have to, He will show us where it is." Kent and Kurt were watching silently as I put my arms around her again and prayed, "Lord, we know nothing is ever lost to you. You said in Your word that 'we have not because we ask not'. We're asking you Lord to send your Holy Spirit to guide us to just where Lisa's cross is. Thank you, Lord." I grabbed my jacket and a flashlight. As we exited our patio I was shocked at how much more snow had come down just in the short length of time I'd been inside. I suddenly had misgivings myself and had to silently rebuke that thought. Everyone had gone inside now and Lisa and I were alone as we climbed the hill to the gate, wading through the deep snow in the dim glow of a street lamp. And there, among the many snow packed grooves from the blades of sleds, the beam of the flashlight landed on the small embedded stone cross.

Lisa was ecstatic, "He did it! He did it! The Lord took us right to it," she shouted. Kent and Kurt were wide-eyed as she triumphantly showed it to them back in the kitchen.

"Well," Kent shrugged his shoulders, "what did you expect? Praise the Lord!" His arms shot heavenward in praise. He would have looked like a small preacher if it hadn't been for the cocoa chocolate moustache around his mouth.

I don't think Lisa was too surprised in that she always asked me to pray with her every time she had a test. Consequently, she was a straight A student. Meanwhile, the Lord was working on a fast track with Eric in high school. When he met his first computer, it was as though he had been born with it in his hand. Data Processing 1 was a snap for him and when he advanced to Data Processing 2, his teacher had him teaching portions of the Data Processing 1 course. While Kurt was not the best student in the class he held his own with the grades. The gift the Lord had seemed to give him was a quiet strength and sense of humor that attracted others to him. He had so many friends at school and in the townhouse complex that I was afraid his popularity might bother Kent. I shouldn't have worried.

As I heard the twins' prayers at bedtime, I always secretly marveled at Kent's faithfulness to pray for the other children at NIH (though fewer now by name as most of his friends had passed on). He also faithfully prayed for all the doctors, plus Dr. Gallo. However, could we have seen into the future, we would have seen that there was to be an orthopedic surgeon in Silver Spring, Maryland who was about to witness his own patient being supernaturally healed. As it happened, Kent was the one who was to have a big part in it. When we stayed home from church one Sunday the following summer, the Lord had a miracle-in-the-making walk right up to our front door... on crutches.

It was now a ritual that whenever the family went to church, climbed the steep blacktop path to Good Shepherd, Kent lovingly pushed me up the hill. I had come to depend on his small hands on my back giving me the steam to deal with the path in high heels. However, one Sunday morning in the summer of the following year, the family stayed home from church. It was a breezy, but humid day and we had gotten back late the night before from camping. I was sitting at the kitchen table with a cup of coffee, reading the Sunday Washington Post when the doorbell rang. Opening the door, I was surprised to find Vi, a surgical nurse who also went to Good Shepherd. She was leaning on crutches.

"What in the world happened to you? Come on in and let me get you seated, hon."

As we moved into the kitchen, she sat down at our kitchen picnic table and stretched out one leg encased in a soft cast onto the bench. Vi giggled slightly, "You're going to think this is the craziest thing. I was water baptized yesterday in the ocean... and broke my leg."

I almost dropped the cup of coffee I had poured for her. "What? How could that have happened?"

"A wave crashed up against me slamming down onto the leg. The doctor I work with in OR is an orthopedic surgeon. He met me at his office on an emergency basis and took X-rays—it's a compound, complex fracture. I'm supposed to be operated on tomorrow morning at 11:00 a.m." She took a sip of coffee, "He warned me that if I don't have it repaired quickly I may never walk again."

"Oh, Vi! How could the Lord let that happen? You were being baptized in His name!"

She shrugged her shoulders. "Sure don't understand it myself." She looked around the kitchen like she was seeing it for the first time. "Another thing I don't quite understand...what am I doing here? I was on my way up the hill to church. Suddenly I just found myself thinking I should come to your house."

"And how did you know we were home? Usually we'd have been at church by now."

We stared at each other for a minute. She finally smiled, "Do you think the Lord's in this somehow. Why does He want me here?"

Meanwhile I'd been silently asking God what His plan was in all this. Obviously He was in it. The thought came so quietly I almost thought it was my own. ***"Pray for her legs to grow out. Have Kent pray."***

"Vi, I think I know exactly what we're to do." I explained to her about praying for leg lengthening and related several testimonies to her, particularly the one about Bob Smith who had had to wear a lift in his shoe. By sharing former testimonies before praying I'd found it increased the faith of everyone praying. I called upstairs for Kent to come down and when he responded, told him we were going to pray for Vi whom he knew from church.

We helped her into a straight backed chair in the dining room. She propped her crutches against the dining room table. We had her sit back as far as possible up against the high ladder back of the chair. I stood by praying as Kent knelt and gently lifted her legs off the floor taking special care. He began saying, "We praise you, Jesus. We thank you, Jesus," repeatedly. Normally it was very apparent when the legs grew out; however, with the cast on one leg it inhibited ascertaining any healing by sight. After a time, Kent must have sensed healing was accomplished for he got up, kissed her on the cheek and left the room to go back upstairs. Soon we heard "Annie's Song" being played—he'd gone back to his records.

The following morning I got an excited telephone call from Vi at the hospital. "Sandy, we've had a miracle!" she said. "Because of the prayers, I insisted before surgery that they do another X-ray. My boss, Dr. Whitlock, thought I was crazy, of course. However, are you ready for this?" She didn't wait for me to answer. "The bone has been healed—completely healed. There's no fracture now. They're not going to have to operate."

"Praise the Lord! That's a blessing directly from Him...a miracle!"

"But...wait 'til I tell you about the extra gift! I've had a congenital hip defect since birth. Jesus healed that too! It showed up on the X-ray too."

"You should see me dancing for joy on this end, Vi." I told her.

"Doc could scarcely believe it...but he did. The X-rays don't lie—the one taken Saturday and then the one taken on Monday. It's made a believer out of him, Sandy."

"The Lord never fails to amaze me and He's full of surprises, isn't He, Vi? I guess now we know why He allowed you to break your leg during baptism. That really stumped me a bit, but He had a miracle planned around it that reached your surgeon. There might not have been any other way to prove to your doctor that Jesus is alive and well - still working miracles."

"That's got to be it. I'm so grateful. Be sure to tell Kent and thank him for praying."

"You bet I will, but he knows better than even you and me that he had little to do with it. I've heard him say before that he just asks and then watches what the Lord does."

"He'll probably be a minister when he grows up."

"He wants to be an architect." I laughed. "He draws pictures of houses with double front doors all the time. Either that or a drummer."

"Well, he's so special. Thank him for me."

I took the stairs two-at-a-time to tell Kent. He was listening to the song "My Sweet Lord". There were two versions and he had taken great exception to the Hare Krishna version when it came out. I was reminded of his godly discernment at a much earlier age also about the television program, "Bewitched." We all liked the program watching Elizabeth Montgomery wiggle her nose. However, one day Kent declared, "I'm not going to watch this anymore—it glorifies witches." We all realized he was right and we never watched it again as a family.

Afterward, as I spent some quiet time praising the Lord for Vi's healing and for Kent and I being present at a miracle, I watched a soft summer rain wash down the patio furniture outside the sliding glass doors. Barnaby Bix leaned against my leg, asking for a scratch under his chin. I felt loved, blessed in the tranquility of the moment.

It was short lived. Bill came home early. He had lost his job at Rockville Glass. It had been a rather rough go financially from the time we had moved in, but the Lord had always provided. Shortly after we had gotten settled, Catherine Marshall introduced me to a minister by the name of Chuck Mottley. He and his father had collaborated on a manuscript titled "The Mustard Seed" and asked me to join the effort to get it into publishable form. This project had helped to pay the bills for awhile. The book was published by Time Warner and on the night it was announced at a press conference, the hotel in Crystal City, Virginia was jammed with photographers and journalists. Dr. Mottley, Chuck's father, Chuck and I were lined up for newspaper photos when suddenly Dr. Mottley announced to everyone, "Good grief! I just realized, here we are: father, son, and holy Ghost." The room exploded with laughter—they all knew my name was "Ghost".

Several months later I had a strange and rather eerie experience. One Saturday night the entire family watched a movie on television. I had made huge bowls of buttered popcorn before we settled down to watch "Born Free", the touching movie about the family in Africa who had raised the beautiful lioness cub named Elsa. It was a true story portrayed in a delicate and loving movie. At the end, the woman realized they had to teach Elsa to survive in the wild—they had to give her up for her own good—let go of her. It was so sad to see how they were torn at losing her, worked with her trying to mold her into capturing her own food. They had to release her for her own sake.

Suddenly I had to slip from the room. I escaped to the kitchen and got as far as the washer and dryer before I burst into tears. I tried to stifle the sobs so they couldn't hear me in the other room as the movie was ending. Why was I touched like this? Why was I filled with some strange grief as though I associated with the character's feelings? I couldn't stop crying so ran into the powder room and locked the door. Was it a warning of some kind pertaining to Kent? Would I be required to release him, I wondered? I wasn't too sure I could.

I set aside those thoughts the following day and attributed them to the fact that I'd been extremely tired. I had a tendency to be too emotional when I hadn't had much sleep, I reasoned. It was quickly forgotten.

Bill still hadn't found another job and spent his days reading every line in the classifieds, just like in Louisville. Now that I wasn't working either, my father's social security was our only source of income. We, of course, didn't let anyone know of our dire financial straits—except the Lord. Two days before the first of the month when the rent of $500 would be due, I brought the mail in and tossed it on the kitchen table. Going through the catalogues and junk mail, I spotted a plain white envelope. It was from an acquaintance that we really didn't know very well. Opening it, I found a note that read:

> *"My husband and I were praying together and felt impressed that we were to send you a check. Now, we have no idea of what your financial situation is. You may have substantial savings, but all we know is that the Lord has told us to send you a check. And He even told us the amount. Please don't try to return this to us or not cash it as you will make us disobedient to God."*

I unfolded the check. It was in the amount of $500, just the amount we needed for the rent as my father's contribution had paid the utilities and bought food. I ran to the living room with it to show Bill. We were so grateful, felt loved, cared for, watched over. I hugged the fact to me that He would always provide. God was good.

And then, the following day we found out Kent had relapsed.

Chapter Twenty-Nine

<img referenced as decorative divider>

*P*erhaps it was my remembrance of the unusual grief I had felt in watching the "Born Free" movie, but I felt more troubled than at any other time in the past over this news of Kent's relapse. One night, after everyone else was in bed, I tried to pray it out. My feeling of anxiety still remained and finally I asked a direct question of the Lord, "Father, are You going to take Kent? Could I ask—as a sort of fleece—that if that's Your plan, You might show me the same scripture about the grain of mustard that You used to guide me when Susie, Kent's girlfriend, crossed over to the other side?"

I had been pacing the floor, but now I turned and picked up a Bible that was on the kitchen table.

"Please let the Holy Spirit guide my hands," I said aloud. My palms were damp and my hands shook as I slowly opened the book at random.

I choked as my eyes stared in disbelief at the words: "The kingdom of heaven is like a grain of mustard seed, which a man took, and sowed in his field; which, indeed, is the least of all seeds; but when it is grown, it is the greatest among herbs, and becometh a tree, so that the birds of the air come and lodge in the branches of it." It was Matthew 13:31-32.

The same scripture I had asked for! The personal implication those words carried seemed to club me senseless momentarily. *Was* it a direct answer or a fluke of my fingers? And then, my mind slowly began to serve up a picture from the past. I saw myself kneeling beside my bed in Kentucky. I had been filled with some strange anxiety for Kent and, like tonight, had asked Jesus for a direct answer in scripture. I had opened immediately to Ecclesiastes 12:6 that read: "Remember your Creator earnestly now... before the whole circulatory system of the blood ceases to function." This experience had proven to be an accurate message to guide us, for the following day we learned that Kent had suffered his first relapse.

As I examined this memory, I realized with a trace of surprise that the cold fear which had accompanied my reading about the mustard seed now seemed to drain away.

I gave myself a pep-talk. *If the Lord is using this to prepare me, then it must be His will. I might possibly be able to accept it if He troubles to etch His will in this across my heart and spells out His intentions in neon across the heavens.*

I know now that the Holy Spirit helped me to a measure of relinquishment of Kent that night. And I had learned from reading Catherine Marshall's books that relinquishment was extremely important to the Father. After years of being bedridden with tuberculosis and trying every avenue of healing—spiritual and physical—she had finally told the Lord, "Alright, if this is what You want, Lord, for me just to lie in this bed, then that's what I want too." She had sincerely given up her own will in the matter. In a number of days she was completely healed after years of fighting with T.B. Bill and I had experienced it ourselves when buying the pink house in Kentucky. When we told the Lord we didn't want it unless He wanted us to have it—He gave it back when there was no hope. But when Kent recovered two months later, I shelved the whole experience into my mental file drawer of spiritual mistakes. Maybe my being confronted with the mustard seed scripture had just been an accident. He had gone back very quickly into remission on a new chemotherapy drug.

Kent, being a research patient, was now the first recipient of a new device to ease the amount of "sticks" a patient would have to have when receiving IV therapy. This was a "hepa-lock" that protected the open site where the IV would be introduced into the vein. The patient would keep it inserted for whenever an IV was required, the cap would then be removed and the tubing inserted after saline or heparin was washed through the device. This was a definite improvement in having to have a needle stick each time there needed to be infusion. Movies were taken of him on a swing, riding his bike and performing different tasks to show that the patient was unencumbered by the new device. The doctors let him know that by accepting this, he would be helping many other patients in the future. He seemed to be proud of his contribution to research.

The family became even more involved in Good Shepherd. Bill and I both were teaching Sunday school and the twins became acolytes. They wore the typical long black skirts with white square necked cassocks with long sleeves. They proudly carried the long gold candle lighters and would start the Sunday service by walking down the aisle and lighting the candles. They ended the service by proudly snuffing them out with the other end of the long gold lighter. My job was to sit in the pew and pray they didn't set each other on fire in those outfits. Good Shepherd was a bit more formal in service than our church back in Kentucky, but Jesus still showed up at every service.

Bill had finally found a job at an auto glass firm. Eric was preparing to graduate from Albert Einstein High School when Kent suddenly relapsed again. It was totally unexpected—no warning from the Lord, nor obvious symptoms from him.

Slowly, a strange thing began to happen, a total departure from anything we might have expected. It had it's inception through an idea that Kent expressed at dinner one night.

"Please pass those little... whaddaya' call them---those little trees." He nudged Lisa and pointed at the vegetable bowl.

She giggled, "You mean the broccoli?"

"That's it! I really like them. If we had a farm we could grow them couldn't we, Mom?"

"I suppose so, sweetheart. What made you think about living on a farm?" I could feel goose bumps begin to erupt on my arms.

He buttered a roll. "I've been dreaming about being a farmer."

I shot a look at Bill. "That's strange. I've been dreaming about living on a farm too." I looked around the table. "Me...of all people. I'm the one who always wants to live with the concrete around me. Yet, I've had dreams about living on a beautiful farm. Maybe it's just because I've seen the beauty of Catherine Marshall's acres of serenity at Evergreen Farm."

Lisa looked pleased with the idea.

"What about it Bill? Could we look at some?" I passed the platter of meatloaf around the table for seconds.

"I guess so. Wouldn't mind getting away from all this traffic."

Kurt had been listening intently. "Could I have chickens?"

"Yes. Probably, son."

"And a goat?"

"Uh...let's stick to a few chickens for now, okay?" I couldn't believe how the idea seemed to be swiftly taking off like a runaway train. Was it really the Lord's guidance for us? Was it what He wanted? Was it time to move again?

A curious transformation seemed to come over Kent as we went on our farm hunting expeditions on weekends. As soon as we got into the countryside, he would become more animated, happy and excited. It was as though the more miles we put between us and the hospital, the more Kent came alive. It was no wonder—he was back on a five day IV protocol that was strenuous, and while he always was so positive and upbeat it obviously began to wear him down. Even the doctors commented on what a hero he was.

We, of course, began looking in places within commuting distance to Bill's job and NIH. While we had prayed about this new direction for our lives in the beginning of our search, we soon became aware of a form of guidance that had to be more than just coincidence. The first two times we left the townhouse to search for a farm, the song "Country Roads Take Me Home" came on the car radio. Kent picked up on it first.

"Listen! Listen to that song!" he exclaimed excitedly. "It's from the Lord. He's saying our new home is a farm!"

"Oh, come on, Kent. It's just a popular song," Eric smiled and patted him on the arm.

But soon none of us could deny the fact that he was right. Every single time we were on our way to look at another farm the song came on the radio. It finally got to the point that a hush would settle over all of us when it came on. It became a reverential form of guidance.

Early one Saturday morning, we began the drive to Myersville, Maryland. We had seen an ad in the Washington Post for a farm that was tantalizing. It had said that the Underground Railroad had hidden runaway slaves there during the Civil War and described a "rippling trout stream" that ran through the property. I had called the night before and made an appointment with Mr. and Mrs. Alexander, the elderly couple who owned the farm. As we turned onto the next state route there was a small brook that followed the highway just as the instructions had said.

"There's the metal bridge, Bill. This is where we turn right." I told him. "The farm should start on the other side."

At that moment, the song "Country Roads Take Me Home" came on the radio. I turned around and looked at Kent in the backseat. He began clapping, "This is it! This is it! The Lord's telling us this is it!" We all began smiling and shaking our heads.

Bill stopped the station wagon at the back of a lovely, white clapboard rambling farmhouse. We could see a barn in the distance. Shortly, Mr. And Mrs. Alexander appeared at the door to welcome us. Kent was fascinated by the outdoor oven. Mrs. Alexander explained that during Civil War times they actually cooked in it. They showed us underneath the front part of the house where slaves had been hidden. Mr. Alexander explained that the owners of the farm had also hidden their horses under there so that the southern soldiers wouldn't steal them. It was a gorgeous home, fraught with a patina of history that was almost possible to touch.

There was a big old mule in the barn that "hee hawed" a welcome at us. Kent fell in love with the mangy and shaggy animal. "We'll just leave him here for you, Kent. We're moving to the city and he won't fit in an apartment," Mr. Alexander told him.

Bill stood looking down at the rippling brook and as we all watched, a trout jumped as if in joy to be alive. That was the exclamation point for him. He shook hands with Mr. Alexander as we prepared to leave, "I'm going to do everything I can to try to buy this place," he told him.

The car was abuzz on the way home. Eric talked about being close enough to the Appalachian Trail to hike on weekends, Kurt went on and on about how he would raise chickens and we could even sell the eggs. Kent wanted to know if we could bake bread in the outdoor oven and Lisa talked about playing her flute on a rock above the trout stream. I couldn't wait to describe the farm to Daddy when we got home. He would adore the rich history we could inherit by buying it.

As the steaming heat of another humid summer approached, Al Houston and Maggie took the youth group, including Lisa, out west to see the Grand Canyon, Bryce Canyon and Zion National Park. Several of the congregation were to take over the services on Sundays. Eric and several friends took off on their trek on the Appalachian Trail. We dropped them off in northern Maryland near the bridge we had seen before on the way to the farm. A picture of him high above on the rainbow-like bridge waving to us below was seared in my mind for weeks with the branding iron of the prayers of a mother's protective, brooding love. I was absolutely convinced that without my daily prayers of claiming the shed blood of Jesus Christ over them they would have been devoured by wolves or attacked by bears.

We were trying to line up financing for buying the farm. Just when everything seemed to be going well... turning a corner—Bill lost his job again. It was so hard to understand how this could possibly be a part of the Lord's plan for us. Why did this keep happening?

Now that we were no longer actively escaping Kensington on the weekends to hunt for farms, the walls of the hospital seemed to be closing in on Kent to smother him in chemotherapy. His protocol called for five days of L-Asparaginase IV's, then the stronger drugs of Donomycin and Vincristine also given intravenously once a week. He seemed to feel great, played outside through this period, and while he couldn't ride his bike because the drugs had taken his platelet count to the hemorrhage level, everything else was normal. We made our daily pilgrimage to the hospital and it got to be grim.

I tried to think of things to keep him entertained when we couldn't really go anywhere as we were anchored to the hospital and the house. On August 16th, Lisa sent a letter from Arizona on the way to the Grand Canyon. She said she was really worried about Kent and had begun to fast. Al and Maggie found out and suggested the entire youth group go on a fast for Kent. She said she had no idea how much love there was in the group. One girl even cried with her as they prayed for Kent.

On Friday, August 23rd, the routine was broken with a surprise. As Kent was lying on the bed in clinic getting his medicines, Dr. Fay came in and announced, "I'm taking him off the L-Asperaginase. I don't think it's doing sufficient good to warrant risking liver damage. I had planned to do a bone marrow on Monday, but next Friday will do. You have a week off from the hospital."

Kent and I could scarcely believe this good fortune—a week's reprieve! It seemed like a gift from heaven. Much later we were to find out that it *was*.

That night I went over to Russ and Ruth Shigley's house. Bill and I again had the Sunday Worship service and Russ had agreed to give the call to worship and announcements that I'd written out. Russ and Ruth had been a dynamic contribution to the Sunday School class Bill and I had taught when we first came to the church. Both had eagerly received the baptism of the Holy Spirit.

Russ' silver recovery business was operated out of their home. As the Shigley's and I sat at the kitchen table, Russ' brother who was in business with him, walked in and placed a stack of company money on the table—the day's receipts.

After Russ' brother had left, Russ grew strangely serious and asked when Kent had his next appointment at NIH for treatment. I told him about our gift of a week off that had come as a surprise just that afternoon.

He leaned forward, blue eyes crackling in a new intensity, and asked, "Lisa's out in Utah having the time of her life with the youth group, right?"

I nodded affirmatively.

"And Eric's hiking with his friends."

I indicated that was right, still puzzled by his attitude. He seemed to be talking more to himself than to Ruth or me.

"And what are you going to do for your twins for a vacation?" His eyes now locked in with mine. It was almost like a statement of confrontation.

The question caught me off-guard. I stammered through an explanation that we had planned to take them to Disney World, but then Bill had lost his job making it out of the question.

Russ cocked his head to one side as though listening to a voice I couldn't hear. "I think you're supposed to leave right after church on Sunday and drive to Florida," he said slowly.

Reaching over to the stack of bills on the table, he pulled a hundred dollar bill to the center of the table. "Now, that's for the trip down." He pulled several more hundreds out of the pile. Ruth and I have a time-share condo in New Smyrna Beach. We'll call and reserve it for you and you can stay there for the week. Orlando is just about an hour and a half from there...two at most. He pushed the bills he'd taken from the pile into the center. "This is for Disney World. You'll love it!" He pushed more bills to the center, "This is for your flight back to Dulles with Kent so he can make it in time for his bone marrow on Friday. And this is for Bill and Kurt to drive back." He pushed more bills to the table's center.

"Oh...Russ...we can't accept this." I realized I was stammering.

"You can't refuse it, Sandy. This is from the Lord. It's for the twins...His provision for them. You'll be disobedient if you don't take it, and you'll make Ruth and me disobedient." She reached over and squeezed her husband's hand.

"This is so...so loving of you, but we'll have to pray about it Russ. I frankly don't think Bill will take it. I can't thank you enough."

"Don't you dare thank me. It's not from me. It's from the Lord for Kent and Kurt."

He practically shoved me out the door with the money stuffed in my purse. When I got home Bill was watching a sports show on television. The twins were in bed. When I related to him what had happened he was as floored as I was.

"Russ acted like he was listening to another voice as he went through counting out the monies. I truly think he was being led by the Holy Spirit, Bill."

"But San, thirteen hundred dollars...we can't accept that."

But after we had prayed and talked some more one thing became clear. Our pride was standing in the way. And we had to consider if this *was* the Lord's provision, it would definitely not be of the Lord to let our pride enter in.

One thing finally seemed solidly framed for guidance—circumstances, timing and then provision. We had received the week off unexpectedly, I had just *happened* to be at Ruth and Russ' that night, provision had been just dumped on the table and the factor of Russ' intense conviction. We decided finally to call him in the morning and accept. We prayed together and thanked the Lord before going to bed.

The following morning, Saturday, Kent and I got up early. As I was fixing his breakfast he suddenly couldn't seem to contain a wave of excitement. "I've got *one whole week off from the hospital!* Couldn't we go away or something?" He sat, chin in hands, "If I could just win that contest on Channel 20 TV we could go to Disney World."

I almost dropped the frying pan, but didn't say a word as I felt Bill should be the one to tell the twins. Later that morning Bill called Russ to tell him of our decision and express our extreme gratitude. Then I called Kurt and Kent downstairs from their Saturday morning bedroom cleaning.

"Sit down, fellas," Bill began. "Something's happened.... something very good. You guys must have been praying about going to Disney World."

Heads nodded.

"Well, God has heard you. He has impressed Mr. Shigley to provide the money for you to go to Disney World."

There was a little-boy-explosion-of-happiness times two!

"Guys we're going to leave right after church tomorrow morning so we have to start packing right after breakfast."

"What about Grandpa, can he go too?" Kent asked.

"No, sweetheart, we have a visiting nurse coming in to stay with him and prepare his meals. She can sleep in Eric's room right next to his." I had told him what had happened that morning when I'd taken his breakfast down to him. He really was not well enough to travel that distance by car and welcomed a nurse. "Get me a pretty one," he'd said.

We left directly after church on Sunday. Bill took the first shift of driving. We figured it would take at least eighteen hours of straight driving with few stops. The twins finally got tired of asking, "Are we there yet?" when we hadn't even made it through Virginia. We stopped for dinner after crossing over into North Carolina.

I took the second driving shift through South Carolina. It seemed like the longest state in the world. It was a dark, cloudy night with no stars in the sky. I was pretty much on my own now as Bill slept in the passenger seat—the twins snored gently in the backseat. The radio was my only company. I had just thought *Will I never reach the Georgia state line?* Just then I recognized the beginning of Ray Charles singing "Georgia on My Mind". I laughed out loud. "You reading my mind again, Lord?" I asked.

Miles and miles later the radio again had my full attention. There was a voice that sounded like Kent's to introduce a song. It said, "Tell me again, Mommy." Then a woman began to sing a song called, "You And Me Against The World", obviously from the lyrics telling a tale of a woman and her child feeling that while the world was against them God was on their side.

Toward the end of the song, unexplainable tears began to well up inside and I felt my spirit crescendo with the music as I heard the words:

> *And when one of us is gone, and one of us is left to carry on*
> *Remembering will have to do, our memories alone will get us through,*
> *Think about the days of me and you... You and me against the world.*

Then the child's voice again: "I love you, Mommy." The woman's voice: "I love you too, baby."

It was over—the disc jockey said it was Helen Reddy, certainly not the voice of God, but my palms were damp on the steering wheel. I had never heard that song before. I had to slow my speed because of the torrent of tears that blurred my vision. Sobs rose up to choke me. Surely this was not just an over-emotional reaction to a sentimental song. The lyrics had touched home and I wondered if the Lord was confirming my thoughts that Kent's time with us was short. The song had hit me like an exclamation point to what I had been thinking at the time—just as it had when "Georgia on My Mind" had been presented.

The lyrics, "When one of us is gone, and one of us is left to carry on" hung over me making it hard to breathe as we crossed the state line into Georgia.

Chapter Thirty

*T*he two bedroom condominium was right on the beach with its own pool and shuffle board court. We were on the second floor with a balcony that afforded a breathtaking view of the ocean. The furnishings were in soft pastels of aqua, blues and mauve. We were exhausted when we first arrived, but had to jump into bathing suits immediately and swim. We swam in the ocean that lapped at us warmly and refreshed us from the lack of sleep.

Tuesday we set out for Disney World early so we could be there when it opened. We were all at a pitch of excitement. I felt like a child myself and as the station wagon started up the long road to the gates and parking lot there were signs informing us to tune our radio to a certain frequency for Disney World information. It was playing "Zippity Doo Dah" as we tuned in. Kent and Kurt sang "My oh my what a beautiful day" from the backseat and I found my eyes filled with tears of gratitude that we could be there.

Kent kept saying, "Thank You, Lord. I can't believe we're really here!" as we walked through the gate. It was like stepping into a world of fantasy. We were there from 9:00 AM until 11:30 PM that night when we straggled to the car nursing our feet. We accomplished the impossible by seeing everything in one day.

However, two things happened there that alerted me spiritually and proved to be of even greater spiritual significance later. We had heard so much about "Small World", one of the attractions, that the four of us decided to go through this ride first so we wouldn't miss it.

As we walked down a long concrete ramp that zigzagged toward waiting boats, the song "Small World" set a mood of excitement. We boarded a replica of a row boat that zipped us through a tunnel and then into a room ablaze with small mechanical dolls dressed in costumes of different lands. They danced and twirled, swung from swings, strummed guitars and as the boat traveled from room to room the song, "It's a Small World After All" crescendoed as did the surroundings.

Finally, around a corner, we entered the last room and I caught my breath. The entire room was filled with dolls dressed in satiny white representing the children of the world. The song reach a pitch of finale that seemed to pulsate through me as the diminutive dolls rode merry-go-rounds, ferris wheels, festooned balloons and knelt before us as the boat passed by.

Kent grabbed my arm. "Mom! That's what the angels are going to sound like!"

He hadn't said, "must sound like"—but "are *going* to sound like." I felt my heart twinge at his words.

Later that evening after dinner, the lights began to wink on softly transforming everything into an even greater scale of fantasy. The four of us were walking toward Cinderella's castle that towered high above us. Suddenly I felt a small hand in mine.

"Mom," Kent said thoughtfully, "is this what heaven is going to be like?"

I smiled and told him, "Yes, sweetheart, I think it's like one big Disney world for the children there."

Now my mind was really beginning to catch up to what I had been feeling in my spirit before. Was our time together short? Was Kent feeling this too? The seriousness of his disease had always seemed to pass over his head, but now I sensed perhaps the Lord was speaking to his spirit as He seemed to be to mine.

I wondered if Bill might be getting any signals about this. Late that night, as just he and I sat on the balcony of the condo listening to the waves roll in, I asked him.

"No. Nothing. No signals."

I dropped the subject. I didn't want to spoil our vacation with ominous portent that might just be my imagination anyway.

The rest of the week was spent in glory. We walked the beach at night, tramping ankle deep in gentle waves through a sparkling pathway of moonlight on the water. An occasional phosphorescent jelly fish popped up like a glob of neon bouncing on the waves in the deep. We got up one morning and were in the ocean as the sun came up spreading God's glory across the horizon, then ran onto the beach that had been swept slate-clean by the tide and wrote, "Praise the Lord" in foot high letters for the early morning beach walkers to hike across. Kent wrote, "Jesus is Lord--King of Kings."

The night before we were to fly home, as I tucked Kent and Kurt in bed, Kent said wistfully, "I wish this week could be like a tape recorder. I just wish we could put it on rewind and start it all over again."

Friday morning as Kent and I boarded an Eastern airlines plane while Kurt and Bill headed back north in the station wagon, my mind whirled backward. It presented me with thoughts of all the air miles Kent and I had logged together since the time of his diagnosis. He hadn't flown in the two and one-half years we had lived in Maryland. And now, 30,000 feet in the air, I wondered if God was giving us one last flight together to commemorate all the happy times we had traveled together. Somehow I felt we were coming full circle in time.

This thought seemed to be punctuated by Kent himself. The flight attendant had pinned an inexpensive set of wings with "Eastern" in blue on the top of his pocket. He smiled at me, reddened a little, ran long fingers through his blond hair and settled back into the seat.

"I'm really too *old* for these, you know," he told me. "But I'm glad I got them for old time's sake."

For old time's sake...just what I'd been thinking. Here we were flying into NIH on Eastern again.

His bone marrow that afternoon was not good. The marrow was apparently packed with leukemia cells and it was impossible after three tries to aspirate any marrow. A biopsy had to be done.

Kent's bravery on the treatment table had always astonished me—there were no tears. But now, as I watched Dr. Fay exert pressure on the larger needle, grinding into the bone for the marrow it was essential to have, I realized Kent was whispering something and leaned my head down to hear. He was repeating the name of Jesus over and over.

There were still a large number of cells present when the reading was made. He was definitely not showing his usual response to the drugs. The marrow the following week was equally discouraging.

On Tuesday, September 10th, Kent had some nausea and stomach pain. As Kurt had just gotten over a bout with the flu, we attributed this to be the culprit or perhaps the usual drug side-effects. We were due to go into the hospital for blood counts the following day and also a conference with the doctor. Dr. Fay had hinted that Kent's lack of response to the chemotherapy might require a switch in drugs and perhaps hospitalization. The threat of being hospitalized was fearful—in all the years since his cerebral hemorrhage he had never had to be back in the hospital again. I realized I was praying now out of fear and that surely couldn't please the Lord.

That afternoon the Lord called an emergency prayer meeting. I say the Holy Spirit called it because people from the church just seemed to appear. C. J., a young minister from the huge youth prayer group, TAG, that Lisa belonged to, came to pray for Kent, also Mary Simmons from Good Shepherd. As we knelt by the bed, I looked up to see Russ and Ruth Shigley in the doorway. They apparently had heard us all upstairs and had just come up too. They smiled, came and knelt with us.

C. J. ministered the Word and then began to pray. In the midst of his prayer he cast out the spirit of leukemia. Directly after the prayer, Kent got out of bed and came downstairs with the rest of us. He was completely free of pain—his usual bouncy, happy self. He told me, "When C. J. cast out the leukemia, I got tears in my eyes. Just to think, Mom, I don't have leukemia anymore!"

Later that afternoon Kent asked me to get some Manaschevitz wine. This seemed like an odd request. I chalked it up to the prednisone that he had to take. It seemed to give him the weird cravings of a pregnant woman—eggs by the dozen if I'd allow it, pickles, donuts, ice cream. I hoped the request for the wine wasn't to be some new craving. I bought it, but told him he could only have a tiny glass.

After dinner, I gave the twins the night off from dishes because there was a special Star Trek program they wanted to watch on television. As I was washing up the pans, Kent appeared at the kitchen door and asked for a cracker. I grabbed the box off the shelf and gave him one. About fifteen minutes later, he came back and asked for the little glass of wine I had promised that he could have. I opened the bottle, poured about a thimble full in the bottom of a jelly glass and handed it to him.

Five minutes later I finished the pans, wiped the counters, turned off the kitchen light and proceeded to go through the dining room to the living room. I stopped short. Kent had dimmed the chandelier and sat at the table with hands folded, head bowed, before the glass of wine and cracker. I hoped the sharp intake of my breath hadn't disturbed him as I silently backed out of the room. I escaped to the powder room to stifle a fresh onslaught of tears. Later he told me, "Jesus served me communion, Mom."

On Wednesday night as I put Kent and Kurt to bed I heard their prayers as usual. Kurt said his first and then Kent, but right at the end he had a very loud, very strong three or four sentences in tongues. We all looked at each other. The children knew, as we adults did, that if the Holy Spirit gave a message in tongues it was scriptural that there be an interpretation. The three of us bowed our heads and waited...and waited...and waited. I had the very loud thought, *Now, don't make anything up... Kent has the interpretation also.*

After a time, Kent spoke these words out loud, *"My son, my son, I would not have you be afraid. I am with you and I love you so much. Take My hand... take My hand, let Me lead you. There is nothing to fear."*

He looked up with a beaming smile. "The Holy Spirit gave me a message in tongues and the interpretation! Wow! Did you hear that, did you, Mom?"

I wrapped my arms around him and hoped he couldn't see the tears in my eyes.

Later, as I was getting ready for bed all my fear returned. Ever since he had received the Holy Spirit, Kent had always leaned heavily on the Lord. But his actions tonight frightened me. It was as though he knew with his spirit that his time was short—although maybe not at all with his mind. Was the Lord getting him ready I wondered?

I gripped the sink in the bathroom and began to cry. "Lord, if this is Your will, I accept it, but please God... please, don't let him suffer."

The words startled me. They sounded familiar. And then I remembered.

283

I had said those very words in the chapel of St. Joseph's hospital the day after Kent had been diagnosed. And for the first time in my life, I had felt God had heard me! I straightened up and wiped the tears away as a current of peace flowed through me.

God *had* heard me that day. He had given us nine and a half beautiful years together after that. I knew I had made a higher step in the relinquishment of Kent that night.

I began to reason that maybe that was all God was requiring. After all the people who had been healed that I'd been privileged to see, to be a part of, surely it was His will for Kent too. Maybe it would be like what God required of Abraham. After all, He had promised Abraham that his offspring would be as "the sands of the sea". But then He told Abraham to take Isaac, his son, up the mountain and sacrifice him. Abraham had been obedient. He built an altar, laid Isaac on it, and just as he raised the knife the Lord provided a ram caught in the thicket for the sacrifice in Isaac's place.

Jesus was the sacrifice for us, He had died in Kent's place, I reasoned. Perhaps this was just a test for us as it had been for Abraham...

Chapter Thirty-One

———ᴄᴠ᷄ᴗ———

*T*hursday afternoon Dr. Fay examined Kent. He had low blood counts from the drugs, but they were not at an unreasonable level. The nausea and stomach pain had returned, but the doctor felt it was either from the drugs or that he had picked up Kurt's "bug". Kent was not a part of our conference, but was in the clinic waiting room with a book. Bill and I had always felt projections could be harmful to his mental well-being.

"I just want to be sure you know where we are," Dr. Fay told us. He then outlined our only remaining choice of treatment left for Kent. We had exhausted all available chemotherapy drugs. He said the staff had conferred and decided that the best course of action to Kent's lack of response to the drugs now being used was to admit him to the hospital on Monday and administer high level doses of methotrexate. While he had had that prior it was not given at the level they intended to use now.

He made it clear that we had the option to refuse after considering the extreme side-effects Kent might encounter. I had a sudden flash back:

When Kent was first admitted when he was two and one-half, there had been a thirteen-year-old boy by the name of Joey in the room next door. By the mother's grapevine I knew they were having to "hit him with everything they had medically". One afternoon I overheard him begging with his mother for a gun to kill himself. I rushed Kent up to the recreation floor so he wouldn't hear. Now, I remembered... I couldn't speak for a moment as raw fear tried to tempt me into a picture I refused to accept. We didn't give him an answer that day. We needed time to pray.

Shortly after we got home from the hospital, Kent began having severe stomach pain. I took his temperature—104 degrees. I gave him Tylenol for pain and fever, but by that evening the pain had increased. I kept imploring, "Kent, you know, I really do think we ought to go over to the hospital and get some help."

But it was always met with, "No! I want to stay home." His tolerance for pain had always been remarkable and I was frightened by the agony he seemed to be in. Finally, at 11:00 PM that night he admitted, "I need help."

I made a call to the doctor on duty at NIH and told him we were coming in. One other call was made to Mary Simmons to start the prayer chain. Bill started the car, I placed a pillow on my lap for Kent's head and we took off.

At 11:30 as Kent lay on a bed in the clinic being examined by the doctor, we looked up and to our surprise saw a crowd gathering in the hall: our minister,

Al Houston and Maggie; Russ and Ruth; Mary Simmons, to name just a few. With a rush I felt an under-girding support. My arms weren't big enough to go around all of them.

The on-call doctor examined Kent carefully, got all of the details from Bill and me. He then telephoned Doctor Fay at home to get a corroborating word on his diagnosis—drug side effects. To our great relief, he told us we could take him home and gave us a prescription for Demerol to pick up at the NIH pharmacy. He had never before had to have such a potent pain killer. In all those years Tylenol had seen him through.

It was highly unusual for Kent to be released. Normally, if a child had low counts, a fever and pain he would be admitted to the hospital. In fact, we had expected Kent would be. He had thought so too and this is why he had resisted going in. We were all relieved.

Our prayer supporters who had been sitting in the waiting room became a cheering section when I told them the news. They filed into the room and one-by-one kissed Kent on the cheek as he still lay on the bed. But as I stood there watching, I had the sudden and distinct impression that they were kissing him "good-bye". I immediately rebuked that thought.

We took Kent home. By this time the pain medication had relieved him considerably and he slept through the night. We changed sleeping arrangements. I slept in Kurt's bed to be near Kent. Kurt slept with Bill.

Earlier in the afternoon Catherine Marshall's new book, *Something More,* had arrived by Federal Express. I marveled over the fact that her book *Beyond Ourselves* had richly laid the foundation for my born again experience. Ironically, our family was now in the sequel. She had graciously shipped us several copies as the story of the healing of Kent's cerebral hemorrhage was Chapter Nine in the book and also the miraculous healing of Maude Blanford's cancer was included. There was a brilliantly instructive chapter on the value of praise, and as I eagerly read that chapter it seemed to leap from the book as a personal instruction.

Now, tonight, it seemed as though God wanted me to praise Him for the pain. As I lay on the other twin bed I resisted. It made no sense until the phone rang around midnight. Two separate couples called who had been alerted by the prayer chain. Both had identical experiences when they began to pray for Kent. The Holy Spirit had spoken to them and said, "The pain is a part of the healing." I couldn't dismiss this word from the mouths of two witnesses although I didn't understand it at the time, but it made it easier to praise when viewing it from that perspective.

The following morning, Friday, Kent needed the pain medication at 8:00 a.m. and again at 11:00 a.m.; although he did seem much more comfortable, the pain was still there. At noon, Dr. Fay called to find out how he was.

"I do want you to bring him in Monday," he told me. "Whether we hospitalize him or not, we might consider giving him blood. In the meantime, if he bats an eyelash the wrong way I want to know about it." I told him I thought we could ride it out.

Kent had on red and white shortie pajamas with little sailboats on them and white crew socks. His record player was beside the bed and he kept playing a new Chicago album he'd just gotten, jiggling his foot in time to the music and looking at the ceiling as though he were waiting for something. His favorite seemed to be the track, "I've Been Searching So Long" and when it would finish, he'd pick up the needle and play the track again. Bill and I both felt the Holy Spirit's guidance for prayer seemed to just be praise. We sat in Kent's room with him, praising silently.

At 1:00 o'clock that afternoon all pain left Kent! "Oh! The pain... it's gone!" he cried and sat straight up in bed smiling. He was a bit lethargic, but seemed to be extremely relieved at the new-found comfort.

I hugged him, "Sweetheart, that's wonderful. Jesus is faithful, isn't he?" He seemed to be a bit sweaty. "I'm going to give you an alcohol rubdown, hon, to cool you off... refresh you a bit, okay?" He nodded and flipped the record.

I got a bottle of alcohol and proceeded to rubdown his legs. When I got to the ankles and feet I noticed a slight discoloration of the skin. I lifted his pajama shirt to do his back with alcohol and discovered the discoloration had traveled upward and spread on his back. I stood looking at it and was totally perplexed, but as I did a warmth began to pour down on me like a mantle of hot oil. I had come to recognize this anointing as the Lord telling me I was in His will and usually truth and healing resulted. It normally came as a reassurance from God that He was there with everything under control. I would have been frightened if this feeling had not been with me now.

"How do you feel, honey?" I asked.

He smiled broadly. "Fine...just fine," he told me. There seemed to be a note of relief to his voice.

Silently pointing out the discoloration to Bill, I signaled for him to follow me out into the hall so Kent wouldn't hear. We agreed I should call the hospital. It was 1:45 p.m.

The NIH doctors wore Page Masters on their belts so they could be located at all times. The signal carried for a radius of twenty-five miles. But Dr. Fay didn't answer the page. This seemed extremely strange at the time. I was on hold for almost ten minutes. As I hung up the telephone I knew I could get another doctor on the leukemia service immediately, or we could put Kent in the car and rush him over there in less than ten minutes.

But I cradled the receiver and as I did, I had the thought,

Will you not watch with Me one hour?

287

This was the same thing Jesus had told the disciples in the Garden of Gethsemane! I looked out the window of our master bedroom and wondered why I would think something like that, or was it the Lord? Sometimes it was difficult to distinguish. It had come so subtly; however, I suddenly felt it would be disobedient to try to contact the hospital again.

I called Bill out into the hall and told him I couldn't reach Dr. Fay, but I didn't describe to him what I thought I'd "heard" from the Lord. I just wasn't sure. Instead, I went into Lisa's room and began to make her bed. It was easier to praise not looking at the circumstances. As I pulled the spread up and smoothed it, it came again...but this time much louder...

Will you not watch with Me one hour?

I looked at Lisa's alarm; it was 2:00 o'clock. As I did, the full meaning swept over me. Jesus had given up His spirit to the Father... at 3:00 o'clock... on a Friday!

I felt no fear, only a deep peace as I went back into Kent's room to keep the vigil I felt that Jesus had instructed. The guidance had come so loudly this time that there was little margin for doubt. But would it be an experience like Abraham had with Isaac? Therefore, I still said nothing to Bill about what I expected.

I bent over Kent and gathering him into my arms, I asked, "How do you feel, honey?"

"Wonderful...warm and wonderful", he smiled up at me as I plumped his pillow and smoothed a few blond stray hairs that had fallen onto his forehead. I sat down on Kurt's bed and picked up *Something More* again to use as a prop for Kent's sake so he'd think I was reading. I began to pray silently. Bill sat in a chair apparently reading too, but I knew he was praying also. Kent had allowed the music to stop now, but occasionally he jiggled a foot in boredom as though in time to some imagined song. I kept asking him how he felt and he always reassured me... "Just fine" or "Warm... wonderful." After a time, I asked Bill what time it was.

He looked at his watch and told me, "Quarter to 3:00."

I got up from Kurt's bed and knelt by Kent's. Bill put down his book and followed suit without asking anything. We laid hands on him and began to praise the Lord aloud. I remember noticing my tongues seemed tinged with a new authority. Kent's breathing seemed to assume a new rapidity. He didn't seem to be struggling to breathe—just breathing faster and more deeply. I took his hand in mine.

Somewhere around five minutes of 3:00 he made a noise as though clearing his throat. I placed my face close to his and again asked how he felt. I noticed there was one small tear glistening in the corner of his eye and at that moment

I realized he couldn't talk. But he was completely conscious and the thought came to me that he knew he was leaving and couldn't tell us.

"Sweetheart, if you feel alright, clear your throat one time. If you don't, do it twice," I told him.

Loud and clear and with great strength, he responded one time and squeezed my hand tightly as though reassuring me.

"I love you, but Jesus loves you more," I told him, kissing him on the cheek so he would know I knew he was leaving us.

Later, Bill told me all of this was completely veiled from him as he continued to pray for healing. As I prayed in the spirit, two things came to mind: *The mercy of the Father,* and *"Blessed in the eyes of the Lord is the death of His saints."* (Psalm 116:15)

Somewhere around 3:00 o'clock Kent just gently crossed over into his new life. It was so gentle that Bill said he didn't even realize what had happened until he noticed Kent had stopped breathing.

Shortly before 3:00 the other children had come in from school. We heard them tiptoe up to the partially opened door of the bedroom and then walk away. They must have seen us kneeling before the bed and figured we were praying for their brother and didn't want to disturb us. Later, it occurred to me that perhaps Kent had waited to cross over until they were there too.

Bill and I kissed him on the lips, then knelt again to pray. I said, "Lord Jesus, we know Kent is receiving his marching orders directly from You now. We know that if his work is not finished You can send him back by raising him up. But we relinquish this completely to Your will."

We continued to pray over his now still, lifeless body until 3:20 p.m. There was a strong awareness within me that Kent was definitely just not in that body any longer. It was as though a shell now lay on his bed. The form that was there now was not Kent. Bill gently closed his eyes and we went downstairs to tell the other children. I could not believe that I was not crying—had not cried. I was overflowing with a warmth and love that I knew to be the Holy Spirit, in His role as Comforter, lifting me above what my eyes and mind told me.

They were gathered in the kitchen having a snack and I just simply said, "Your brother's spirit left his body to be with Jesus just a few minutes ago." The under-girding power of the Comforter must have wrapped His arms around each one as we told them. Only Kurt cried, and then just for a few short minutes as we explained how merciful, loving and gentle it had been. We also told them that Kent would have had to be hospitalized on Monday and endured horrendous pain and suffering from a last ditch effort of chemotherapy to save him. God had mercifully spared him that.

We called Al Houston, our minister, and then I called NIH and got Dr.

Fay on the line. I felt a deep wave of concern for this kind and dedicated man who seemed to care so much about Kent. I wondered just how to express to him what had happened. Trying to use medical terms so he would have instant understanding I said, "Dr. Fay, Kent expired around 3:00 o'clock and we need to know what to do now."

There was silence for a moment on the other end and then, "Expired? What do you *mean* expired?"

I had the feeling he thought I was using the wrong word to express a symptom. "Kent died around 3;00 o'clock, Dr. Fay, and we need to know what to do now," I told him, amazed at the calm manner in which I was able to put it into words.

"Well... well,... I..." he stammered. "This must be a *terrible* shock for you," he said, his own raw shock coming across the line to me in his voice. "Did you know this...I mean, did you know he was dying?"

"Yes, I thought he might be around 2:00 o'clock. I did try to get you on the telephone, but I don't want you to feel guilty in any way that I didn't reach you. I could have gotten another doctor or brought him in. I take full responsibility for this."

This strong and positive man whom we thought more of than any other doctor we had had on the service other than Kent's first, Dr. Gallo, still seemed stunned beyond words.

"I'll have to call you back after I've made arrangements. I'm so sorry about this, Mrs. Ghost." I sensed he was trying to control tears. I knew he really cared-- just as Dr. Gallo had cared so deeply when he told me, with tears in his eyes, that Kent was dying of a cerebral hemorrhage those nine and one-half years ago.

In the interim Al and Maggie Houston arrived. Al was crying as they came in the door. "Oh don't, Al. It's a miracle the way it happened. As soon as I get a chance to tell you all the details, you won't be sad." (I couldn't believe how I was dry-eyed, lifted up and able to minister to others. I was actually ministering to the *minister*.)

When Dr. Fay did call back a few minutes later it was to say that an NIH ambulance had been dispatched for Kent's body. Would we please accompany it as there were papers to be signed and pronouncement to be made? Bill and I felt we should spare the other children the unhappy memory of seeing the ambulance come for Kent's body, so Margaret took them to their home. I ran downstairs to explain to Daddy what had happened. He gasped and bit a knuckle, "My little guy! My sidekick!" I could see he was trying not to break down for my sake.

I hugged him tightly. "Will you be alright? I hate to leave you alone, but Bill and I have to accompany Kent's body to the hospital. The ambulance is on the way."

"Don't you worry about this tough old bird," he said and waved me away, but I knew he would grieve alone when we left.

Al prepared to make the trip with us in his car. The telephone rang. It was Russ Shigley wanting to know how Kent was. When I told him Kent had quietly begun his new life around 3:00 o'clock, Russ began to weep uncontrollably. At that moment, the long white NIH ambulance came slowly through the gates and I was concerned about breaking off with Russ so abruptly until I had made certain that Ruth was with him.

"Don't cry, please," I told him. "Once you hear how mercifully the Lord took him you won't be sad. God didn't let him suffer." I promised him Bill and I would come to their house just as soon as we finished at NIH

I said a quick prayer, "Lord, please let the drivers be someone who will have a sense of reverence for Kent's body."

The front door was partially open and I ran up to the bedroom. "Up here!" I called to them. And as they rounded the bend in the stairway I saw Jesse and Mr. Bates, two Patient Care Technicians whom Kent had adored. For the past two years there had been scarcely one bone marrow or spinal tap that Kent had experienced that Mr. Bates hadn't been there to assist, not only professionally, but as an encouraging friend.

"Oh, I'm so glad it's *you,*" I told them both, hugging Mr. Bates as I said the words. I couldn't help notice he had tears in his eyes. Everybody seemed to be crying except me—the usual cry baby. It had to be the Lord's help.

"I'm so sorry, Mrs. Ghost, you'll never know how much I thought of that little guy," he told me, while patting my shoulder.

Mr. Bates picked up Kent's limp body and wrapped a white sheet around it. He personally carried Kent's body to the waiting ambulance in his arms, tears streaming unashamedly down his face. Jesse followed with the empty, unused stretcher.

Neighbors gathered questioning, crying, caring...

I had to go. Al and Bill were waiting in Al's car behind the ambulance. It was time... Kent's last trip to NIH. I could praise for that!

Al, Bill and I followed the ambulance as it slowly made its way through the late afternoon traffic down Cedar Lane. The trees were just beginning to change color and hazy rays of sunlight winked off the smoky leaves magnifying their color.

I still couldn't comprehend the calm I felt. I knew the Holy Spirit had to be providing tremendous support for both Bill and me. But still, my precious, irreplaceable child had died before my very eyes and I had scarcely shed a tear. Two thoughts crossed my mind: My tears for Kent had been shed each time I had relinquished him. Today, when the Lord had proven clearly it was His intent to take Kent, I had been able to accept his Will with the help of the Holy

Spirit. Bill seemed to be lifted up also. He had only teared up a couple of times, usually in response to being touched by either Al or Russ crying.

We were taken and seated in Dr. Fay's office with a social worker, Al, and Dr. Brigid Leventhal, Chief of the Chemo Immunotherapy Section. She had just come through the door, sagged onto a stool and through obvious tears herself told us, "I am having a terribly hard time with this...so totally unexpected."

"Please let me tell you both exactly what happened," I said, "and when I do, I think you will know that God had a strong merciful hand in this. As you know, we were considering hospitalizing Kent on Monday, hitting him with our last bit of ammunition. Instead, let me recount the time frame of what occurred. Dr. Fay, when you hear what I'm about to tell you I'm sure you could not possibly feel guilty about not taking my call. The Lord stuffed cotton in your ears so you couldn't take my page." I proceeded to tell them everything, leaving nothing out. I recounted what I had heard, "Will you not watch with Me one hour?" and the timing involved—one hour exactly. I realized by looking at Bill and Al's faces that this was the first time they had heard it too.

Dr. Leventhal shook her head slowly from side-to-side. "It had to be God, Sandy. We doctors can't even predict the time of death."

"I feel so much better, Mrs. Ghost." Dr Fay added. "That's beautiful. We would know more, of course, of what happened internally if you permit us to do an autopsy. Will you?"

I looked at Bill. "Can we have time to pray about it?"

"Well, we're under a bit of a time constraint. Please call me by noon tomorrow."

We assured them we would and said we were grateful Kent had been spared so much suffering. Both doctors nodded in understanding and I wondered just how many children's deaths had been scarred into their memories—the lingering agonies of pain that usually thresholds death by leukemia. Only those doctors could truly appreciate the merciful gift from God that we had just witnessed. We had known Dr. Leventhal ever since Kent had first become a research patient. While the service doctors came and went, she had been the solid unmoving pillar of wisdom we had come to rely on through the years.

The social worker explained to us that NIH would take care of all financial aspects of the funeral and burial. Bill and I stared at each other across the office. His expression told me his thoughts must be following mine. The Lord was providing for something He had shown us was His will. But also, my mind spun backward to the thousands of dollars and years of care NIH had invested in trying to help Kent. And now to find this was provided for too was overwhelming. We were told there was a cemetery plot provided in southwest

Washington. The generous offer of this plot seemed the only thing that was not quite right.

"Somehow I feel Kent should be buried in Myersville, Bill. You know how he adored the Alexander farm we wanted to buy. He always talked about it in such a positive way, 'When we get the Myersville farm, when I live there, we'll plant squash, bake bread in the outdoor oven.'"

"I think you're right, San. That fits."

"There are two Brethren churches near Myersville," Al told us. "Both have cemeteries. We could go up there and take a look tomorrow."

"We can only transport for a fifty mile radius," the social worker told us. We had no way of knowing at the time that this would prove to be another loving sign from God that we were doing what He wanted us to do. Remarkably, the cemetery we ended up picking out was exactly fifty miles.

A rippling wake of sympathy from the personnel followed us through the revolving doors of the Clinical Center. We stood outside on the sidewalk dwarfed by the handsome marble portico. It was the first time in nine and one-half years that I had walked through those doors without Kent. The Lord was with us in such a remarkably sustaining way that my eyesight seemed to be fixed in a laser-beam heavenward. Grief would set in later. But for now, I could feel gratitude for the suffering Kent had been spared, the monumental help we had received from NIH. Now, Kent lived in a splendor where there were no more bone marrows, no more IV's, no more side-effects, no more pain. With a start I realized I was grateful—not for his death—but for his gain. I had no idea just how much he was experiencing, but was in for a heavenly surprise the next day.

Chapter Thirty-Two

————— ⌒ —————

e had to get up early to meet Pastor Al and drive to Myersville the following morning. As I climbed into bed I thought: *Tomorrow the bubble will burst. Tomorrow I'll know Kent's gone... it will sink in and I will sink with the realization. Tomorrow I'll hit bottom.*

However, the following day began with a new message direct from the Holy Spirit.

The alarm rang. I stumbled out of bed and into the bathroom, still half-asleep, but as my body responded to the cold ceramic tiles on my feet, I suddenly realized some deep part of my mind was already awake. There was something pulsing insistently through it as though saying, ***Pay attention to me!***

I stood dead center on the cold tile floor and tried to identify what was going on. Loudly, clearly, but with new words the song from Disney World, "It's A Small World" coursed through my mind with a volume incapable of pure thought.

> *"It's a land of laughter*
> *A land of cheer*
> *It's a land of love*
> *It's a land so near.*
>
> *There's so much that we share*
> *It is time we're aware*
> *It's a small world after all!"*

It was a chorus of children's voices singing—just like the children of the world. The last stanza was exactly as we had heard it in Disney World. The first was almost the same, but a few words had been changed so that now it took on an entirely different significance. It was not as though Kent was trying to communicate directly with me; the voices were not his, the song was a blend of many children's voices. But it was a decided message to describe that heaven was indeed like this. He had asked me while we were in Disney World if heaven would be like that. And now, it was as though the Lord was allowing him to indirectly confirm that heaven was like what we had pictured it to be together. Our family knew it was not scriptural to try to communicate with someone on the other side directly—but this wasn't direct, it was filtered through the Holy Spirit.

It continued as I showered and brushed my teeth. One line stood out as a singular message for me. ***There's so much that we share, it is time we're*** *aware, it's a small world after all.* It seemed to mean the communion of the saints from this side to the other. And also, I had the impression that it was just a short step from this world into the next.

For the entire day the song, "Small World" played in the foreground of my mind. It wasn't that I promoted it. I made tiny experiments of trying to dismiss it, but it coursed through my conscious and apparently subconscious minds until late that night. However, I thought I was having a unique experience. Not until much later that day did I discover that was not so. But when I did, it only confirmed that this had not been some grasping effort for comfort stirred up by my imagination, but a gift from God.

I dressed and wakened Bill after the alarm had rung. "Small World" still chorused through my mind, but I said nothing to him about it. We were to meet Al and drive to Myersville to look for a cemetery lot. A sense of deep gratitude enveloped me again as our minister got into the car. What a strong arm of help he had always been to us. Handsome, but small of stature, Bill had described him to perfection the night before, "A giant in boy's clothing", he had said. Al seemed seven feet tall as he ministered to us during the long drive to Myersville. We looked at the first cemetery. It was lovely, in a serene valley surrounded by mountains, but we were searching for God's guidance in this and not one bell went off mentally with either of us.

We headed out Route 40 to take a look at the other one with Al giving directions. Suddenly the scenery became familiar. I gasped. The stream paralleled the highway. We were on the road to the farm! We passed right by the metal bridge and about a mile up the road stopped in front of a small red brick church. The cemetery rose high above the churchyard on a hill that was surrounded by mountains. The same stream that ran in front of the Alexander farm wound in front of the cemetery. I put on dark glasses... now I was crying for the first time—not because of grief, but because I could see the Lord's caring hand in where we were, His gentle guidance. As we climbed the hill together, in the distance I could see the farm Kent had loved so much.

Was it a fluke of circumstances or the Lord again that we couldn't find a telephone to contact the local undertaker to make arrangements for the vault? Finally, we drove up to the farm to ask Mrs. Alexander if we could impose on her. She asked where the children were and we told her our purpose for being in the area. Kent had died and because he had loved her farm so much we were having burial made at the Brethren church.

Her warm sympathy was instant. We had coffee together while Al and Bill drove into town to make arrangements and talk with the minister about the plot. Although we hadn't seen each other for months, she told me she had been thinking of Kent just the day before. An advertisement for the Leukemia Society had come on television and she had decided to send Kent a check as contribution and have him present it to the Society. She asked me what time he had started his new life and when I told her she gasped.

"Sandy," she took my hand, "it was on the 3:00 o'clock station break that the ad came on. I must have been thinking about him just as he was dying, dear."

"I've come to believe that there are absolutely no coincidences in life," I told her. "The Lord orchestrates more than what we ever suspect. Right now I'm struggling with giving permission for NIH to do an autopsy. I just can't bear to think about his little body being mutilated in any way...he's been through so much."

She patted my hand as though to encourage me to talk.

"But, this morning just as we were getting ready to leave—Bill and I had prayed about it last night, but didn't get any kind of guidance. But today, as we were getting ready to leave to come up here I had the strangest feeling that we would *miss a blessing* if we didn't permit it to be done. Isn't that odd?"

She patted my hand again and then tucked up a whisp of gray hair that had come loose. "Well, the way I see it...if it helps the boy next door what are you waiting for?"

I felt like I'd been hit in the stomach with the reality of her statement. Why hadn't I thought of that? "Could I... could I impose on you further to use your phone to call NIH? You're absolutely right! Bill had said it was up to me and you just hit me over the head with truth. I have to call before noon."

Mrs. Alexander beamed, "Good girl! You're doing the right thing." She led me to the phone where I called Dr. Fay and granted permission. When Bill and Al got back, all arrangements had been taken care of and Mrs. Alexander and I hugged each other tightly. We still hoped to be able to get the farm, but of course had told her that Bill had quite unexpectedly lost his job and that had put a crimp in planning for now. She reassured us that they perfectly understood. I kissed her goodbye and felt like the Lord had made the Alexanders a part of our family.

The song, "Small World" seemed even louder as we traveled back home. But that day held yet another surprise. Around midnight, Bill and I sat together at the kitchen table. The children were in bed. It was the first time we had had a chance to be alone and talk. Friends from the church and neighbors had deluged us with sympathy and food in an endless procession of compassion from the time we had returned from Myersville.

Even steaming, hot coffee couldn't seem to wipe away the cobwebs of fatigue; however, we still felt a need to sit up and talk. Bill, with chin resting on the palms of his hands said, "San I've had the strangest thing happening to me today. It started the minute I got up this morning."

I sensed what he was about to tell me was extremely important.

"You know the song we heard in Disney World... 'Small World'?"

I held my breath. Was it happening to him too?

"Well, as soon as I got up this morning that song began circling through my mind...over and over. It's been like that all day. It's still there."

I grabbed his hand and squeezed it, "Bill, the same thing has been going on inside my head! It started as soon as I got up this morning and I'm still hearing it in the background of everything that's gone on today." I shared with him the impressions I had had about what it meant—the Lord was allowing it to impress us that Kent's new life was "a land of laughter" and a "land so near". I said what had really struck me were the words, "It is time we're aware it's a small world after all."

"In other words," I told him, "I think we're being allowed to see that it's just a small step between this world and the next, and being permitted to know Kent is in a land of laughter and cheer. Don't you think?"

"Yes, I take it to mean Kent's in a wonderful place."

"But you know, there's something else... I think it also means there are no coincidences. People always say, 'Gee! It sure is a small world!' when they encounter some colossal coincidence like meeting their neighbor in a different state they both happen to be in. Look at all the things we could have chalked up to coincidence, but we know very well that these were occurrences orchestrated by the Holy Spirit. It's time we're aware (like the song says) that there are no coincidences."

"Is there scripture for that, San?"

"I don't know, but I'll try to find out when things calm down a bit." I told him.

What may have seemed like two parents just grasping at spiritual straws gained further proof the following day.

We told no one else about what we had experienced. Sunday night, Bill and I went in to kiss Kurt goodnight and hear his prayers. He sprawled on his bed, a tangle of lanky arms and legs and propped himself up on one elbow, "Can God speak to you in a song, Mom?" he asked.

Bill's eyes met mine. "Why, son?"

"Because all day today—even through church, the song 'Small World' has been playing like a loud record in my mind."

I sat down on the bed and put my arms around him. "You remember how Kent's been absolutely sure that the song, 'Country Roads' has been a message from the Lord?"

He nodded his agreement.

"In the Old Testament the Lord spoke to Balaam through a donkey. I guess He can speak to us through anything," I told him.

"A *donkey?*" He started to giggle.

"I think Jesus is using the song 'Small World' to speak to all of us, sweetheart. Your Dad and I have had the very same thing happening to us too. I think we're being allowed to have a peek at the wonders Kent's experiencing—heaven's a wonderful world. We're all going to miss him terribly, but we can truly praise the Lord that he's not in the hospital, can't we? And we know we'll see him again."

He reached up and hugged me tightly.

Later, we told Lisa and Eric about what Bill, Kurt and I had experienced.

"Why didn't that happen to us?" Lisa pouted slightly.

"Maybe because it was only the four of us that went to Disney World and went through the ride 'Small World', don't you think?"

She smiled. "That makes me feel better. I kinda' felt left out."

"I had somewhat of an experience, Mom." Eric took off his glasses and cleaned them. "I was sitting here in the kitchen, working on putting together a pair of leather moccasins from a craft kit. They were for Kent and it was the night you had to rush him to the hospital. There was a leaflet on the table with the Twenty-third Psalm on it." He swallowed hard a couple of times and I realized it was a struggle for him to tell us.

"Go on, hon, what happened?"

"Well, when I looked at the words, 'Yea though I walk through the valley of the shadow of death' just seemed to be in big bold letters... it was more of an impression than anything I actually saw. But I had a... kind of an inner... knowing."

"The Lord was gently trying to prepare all of us. Lisa had her moments of 'knowing' out West when she was led to fast." I turned toward her.

"Yes... I think a part of me had begun to suspect." She wiped at a tear with her sleeve.

I put my arms around her. "We've got to focus on how very much Jesus was with all of us and with Kent. And also know we'll see him again. He's alive!"

I needed to be alone and sort out something that kept prodding me now that I knew Bill and Kurt had experienced the same thing as I had in the supernatural. I escaped to the powder room—my prayer closet—and locked the door. My mind spun backward to that night when I had been driving toward Florida with Bill and the twins asleep in the back of the station wagon. I wondered if the Lord could use secular music as a message from Him when the song, "Georgia on My Mind" popped up on the radio just as I was thinking about getting to the Georgia state line. That had to be pure coincidence, I reasoned. But what if there were no coincidences? What if the Lord orchestrated guidance from Him in all manner of ways?

Then "You And Me Against The World" had played softly on the radio. The words had seemed to sear into me with new knowledge that Kent wouldn't be with us much longer.

> *"When one of us is gone*
> *And one of us is left to carry on*
> *Memories will have to do..."*

That had, indeed, proven to be accurate guidance. But there was something more that struck me about the two songs—they both had the word "world" in them. I turned this over and over mentally. "You And Me Against The World—"It's A Small World After All" I remembered that was the full title. Now that I knew, without a doubt, that God had spoken through the first song, I suddenly saw something else! It's not just us struggling alone against the world. 'Small World' told us: "There's so much that we share, it's time we're aware." Could that mean the help of the Holy Spirit, the communion of the saints, the angels helping from the Other Side to this? And the Lord seemed to be strongly doing everything He could to prove to us that He *was* and *had been* helping, orchestrating details, large and small. Something else, another piece to the puzzle played tug-of-war with my mind, but I couldn't seem to grasp it. Perhaps at another time...

That afternoon Al had come by our townhouse and we had planned Kent's celebration of his life. I refused to call it a funeral. Bill, Al and I sat at the kitchen table and idea contributions seemed to just float down into place. It was to be a service of worship and praise—a stark contrast to the usual solemn, heavy funeral. We had planned it for Monday, but the Lord had other much more significant plans. It was changed to Tuesday because the funeral home couldn't handle it on Monday. Later, we saw the exquisite wisdom of this. There was no school on Tuesday. As it turned out half of Kent's classmates, plus most of the faculty at Rock Creek Palisades school could be there—they were mostly Jewish. Tuesday, September 17th was the Jewish New Year! Therefore, all those dear people who would have been in their synagogue, sat in a church hearing about Kent's relationship with Jesus Christ and how it was possible to have salvation through Christ as the Messiah. Rock Creek Palisades School had put their flag at half-mast for Kent.

And as it might have been a new beginning for some of Kent's classmates and teachers, little did I know that my own son's funeral was to be a beginning for me. I *knew* and I can't say it was even a gentle urging, but more of a command that I should speak at the beginning of the service. I balked and warred inwardly at this, mainly because of my emotional nature. Ever since I had become a Christian a certain hymn, people coming down the aisle to accept Christ, personal words seeping through a sermon always produced tears in church. While I realized the Holy Spirit had been carrying me around on a spiritual cloud since Friday so that I was above tears, I was afraid this could evaporate at Kent's service.

How could I possibly get up and speak at my son's funeral? The idea frightened me. I was afraid I would just be able to blubber out a few words and sit down, only making those who attended more uncomfortable. I confessed all of this to Al across our kitchen table the afternoon we were planning the service.

"Sandy, he said, eyes intent but understanding behind his glasses, "don't you think that if God is leading you to do this, He'll support you in it?"

"I know what I should say but..." I could feel the start of my eyes welling up just thinking about doing it.

"Okay," Al set his cup down on the saucer. "I feel confident the Holy Spirit will support you, but this suggestion might make you more comfortable. After the first hymn I'll nod to you. If you think you can't make it, just shake your head and I'll stand up and go to the next segment."

"I'm not really going to know until the last minute," I told him.

The night before the service, long after all of Bill's relatives from Pennsylvania had gone to bed, I sat up fidgeting with what I felt I had to do the next day, trying to record it on paper. Nothing super spiritual really happened. But when I called on the Lord for help, an answer came that was much bigger than my immediate problem.

Chapter Thirty-Three

I sat in a corner of the living room, pencil and pad in hand. All the lights were out except for the tall floor lamp behind my wing chair. It was as though Jesus lovingly pulled me onto His lap and began explaining, *You've been searching for years for your identity, Sandy. I've heard all your questionings about who you are. Long before you knew Me, I knew you. I smiled as you tried to sort out who you were through being a housewife... yes, and I was even with you when you were a singer. You see, I knew someday you would give yourself totally to Me. I'm sure you realize I've spoken to you so many times in songs...in lyrics.*

I felt so loved and didn't want this ever to stop. While it was more of an impression than hearing the words aloud like I had before, I knew it was definitely the Lord.

You found Me through the illness of this precious child, but also, it was then you discovered your role of mother—you traded singer for mother gladly. You became a Christian and discovered I was real and cared about you and your family. Again you shouted, "Who am I?" as you rallied to crusade for Me. But I showed you that you were first a wife and a mother.

It was late and I was tired, but the depth of truth that now swirled around me seemed to open up a whole new world. The impression within me continued:

I say again, I knew you long before you knew Me. Every experience, every role you have felt placed in was not coincidence but My guidance. These made up the composite of experiences from which you are made. Yes, even when you were a singer and had to appear before people—this is the experience I would have you draw upon tomorrow, plus the power of My Holy Spirit that will equip you. You prayed over Kent's body to see if I would raise him up, but I would have you consider that it was My timing and his desire to go." Scripture tugged at my mind reminding that Paul said he could choose to go to be with the Lord, but it was better that he stay for the sake of the disciples.

I put my pencil down. Something inside me had experienced birth. Suddenly I was at peace with myself.

Not the alarm clock, but the sun wakened me the next morning. With a flash, I realized it was the day of Kent's service. I shut off the alarm and looked out the window. The trees in the park blazed with colors of red and gold.

Suddenly the thought came, *Those leaves are really dead. Their life's blood, the sap, doesn't run through them anymore, but they're more beautiful in death than they ever were in life. I miss Kent more than anyone will ever know, but I wouldn't bring him back to this life for one minute. He has so much more now.*

We had stipulated no flowers; instead contributions of sympathy might be made to Candle-Lighters. This was an organization we belonged to that had been formed for the purpose of conquering cancer through research.

We each placed one red rose for each member of our family on the small closed casket the funeral directors had placed at the back of Good Shepherd's sanctuary. They tried to put it up front and I instructed them we wanted it to be in the back so that the focus of attention would be on Jesus. I then took my place in the first pew with the rest of our family. I refused to wear somber black. This was a celebration and I picked out a bright aqua suit with gold buttons that was lively.

And then they came—Kent's teachers, his principal, the superintendent of schools, classmates, neighbors, members of our church, people from NIH. Men obviously had taken time off from their jobs. The chaplains from NIH were there, surely acting above and beyond the call of duty.

As I watched the people file in I was suddenly filled with an overwhelming love for all of them because they had cared about Kent. The little church that sometimes saw an attendance of sixty people or less on a Sunday morning now bulged at the seams. I could scarcely believe what was happening. We sang the first hymn. Al, from his sitting position facing the congregation nodded to me. Could I do it?

I stood up, turned around and faced the sea of faces. My mouth was dry. I could hear my heart pounding in my ears.

"Kent should have died nine years ago when he was first diagnosed with leukemia." I heard my voice saying. "He had a severe cerebral hemorrhage, was paralyzed and in a coma. The doctors had given up all hope for the seven hours he laid there. Mr. Botts, an elevator operator at NIH prayed for him and within twenty minutes he was sitting up in bed, completely normal. This was our family's introduction to Jesus Christ and His power."

I continued, telling more about the reality of Christ in Kent's life, some of the miracles along the way and the miracle of his death being so merciful. "Never in nine and one-half years was he hospitalized or transfused with blood except in the beginning. A fantastic track record with leukemia!" (I saw several of the NIH staff nodding in agreement.) I ended by stressing that this same miraculous power was available to everyone by receiving Jesus Christ as Lord and Savior. Perhaps another miracle was that I did not shed a tear. Me...Sandy Ghost... the one who cried through most normal church services didn't feel a need to throughout the entire service. The Lord had promised me support and I got it as did Bill and the rest of the family.

I noticed Diane Simmons dabbing at her eyes. Thirteen year old Diane had taken Kent under her wing as her little brother. Just the Friday before she had given Kent a beautiful cross necklace and her very own Bible with many personal notes about scriptures. Before church on Sunday, the same week he went to be with the Lord, we had taken a picture of him wearing that cross and holding up the Bible she had given him. Her mother, Mary Simmons, had come to see us the night of Kent's crossing. She confessed that the same day of Kent's last relapse the Lord had let her know his time on earth was short. The Holy Spirit had given her a song for Kent. The words and music were inspired and very upbeat. We had gone to her house the night before the service and recorded it with Eric playing bass and Lisa flute. Mary sang. We didn't feel we could do it live as that might be asking too much of us emotionally so it was taped. It played over the loud speakers in the church:

> *There are loved ones gone before us*
> *And we praise His holy name*
> *That they're resting in His bosom*
> *And we long to do the same,*
> *But 'til then we'll tell of Jesus*
> *For He is the only Way*
> *Then we'll walk with them in glory*
> *In a new and brighter day.*

Al then gave a glowing picture of Kent's walk with the Lord. His intent and ours, and we knew it would be Kent's, was to proclaim to all who didn't know Jesus Christ personally that the death of a Christian should be an occasion for praise. The theme of the service was to be victory; his death most assuredly was not a defeat. Our main concern was that our family could be joyous witnesses for Christ and that was the only reason I was so concerned that I not cry.

The last song was to be the happy, crisp tempo, spiritual "Do Lord". We hoped the verses, "I've got a home in Glory Land that outshines the sun" and "I took Jesus as my Savior, you take Him too," might speak personally as though from Kent to anyone who had known him, but who didn't know Christ.

It was planned and announced by Al that everyone file out, row by row, beginning with the back and leave the church still singing and clapping. In some manner this was contrived to not only keep the joyous nature of the service, but to serve as a mental cushion for the family to recover emotionally as we were in the first row; therefore, we were the last to leave the sanctuary.

However, to my own astonishment, I was still dry-eyed and buoyed high by a current of the Holy Spirit's power. A glance at Bill and the children seemed to confirm that they were experiencing this same arm of strength as they were clapping and singing lustily. But the unexpected almost threw me.

We had asked that everyone leave the church singing, we were the last except for the casket, but when we walked out into the sunlight of the warm fall day, we were met with a scene that totally surprised us. The entire body of people who had just left the church were standing on the sidewalk, facing the church, still singing and clapping their hands in time to the music. It was as though it was their contribution to the family and Kent. Momentarily, my knees almost buckled.

The Holy Spirit seems to have an exquisite knack for precise timing. While God operates in eternity, we've come to understand that many times He honors our time here on earth to prove a point. Although it was certainly not planned by us, we reached the cemetery in Myersville after the long drive, at exactly 3:00 o'clock—the same time as Kent's passing. And so, Kent's earthly body was buried exactly three weeks to the day from the Tuesday we had spent in Disney World—one week to the day from the Tuesday he had said Jesus had served him communion.

On the way back in the funeral home's limousine, I happened to glance down at my ring hand. With a start, I realized one of the diamonds in my engagement ring was missing. The ring had a large diamond in the center with two smaller diamonds on either side of the large stone. I had always regarded that ring as a symbol of our family—our marriage in the center with four children total—two on each side. I marveled that Kent's stone was now missing. I didn't look for it.

Slowly, gently at first, I began experiencing the grief I knew had to come eventually. I wandered the house, fingered Kent's clothes in the closet, knelt by his bed and cried for the first time with an emptiness that was so painful it felt like a raw sore. The Holy Spirit let me gently back down to earth, continued to sustain me, but I was now allowed to experience the emotions I normally would have had. It was tough. As grief came flooding in on a tidal wave, I realized just how much I had been spared when I had needed the strength.

Several days later the unsolved piece in the puzzle of guidance that had played tug-of-war with my mind, seemed to pull at my sleeve again. It was as though there was something I hadn't been able to grasp yet. The feeling had begun when I had discovered that the Lord had spoken through the songs, "You And Me Against The World" and "Small World".

Kurt and Lisa were in school. Eric was now employed by Boeing Computer Service, Bill was on a job interview and Daddy was taking a nap after a roast beef sandwich and onion soup for lunch. I decided to make a cup of tea and put on my thinking cap—see if I could get the mind of the Lord on what it was He wanted me to learn. Through the sliding glass doors, sunbeams danced on the patio beckoning for me to come out and play. Instead I opened the door, sat drinking my tea and prayed silently. My mind sifted back over the incredible ways that guidance and communication had come from the Lord during the years since our family had come to know Him.

It had really begun that day, eight years ago, when I had knelt by my bed to pray. I had been in a panic because we thought Kent was having a second cerebral hemorrhage. I had heard, as a loud thought, "the effectual fervent prayers of a righteous man availeth much." I couldn't attribute the words to my own mind, they couldn't have originated there as I was a new Christian and hadn't known that scripture from James.

While kneeling by a bed in the motel, much later, the Lord had spoken again in the same manner as I had prayed for little Kim Griggs, who was dying on 2E at NIH. Sentences had seemed to float down into my mind—sentences that again didn't seem to be originating from my own mind. It seemed I was to repeat what I'd "heard" to Kim. When I obeyed and repeated the words to him the following day, he had received Jesus and been miraculously healed in that particular time of crisis. And then there was the time that Kent and I were on our way in to Bethesda and I felt I was to pray in the spirit on the plane. As we got to the hospital it became much more urgent to do so. When the doctor started to give him the drugs, the syringe broke spilling the medicine all over the bed. The pharmacy had sent the wrong strength drugs and had it not spilled it would have killed Kent. Strong guidance to pray in the spirit for protection.

And then the most recent incident of that small, internal voice of the Lord coming again, "Will you not watch with Me one hour?"

The Bible quotes Jesus as saying, "My sheep know My voice." And even though my mind had wavered in doubt and questioned at the time, I knew today as I sipped my tea, that if Jesus had not proven to me in times past that He could use this manner of the internal still, small voice to speak to me, I would have missed His voice entirely the day Kent died. Dr. Leventhal had said that had we put him in the car to rush him to the hospital, he most likely would have died on the way, and it could have been devastating for all of us.

A parade of the differing methods of guidance the Lord had used in the past marched though my mind as I set my cup down and picked up a pencil to list them.

He had spoken through an anointing—a purely physical feeling as though a mantle of warm, tingling oil was being poured upon me. The Lord had also used this feeling at times to confirm that He was present and in control of a particular situation. The day Kent crossed over and I had first noticed the discoloration of his skin, the feeling of an anointing had lifted me above what I was seeing. By this the Lord seemed to be saying, "It's alright." Had He not given me previous experience with this physical form of guidance, I'm sure I would have panicked and been disobedient to His ultimate will for Kent.

He had spoken in the past by visions: Eric's vision of a column of light and ball of fire the night he received the Holy Spirit.

He had spoken to all of us in dreams I recalled, remembering my dream of Kent on the roller coaster. He had spoken by manipulating circumstances it occurred to me: provision to the penny for the purchase of the Pink House; an eighty-eight passenger jet plane, emptied, except for Kent and me and the two flight attendants who later had accepted Christ.

Someone once had challenged me on the fact that God didn't create circumstances for us to encounter to guide us in the path He wanted. I searched the scriptures and prayed for help to know the truth. And then I found it! Mark 14:12-14

> *"On the first day of the Feast of Unleavened Bread*
> *when they killed the Passover lamb, Jesus' disciples*
> *said to Him, Where do You wish us to go and prepare*
> *the Passover for You to eat?*
>
> *And He sent two of His disciples and said to them, Go*
> *into the city, and a man carrying an earthen jar or*
> *pitcher of water will meet you; follow him.*
> *and whatever house he enters, say to the master of*
> *of the house, The Teacher says: Where is My*
> *guest room, where I may eat the Passover with*
> *My disciples?"*

It was obvious that Jesus knew (and arranged) the exact moment when the disciples, as they were walking, would intersect with the man carrying the pitcher of water. He also arranged for them to meet this same exact person who would lead them to a house that was perfectly fitted for the Passover Supper. This scripture was proof positive to support that there are no coincidences. My study also revealed that there is no Hebrew word for "coincidence"!

The thing that had been tugging at my mind seemed to explode as suddenly I remembered another plane ride where I had felt the Lord had intervened and the entire scenario was beyond coincidence! Something today seemed to urge me on with the importance of this memory. It had been one of our customary flights into NIH; however, as we approached National Airport the pilot announced that there was a fast moving, fast approaching snow storm.

National and Dulles airports were both closed. Friendship in Baltimore had just shut down. He chuckled and said, "When I find out where I'm gonna' set this thing down, I'll let you know."

Strangely enough, just before his announcement, I had felt extremely led to pray. I really put a shoulder to my prayers after his dour announcement. I worked harder than the crew to get us on the ground. At least I thought that was the purpose of my alerting, but I was silently praying in the spirit and letting the Holy Spirit make intercession for us.

The pilot made two more bleak announcements. He told us cheerfully that Atlanta was closed now, and then much later that we were one-hundred miles south of Philadelphia, had requested permission to land that had been denied as Philadelphia was closing. I would have settled for a cow pasture at this point. My knuckles were white from clutching the arm of the seat.

Finally we made it down in Newark just before they closed up their runways. The terminal there was a seething mass of air refugees who should have landed in other parts of the country, but had also ended up in New Jersey. There were buses to take us to the train station. I took Kent by the hand and headed for a bus. It was then I realized I still had a gentle urging to pray. I didn't see a need for it now that we were safely on the ground, but continued to pray silently in the spirit. Sky caps loaded our luggage under the bus and I realized I would be responsible for the suitcase from this point forward.

I put Kent on my lap after we had boarded; he was just about four years old when this incident occurred. A distinguished looking man, slightly gray at the temples, sat down beside me. It seems when people are inconvenienced by emergency the barriers of sophistication are lowered and they talk to strangers.

"I'd have worn a topcoat when I left Houston this morning if I'd known about this storm," he told me.

"Where should you have landed?" I asked.

"Washington National. I'm headed for Bethesda, Maryland by way of New Jersey," he grumbled.

"My, what a coincidence! That's where we're going too, but we came in on a plane from Louisville." I told him we were going to NIH

He asked if my son was the patient and then asked if Kent was getting some kind of chemotherapy. He must have noticed a hike in my eyebrows at his acuity. He introduced himself and I almost went into shock. I was sitting next to the chief surgeon of the M. D. Anderson Cancer Clinic! *Is this coincidence or the Lord?* I wondered at the time. But when we went our separate ways at the train station, I chalked it off to a colossal coincidence that two people, starting from locations of a thousand miles apart, on different flights, but going to Bethesda,

Maryland would end up on the same bus, the same seat on the way to a train station.

The train platform was a crush of elbowing people trying to manage their luggage and press toward the cars. The scene reminded me of the stations during World War II.

Unexpectedly, the doctor from Texas appeared at my elbow. "Here, let me take your luggage and run interference for you and your son," he said, taking our suitcase.

We threaded our way toward the coach section. People sat on suitcases in the aisles and the three of us had to stand as our train lurched through the state of New Jersey. Somewhere in Delaware two seats vacated on one side of the coach, and one more directly across the aisle. I had tried to play up the fact to Kent that we were going to take an exciting ride on a real train. After awhile, he complained, "I want to get off this dirty old train." Everybody around us laughed—they probably all felt the same way.

Strange, I thought, *that in this crowd the doctor and I should be seated together.* I wondered again if the Lord happened to be in this somewhere. Because he and I had the aisle seats, we continued talking about clinical procedures, new drugs and techniques while Kent looked out the window and ate a sandwich.

Lord, do You want me to talk to this man about You? The question framed itself in my mind. *If You do, would You cause Kent to go to sleep as a sign to me and also take care of any interruptions?*

I looked at Kent who had been munching a cookie. His head nodded slightly and his eyes closed. I'd asked, but I couldn't believe how quickly it had happened. I'd asked for a sign—now I couldn't back out. I hoped we had talked enough medicalese that he would know I wasn't some kind of fanatic.

"Have you ever seen what we laymen would call a 'healing', but you might term a 'spontaneous remission'?" I asked him.

Wrinkles appeared around his eyes as he smiled, "Yes, I have." He nodded his head.

"Well, what would you attribute this to?" I realized my palms were damp.

He pursed his lips slightly, stared into the distance and seemed to choose His words carefully. "I believe a force can come into a body and completely reverse an existing condition."

"Would you be willing to say this force could be from God?" I tried to pin him down.

The smile wrinkles appeared again. "Definitely!" To my surprise, he offered that he had been witness to many cases that would fit into this category. "We see many patients that fit the description of a healing; however, we don't usually document them as a 'healing' for fear of being branded as quacks," he chuckled.

I shared Kent's experience in response to the prayer of Mr. Botts, an elevator operator at NIH "His recovery went on his chart as 'medically unexplainable recovery'."

"Surely a miracle," he agreed.

"Have you ever asked the Lord for the answer to cancer?" I asked.

He looked as though I'd hit him over the head with my suitcase.

"Is that so unreasonable?" I continued. "I think God wants to give us the answer to this. Look how the answer to polio came—they said it was a laboratory mistake. I don't think it was a mistake at all. I think God gave the answer."

"That's an interesting hypothesis." He stroked his chin lightly as though in deep thought.

The fact that he seemed genuinely interested encouraged me to go on. "Edison admitted his inventions were not entirely his own. They came 'out of the air' as he put it, or sometimes in a vivid thought when he wakened from sleep."

"This is fascinating. I've never considered this aspect," he told me.

I said that I had approached Kent's first doctor, Robert Gallo, who had since gone into research at NIH with this same question—would he ask for the answer? "He didn't think he could ask, he very truthfully told me. Said it might be too 'ego slaying', but I thought he might be pulling my leg with that reason."

"Does he have some spiritual axe to grind?" the doctor asked.

I smiled at his perception. "I guess anyone who has lost a relative to cancer might have an axe to grind. Dr. Gallo's sister died of leukemia—that's what led him into cancer research."

We were nearing Union Station in Washington and this announcement from the conductor had snapped a lid on our conversation. I thanked him for all his help as he carried our suitcase off the train for us. We shook hands and he said we might see each other again at NIH. Someone was yelling, "Mrs. Ghost! Mrs. Ghost!" It was Jesse from NIH with a car to pick us up.

"How in the world did you know we were coming in by train, Jesse?"

He threaded the car through the snowy snarl of traffic at the station. "Oh, I don't know...somebody in the AOD's office told me to pick you up."

"But how would they know? Passengers from the airport were just being jammed on trains. How did the AOD know that my plane had landed in Newark?" It was too strange.

And when we got into NIH, Jesse and I both checked in the AOD's office because he couldn't remember who had told him to get us. Absolutely nobody in the office said they had given him the order for pickup. Had it come from the Lord?

Now, many years later, as I remembered this incident the memory perplexed me. Nothing had ever come of this conversation on a train to my knowledge. All signs pointed to more than coincidence in our meeting and conversation. And yet, why would the Lord pointlessly trouble to arrange all the breathtaking coincidences involved? It didn't make sense.

I made another cup of tea and looked at the list of guidance we'd had. The answer shimmered in front of me, but I still couldn't quite reach it. The same mind-bending mental tug-of-war that had caused me to sit down and list the manner in which God's guidance had come to us in the past nine years now beckoned to me. Why had the memory of the meeting on the train seemed so important today?

"What is it, Lord?" I asked in desperation. "Is there something I must do—something You want me to see?"

My eyes fastened on a plain, brown mailing carton that sat on the top of the dryer. I still had to deliver the publisher's complimentary copy of Catherine Marshall's new book, *Something More*, to Dr. Gallo. The story of Kent's cerebral hemorrhage and miraculous recovery had been included in her book. The publisher had sent me Gallo's complimentary copy because he appeared in the book as Kent's attending physician at the time.

Suddenly the abstract became tangible—the last piece of the jigsaw puzzle snapped into place—Dr. Gallo! I pictured myself taking the book to him, telling all the details of Kent's unusual crossing. And then, as I had done eight years before, suggesting he ask God for the answer to cancer. I had learned the lesson of God's precise timing---maybe now it was the Lord's timing to give us the answer to this dread disease.

The first time guidance had come to me directly from the Lord, I had questioned that the same God who had spoken to Abraham and Moses could speak to a housewife. But from a panoramic view of eight years, I had come to know that through the acceptance of salvation through Jesus Christ this is possible. Now I knew beyond the shadow of a doubt, that if God could speak to a plain ordinary housewife, He could certainly speak the answer to cancer to a dedicated doctor.

I dialed Dr. Gallo's office and made an appointment with him for 2:00 o'clock, September 25th—eight days after Kent's earthly body had been buried.

Chapter Thirty-Four

I tried to dress attractively the day of the appointment. Bob Gallo and I hadn't seen each other in several years except to nod in elevators. Not until I was in the car, Catherine's book on the seat beside me, did I realize I had chosen the same aqua suit that I had worn the day of Kent's funeral. Somehow this thought strengthened me.

I told the receptionist my name and was admitted to the secretarial pool that was in the foyer of Dr. Gallo's office. They were friendly, casual and put me at ease. I sat on a straight backed chair, Catherine's book on my lap, as I watched the clock. Two o'clock now became two-thirty. I wondered if I had been forgotten. Scientists ran in and out. The secretaries responded to calls internally and from without the building with mind-boggling dispatch. I secretly was glad I didn't work there in the midst of such a swirl of activity. There seemed to be a super-charged atmosphere present in this office that kept pace with the intensity I'd known to be a part of Dr. Gallo's personality in the past.

I picked lint off my skirt. It was now a quarter to 3:00 PM—my appointment had been for 2:00 PM. Perhaps the Lord wasn't in my invasion into this world of scientists at all, I told myself. I began to feel increasingly more foolish.

A familiar face appeared at the door—a lab technician I hadn't seen in years. "Mrs. Ghost!" she exclaimed, "It's been so long. How have you been?"

I told her everything was great, adding that I was so happy to see her.

"Well... it's a small world!" she said and disappeared down the hall.

Just those words, "it's a small world" were enough to buck me up with a new measure of confidence that I was there with the Lord's guidance.

Three o'clock had seemed to figure as important timing in relation to God's time clock. And now, it was at exactly 3:00 o'clock when Dr. Gallo waved for me to come into his office. *Could the delay have been for my benefit so I'd feel encouraged the Lord was indeed in it?* Somehow, as I waited, I had felt that God would work out the timing. Obviously Dr. Gallo's time was at a premium. How would I ever bring my message without interruption from the chaos of activity I had been witness to in the hour I had sat in the secretarial pool?

I had forgotten how Bob Gallo's boyish smile could melt my heart. He picked up a stack of books off a chair and gestured for me to sit down. Piles of medical records in file folders formed random columns on the floor. His desk erupted in a tidal wave of papers. He looked much as I had remembered him, horned rimmed glasses, piercing dark eyes that could change instantly to softness when he grinned. There was only one change—his black hair that had been touched with gray at the temples was salted more liberally now.

"Great to see you," he shook my hand. "I'm afraid I let our appointment time slip by. Sorry... it's been one heck-of-a-day!" He ran fingers through his hair.

I felt presumptuous but said, "For old time's sake, can I have fifteen uninterrupted minutes of your time, Bob?"

He looked at the clock, "Hey, we're in luck. It's my secretary's birthday. They're having a party at 3:00 o'clock. Nothing will *move* in that outside office 'til they get back."

He picked up the phone, "Please put all lines on hold when you leave," he told his personal secretary. "I don't want any interruptions."

The Lord seemed to favor 3:00 o'clock in His timing; His death on the cross and using that to point up Kent's death, his burial service at precisely 3:00, but now I saw that while this timing had a meaningful significance to me, today it served again as heavenly timing. At no other time could I have seen Dr. Gallo on an uninterrupted basis. Surely at 2:00 o'clock it couldn't have happened. Because of the intricate timing and a birthday celebration, I would have time alone with him.

He closed the door, sat down at his desk and smiled again, "Now, what's on your mind?"

I handed him Catherine's book and he eagerly turned to the chapter about Kent's cerebral hemorrhage. As he had approved the galley proofs, he had read the story before. "It reads the same, but there's something more exciting about seeing it in print," he told me.

I wondered, *Has he heard that Kent died just a week ago?*

"How's Kent doing?" The question answered my thoughts.

"I didn't just come to bring you the book. You apparently didn't hear that Kent died last week, Bob. Some staff from NIH were at the funeral and the chaplains, but they were people who were involved with his current care. I'm sure the news didn't reach into the labs." I could tell by the tears that sprang up instantly, he still had a soft spot in his heart for Kent.

He turned from me and took off his glasses. "No, I didn't know." His voice wavered.

Apparently, even seven years of research, removed from the clinical aspects, had not changed his affection for his former patients. Kent had seemed special to him as he'd been Bob Gallo's first pediatric patient.

When he turned back to face me, he had recovered his professional mask, but the eyes were gentle, still a little moist. "I'm so sorry. You were fortunate though, he went a long time—nine and one-half years."

"We *were* fortunate. He never had to have a blood transfusion at NIH—just at the hospital in Louisville. He was never hospitalized except initially when he was your patient. He died at home, Bob, in his own bed with no pain."

He shook his head, "Was there an autopsy?"

"Yes, septicemia and he went into liver shock."

He winced. "Was he in a coma?"

"No. In fact he was conscious and responding right up until the end."

Until that moment I had not had medical proof of what we had felt was God's gracious mercy in Kent's death. Until now...."But he *should* have gone into a deep lingering coma!" Bob grew excited. "That defies precedent of death from shock."

I suddenly remembered an inner promise that we would *miss a blessing* if we denied NIH the opportunity to conduct an autopsy. "I think when I tell you the whole story Bob, you'll see just how unusual it was,"

He momentarily looked out the window as if reflecting on something. "I almost died myself", he smiled a bit self-consciously. "I was at a medical conference in Israel."

I remembered that several years ago he had made a major contribution in discovering an enzyme present in the leukemia cell that is not present in a normal cell. Since then he had been in demand as a major speaker when cancer research scientists convened in different parts of the world.

"The jet I *should* have taken back crashed."

"There are no coincidences, Bob. I truly believe you were protected."

"It was a good trip though, I saw the Holy land—even slept on the Mount of Olives and saw the Garden of Gethsemane."

Will you not watch with Me one hour?... floated across my mind. I couldn't believe how the Lord was opening doors.

"I have a story to tell you, and that's really why I've come today. Since you saw the Garden of Gethsemane recently, it should be rather meaningful at one particular point. And when I'm done, you may be able to see that a Higher Hand than chance kept you off the plane that was ill fated."

I told him the entire story of Kent's death, stressing the loud thought that had proven to be God's voice asking, *Will you not watch with Me one hour?*

At that point, Dr. Gallo's dark, bushy eyebrows shot above the frames of his glasses. "Just like at Gethsemane," he mumbled more to himself than to me. He seemed to be analyzing and weighing my words. "And so you had the strong impression Kent would die at 3:00 o'clock and he wasn't to be moved?"

"Not just a strong impression. It came outside my own mind. I dismissed it until it came again—more loudly the second time. It proved to be true."

He shook his head slowly from side-to-side probably trying to bracket my experience into a world of more substantial and realistic terms. "That's highly unusual. Not even a doctor can pinpoint the time of death. You mean you really think God spoke to you?"

He wasn't making fun of me. The statement was made in the tone of a researcher's prying, inquisitive, sensitive search for truth. I told him, "You've just repeated verbatim what Brigid Leventhal said directly afterward, 'Not even we doctors can pinpoint the time of death.' She added, 'It must have been the Lord.'"

"You told this to Brigid?"

"The NIH ambulance transported Kent's body and we followed it to the Clinical Center. We met with Brigid, Dr. Fay and a social worker afterward, Bob. I told them the entire story."

"Fay's terrific. He's joining my research team when his term on the service is at an end."

"Of all the doctors Kent had, changing every six months for nine and one-half years, you and Dr. Fay were the best—the first and the last." His interest encouraged me. "Do you remember, just before you left the leukemia service I came to you and told you I had had an experience with Jesus Christ? I asked you at that time to pray and ask God for the answer to cancer, remember?"

He seemed embarrassed by that remembrance. I had been a new Christian then and my exuberance and zeal had caused me to come on too strong. (In fact, years later I told someone that in the beginning I had charged out to save the world and then finally figured out Jesus had already done it.) I must have seemed like any other distraught mother groping for help for her child.

But now I told him of the strange chain of events and circumstances that had led me into the conversation on the train with the chief surgeon of the M. D. Anderson Cancer Clinic. As Dr. Gallo listened, I sensed he seemed to have respect for this colleague who had admitted he had seen occasions when God had intervened... "A force that can come into a body and completely reverse an existing condition," he had said.

"Bob, I hope you don't mind, but I related the part about asking God for the answer to cancer, told him I had asked you to do it. His remark in answer to this was perceptive, 'If Gallo felt he couldn't do it, perhaps he has an axe to grind with God.'"

He winced.

"Maybe it's painful for you, but significant to me," I continued, fueled by a new source of strength. "You had a sister who died of leukemia. Her short life influenced the direction of your own tremendously. You told me, the first time I talked to you about this, 'Don't you think we prayed! We prayed for her around the clock and she *died*. Where was God?'"

I could see pain in his eyes as I went on, "Maybe God had a higher plan by using your sister's life. By her death you were led into hematology. You ended up with the National Cancer Institute and already you've made a brilliant contribution to science."

He fidgeted in obvious embarrassment.

"Isn't it possible that all of those prayers for your sister laid a foundation for the answer? I would like to think Kent's death, as a research patient, served this purpose. We've prayed from the point of his diagnosis that God would use him for the answer to this disease."

He still remained silent.

"My point is this, Bob, if you haven't already ruled out that indeed God did speak to me," I held my breath praying the Lord would drive my words home, "if He can speak to an ordinary housewife, why couldn't He speak to a dedicated doctor who is earnestly digging for the answer to cancer?"

He shuffled his feet and stared at one brown shoe.

"I'm here to ask you again to ask God for the answer to this disease."

"That's a tall order." He smiled. "At least for me."

"Can you do it as an experiment? Approach it on a laboratory basis?"

I did not get a formal commitment from Dr. Gallo that day. He indicated that he might ask, but my suggestion—while well received—seemed to cut across the grain of everything this scientist's analyzing, calculating mind had been trained for.

As we shook hands at the door, there seemed to be an unseen bond between us. Perhaps it was my imagination, or did he feel it too? Did he feel the bond that stretched from the past when he had cared for Kent to the present? We had both lost loved ones to our common enemy—leukemia. One thing I felt sure of, we both shared the driving desire to defeat this disease forever.

His dark eyes made their change from granite to liquid. "Sandy, it's been so good to see you," he told me.

"I know I've placed quite a responsibility on you by asking that you open yourself up to God's help in this. But think of the responsibility *you* assume if you don't, Bob."

He shook his head in understanding and stared at his shoes again. I was suddenly reminded of a letter he had sent Kent once. Kent had called him "Dr. Jello". Their relationship had been unique. Gallo was a good-looking man, but in the intensity of his duties on the service, he many times appeared with hurriedly tied, broken shoe laces. Kent and I had always kidded him about it and Kent had sent him a pair of laces from Kentucky as a joke.

He had written Kent a thank you note. "I guess now," he had written, "I have no excuse to be (as my grandmother used to call me) 'the peacock'. Always keeps his hair in place, but never minds his feet." It had been signed, "Robert Gallo (alias Dr. Jello)."

"Well, the 'peacock's' finally looking at his feet.'" I kidded him.

He exploded with rich laughter. "My letter to Kent!"

"Can I push it one step farther? Your grandmother didn't tell you to forget about your head entirely and just concentrate on your feet. I'm not asking you to do that either. The experience and research knowledge you have could be the ripe tools for the answer. You may not actually hear the same still, small Voice I did...it could be a collision of circumstances, or even just being headed down the right track. But I still feel, if you'll ask, you're God's man for the answer!"

"I sure wish I could be confident of that," he leaned against the doorjamb and smiled.

The secretaries were just beginning to return from their office party. The timing had been perfect.

September turned to October. October 1974 surrendered its life to a gray November. The colorful leaves I had compared to the beauty of death turned an ugly brown, swirled in small tornadoes onto the patio and beat against the glass doors as though demanding entry from the cold.

Occasional bouts with my sense of loss pockmarked my life: a song on the radio Kent and I had heard while driving to the hospital; the sight of his bongo drums; Kurt's summer pajamas put away in the drawer—identical to those Kent had worn the day he died.

He has so much more now... no more needles... no more hospitals, I would tell myself and be able to drift into genuine praise to the Lord. This would stabilize me until another memory would resurrect fresh grief. Other than the night we had taken communion as a family, the week after Kent died, and had all broken down, we managed to hide it fairly well. Bill seemed to have the same occasional onslaught I was having—but we both kept it behind closed doors. I was to find this was a gross mistake with Kurt.

It all surfaced over a small thing. Kurt came to me and asked if we could take Kent's bed down to make more room. I told him we needed an extra bed for guests and besides, there was no room in the storage room. It was out of the question.

Kurt bit his lip and tears splashed down his cheeks. He whirled and ran upstairs. His emotions had seemed to sit on his sleeve lately.

I peeled another potato and suddenly it burst over me that I had just served up excuses to hide what I really felt. I just couldn't bear to have Kent's bed taken down yet. I ran up the stairs two-at-a-time and found Kurt, lying on his bed, the tears still trickling down his cheeks.

I sat down beside him. "Kurt, I just realized I wasn't telling you the truth. It's not that we need the bed for guests or no room in the storage. The plain truth is..." I choked out the words, "I'm going through a period of missing Kent terribly."

Tears continued to stream across his freckles.

316

"Do you ever feel that way?"

He nodded. A fresh wave erupted in his blue eyes.

"And I just can't bear to think of taking Kent's bed down yet. Not that we can't later..." I was crying now.

Suddenly he threw himself into my arms—the first time since his twin had died. I saw something I had not seen before, and as I did, my heart threatened to burst apart at the seams.

The great strength given to me at the time of Kent's death, had been misinterpreted by Kurt. He must have thought I didn't really love Kent! And if I didn't care if Kent died, then it would follow I didn't care about him either.

What could have been a scarring mistake, dissolved in salty tears as we sat with arms around each other and cried.

I dreaded facing Christmas without Kent, but the entire family seemed to have a return of the Holy Spirit's strengthening arm. Surprisingly, it was a festive, fun time. We welcomed 1975 by banging on pots and pans on the patio at midnight. It had to be a better year!

On the morning of January 9th, I zipped on my heavy robe, gave the alarm clock a nasty look, and wakened Kurt and Lisa for school. I felt my way downstairs, mind still fuzzy with sleep and trying to cope with the heavy decision of oatmeal or cold cereal.

Suddenly a shaft of sunlight shone on a plaque that hung by the front door—the same Irish Blessing that had always hung near the door of every home we'd ever had.

There was a strange insistence, compelling me to read it. I fought the notion. I *knew* what it said!

But the same feeling persisted to beckon me toward the plaque. And as I read it, it was almost as though Kent stood beside me.

May the road rise to meet you,
May the wind be always at your back
(the times he'd pushed me up the hill to the church—
two small hands on my back)
May the rain fall soft upon your fields
(the Myersville farm he loved)
I gasped at the last words...
And until we meet again, may God
Hold you in the palm of His Hand.

A warmth spread slowly through me. Yes, we would meet again.

I opened the front door to get the morning newspaper. The cold concrete on my bare feet sent teeth-chattering chills up my spine. And then I saw it!

On the front page of the Washington Post, in the lower left-hand corner was

Dr. Gallo's picture. I slammed the door and sank onto one of the kitchen table benches with the paper. "Virus Linked to Human Cancer Believed Isolated by Scientists" the headline proclaimed and under his picture, "Dr. Robert Gallo heads scientists."

As my eyes skimmed through the words, my heart pounded. Gallo's team had isolated a newly discovered virus that "emerged to be the strongest candidate ever to be the first human cancer virus to be isolated by scientists."

"Finding a human cancer virus," the article continued, "would open the door to new ways to diagnose, treat and detect cancer, the second greatest killer of Americans."

It went on to say, "Dr. Robert Gallo, who headed the National Cancer Institute scientists who isolated the virus, said he would not have allowed the Cancer Institute to announce the findings yesterday if he was not sure that it was a virus associated with human cancers." The article continued to quote Gallo as the complexities of the lab techniques involved were described. It also stated that "Gallo has been systematically studying acute myelogenous leukemia in man and animals for six years hunting for its cause."

I couldn't believe what I'd just read. I yelled for Bill. Lisa and Kurt caught my excitement too. They had known of my trip to Dr. Gallo's office and had been a part of the team of people we had enlisted to pray specifically for him.

While it was far from the complete answer to cancer, even the press had described it as a "door". Did God speak to Dr. Gallo? I may never have that question answered. Out of a sense of both reverence and respect, I feel that answer should remain between him and the Lord.

But then, if it was coincidence, this book from first to last page contains merely coincidence piled upon coincidence. It would not then be a record of the supernatural Hand of God at work in the lives of an ordinary family.

It's a small world, after all...

After Thoughts

*N*o longer tied to the Bethesda, Maryland area, we still felt the Lord's Hand of guidance to continue to look for a farm. We finally found a beautiful relic from the Civil War days. A retiree from the Library of Congress had purchased an authentic log cabin from the 1700's sited on 140 acres in the Blue Ridge Mountains in Linden, Virginia. He lovingly began to add rooms in wings using the log cabin itself as the central room. On the Civil War maps Fiery Run, the brook that ran past Harrell's Corners, wound its way through the farm. Descendants of the Harrell family still lived at the corner of the road.

Two attorneys from Washington, DC had purchased the farm to run Black Angus cattle and intended to rent the farm house. It seemed to be a match made in heaven for us, but no Voice of guidance came to confirm it; yet for some reason we felt it was where we were supposed to be. The mountains of the Skyline Drive were framed by the huge picture window in the living room. Oak beams and a large stone fireplace cried out for restoration and cleaning, but once finished with yellow chintz curtains in the log room and newly painted walls in the living room I knew it could be a show place. There were two closets in the living room and I lugged a hot bucket of soapy water to wash down the shelves. Climbing on the ladder, my fingertips touched a piece of paper on the top shelf. Bringing it down into view, I caught my breath. On lined notebook paper were penned the words we had always heard when looking for our farm with Kent—the words to the song, "Country Roads... Take me home, to the place I belong..." There was nothing else left by former tenants in any of the other closets.

Coincidence?

Made in the USA
Monee, IL
07 July 2020